A
CAESAR
Workbook

Teacher's Manual

LLWS

Latin Literature Workbook Series

A Series Edited by LeaAnn A. Osburn
and Donald E. Sprague

A Horace Workbook (2005)

A Horace Workbook Teacher's Manual (2006)

A Vergil Workbook (2006)

A Vergil Workbook Teacher's Manual (2007)

An Ovid Workbook (2006)

An Ovid Workbook Teacher's Manual (2007)

A Catullus Workbook (2006)

A Catullus Workbook Teacher's Manual (2007)

A Cicero Workbook (2006)

A Cicero Workbook Teacher's Manual (2007)

A Vergil Workbook 2ⁿᵈ Edition (2012)

A Vergil Workbook 2ⁿᵈ Edition Teacher's Manual (2012)

A Caesar Workbook (2012)

A Caesar Workbook Teacher's Manual (2012)

A
CAESAR
Workbook

Teacher's Manual

Rose Williams
& Debra L. Nousek

x

Bolchazy-Carducci Publishers, Inc.
Mundelein, Illinois USA

Series Editors: LeaAnn A. Osburn and Donald E. Sprague
Volume General Editor: Donald E. Sprague
Volume Contributing Editor: Laurel Draper
Design & Layout: Adam Phillip Velez

A Caesar Workbook Teacher's Manual

Rose Williams and Debra L. Nousek

AP is a registered trademark of the College Entrance Examination Board, which was not involved in the production of, and does not endorse, this product.

Bolchazy-Carducci Publishers, Inc.
1570 Baskin Road
Mundelein, Illinois 60060
www.bolchazy.com

Printed in the United States of America
2013
by Publishers' Graphics

ISBN 978-0-86516-755-1

CONTENTS

FOREWORD

All Latin teachers want their students to read ancient authors in the original. Yet to study the authentic Latin of an ancient Roman author is a complex task. It requires comprehension of the text and its grammatical underpinnings; an understanding of the world events and the culture in which the work of literature was produced; an ability to recognize the figures of speech the author uses and to grasp the impact they have on the text; sensitivity to the way sound effects, including meter if a passage is poetry, interact with the meaning of the text; and the ability to probe whatever thoughts and ideas the author may be expressing. To be successful in this multifaceted task, students need not only a comprehensive textbook but also exercises of different kinds, in which to practice their newly developing literary and critical skills.

Students often need extensive drill and practice material—something not available in the traditional Latin author textbook—to help them master the grammar and syntax of the Latin text as well as the literary skills that the text demands of its readers. Teachers, too, no matter how many questions they ask in class to help their students analyze the syntax and the literary qualities of the text, often need and want more questions to be available. Realizing this need on the part of both students and teachers, Bolchazy-Carducci Publishers developed a series of workbooks to accompany Advanced Placement author textbooks. Initially, the series comprised five workbooks, one for each advanced placement author at the time: Catullus, Cicero, Horace, Ovid, and Vergil. A team of authors—one, a university scholar with special expertise in the Latin literary text and the other, a high school Advanced Placement Latin teacher—wrote each workbook.

Upon the announcement of a major revision of the AP Latin Curriculum beginning with the 2012–2013 school year, Bolchazy-Carducci commissioned the revision of *A Vergil Workbook* and the development of the new *A Caesar Workbook*. These workbooks contain the Latin text as delineated on the Advanced Placement Syllabus.

All the texts in the series provide exercises that drill grammar, syntax, and figures of speech. In addition, multiple choice questions that focus on the student's comprehension of the passage and on items of literary analysis are included. The workbooks also feature scansion practice, essays to write, and other short analysis questions in each section. By reading and answering these types of questions, students will gain experience with the types of questions that are used in upper level Latin classes on the college level as well as on the Advanced Placement Examinations. Students at the college level will also benefit from the additional practice offered in the workbooks.

These workbooks contain neither textual notes nor vocabulary on the page with the text nor on the facing page. The absence of these traditional features of textbooks will allow students, after reading the Latin passage in the textbook, to practice in the workbook what they have learned and to assess how much they have mastered already and what needs more study. The workbooks do, however, contain a Latin to English Vocabulary at the back of the book.

We are confident that this series of workbooks has a unique role to play in fostering students' understanding of authentic Latin text and will be a significant addition to the Advanced Placement and college materials that already exist.

LeaAnn A. Osburn and
Donald E. Sprague
Series Editors

PREFACE TO THE STUDENT WORKBOOK

This book is intended to enhance students' ability to read and comprehend Caesar's *Commentaries on the Gallic War*, whether in an Advanced Placement course or not. Each Latin author presents his own set of challenges. Each has personal syntax and vocabulary preferences and is influenced by his era and his experiences. The selections in this book have been carefully chosen to familiarize the students with Caesar's preferences in such areas so that they can approach the body of Caesar's works with confidence. Whether the students have the intention of taking the AP exam or understanding Caesar in general, careful practice underscoring his unique qualities can be of use. The selections included are from the AP Syllabus.

The book features several types of questions, some of which parallel the AP test format, and others designed to facilitate student progress through the text. Each target passage is divided into manageable sections. At the beginning of each section, the text is provided.

The Latin text with some minor variation and different line breaks is taken with permission from *Caesar: Selections from his Commentarii De bello Gallico* by Hans-Friedrich Mueller (Bolchazy-Carducci Publishers 2012).

I. Preparatory Questions

Following the text are Preparatory Questions. These are prompts that guide the students through the text line by line, asking them to identify constructions of syntax and their components in order to understand the relationships among them that are critical to comprehension. Sometimes a question involving several lines will appear before those questions involving a single word in a given line. This arrangement is meant to promote recognition of the major clauses and aid to the student to see the big picture. Lines in the text are provided for written answers.

II. Multiple Choice Questions

Next come multiple choice questions that are meant to be done after the student has completed the translation. These cover a variety of topics, including agreement, reference, translation, syntax, comprehension, and figures of speech. As these, for the most part, replicate the multiple choice sections of the AP exam, time limits are suggested for each. Teachers may want to break the lengthier multiple choice sections into two assignments. The multiple choice section on the AP exam consists of approximately fifty questions to be completed in an hour.

III. Translation

A passage for translation follows, approximately the same length as those found on the AP exams. Students should provide as literal a translation as possible, paying particular attention to maintaining the original voice and tense of verbs.

IV. Short Analysis Questions

Short analysis questions, similar to those found in AP exams, are designed to help the students focus on key ideas in the passage. They often ask students to quote and translate accurately specific words or phrases in support of their answer. Insight and brevity are essential here.

V. Essay Questions

Finally, for each chapter or section an essay question is provided, in which students will gain valuable experience with in-depth literary analysis. Consistent with AP expectations for short essays, students should formulate cogent arguments with appropriate support from the Latin text to demonstrate their understanding of the passage.

VI. How to Interpret Question Prompts

The following is a guide to the correct way to formulate answers to the various types of questions asked in the Workbook, primarily in the Preparatory Questions, but also throughout the Workbook. Students will benefit from developing a standard pattern for parsing Latin words since knowing which elements of the word's form and usage are required will enable the student to provide full identifications of the word.

Question Prompt	Expected Answer
Identify the case and use of X	provide case + type of use (e.g., ablative of means, partitive genitive)
Identify the tense and voice of X	provide the required components of the verb form (e.g., present active)
Identify the tense and mood of X	provide the required components of the verb form (e.g., imperfect subjunctive)
Identify the form and syntax of X (noun)	provide gender, case, number + grammatical function in the clause
Identify the form and syntax of X (verb)	provide person, number, tense, mood, and voice + grammatical function in the clause
Identify the form and case of X (participle)	provide the type of participle and its case (e.g., perfect passive participle, ablative)
What does X modify?	identify the adjective, noun, or verb with which the adjective or adverb agrees
What is the dictionary entry of X (noun)?	provide the nominative singular form of the noun
What is the dictionary entry of X (verb)?	provide the first principal part of the verb
What construction is X?	provide the grammatical explanation for the word or phrase (e.g., gerundive of purpose)

PREFACE TO THE TEACHER'S MANUAL

The purpose of the Teacher's Manual is to provide teachers assistance in evaluating their students' work with the exercises of *A Caesar Workbook*. Such feedback is intended to help teachers as they, in turn, help students better understand the content, context, and style of Caesar's writing. The Teacher's Manual supplies answers for all questions contained in the student text.

Each section of *A Caesar Workbook* contains questions carefully written to replicate the style of questions found on the AP Latin examination. It contains short answer, multiple choice, translation, short analysis, and essay questions. In conjunction with our stated goal of enhancing students' ability to read and comprehend Caesar's work, our selections follow the targeted AP selections with special emphasis on his personal syntax and vocabulary preferences.

Whether the students have the intention of taking the AP Latin Exam or just improving their understanding of Caesar, diligent practice underscoring his unique qualities can be of use.

Preparatory Questions

The preparatory questions encourage students to deconstruct a sentence, considering each syntactical element individually and in relationship to the whole. They are sequential, guiding the students line by line to make critical decisions about the passage elements. These are prompts to create a mental checklist of important elements. This section includes questions that ask about form and syntax, questions helping students see connections between words, questions designed to foster associations into subordinate clauses, signal words that herald each type of clause, and questions asking students to name the clauses to facilitate translation. Some answers provide information in parentheses. This information is relevant to the question but not specifically requested in the question.

Multiple Choice Questions

Multiple choice question exercises are meant to be undertaken after the students have read the passage carefully. They cover such topics as agreement, reference, translation, syntax, comprehension, and figures of speech. All this affords practice with the type of questions found on the AP Latin Exam. Teachers may wish to break the longer passages into two assignments.

Translation

Translation passages are broken into segments or chunks similar in length to those found on the AP exam. This enables students to understand the AP expectation for translation and to evaluate their own performance in that light. Teachers should advise students to translate these passages as literally as possible. Care should be taken to render the tense and voice of verbs exactly, and to stay very close to the standard definitions of words. Of course alternatives are possible, but emphasis should always be on an accurate, literal translation. Please note that we have rendered historical presents as presents when translated into English. Teachers may prefer to render them in the past tense.

We have divided each of the translation sections into grammatical/syntactical units, or "chunks," for scoring. Teachers should use discretion in considering synonyms students might use in their translations as we usually provide only one or two English equivalents for the Latin. We encourage teachers to use this "chunking" system for grading translations.

Short Analysis Questions

Short analysis questions are designed to help students focus on key ideas in a short Latin excerpt. They usually ask students to cite and accurately translate specific words or phrases in support of their answer. In some instances the question did not ask the students for Latin citation but the bracketed citation is provided for teachers.

Essay Questions

Each section provides an essay question so that students will gain experience with in-depth literary analysis. These essays usually involve the analysis of a single passage from the lesson's Caesar text. For each essay we provide a sample essay answer containing the information that should be included in a comprehensive and thoughtful answer. Of course there will be variation in acceptable answers, and what is offered here is only one approach, not the only acceptable one. These are provided to assist both teacher and student to understand the components of a well developed response.

Essays receiving the highest scores are analytical and interpretive rather than merely descriptive or narrative. These essays require specific reference to the Latin throughout the passage, with appropriate citation, to support and document a student's analysis. For such reference to the Latin, students must write out the Latin and/or cite line numbers. They must also translate, accurately paraphrase, or otherwise make clear in their discussion that they understand the Latin. When referring to a relatively long portion of Latin text, they may either cite the line numbers or use ellipsis ("word . . . word"). When referring only to words or phrases, they should write the Latin out. The responsibility rests with the students to convince the reader that they are drawing conclusions from the Latin text and not from a general recall of the passage. Such careful citation of the Latin is critical as is noted in the essay grading rubrics printed below.

The following essay rubrics are adapted from the College Board's *AP Latin Course and Exam Description Effective Fall 2012*. While the rubrics address an essay that discusses two Latin passages, they are readily applied to essays in *A Caesar Workbook* that address a single Latin passage. The AP Latin exam always pairs two passages for discussion and analysis; these pairs consist of one of the following combinations: one passage from Vergil and one from Caesar, two passages from Caesar, or two passages from Vergil. All the essay questions in the student workbook help students prepare for essays that are based in whole or in part on Caesar. However, with the exception of two essays that require students to discuss two or more passages from Caesar, the essays in the workbook are not identical in format to the current AP Latin exam essay. To assist students with essays that require the analysis of two Latin passages, we provide four such essays (two pairing a Vergil and Caesar passage and two pairing two Caesar passages) and suggested answers in this manual. Teachers may duplicate these essays for use in their classes.

Essay Scoring Guidelines

5 – Strong

- The essay provides a well-developed, nuanced analysis of the passages.
- The analysis is supported by relevant details and evidence drawn from throughout both passages.
- References to the Latin are accurate, specific, and relevant.
- Inferences made and conclusions drawn fully support the analysis.
- Any examples of language usage and/or stylistic features are well developed and support the analysis.
- Any contextual references are specific and accurate, and support the analysis.

4 – Good

- The essay provides analysis though it may not be nuanced.
- The analysis is supported by the citation of main ideas and some supporting details, with evidence drawn from throughout both passages.
- References to the Latin are accurate, specific, and generally relevant.
- Some inferences may be drawn but the essay relies more on what is directly stated in the passages; occasional errors in inferences may occur.
- Any examples of language usage and/or stylistic features may not be well developed and/or may not support the analysis.
- Any contextual references used to support the argument may not be specific and/or accurate.

3 – Fair

- The essay provides discussion of the question but it may be uneven, inadequately developed, and/or primarily focused on only one of the passages.
- The discussion is supported by main ideas but few supporting details and relies on summary rather than analysis.
- References to the Latin are accurate but may be limited or not connected to the focus of the discussion.
- The essay may show partial understanding of information that is not stated but implied; few inferences are made.
- Any examples of language usage and/or stylistic features may not be connected to the discussion.
- Any contextual references made are not connected effectively to the discussion.

2 – Weak

- The essay provides discussion of the question but the discussion may be confusing and lack organization.
- There may be limited discussion of both passages or an adequate discussion of one passage and failure to recognize the other.
- The discussion consists of summary, not analysis.

- References to the Latin, if any, are limited and there is little or no understanding of the meaning and context.
- Inferences based on the passages are not accurate, and assumptions are incorrect.
- No meaningful examples of language usage and/or stylistic features are provided.
- No meaningful contextual references are made.

1 – Poor

- The essay shows some understanding of the question but contains no meaningful discussion. It provides some correct, relevant information.
- Either no Latin or only individual words are cited; no understanding of the meaning and context of either passage is demonstrated.
- The essay makes no inferences based on the passages.
- No meaningful examples of language usage and/or stylistic features are provided.
- No meaningful contextual references are made.

0 – Unacceptable

- The response is totally irrelevant, totally incorrect, or merely restates the question.
- The response demonstrates no understanding of the Latin in context.

—

- The page is blank or the response is off-task (e.g., drawing, personal letter).

NB: We call your attention to a set of errata on page 262 for the 2012 printing of the student workbook.

TEXT SELECTIONS FROM
DE BELLO GALLICO
WITH EXERCISES
& ANSWERS

GAIUS JULIUS CAESAR
DE BELLO GALLICO
CHAPTER 1: BOOK 1.1
THE NATURE OF GAUL

[1] Gallia est omnis divisa in partes tres, quarum unam incolunt
Belgae, aliam Aquitani, tertiam qui ipsorum lingua Celtae, nostra Galli
appellantur. Hi omnes lingua, institutis, legibus inter se differunt.
Gallos ab Aquitanis Garumna flumen, a Belgis Matrona et Sequana
5   dividit. Horum omnium fortissimi sunt Belgae, propterea quod a cultu
atque humanitate provinciae longissime absunt, minimeque ad eos
mercatores saepe commeant atque ea quae ad effeminandos animos
pertinent important, proximique sunt Germanis, qui trans Rhenum
incolunt, quibuscum continenter bellum gerunt. Qua de causa Helvetii
10 quoque reliquos Gallos virtute praecedunt, quod fere cotidianis proeliis
cum Germanis contendunt, cum aut suis finibus eos prohibent aut ipsi
in eorum finibus bellum gerunt. Eorum una pars, quam Gallos obtinere
dictum est, initium capit a flumine Rhodano, continetur Garumna flumine,
Oceano, finibus Belgarum, attingit etiam ab Sequanis et Helvetiis flumen
15 Rhenum, vergit ad septentriones. Belgae ab extremis Galliae finibus
oriuntur, pertinent ad inferiorem partem fluminis Rheni, spectant in
septentrionem et orientem solem. Aquitania a Garumna flumine ad
Pyrenaeos montes et eam partem Oceani quae est ad Hispaniam pertinet;
spectat inter occasum solis et septentriones.

Preparatory Questions

Line 1   Identify the case and use of *omnis*. **nominative; modifies *Gallia* (the subject of
the sentence)**

What is the antecedent of *quarum*? ***partes***

Lines 1–2   What three words modify the understood noun *partem*? ***unam, aliam, tertiam***

Line 2   Identify the case and use of *ipsorum*. **genitive of possession**

Identify the case and use of *lingua*. **ablative of respect or specification**

Line 3   Identify the tense and voice of *appellantur*. **present passive**

To what does *se* refer? ***Hi***

Line 4   Identify the case and use of *Aquitanis.* **ablative of separation**

Line 5   What are the subjects of *dividit*? ***Garumna flumen, Matrona et Sequana***

          Identify the case and use of *horum.* **partitive genitive (with *fortissimi*)**

          Identify the form and syntax of *fortissimi.* **nominative plural masculine (superlative) adjective modifying the subject *Belgae***

          What kind of clause does *propterea quod* introduce? **a causal clause**

Line 6   What does *longissime* modify? ***absunt***

Line 7   *Saepe* is complemented by what word in line 6? ***minime* (line 6)**

          Identify the form and use of *effeminandos.* **gerundive accusative plural masculine modifying *animos***

          Find a relative clause. ***quae ... pertinent***

Line 8   What is the subject of *important*? ***mercatores* (line 7)**

          What is the antecedent of *qui*? ***Germanis***

Line 9   What part of speech is *continenter*? **adverb**

Line 10   What is the subject of *praecedunt*? ***Helvetii* (line 9)**

          What part of speech is *quod*? **conjunction**

          What does *fere* modify? ***cotidianis***

Line 11   Explain the use and syntax of *suis.* **(possessive) adjective modifying *finibus* (ablative of separation)**

Lines 11–12   To whom do *eos* and the <u>first</u> *eorum* refer? ***Germanis***

Line 12   What is the antecedent of *quam*? ***pars***

          Find an indirect statement. ***quam Gallos obtinere***

Line 13   Identify the tense and voice of *dictum est.* **perfect passive**

Lines 12–15   *Una pars* is the subject of what four verbs? ***capit* (line 13), *continetur* (line 13), *attingit* (line 14), *vergit* (line 15)**

Line 14   What words are governed by *ab*? ***Sequanis et Helvetiis***

Line 15   What does *extremis* modify? ***finibus***

Line 16   Identify the form and syntax of *oriuntur.* **third person plural present indicative passive (deponent), main verb of sentence**

          Identify the case and use of *inferiorem.* **accusative modifying *partem***

          What words does *ad* govern? ***inferiorem partem***

Line 19   What words does *inter* govern? ***occasum solis et septentriones***

Multiple Choice Questions *Suggested time: 25 minutes*

1. In line 1 *quarum* is
    - a. a plural adjective
    - **b. a relative pronoun**
    - c. a demonstrative pronoun
    - d. an interrogative pronoun

2. In line 1 *unam* is translated
    - a. unique
    - b. one nation
    - **c. one part**
    - d. universal

3. In line 2 *qui* introduces
    - a. a gerund
    - **b. a relative clause**
    - c. a result clause
    - d. a verbal phrase

4. In line 3 we learn that
    - a. the Gauls are closely united
    - b. the Gauls have a common culture
    - **c. the Gauls differ in major cultural aspects**
    - d. all Gauls are called Celts

5. In line 4 *Gallos* is
    - a. an appositive
    - b. subject of a verb
    - **c. direct object of a verb**
    - d. a modifier

6. In lines 4–5 we learn that rivers
    - a. matter little to the Gauls
    - **b. form the major territorial divisions**
    - c. hinder the Gauls
    - d. provide recreation for Gauls

7. In line 5 *omnium* is
    - **a. a partitive genitive**
    - b. a genitive of possession
    - c. an accusative singular
    - d. a genitive of separation

8. In line 5 *propterea quod* is translated
    - a. before
    - b. after
    - **c. because**
    - d. although

9. In line 7 *ad effeminandos animos* is
    - a. a participial phrase
    - b. a clause
    - c. a gerund phrase
    - **d. a gerundive phrase**

10. The subject of *sunt* (line 8) is
    - a. *mercatores* (line 7)
    - **b. *Belgae* (line 5)**
    - c. *Germanis* (line 8)
    - d. *Gallos* (line 10)

11. In line 9 *quibuscum* is translated
    a. wherever
    c. with whom
    b. by whom
    d. who

12. In line 9 *qua de causa* refers to
    a. narrow boundaries
    c. proximity to Germans
    b. education
    d. determination

13. In line 10 *virtute* is
    a. an ablative absolute
    c. an ablative of manner
    b. an ablative of specification
    d. an ablative of association

14. In line 11 the first *cum* is translated
    a. with
    c. when
    b. under
    d. over

15. In line 11 *ipsi* is
    a. a reflexive pronoun
    c. an intensive pronoun
    b. a demonstrative pronoun
    d. a personal pronoun

16. The subject of *capit* (line 13) is
    a. *Gallos* (line 12)
    c. *una pars* (line 12)
    b. *Rhodano* (line 13)
    d. *initium* (line 13)

17. In line 14 *attingit* is translated
    a. it touches
    c. it avoids
    b. it stops
    d. it maneuvers

18. In line 15 *septentriones* is translated
    a. seventh
    c. south
    b. north
    d. seventy

19. The subject of *spectant* (line 16) is
    a. *Galliae* (line 15)
    c. *Belgae* (line 15)
    b. *Helvetiis* (line 14)
    d. *Rheni* (line 16)

20. In line 18 *quae . . . pertinet* is
    a. a relative clause
    c. a purpose clause
    b. a relative clause of purpose
    d. an indirect statement

21. In line 19 *occasum solis* is translated

    a. settled

    b. the west

    c. home of the sun

    d. heat wave

Translation *Suggested time: 15 minutes*

Gallia est omnis divisa in partes tres, quarum unam incolunt Belgae, aliam Aquitani, tertiam qui ipsorum lingua Celtae, nostra Galli appellantur. Hi omnes lingua, institutis, legibus inter se differunt. Gallos ab Aquitanis Garumna flumen, a Belgis Matrona et Sequana dividit.

20 chunks. 10 points, ½ point each.

Gallia . . . omnis	all Gaul
est divisa	is divided
in partes tres	into three parts
quarum	of which
unam	one
incolunt Belgae	the Belgians inhabit
aliam Aquitani	another, the Aquitani
tertiam	the third
qui . . . appellantur	(those) who are called
ipsorum lingua Celtae	in their own language Celts
nostra Galli	in ours Gauls
Hi omnes	all these
lingua, institutis, legibus	in language, institutions, (and) customs
inter se differunt	differ among themselves
Gallos	the Gauls
ab Aquitanis	from the Aquitani
Garumna flumen	the Garonne River
a Belgis	from the Belgians
Matrona et Sequana	the Marne and the Seine
dividit	divides

Short Analysis Questions

> Gallia est omnis divisa in partes tres, quarum unam incolunt Belgae, aliam
> Aquitani, tertiam qui ipsorum lingua Celtae, nostra Galli appellantur. Hi
> omnes lingua, institutis, legibus inter se differunt. Gallos ab Aquitanis
> Garumna flumen, a Belgis Matrona et Sequana dividit.

1. How does Caesar attempt to set up an overview of Gaul for his Roman readers?

   He shows them that Gaul is not a cohesive whole, but is divided by various factors.

2. What important cultural facts does Caesar perceive? How could these impact his mission and intentions? Cite the Latin that supports your answer and translate or accurately paraphrase.

   In line 3 he says that the Gauls differ in the aspects of life that might bind them together—institutions and laws—*institutis*, *legibus* (line 3). They also differ in language, *lingua* (line 3), which makes communication and understanding difficult if not impossible.

3. What geographical boundaries does he mention? Explain how these could be helpful to Caesar or not?

   Lines 3–4 indicate that the Gauls are in the middle of the country, and that they separate the Aquitani from the Belgae. One river, the Garonne, separates Gauls from the Aquitani, and two, the Marne and the Seine, separate them from the Belgians. Such divisions between his enemies makes their uniting against him more difficult. Students may also note that the geographical features also serve to some degree as barriers for the movement of Roman troops.

Essay *Suggested time: 20 minutes*

Horum omnium fortissimi sunt Belgae, propterea quod a cultu atque
humanitate provinciae longissime absunt, minimeque ad eos mercatores
saepe commeant atque ea quae ad effeminandos animos pertinent
important, proximique sunt Germanis, qui trans Rhenum incolunt,
5   quibuscum continenter bellum gerunt. Qua de causa Helvetii quoque
reliquos Gallos virtute praecedunt, quod fere cotidianis proeliis cum
Germanis contendunt, cum aut suis finibus eos prohibent aut ipsi in
eorum finibus bellum gerunt.

In this passage Caesar discusses the factors that he believes contribute to the bravery of the Belgians and then of the Helvetians. In a short essay, discuss these factors and point out which one he does not mention as operating in the case of the Helvetians. What does this omission indicate?

Support your assertions with references to the Latin text throughout the passage above. All Latin words must be copied or their line numbers provided, AND they must be translated or paraphrased closely enough that it is clear that you understand the Latin. It is your responsibility to convince the reader that you are basing your conclusions on the Latin text and not merely on a general recollection of the passage. Direct your answer to the question; do not merely summarize the passage. Please write your essay on a separate piece of paper.

Teachers should review the Essay Scoring Guidelines given at the beginning of this manual with students.

Students should be very aware of the meaning of *humanitas* (line 2) and discuss the effect that Caesar indicates this quality in neighbors can have in making men less *fortis*. The balance between *mercatores* (line 2), their activities, and *effeminandos animos* (line 3) should be explored. Also important is the effect that living close to the Germans has upon peoples. The introduction of the Helvetii, who are just now coming into the discussion, should be noted. The province does not seem to affect them, and Caesar credits their ferocity totally to the exercise provided by the Germans. Various cultural experiences contribute to the bravery of these peoples.

Notes

CHAPTER 2: BOOK 1.2-3
THE CONSPIRACY OF ORGETORIX

[2] Apud Helvetios longe nobilissimus fuit et ditissimus Orgetorix.
Is M. Messala et M. Pupio Pisone consulibus, regni cupiditate inductus,
coniurationem nobilitatis fecit et civitati persuasit ut de finibus suis cum
omnibus copiis exirent: perfacile esse, cum virtute omnibus praestarent,
5 totius Galliae imperio potiri. Id hoc facilius eis persuasit, quod undique
loci natura Helvetii continentur: una ex parte flumine Rheno latissimo
atque altissimo, qui agrum Helvetium a Germanis dividit; altera ex
parte monte Iura altissimo, qui est inter Sequanos et Helvetios; tertia
lacu Lemanno et flumine Rhodano, qui provinciam nostram ab Helvetiis
10 dividit. His rebus fiebat ut et minus late vagarentur et minus facile
finitimis bellum inferre possent; qua ex parte homines bellandi cupidi
magno dolore adficiebantur. Pro multitudine autem hominum et pro
gloria belli atque fortitudinis angustos se fines habere arbitrabantur, qui
in longitudinem milia passuum CCXL, in latitudinem CLXXX patebant.
15 [3] His rebus adducti et auctoritate Orgetorigis permoti constituerunt ea
quae ad proficiscendum pertinerent comparare, iumentorum et carrorum
quam maximum numerum coemere, sementes quam maximas facere, ut
in itinere copia frumenti suppeteret, cum proximis civitatibus pacem et
amicitiam confirmare. Ad eas res conficiendas biennium sibi satis esse
20 duxerunt; in tertium annum profectionem lege confirmant. Ad
eas res conficiendas Orgetorix deligitur. Is sibi legationem ad civitates
suscepit. In eo itinere persuadet Castico, Catamantaloedis filio,
Sequano, cuius pater regnum in Sequanis multos annos obtinuerat et a
senatu populi Romani amicus appellatus erat, ut regnum in civitate sua
25 occuparet, quod pater ante habuerat; itemque Dumnorigi Aeduo, fratri
Diviciaci, qui eo tempore principatum in civitate obtinebat ac maxime
plebi acceptus erat, ut idem conaretur persuadet eique filiam suam
in matrimonium dat. Perfacile factu esse illis probat conata perficere,
propterea quod ipse suae civitatis imperium obtenturus esset: non
30 esse dubium quin totius Galliae plurimum Helvetii possent; se suis
copiis suoque exercitu illis regna conciliaturum confirmat. Hac oratione
adducti inter se fidem et ius iurandum dant et regno occupato per tres
potentissimos ac firmissimos populos totius Galliae sese potiri posse
sperant.

Preparatory Questions

Line 1 In what degree are the adjectives *nobilissimus* and *ditissimus*? **superlative**

Line 2 What does the phrase *M. Messala et M. Pupio Pisone consulibus* communicate?

    This statement (an ablative absolute) gives the year, as teams of consuls served one year.

    Identify the form and case of *inductus*. **perfect participle passive, nominative**

Lines 3–4 Find an indirect command. **ut … exirent**

Line 4 In what tense and mood is *exirent* and why? **imperfect subjunctive in an indirect command following a secondary main verb**

    Find a *cum* clause. **cum … praestarent**

    What kind of *cum* clause is it? **cum causal**

Line 5 What does *quod* mean in this sentence? **because**

Line 6 Identify the case and use of *natura*. **ablative of means**

Line 7 What is the antecedent of *qui*? **flumine Rheno (line 6)**

    To what phrase in line 6 does *altera ex parte* compare? **una ex parte**

    What is the subject of *dividit*? **qui**

Line 9 What is the antecedent of *qui*? **flumine Rhodano**

Line 10 What result clause is the subject of *fiebat*? **ut et minus … possent**

    Identify the form and syntax of *vagarentur*. **third person plural imperfect subjunctive (deponent) in result clause following a secondary main verb**

Line 11 Identify the form and use of *bellandi*. **objective genitive gerund (with *cupidi*)**

Line 13 What is the antecedent of *se*? **they (in verb)**

Line 14 Identify the case and use of *longitudinem* and *latitudinem*. **accusative of extent**

Line 15 To what does the phrase *his rebus* refer? **the geographical circumstances**

Lines 16–19 Find four infinitives that form an indirect statement with *constituerunt*.

    comparare (line 16), coemere (line 17), facere (line 17), confirmare (line 19)

Line 17 Identify the syntax of *quam maximum*. **idiom used as modifier**

    What does it modify? **numerum**

Lines 17–18 Find a purpose clause. **ut … suppeteret**

Line 18 Identify the use of *cum*. **preposition "with" expressing accompaniment**

Line 19	What is the syntax of *ad eas res conficiendas*? **gerundive of purpose**
Line 20	Identify the case and use of *lege*. **ablative of means**
Line 21	Identify the case and use of *sibi*. **dative (reflexive), indirect object (of *suscepit*, line 22)**
Line 24	Who is the subject of *appellatus erat*? ***pater* (line 23)**
Line 26	What is the antecedent of *qui*? ***Diviciaci***
Line 27	To whom does *eique* refer? ***Dumnorigi* (line 25)**
Line 29	Identify the form and use of *obtenturus*. **future active participle in verb phrase**
Lines 30–31	Identify the case and use of *suis copiis suoque exercitu*. **ablative of means**
Line 32	What is the syntax of *regno occupato*? **ablative absolute**
Line 33	Identify the case and use of *sese*. **accusative; subject of infinitive in indirect statement**

Multiple Choice Questions *Suggested time: 40 minutes*

1. In line 1, *Helvetios* is
   a. **accusative object of preposition**
   b. accusative direct object
   c. nominative subject
   d. nominative appositive

2. In line 1 *longe* is
   a. a noun
   b. a verb
   c. an adjective
   d. **an adverb**

3. In line 2 we learn that Orgetorix
   a. is a Helvetian
   b. has lots of friends
   c. wants money
   d. **wants to be ruler**

4. The subject of *fecit* in line 3 is
   a. *Messala* (line 2)
   b. ***Is* (line 2)**
   c. *nobilitatis* (line 3)
   d. *inductus* (line 2)

5. In line 3 the object of *persuasit* is
   a. *coniurationem* (line 3)
   b. ***civitati* (line 3)**
   c. *finibus* (line 3)
   d. *copiis* (line 4)

6. The object of *potiri* in line 5 is
   a. *Galliae* (line 5)
   b. *virtute* (line 4)
   c. ***imperio* (line 5)**
   d. *omnibus* (the first in line 4)

7. In lines 5–6 *undique loci natura Helvetii continentur* we learn that the
   a. Helvetian boundaries were growing
   b. Helvetians were happy
   c. Helvetians were constricted
   d. Helvetians were warlike

8. In line 6 the word *latissimo* is translated
   a. very pretty
   b. somewhat wide
   c. somewhat pretty
   d. very wide

9. In lines 6–8 *una ex parte, altera ex parte,* and *tertia* introduce
   a. the limitations of Helvetian territories
   b. the extent of military strongholds
   c. a litany of scenic beauties
   d. the number of settlements or villages

10. In line 10 the word *minus*, used twice, is
    a. an adjective
    b. an adverb
    c. a noun
    d. a predicate adjective

11. In line 11 *qua ex parte* is best translated
    a. on that side
    b. on which side
    c. for which (this) reason
    d. on that hand

12. *bellandi cupidi* in line 11 modifies
    a. *homines* (line 11)
    b. *dolore* (line 12)
    c. *parte* (line 11)
    d. *adficiebantur* (line 12)

13. In line 13 *angustos se fines habere arbitrabantur* is best translated
    a. they thought about their boundaries
    b. they had limits
    c. they liked limits
    d. they thought they had narrow boundaries

14. In line 14 *longitudinem* and *latitudinem* mean
    a. longitude and latitude
    b. seriousness and breadth
    c. length and width
    d. depth and height

15. In line 15 *adducti* and *permoti* modify
    a. Orgetorix
    b. they
    c. those things
    d. authority

16. In line 16 *proficiscendum* is
    a. a major verb
    b. an adjective
    c. a gerund
    d. a helping verb

17. In line 17 *sementes quam maximas facere* means
    a. they would travel as widely as possible
    b. they would pack everything possible
    c. they would repel attacks as strongly as possible
    d. they would plant as much food as possible

18. In line 18 *cum* is translated
    a. with
    b. when
    c. since
    d. although

19. In line 19 *biennium* is
    a. the subject of *duxerunt* (line 20)
    b. an adverb
    c. the subject of an infinitive
    d. the object of *duxerunt* (line 20)

20. In line 20 what is planned for the third year?
    a. a battle
    b. a conference
    c. a revolution
    d. an exodus

21. In line 20 we learn that
    a. progress will be evaluated
    b. alternatives will be discussed
    c. by law everyone must depart
    d. new leaders will be elected

22. In line 21 *deligitur* is translated
    a. chooses
    b. is chosen
    c. delights
    d. is delighted

23. In lines 21–22 we learn that Orgetorix
    a. goes to visit other states
    b. oversees the grain supply
    c. amasses an army
    d. departs with his family

24. *persuadet* (line 22) governs
    a. *itinere* and a phrase (line 22)
    b. *regnum* and an adjective (line 24)
    c. *Castico* (line 22) and an *ut* clause (line 24)
    d. *occuparet* and a place (line 25)

25. In line 25 *quod* is translated
    a. because
    b. which
    c. that
    d. what

26. In lines 26–27 we learn that the leader of the Aeduans is
    a. Dumnorix
    b. Diviciacus
    c. Orgetorix
    d. Casticus

27. In line 27 *idem* refers back to
    a. **regnum in civitate sua occuparet (lines 24–25)** b. *persuadet Castico Sequano* (line 22)
    c. *eo itinere* (line 22) d. *quod pater* (line 25)

28. In lines 27–28 Orgetorix gives Dumnorix
    a. *principatum* (line 26) b. *civitate* (line 26)
    c. *imperium* (line 29) d. **filiam (line 27)**

29. In line 31 the elliptical phrase *conciliaturum* is completed by the understood
    a. *sunt* b. *habet*
    c. **esse** d. *dicit*

30. In line 32 *inter se* is translated
    a. for all b. for each other
    c. **among themselves** d. faithfully

31. In line 32 *regno occupato* is
    a. an ablative of time b. an ablative of means
    c. **an ablative absolute** d. an ablative of manner

32. In lines 32–34 we learn that the goal of the men is
    a. *potentissimos populos* (line 33) b. *sperant* (line 34)
    c. *ius iurandum* (line 32) d. **totius Galliae potiri (line 33)**

Translation *Suggested time: 15 minutes*

His rebus adducti et auctoritate Orgetorigis permoti constituerunt ea quae
ad proficiscendum pertinerent comparare, iumentorum et carrorum quam
maximum numerum coemere, sementes quam maximas facere, ut in itinere
copia frumenti suppeteret, cum proximis civitatibus pacem et amicitiam
5   confirmare.

20 chunks. 10 points, ½ point each.

His rebus	**By these things**
adducti	**influenced/prompted**
et auctoritate	**and by the authority**
Orgetorigis	**of Orgetorix**
permoti	**deeply moved/greatly influenced**
constituerunt	**they decided**
ea quae . . . pertinerent	**those things which . . . pertain**
ad proficiscendum	**to setting out**
comparare	**to prepare**
iumentorum et carrorum	**of beasts and carts**
quam maximum numerum	**as great a number as possible (the greatest possible number)**
coemere	**to buy up**
sementes quam maximas	**as great a planting as possible**
facere	**to make**
ut . . . .suppeteret	**so that . . . there might be**
in itinere	**on the journey**
copia frumenti	**a supply of grain/food**
cum proximis civitatibus	**(and) with neighboring states**
pacem et amicitiam	**peace and friendship**
confirmare	**to establish**

Short Analysis Questions

Apud Helvetios longe nobilissimus fuit et ditissimus Orgetorix. Is
M. Messala et M. Pupio Pisone consulibus, regni cupiditate inductus,
coniurationem nobilitatis fecit et civitati persuasit ut de finibus suis cum
omnibus copiis exirent: perfacile esse, cum virtute omnibus praestarent,
5   totius Galliae imperio potiri. Id hoc facilius eis persuasit, quod undique
loci natura Helvetii continentur: una ex parte flumine Rheno latissimo
atque altissimo, qui agrum Helvetium a Germanis dividit; altera ex
parte monte Iura altissimo, qui est inter Sequanos et Helvetios; tertia
lacu Lemanno et flumine Rhodano, qui provinciam nostram ab Helvetiis
10   dividit. His rebus fiebat ut et minus late vagarentur et minus facile
finitimis bellum inferre possent; qua ex parte homines bellandi cupidi
magno dolore adficiebantur. Pro multitudine autem hominum et pro gloria
belli atque fortitudinis angustos se fines habere arbitrabantur, qui in
longitudinem milia passuum CCXL, in latitudinem CLXXX patebant.

1. According to Caesar why does Orgetorix decide to talk his people into abandoning their homes? Cite the Latin that supports your answer and translate or accurately paraphrase.

    Caesar flatly says that Orgetorix is *regni cupiditate inductus* (line 2)—he wants a kingdom. [He makes a plot, *coniurationem* (line 3), among the nobles and then proceeds with the persuasion of everybody else—*civitati persuasit* (line 3).]

2. Why can the Helvetians not simply expand slowly, filching small amounts of land from their neighbors?

    They are hemmed in on all sides by the nature of the place. [*undique loci natura*]

3. In lines 11–12, what does Caesar say is a "grief" to some Helvetians? Could this statement be ironic? Cite the Latin that supports your answer and translate or accurately paraphrase.

    The men who like to fight—*homines bellandi cupidi* (line 12)—are grieved by this—*qua ex parte . . . magno dolore adficiebantur* (lines 11–12). For which reason—*qua ex parte*—refers back to lines 10–11, which states that it is difficult because of the nature of the place to fight with their neighbors—*minus facile finitimis bellum inferre*. The statement may well be ironic because of the use of the words *cupido* and *dolore* in connection with waging war. This is especially the case with *dolore* as we are accustomed to thinking of war in terms of grief while the Helvetians find it a grief not to be able to engage in war.

4. In lines 13–14 what two factors make the Helvetians think they need more land?

    The number of their population [*multitudine hominum*] and the pursuit of the glory of war. [*pro gloria belli*]

His rebus adducti et auctoritate Orgetorigis permoti constituerunt ea
quae ad proficiscendum pertinerent comparare, iumentorum et carrorum
quam maximum numerum coemere, sementes quam maximas facere, ut
in itinere copia frumenti suppeteret, cum proximis civitatibus pacem et
5   amicitiam confirmare. Ad eas res conficiendas biennium sibi satis esse
duxerunt; in tertium annum profectionem lege confirmant. Ad
eas res conficiendas Orgetorix deligitur. Is sibi legationem ad civitates
suscepit. In eo itinere persuadet Castico, Catamantaloedis filio,
Sequano, cuius pater regnum in Sequanis multos annos obtinuerat et a
10   senatu populi Romani amicus appellatus erat, ut regnum in civitate sua
occuparet, quod pater ante habuerat; itemque Dumnorigi Aeduo, fratri
Diviciaci, qui eo tempore principatum in civitate obtinebat ac maxime
plebi acceptus erat, ut idem conaretur persuadet eique filiam suam
in matrimonium dat. Perfacile factu esse illis probat conata perficere,
15   propterea quod ipse suae civitatis imperium obtenturus esset: non
esse dubium quin totius Galliae plurimum Helvetii possent; se suis
copiis suoque exercitu illis regna conciliaturum confirmat. Hac oratione
adducti inter se fidem et ius iurandum dant et regno occupato per tres
potentissimos ac firmissimos populos totius Galliae sese potiri posse
20   sperant.

5.   What two considerations influenced the Helvetians to leave everything they had ever known?
Cite the Latin that supports your answer and translate or accurately paraphrase.

**The feelings cited in the statements above—*his rebus adducti* (line 1)—and the influence of
Orgetorix—*et auctoritate Orgetorigis* (line 1).**

6.   In lines 2–5 Caesar discusses three essentials for the success of this undertaking. Cite and
translate an indirect statement describing each of these.

**A) *iumentorum et carrorum quam maximum numerum coemere* (lines 2–3)—to buy as many
carts and beasts as possible
B) *sementes quam maximas facere* (line 3)—to plant as much grain (food) as possible
C) *cum proximis civitatibus pacem et amicitiam confirmare* (lines 4–5)—to establish friendly
relations with the neighbors.**

7.   In lines 7–8 Orgetorix concerns himself with which one of these three essentials?

relationships with the neighbors—*Is sibi legationem ad civitates suscepit.*

8.   How does Orgetorix go far beyond the simple establishment of friendly relations? Cite the
Latin that supports your answer and translate or accurately paraphrase.

**He makes a conspiracy with powerful neighboring men, Casticus the Sequanus and
Dumnorix the Aeduan, to seize power in their lands—*regnum in civitate sua occuparet* (lines
10–11).**

Essay *Suggested time: 20 minutes*

In eo itinere persuadet Castico, Catamantaloedis filio, Sequano,
cuius pater regnum in Sequanis multos annos obtinuerat et a senatu
populi Romani amicus appellatus erat, ut regnum in civitate sua occuparet,
quod pater ante habuerat; itemque Dumnorigi Aeduo, fratri Diviciaci,
5   qui eo tempore principatum in civitate obtinebat ac maxime plebi acceptus
erat, ut idem conaretur persuadet eique filiam suam in matrimonium
dat. Perfacile factu esse illis probat conata perficere, propterea quod ipse
suae civitatis imperium obtenturus esset: non esse dubium quin totius
Galliae plurimum Helvetii possent; se suis copiis suoque exercitu illis
10   regna conciliaturum confirmat. Hac oratione adducti inter se fidem et ius
iurandum dant et regno occupato per tres potentissimos ac firmissimos
populos totius Galliae sese potiri posse sperant.

In this passage we see how Orgetorix means to use the dissatisfaction of Helvetians and others for his own ends. Discuss Orgetorix's ultimate goal, the allies he chose, why he probably chose them, what he wanted them to do, and what he promised that he himself would do.

Support your assertions with references to the Latin text throughout the passage above. All Latin words must be copied or their line numbers provided, AND they must be translated or paraphrased closely enough that it is clear that you understand the Latin. It is your responsibility to convince the reader that you are basing your conclusions on the Latin text and not merely on a general recollection of the passage. Direct your answer to the question; do not merely summarize the passage. Please write your essay on a separate piece of paper.

Teachers should review the Essay Scoring Guidelines given at the beginning of this manual with students.

Orgetorix's ultimate goal is power or rulership over all Gaul—*totius Galliae sese potiri* (line 12). His chosen allies were powerful men very close to supreme power in their own lands. The first, Casticus the Sequanus, was the son of the former ruler of his nation—*pater regnum in Sequanis multos annos obtinuerat* (line 2). It must have been fairly easy to persuade him that he should have this power. A further consideration was Casticus's father's friendship with Rome; he was designated a friend of the Romans—*populi Romani amicus appellatus* (line 3). To detach Casticus and his nation from this alliance would probably weaken Roman influence and make Casticus more dependent on Orgetorix.

Dumnorix was the brother of the Aeduan leader Diviciacus, *fratri Diviciaci, qui . . . principatum in civitate obtinebat* (lines 4–5). A bit of sibling rivalry would make Dumnorix more eager to undercut his brother and at the same time deprive him of that brother's aid and make him more dependent on Orgetorix. Orgetorix gave his daughter in marriage to Dumnorix to cement the friendship, and persuades Casticus and Dumnorix to seek supreme power in their realms—*ut regnum in civitate sua occuparet* (line 3). He promised to do the same in his own land—*ipse suae civitatis imperium obtenturus esset* (lines 7–8).

CHAPTER 3: BOOK 1.4–5
THE PREPARATIONS OF THE HELVETIANS

[4] Ea res est Helvetiis per indicium enuntiata. Moribus suis Orgetorigem
ex vinclis causam dicere coegerunt. Damnatum poenam sequi oportebat
ut igni cremaretur. Die constituta causae dictionis Orgetorix ad iudicium
omnem suam familiam, ad hominum milia decem, undique coegit, et
5   omnes clientes obaeratosque suos, quorum magnum numerum habebat,
eodem conduxit; per eos ne causam diceret se eripuit. Cum civitas ob eam
rem incitata armis ius suum exsequi conaretur multitudinemque hominum
ex agris magistratus cogerent, Orgetorix mortuus est; neque abest suspicio,
ut Helvetii arbitrantur, quin ipse sibi mortem consciverit. [5] Post eius
10   mortem nihilo minus Helvetii id quod constituerant facere conantur,
ut e finibus suis exeant. Ubi iam se ad eam rem paratos esse arbitrati
sunt, oppida sua omnia, numero ad duodecim, vicos ad quadringentos,
reliqua privata aedificia incendunt; frumentum omne, praeter quam quod
secum portaturi erant, comburunt, ut domum reditionis spe sublata
15   paratiores ad omnia pericula subeunda essent; trium mensum molita
cibaria sibi quemque domo efferre iubent. Persuadent Rauracis et Tulingis
et Latobrigis finitimis, uti eodem usi consilio oppidis suis vicisque exustis
una cum eis proficiscantur, Boiosque, qui trans Rhenum incoluerant et in
agrum Noricum transierant Noreiamque oppugnarant, receptos ad se
20   socios sibi asciscunt.

Preparatory Questions

Line 1   Identify the case and use of *Orgetorigem*. **accusative; direct object (of *coegerunt*, line 2)**

Line 2   What part of speech is *damnatum*? **(verbal) adjective (perfect passive participle)**

Identify the use of *oportebat*. **impersonal verb**

Line 3   Identify the tense, mood, and voice of *cremaretur*. **imperfect subjunctive passive**

Identify the case and use of *Die constituta*. **ablative absolute**

Line 4   What does *omnem* modify? **familiam**

Find two objects of *coegit*. **familiam (line 4), clientes (line 5)**

Line 5   What is the antecedent of *quorum*? **clientes obaerotosque**

Line 6   Identify the case and use of *eos*. **accusative, object of the preposition *per***

Find a negative clause of purpose. **ne causam diceret**

What is the tense and voice of *eripuit*? **perfect active**

Lines 6–7 Find a *cum* clause. ***Cum civitas ... conarentur***

What kind of *cum* clause is it? ***Cum* circumstantial**

Line 7 What is the tense and voice of *conaretur*? **imperfect deponent**

Line 8 Identify the case and use of *magistratus*. **nominative, subject (of *cogerent*)**

What is the tense and voice of *mortuus est*? **perfect deponent**

Line 9 Identify the tense of *consciverit*. **perfect (subjunctive)**

Line 10 What is the antecedent of *quod*? ***id***

What is the subject of *conantur*? ***Helvetii***

Line 11 Find an *ut* clause. ***ut e finibus suis exeant***

What kind of *ut* clause is it? **(substantive clause of) result**

Line 12 Identify the case and use of *numero*. **ablative of specification**

Lines 12–13 Find three objects of *incendunt*. ***oppida, vicos, aedificia***

Line 13 Identify the case and use of *frumentum*. **accusative, direct object (of *comburunt*, line 14)**

Line 14 Identify the form and use of *portaturi*. **future active participle, part of verb**

Identify the case and use of *spe sublata*. **ablative absolute**

Line 15 What does *molita* modify? ***cibaria* (line 16)**

Line 16 Identify the form and syntax of *efferre*. **present active infinitive after *iubent***

Line 17 Identify the form and use of *finitimis*. **dative plural masculine appositive to *Rauricis*, etc., dative object of *persuadent* (line 16)**

Line 18 What is the antecedent of *qui*? ***Boios***

Identify the tense and voice of *incoluerant*. **pluperfect active**

Line 20 To what word is *socios* an appositive? ***Boios* (line 18)**

Multiple Choice Questions *Suggested time: 35 minutes*

1. In line 1 *Ea res* refers to
   a. the weather
   b. Orgetorix's plan
   c. Caesar's arrival
   d. the departure

2. In line 2 the phrase *ex vinclis* is translated
   a. at home
   b. in jail
   c. in absentia
   d. in chains

3. In line 2 *causam dicere* is translated
   a. to write a story
   b. to call the roll
   c. to plead his case
   d. to give instructions

4. In lines 2–3 we learn that the Helvetian punishment for treason was
   a. exile
   b. a fine
   c. death by stoning
   d. death by fire

5. *ad hominum milia decem* (line 4) modifies
   a. *Orgetorix* (line 3)
   b. *iudicium* (line 3)
   c. *familiam* (line 4)
   d. *clientes* (line 5)

6. In line 4 *coegit* is translated
   a. compelled
   b. collected
   c. addressed
   d. saw

7. The object of *conduxit* (line 6) is
   a. *clientes* (line 5)
   b. *numerum* (line 5)
   c. *familiam* (line 4)
   d. *eos* (line 6)

8. In line 6 *eodem* is translated
   a. all together
   b. to the same place
   c. a few at a time
   d. at that time

9. In line 6 *ne* is translated
   a. never
   b. not many
   c. none
   d. so that ... not

10. In line 6 we learn that Orgetorix
    a. escaped pleading his case
    b. begged forgiveness
    c. persuaded the judges of his case
    d. led a revolution

11. In line 8 *neque abest suspicio* is an example of the figure of speech
    a. alliteration
    c. litotes
    b. metaphor
    d. chiasmus

12. In line 9 *quin . . . consciverit* is translated
    a. that he died
    c. that he was not killed
    b. that he was killed
    d. that he decided on suicide

13. In lines 9–11 we learn that the Helvetians
    a. gave up hope of emigrating
    c. made new plans
    b. tore down the statues of Orgetorix
    d. continued the emigration plan

14. In line 11 *ubi* is translated
    a. where
    c. under
    b. when
    d. eventually

15. In line 11 *paratos* modifies
    a. *finibus* (line 11)
    c. se (line 11)
    b. *rem* (line 11)
    d. *oppida* (line 12)

16. In line 12 *duodecim* refers to
    a. *se* (line 11)
    c. *rem* (line 11)
    b. oppida (line 12)
    d. *vicos* (line 12)

17. In lines 12–13 we learn that the Helvetian cities and villages
    a. were all burned
    c. were carefully preserved
    b. were extensive and beautiful
    d. were widely scattered

18. In line 14 *portaturi erant* is translated
    a. they were carried
    c. they were going to carry
    b. they will carry
    d. they had carried

19. In line 14 *domum reditionis* depends upon
    a. spe (line 14)
    c. *secum* (line 14)
    b. *comburunt* (line 14)
    d. *frumentum* (line 13)

20. In line 14 *secum* is translated
    a. seed
    c. with them
    b. grain
    d. lonely

21. In line 15 *paratiores* is
    - a. a comparative adverb
    - **b. a comparative adjective**
    - c. a verb form
    - d. a nominative noun

22. In line 15 *subeunda* is
    - a. an infinitive
    - b. a noun
    - **c. a gerundive**
    - d. a verb

23. In line 15 *trium mensum* is
    - **a. a genitive of measure**
    - b. a genitive of possession
    - c. an accusative singular phrase
    - d. an appositive

24. In line 16 *quemque* is translated
    - **a. each one**
    - b. that one
    - c. whoever
    - d. whatever

25. In line 17 *uti* is a variation of
    - a. *utor*
    - b. *usque*
    - **c. *ut***
    - d. *ultimus*

26. In line 18 *una cum* is translated
    - a. one alone
    - **b. along with**
    - c. unique
    - d. one by one

27. The subject of *transierant* (line 19) is
    - a. *Tulingis* (line 16)
    - b. *Rhenum* (line 18)
    - **c. *qui* (line 18)**
    - d. *oppidis* (line 17)

28. In lines 18–19 the Boii
    - a. were just crossing the Rhine
    - **b. had come into Norican land**
    - c. were attacking the Helvetians
    - d. asked for peace

29. In lines 18–19 the Helvetians
    - a. repelled the Boii
    - b. ignored the Boii
    - c. helped the Noreians
    - **d. made allies of the Boii**

Translation *Suggested Time: 15 Minutes*

frumentum omne, praeter quam quod secum portaturi erant, comburunt,
ut domum reditionis spe sublata paratiores ad omnia pericula subeunda
essent; trium mensum molita cibaria sibi quemque domo efferre iubent.

12 chunks. 6 points, ½ point each.

Frumentum omne . . . comburunt	**all the grain they burn**
praeter quod	**except (that) which/what**
secum	**with them**
portaturi erant	**they were going to carry**
ut . . . paratiores . . . essent	**so that they might be more prepared**
domum reditionis	**of returning/the return home**
spe sublata	**the hope having been destroyed/since hope had been destroyed**
ad omnia pericula subeunda	**for all dangers to be undergone**
trium mensum molita cibaria	**a three month's ground flour allowance**
sibi . . . quemque	**for himself each one**
domo efferre	**to carry out from home**
iubent	**they command**

Short Analysis Questions

Ea res est Helvetiis per indicium enuntiata. Moribus suis Orgetorigem ex
vinclis causam dicere coegerunt. Damnatum poenam sequi oportebat
ut igni cremaretur. Die constituta causae dictionis Orgetorix ad iudicium
omnem suam familiam, ad hominum milia decem, undique coegit, et
5   omnes clientes obaeratosque suos, quorum magnum numerum habebat,
eodem conduxit; per eos ne causam diceret se eripuit. Cum civitas ob eam
rem incitata armis ius suum exsequi conaretur multitudinemque hominum
ex agris magistratus cogerent, Orgetorix mortuus est; neque abest suspicio,
ut Helvetii arbitrantur, quin ipse sibi mortem consciverit.

1. In lines 4–7 how powerful a man is Orgetorix shown to be and how does that aid him? Cite the Latin that supports your answer and translate or accurately paraphrase.

    Orgetorix has ten thousand members of his immediate household—*familiam, ad hominum milia decem*—and a great number of clients and debtors—*clientes obaeratosque suos, . . . magnum numerum*. Through them he escaped—*per eos . . . se eripuit*. Obviously he is more powerful than the civil authority and they cannot contain him.

2. In lines 7–9 to what lengths did the Helvetians have to proceed in order to attempt to bring Orgetorix to the court of justice? Cite the Latin that supports your answer and translate or accurately paraphrase.

    The authorities have to call out a great number of citizens from their agricultural labors—*multitudinemque hominum ex agris magistratus cogerent* (lines 7–8).

3. In line 9, how did they believe he had escaped that justice? Cite the Latin that supports your answer and translate or accurately paraphrase.

They think he had chosen suicide to escape trial—*Helvetii arbitrantur . . . ipse sibi mortem consciverit.*

Essay *Suggested time: 20 minutes*

> Ubi iam se ad eam rem paratos esse arbitrati sunt, oppida sua omnia,
> numero ad duodecim, vicos ad quadringentos, reliqua privata aedificia
> incendunt; frumentum omne, praeter quam quod secum portaturi erant,
> comburunt, ut domum reditionis spe sublata paratiores ad omnia pericula
> 5   subeunda essent; trium mensum molita cibaria sibi quemque domo efferre
> iubent. Persuadent Rauracis et Tulingis et Latobrigis finitimis, uti eodem
> usi consilio oppidis suis vicisque exustis una cum eis proficiscantur,
> Boiosque, qui trans Rhenum incoluerant et in agrum Noricum transierant
> Noreiamque oppugnarant, receptos ad se socios sibi asciscunt.

In this passage the extensive preparations that the Helvetians made for setting out from home *en masse* are discussed. In a short essay, discuss the drastic measures they took at home, why they thought these necessary, and the preparations made here for the journey.

Support your assertions with references to the Latin text throughout the passage above. All Latin words must be copied or their line numbers provided, AND they must be translated or paraphrased closely enough that it is clear that you understand the Latin. It is your responsibility to convince the reader that you are basing your conclusions on the Latin text and not merely on a general recollection of the passage. Direct your answer to the question; do not merely summarize the passage. Please write your essay on a separate piece of paper.

Teachers should review the Essay Scoring Guidelines given at the beginning of this manual with students.

A good essay should stress the measures taken to prevent anyone's refusing to leave or trying to sneak back. Their twelve cities, their four hundred villages, private buildings, and all food that could not be taken on the journey were burned—*oppida . . . ad duodecim, vicos ad quadringentos, reliqua privata aedificia incendunt; frumentum omne, praeter quam quod secum portaturi erant, comburunt . . .* **(lines 1–4). These things were necessary, they said, in order to stiffen everyone for the hard journey by taking away the possibility of going back**—*ut domum reditionis spe sublata paratiores ad omnia pericula subeunda essent* **(lines 4–5). After they did this, they turned their attention to the food necessary for the journey, which everyone had to provide for himself**—*molita cibaria sibi quemque domo efferre iubent* **(lines 5–6). They persuaded three tribes to destroy their homes and go with them.** *Persuadent Rauracis et Tulingis et Latobrigis finitimis, uti . . . oppidis suis vicisque exustis una cum eis proficiscantur* **(lines 6–7). They made an alliance with another tribe, the Boii, who had attacked Noreia.** *Boiosque, qui . . . in agrum Noricum transierant Noreiamque oppugnarant, receptos ad se socios sibi asciscunt* **(lines 8–9).**

Notes

CHAPTER 4: BOOK 1.6–7
THE HELVETIANS REQUEST PASSAGE

[6] Erant omnino itinera duo, quibus itineribus domo exire possent:
unum per Sequanos, angustum et difficile, inter montem Iuram et flumen
Rhodanum, vix qua singuli carri ducerentur, mons autem altissimus
impendebat, ut facile perpauci prohibere possent; alterum per provinciam
5   nostram, multo facilius atque expeditius, propterea quod inter fines
Helvetiorum et Allobrogum, qui nuper pacati erant, Rhodanus fluit
isque non nullis locis vado transitur. Extremum oppidum Allobrogum
est proximumque Helvetiorum finibus Genava. Ex eo oppido pons ad
Helvetios pertinet. Allobrogibus sese vel persuasuros, quod nondum bono
10   animo in populum Romanum viderentur, existimabant vel vi coacturos
ut per suos fines eos ire paterentur. Omnibus rebus ad profectionem
comparatis diem dicunt, qua die ad ripam Rhodani omnes conveniant. Is
dies erat a. d. V. Kal. Apr. L. Pisone, A. Gabinio consulibus. [7] Caesari
cum id nuntiatum esset, eos per provinciam nostram iter facere conari,
15   maturat ab urbe proficisci et quam maximis potest itineribus in Galliam
ulteriorem contendit et ad Genavam pervenit. Provinciae toti quam
maximum potest militum numerum imperat (erat omnino in Gallia
ulteriore legio una), pontem, qui erat ad Genavam, iubet rescindi. Ubi
de eius adventu Helvetii certiores facti sunt, legatos ad eum mittunt
20   nobilissimos civitatis, cuius legationis Nammeius et Verucloetius
principem locum obtinebant, qui dicerent sibi esse in animo sine ullo
maleficio iter per provinciam facere, propterea quod aliud iter haberent
nullum: rogare ut eius voluntate id sibi facere liceat. Caesar, quod
memoria tenebat L. Cassium consulem occisum exercitumque eius ab
25   Helvetiis pulsum et sub iugum missum, concedendum non putabat; neque
homines inimico animo, data facultate per provinciam itineris faciendi,
temperaturos ab iniuria et maleficio existimabat. Tamen, ut spatium
intercedere posset dum milites quos imperaverat convenirent, legatis
respondit diem se ad deliberandum sumpturum: si quid vellent, ad Id.
30   April. reverterentur.

Preparatory Questions

Line 1   What is the antecedent of *quibus*? **itinera**

Identify the form and use of *exire*. **present active infinitive, complementary with possent**

Identify the case and use of *domo*. **ablative of place from which (with *exire*)**

Line 2	What does *difficile* modify? **unum (iter)**
	What are the objects of *inter*? **montem Iuram et flumen Rhodanum**
Line 3	What is the tense, mood, and voice of *ducerentur*? **imperfect subjunctive passive**
Line 4	Find a result clause. **ut ... possent**
	What is the subject of *possent*? **perpauci**
Line 5	What is the case and use of *multo*? **ablative degree of difference**
	Identify the part of speech and degree of *facilius*. **comparative adjective**
Line 6	Find a relative clause. **qui ... pacati erant**
	What kind of relative clause is it? **adjectival or parenthetical**
Line 7	What does *–que* connect? **Rhodanus and is**
	Identify the case and use of *vado*. **ablative of means**
	Identify the case and use of *Allobrogum*. **genitive of possession**
Line 8	What does *proximum* modify? **oppidum (line 7)**
	Identify the case and use of *Genava*. **nominative, subject**
	To what does *eo oppido* refer? **Genava**
Line 9	What is the form and use of *persuasuros*? **future active participle with understood "esse"**
Line 10	What is the subject of *existimabant*? **"they," i.e., the Helvetii**
	What does *coacturos* modify? **sese (line 9)**
Line 11	Find an *ut* clause. **ut ... paterentur**
Lines 9–12	Find an indirect statement. **sese persuasuros (esse) ... vel coacturos (esse)**
Line 12	Identify the case and use of *qua die*. **ablative of time when**
Line 13	What information does the phrase *L. Pisone, A. Gabinio consulibus* give?
	the year or date of the event
Line 14	Find a *cum* clause. **cum ... esset**

What kind of *cum* clause is it? **cum circumstantial**

To whom does *eos* refer? **the Helvetians**

What is the subject of *conari*? **eos**

Line 15   Identify the form and use of *proficisci*. **present infinitive deponent, complementary with *maturat***

Line 17   Give the dative and accusative objects of *imperat*. **Provinciae, numerum**

Line 18   Identify the case and use of *pontem*. **accusative subject of infinitive *rescindi* (following *iubet*)**

Line 19   To whom does *eius* refer? **Caesar**

Line 20   What does *nobilissimos* modify? **legatos (line 19)**

Line 22   Identify the case and use of *iter*. **accusative, direct object of *facere***

Line 23   What does *nullum* modify? **iter**

Identify the form and use of *liceat*. **impersonal third person singular present subjunctive active in an indirect command**

Line 24   What does *occisum* modify? **Cassium**

Line 25   Identify the form and use of *concedendum*. **gerundive in a passive periphrastic with understood *esse* and *id* (line 23)**

Line 27   What does *temperaturos* modify? **homines (line 26)**

Lines 27–29   Find a purpose clause. **ut spatium ... posset**

Line 29   What construction is *ad deliberandum*? **gerund of purpose**

How does the word *si* change the meaning of *quid*? **quid becomes "anything" (aliquid)**

Multiple Choice Questions *Suggested time: 37 minutes*

1.   In line 1, *itinera* is translated
   a. methods   **b. routes**
   c. groups   d. countries

2.   In line 2, *unum* stands for the understood noun
   a. iter   b. *domo*
   c. *flumen*   d. *montem*

3.   In line 3, *singuli* is translated
   a. unusual   b. loaded
   c. one at a time   d. unique

4. In line 3, *autem* is
   a. an adjective
   c. an accusative noun

   b. a helping verb
   d. an adverb

5. In line 3 *vix qua . . . ducerentur* is
   a. a relative clause
   c. an indirect question

   b. a relative clause of characteristic
   d. a conditional clause

6. In line 4, *perpauci* is translated
   a. armies
   c. very few

   b. enemies
   d. spies

7. The figure of speech in line 4 is
   a. litotes
   c. alliteration

   b. metaphor
   d. simile

8. In line 5, *propterea quod* is translated
   a. whenever
   c. property

   b. because
   d. which

9. In line 6 we learn that the Allobroges
   a. were old friends of the Romans
   c. had recently been subdued

   b. hated the Helvetians
   d. had great wealth

10. In line 7, *non nullis* is translated
    a. never
    c. unlikely

    b. some
    d. none

11. In line 8 we learn that Genava is
    a. a city of the Helvetians
    c. a Helvetian camp

    b. a city near Helvetia
    d. a lake near Helvetia

12. The subject of *pertinet* (line 9) is
    a. *pons* (line 8)
    c. *oppido* (line 8)

    b. *Genava* (line 8)
    d. *Helvetios* (line 9)

13. *paterentur* (line 11) comes from the verb
    a. *pateo*
    c. *paro*

    b. *patior*
    d. *patro*

14. In lines 11–12, *omnibus rebus comparatis* is
   a. an indirect statement
   b. a gerund phrase
   c. an ablative absolute
   d. a gerundive clause

15. In line 13, *a. d. V. Kal. Apr.* is in the month of
   a. April
   b. March
   c. May
   d. June

16. In line 14, *eos per provinciam nostram iter facere conari* explains
   a. *eos* (line 14)
   b. *Caesari* (line 13)
   c. *id* (line 14)
   d. *nostram* (line 14)

17. In line 15, *quam maximis itineribus* <u>literally</u> means
   a. whatever routes possible
   b. by the greatest marches possible
   c. by the longest routes
   d. with great labor

18. In lines 15–16 we learn that Caesar hurries to
   a. Rome
   b. the army camp
   c. headquarters
   d. Genava

19. In line 17, *imperat* is translated
   a. he is impertinent
   b. he seeks
   c. he requisitions
   d. he praises

20. In lines 17–18 we learn that Caesar's strategic aim in Genava is
   a. to confront the Allobroges
   b. to train his troops
   c. to make speeches
   d. to destroy the bridge to Helvetia

21. In line 19, *certiores facti sunt* is translated
   a. they were told
   b. they were informed
   c. they were asked
   d. they said

22. In line 21, *esse in animo* is translated
   a. to have in mind
   b. to trust
   c. to promise
   d. to request

23. In line 22, the second *iter* is modified by
   a. *aliud nullum* (lines 22–23)
   b. *sibi* (line 21)
   c. *provinciam* (line 22)
   d. *facere* (line 22)

24. In lines 23–25 Caesar recalls
    a. Helvetians have been friends to the Romans
    b. Helvetians previously defeated the Allobroges
    c. Helvetians killed a Roman consul and sent his army under the yoke
    d. Helvetians previously invaded the Roman province before

25. In line 25, *concedendum* modifies
    a. *id* (line 23)
    b. *missum* (line 25)
    c. *homines* (line 26)
    d. *animo* (line 26)

26. In line 27, *temperaturos* is translated
    a. going to count
    b. going to restrain themselves
    c. going to help
    d. going to visit

27. In line 27, *iniuria et maleficio* are
    a. ablative absolutes
    b. ablatives of separation
    c. datives
    d. ablatives of means

28. In line 27, *ut* introduces
    a. a purpose clause
    b. a result clause
    c. a relative clause
    d. a negative clause

29. In line 28, *dum* is translated
    a. over
    b. so that
    c. until
    d. after

30. In lines 28–30 Caesar says that
    a. he is willing for them to pass
    b. he wants to think about it
    c. he will not allow it
    d. he really likes the idea

31. In line 29, *quid* after *si* is translated
    a. which
    b. where
    c. anything
    d. something

Translation *Suggested time: 15 minutes*

Caesari cum id nuntiatum esset, eos per provinciam nostram iter facere conari, maturat ab urbe proficisci et quam maximis potest itineribus in Galliam ulteriorem contendit et ad Genavam pervenit. Provinciae toti quam maximum potest militum numerum imperat (erat omnino in Gallia
5   ulteriore legio una), pontem, qui erat ad Genavam, iubet rescindi.

19 chunks. 20 points, ½ point each.

Caesari	to Caesar
cum id nuntiatum esset	when it had been announced
eos	them/that they
per provinciam nostram	through our province
iter facere conari	to try/were trying to make a journey
maturat . . . proficisci	he hurries . . . to set out
ab urbe	from the city
et quam maximis potest itineribus	and by the greatest possible marches
in Galliam ulteriorem	into further Gaul
contendit	he made his way/hastened
et ad Genavam	and at Genava
pervenit	he arrived
Provinciae toti	the whole province
quam maximum potest militum numerum	the greatest number of soldiers he could
imperat	he requisitions
erat . . . legio una omnino	there was in all one legion
in Gallia ulteriore	in further Gaul.
pontem . . . iubet rescindi	He orders the bridge to be torn down
qui erat ad Genavam	that was at Genava

Short Analysis Questions

> Erant omnino itinera duo, quibus itineribus domo exire possent: unum per
> Sequanos, angustum et difficile, inter montem Iuram et flumen Rhodanum,
> vix qua singuli carri ducerentur, mons autem altissimus impendebat,
> ut facile perpauci prohibere possent; alterum per provinciam nostram,
> 5 multo facilius atque expeditius, propterea quod inter fines Helvetiorum
> et Allobrogum, qui nuper pacati erant, Rhodanus fluit isque non nullis
> locis vado transitur. Extremum oppidum Allobrogum est proximumque
> Helvetiorum finibus Genava. Ex eo oppido pons ad Helvetios pertinet.
> Allobrogibus sese vel persuasuros, quod nondum bono animo in populum
> 10 Romanum viderentur, existimabant vel vi coacturos ut per suos fines eos
> ire paterentur.

1. From lines 1–4, give two major difficulties with the first route of departure that the Helvetians considered. Cite the Latin that supports your answer and translate or accurately paraphrase.

   The path through the territory of the Sequani was narrow and hard, running between mountains and a river—*unum per Sequanos, angustum et difficile, inter montem Iuram et flumen Rhodanum* (lines 1–2). In addition, it was so narrow that only one cart could pass at a time, and overhanging mountains allowed a very few people to stop the progress—*vix qua singuli carri ducerentur, mons autem altissimus impendebat, ut facile perpauci prohibere possent* (lines 3–4).

2. Discuss the great geographical advantages of the second route as outlined in lines 5–7.

   There was only a river, fordable in several places, between the Helvetians' land and the Roman province—*inter fines Helvetiorum et Allobrogum . . . Rhodanus fluit isque non nullis locis vado transitur.*

3. Caesar elliptically comments on what recent experience of the Allobroges?

   They had been "pacified" or brought under Roman control—*qui nuper pacati erant* (line 6). They don't seem yet reconciled to Roman control—*nondum bono animo in populum Romanum viderentur* (lines 9–10).

4. What is the strategic importance of Genava (lines 7–8)? Cite the Latin that supports your answer and translate or accurately paraphrase.

   Genava is at the edge of the Allobroges' territory and nearest to the Helvetians—*Extremum oppidum Allobrogum est proximumque Helvetiorum finibus Genava* (lines 7–8).

5. What do the Helvetians hope to do about the Allobroges? Cite the Latin that supports your answer and translate or accurately paraphrase.

   They think they can either persuade or force the Allobroges to let them pass—*existimabant vel vi coacturos ut per suos fines eos ire paterentur* (lines 10–11).

Caesari cum id nuntiatum esset, eos per provinciam nostram iter facere
conari, maturat ab urbe proficisci et quam maximis potest itineribus
in Galliam ulteriorem contendit et ad Genavam pervenit. Provinciae
toti quam maximum potest militum numerum imperat (erat omnino in
5   Gallia ulteriore legio una), pontem, qui erat ad Genavam, iubet rescindi.
Ubi de eius adventu Helvetii certiores facti sunt, legatos ad eum mittunt
nobilissimos civitatis, cuius legationis Nammeius et Verucloetius
principem locum obtinebant, qui dicerent sibi esse in animo sine ullo
maleficio iter per provinciam facere, propterea quod aliud iter haberent
10   nullum: rogare ut eius voluntate id sibi facere liceat.

6.   In lines 1–3 what does Caesar do when he hears of the Helvetian plans?

He rushes to Genava. [*maturat . . . in Galliam ulteriorem contendit et ad Genavam pervenit.*]

7.   In lines 3–5, what two actions does Caesar take upon arrival in Genava?

He levies as many soldiers as possible [*quam maximum potest militum numerum imperat* (line 4)] and orders the bridge to Helvetia to be destroyed [*pontem, qui erat ad Genavam, iubet rescindi* (line 5)].

8.   What do the Helvetian envoys say to Caesar?

They say they want to cross his province without doing any harm. [*dicerent sibi esse in animo sine ullo maleficio iter per provinciam facere* (lines 8–9)].

9.   Why do they say this is necessary?

They have no other route. [*aliud iter haberent nullum* (lines 9–10)].

10.   What do they ask of him?

They ask that he grant them passage. [*ut eius voluntate id sibi facere liceat* (line 10)].

Essay *Suggested time: 20 minutes*

> Caesar, quod memoria tenebat L. Cassium consulem occisum exercitumque
> eius ab Helvetiis pulsum et sub iugum missum, concedendum non
> putabat; neque homines inimico animo, data facultate per provinciam
> itineris faciendi, temperaturos ab iniuria et maleficio existimabat. Tamen,
> 5   ut spatium intercedere posset dum milites quos imperaverat convenirent,
> legatis respondit diem se ad deliberandum sumpturum: si quid vellent, ad
> Id. April. reverterentur.

In this passage Caesar gives his thoughts on and his reaction to the Helvetian request. In a short essay, discuss the factors Caesar weighed when considering the request, his publicly stated reason for delay, and his private and practical reason. Comment on his ability as a leader as shown in this passage.

Support your assertions with references to the Latin text throughout the passage above. All Latin words must be copied or their line numbers provided, AND they must be translated or paraphrased closely enough that it is clear that you understand the Latin. It is your responsibility to convince the reader that you are basing your conclusions on the Latin text and not merely on a general recollection of the passage. Direct your answer to the question; do not merely summarize the passage. Please write your essay on a separate piece of paper.

Teachers should review the Essay Scoring Guidelines given at the beginning of this manual with students.

Caesar carefully considers a previous encounter between Romans and Helvetians. There had been a battle in which the Helvetians killed a Roman consul and sent his army under the yoke—*memoria tene-bat L. Cassium consulem occisum exercitumque eius ab Helvetiis pulsum et sub iugum missum* (lines 1–2). This memory makes him feel that their request should not be granted—*concedendum non putabat* (lines 2–3)—as they must be considered unfriendly to the Romans. He does not think that these unfriendly men—*homines inimico animo* (line 3)—are going to refrain from destructive deeds—*temperaturos ab iniuria et maleficio* (line 4)—if they are allowed into the province. This thinking provides him a very practical reason for forbidding their crossing, but he does not think it is wise to say so at the outset. He tells them he wants to think about it—*diem se ad deliberandum sumpturum* (line 6)—and bids them come back later. Caesar is a very astute leader. He weighs the facts and decides that Helvetians roaming through the province are not a good idea, but he wants a bit of time to prepare for their reaction to a negative response. Therefore he tells them to come back, and gives them a specific day for doing so—*ad Id. April. reverterentur* (lines 6–7). This both delays any unpleasant reaction they may show to being refused and gives them hope that perhaps he may allow the crossing.

CHAPTER 5: BOOK 4.24–25
CAESAR'S TROOPS ARRIVE OFF
THE COAST OF BRITAIN

[24] At barbari, consilio Romanorum cognito praemisso equitatu et
essedariis, quo plerumque genere in proeliis uti consuerunt, reliquis
copiis subsecuti nostros navibus egredi prohibebant. Erat ob has causas
summa difficultas, quod naves propter magnitudinem nisi in alto constitui
5   non poterant, militibus autem, ignotis locis, impeditis manibus, magno
et gravi onere armorum oppressis, simul et de navibus desiliendum et
in fluctibus consistendum et cum hostibus erat pugnandum, cum illi aut
ex arido aut paulum in aquam progressi, omnibus membris expediti,
notissimis locis, audacter tela coicerent et equos insuefactos incitarent.
10   Quibus rebus nostri perterriti atque huius omnino generis pugnae
imperiti, non eadem alacritate ac studio quo in pedestribus uti proeliis
consuerant utebantur. [25] Quod ubi Caesar animadvertit, naves longas,
quarum et species erat barbaris inusitatior et motus ad usum expeditior,
paulum removeri ab onerariis navibus et remis incitari et ad latus apertum
15   hostium constitui atque inde fundis, sagittis, tormentis hostes propelli
ac summoveri iussit; quae res magno usui nostris fuit. Nam et navium
figura et remorum motu et inusitato genere tormentorum permoti barbari
constiterunt ac paulum modo pedem rettulerunt. Atque nostris militibus
cunctantibus, maxime propter altitudinem maris, qui decimae legionis
20   aquilam ferebat, contestatus deos, ut ea res legioni feliciter eveniret,
"Desilite," inquit, "milites, nisi vultis aquilam hostibus prodere: ego
certe meum rei publicae atque imperatori officium praestitero." Hoc cum
voce magna dixisset, se ex navi proiecit atque in hostes aquilam ferre
coepit. Tum nostri cohortati inter se, ne tantum dedecus admitteretur,
25   universi ex navi desiluerunt. Hos item ex proximis primis navibus cum
conspexissent, subsecuti hostibus appropinquarunt.

Preparatory Questions

Line 1   Identify the case and use of *barbari*. **nominative, subject of *prohibebant* (line 3)**

            Identify the case and use of *cognito*. **ablative absolute**

            What words does *praemisso* modify? **equitatu et essedariis**

Line 2   Find a relative clause. **quo plerumque genere in proeliis uti consuerunt**

            Identify the case and use of *genere*. **ablative, object of *uti***

	Identify the form and use of *uti*. **present infinitive deponent (of *utor*), complementary**
Line 3	Identify the form and use of *nostros*. **masculine accusative plural (of *noster*), direct object of *prohibebant***
	Identify the tense and voice of *prohibebant*. **imperfect active**
Lines 4–5	What kind of clause does *quod* introduce? **causal**
Line 5	What is the subject of *poterant*? ***naves* (line 4)**
	Identify the case and use of *militibus*. **dative of agent**
Lines 5–6	Find two ablative absolutes. ***ignotis locis, impeditis manibus***
Line 6	What words modify *onere*? ***magno et gravi***
Lines 6–7	Find three gerundives. ***desiliendum, consistendum, pugnandum* (each of which operates with the *erat* in line 7)**
Line 7	To whom does *illi* refer? **the Britons**
Line 9	What part of speech is *audacter*? **adverb**
	Identify the case and use of *tela*. **accusative, direct object of *coicerent***
Line 10	What word does *huius* modify? ***generis***
Line 11	Find a relative clause. ***quo in pedestribus uti proeliis consuerant***
	What kind of relative clause is it? **comparative**
	Identify the form and use of *uti*. **present infinitive deponent (of *utor*), complementary**
Line 12	Identify the tense and voice of *utebantur*. **imperfect deponent**
Line 13	What is the antecedent of *quarum*? ***naves* (line 12)**
	Identify the case and use of *barbaris*. **dative of reference**
	What is the degree and part of speech of *expeditior*? **comparative adjective**
Line 14	Identify the case and use of *remis*. **ablative of means**
	Identify the tense and voice of *incitari*. **present passive**
	What word does *apertum* modify? ***latus***
Line 15	Identify the case and use of *hostium*. **genitive of possession**
	Identify the case and use of *hostes*. **accusative, subject of *propelli* (line 15) and *summoveri* (line 16) in indirect statement**
Line 16	Who or what is the subject of *iussit*? ***Caesar* (line 12)**
	Identify the case and use of *magno*. **dative modifying *usui* (dative of purpose)**

	Identify the case and use of *nostris*. **dative of reference**
Lines 16–17	Find three instances of an ablative of means. ***figura, motu, inusitato genere***
Line 18	What is the subject of *constiterunt*? ***barbari* (line 17)**
	What does *paulum* complement? ***modo***
Line 19	Identify the form and syntax of *cunctantibus*. **ablative plural masculine present active participle, ablative absolute**
	What word does *propter* govern? ***altitudinem***
	What is the understood antecedent of *qui*? ***miles* (alternatives: *is, ille, unus homo,* etc.)**
Line 20	Identify the form and use of *contestatus*. **perfect passive participle (of *contestor*— deponent), nominative modifying subject (of *inquit*, line 21)**
	Identify the type of clause introduced by *ut*. **indirect command**
	What does *feliciter* complement? ***eveniret***
Line 21	Identify the form and syntax of *desilite*. **plural present imperative (of *desilio*)**
Line 22	Identify the form and syntax of *praestitero*. **first person singular future perfect indicative active (of *praesto*), main verb of clause (indicates futurity of action within the narrative of the past)**
Line 23	Identify the tense and mood of *dixisset*. **pluperfect subjunctive**
	To whom does *se* refer? **the standard-bearer (*qui* clause, lines 19–20)**
	Identify the form and syntax of *ferre*. **present infinitive active (of *fero*), complementary infinitive with *coepit* (line 24)**
Line 25	Identify the case and use of *navi*. **ablative, place from which (with *desiluerunt*)**
Line 26	Identify the tense and mood of *conspexissent*. **pluperfect subjunctive**
	Identify the tense and voice of *appropinquarunt*. **pluperfect active**

Multiple Choice Questions *Suggested time: 40 minutes*

1. In line 1 the phrase *consilio . . . cognito* is
   a. an ablative of means
   c. a double dative
   b. a relative clause
   d. an ablative absolute

2. In line 2 *uti* governs
   a. *quo genere* (line 2)
   c. *plerumque* (line 2)
   b. *proeliis* (line 2)
   d. *consuerunt* (line 2)

3. In line 4 *quod* introduces
    a. a relative clause
    c. a purpose clause
    b. an explanatory clause
    d. a result clause

4. In line 4 *nisi* is best translated as
    a. except
    c. without
    b. if
    d. within

5. In lines 4–6 we learn that
    a. the Britons fight with war chariots
    c. the waves are dangerous
    b. the Romans are at a disadvantage
    d. the Roman soldiers lost their weapons

6. In line 6 *de navibus desiliendum* is
    a. a clause
    c. a passive periphrastic
    b. a participial phrase
    d. a relative clause

7. In line 8 *omnibus membris expeditis* is
    a. an ablative absolute
    c. an ablative of specification
    b. an ablative of means
    d. an ablative of manner

8. What is the relationship of *equos* (line 9) to the verb *incitarent* (line 9)?
    a. subject
    c. direct object
    b. explanatory participle
    d. accusative of respect

9. In line 10 *Quibus* refers to
    a. the horses
    c. the deep water
    b. the weapons
    d. the whole situation

10. In line 10 *omnino* is
    a. an ablative
    c. an adjective
    b. an adverb
    d. a noun

11. *imperiti* (line 11) modifies
    a. *pugnae* (line 10)
    c. *omnino* (line 10)
    b. *generis* (line 10)
    d. *nostri* (line 10)

12. In line 12 *naves longas* is translated
    a. long ships
    c. transport ships
    b. long shores
    d. war ships

13. In line 13 *quarum* is
    a. a partitive genitive
    b. a possessive genitive
    c. a genitive of specification
    d. a genitive of value

14. *expeditior* (line 13) modifies
    a. *usum* (line 13)
    b. *species* (line 13)
    c. *motus* (line 13)
    d. *Caesar* (line 12)

15. In line 14 *incitari* is
    a. an infinitive
    b. a participle
    c. a comparative adjective
    d. an adverb

16. In line 15 the phrase *fundis, sagittis, tormentis* is an example of
    a. alliteration
    b. asyndeton
    c. anaphora
    d. hyperbole

17. In line 16 *nostris* and *magno usui* are examples of
    a. a double dative
    b. an ablative of means
    c. an ablative of comparison
    d. a dative of reference

18. In lines 16–17 the repetition of *et* is an example of
    a. anaphora
    b. asyndeton
    c. alliteration
    d. tmesis

19. In line 18 the word *modo* is
    a. an adjective
    b. a verb
    c. a noun
    d. an adverb

20. The subject of *constiterunt* (line 18) is
    a. *Caesar* (line 12)
    b. *permoti* (line 17)
    c. *barbari* (line 17)
    d. *figura et motu* (line 17)

21. In line 18 the phrase *pedem rettulerunt* is translated
    a. retreated
    b. were destroyed
    c. carried a foot
    d. restored the infantry

22. In line 19 *altitudinem* is translated
    a. height
    b. depth
    c. attitude
    d. waves

23. In line 19 *qui* introduces
    a. a relative clause of characteristic
    c. an indirect statement
    b. an indirect command
    d. a relative clause

24. The case of *decimae* in line 19 is
    a. nominative
    c. dative
    b. genitive
    d. ablative

25. In line 21 *desilite* is an example of
    a. an imperative
    c. an infinitive
    b. an impersonal verb
    d. a subjunctive verb

26. In line 21 the phrase *nisi vultis aquilam hostibus prodere* is
    a. a conditional clause
    c. an indirect statement
    b. an apodosis
    d. a result clause

27. In line 21 *ego* refers to
    a. Caesar
    c. a member of the Roman army
    b. the British commander
    d. the narrator

28. In line 22 *cum* is translated
    a. when
    c. since
    b. with
    d. although

29. In line 23 *se* refers to
    a. the ships
    c. Caesar
    b. the Britons
    d. the aquilifer

30. In line 24 *ne tantum dedecus admitteretur* is
    a. an indirect command
    c. a purpose clause
    b. a result clause
    d. a negative condition

31. In line 25 *universi* is translated
    a. as a body
    c. the universe
    b. universal
    d. with one verse

32. In line 26 *hostibus* is
    a. ablative
    c. genitive
    b. dative
    d. accusative

33. In line 26 an alternative way of writing *appropinquarunt* is

a. *appropinquere*

b. *appropinquerunt*

c. appropinquaverunt

d. *appropinquaverant*

Translation *Suggested time: 15 minutes*

> Quod ubi Caesar animadvertit, naves longas, quarum et species erat
> barbaris inusitatior et motus ad usum expeditior, paulum removeri ab
> onerariis navibus et remis incitari et ad latus apertum hostium constitui
> atque inde fundis, sagittis, tormentis hostes propelli ac summoveri iussit;
> 5   quae res magno usui nostris fuit.

26 chunks. 13 points, ½ point each.

Quod	**Which (situation)**
ubi Caesar	**when Caesar**
animadvertit	**noticed (it)**
naves longas	**the war ships**
quarum	**of which**
et species	**both the appearance**
erat	**was**
barbaris	**to the foreigners**
inusitatior	**more unusual**
et motus	**and the movement**
ad usum	**for use**
expeditior	**more convenient**
paulum removeri	**to be withdrawn a little**
ab onerariis navibus	**from the transport ships**
et remis incitari	**and to be hastened by means of the oars**
et ad latus apertum	**and near the open flank**
hostium	**of the enemy**
constitui	**to be stationed**
atque inde	**and from there**
fundis, sagittis, tormentis	**with slings, arrows, and missiles**
hostes	**the enemy**
propelli ac summoveri	**to be driven back and removed**
iussit	**he ordered**
quae res	**which thing**
magno usui nostris	**(for the purpose) of great use to our men**
fuit	**was**

Short Analysis Questions

> Erat ob has causas summa difficultas, quod naves propter magnitudinem
> nisi in alto constitui non poterant, militibus autem, ignotis locis,
> impeditis manibus, magno et gravi onere armorum oppressis, simul et
> de navibus desiliendum et in fluctibus consistendum et cum hostibus
> 5 erat pugnandum, cum illi aut ex arido aut paulum in aquam progressi,
> omnibus membris expediti, notissimis locis, audacter tela coicerent et
> equos insuefactos incitarent. Quibus rebus nostri perterriti atque huius
> omnino generis pugnae imperiti, non eadem alacritate ac studio quo in
> pedestribus uti proeliis consuerant utebantur.

1. What difficulties do the Roman soldiers face in lines 1–5? Cite the Latin that supports your answer and translate or accurately paraphrase.

   The ships cannot be beached on the shore—*nisi in alto constitui non poterant*; the Roman soldiers face unknown places (*ignotis locis*), have their hands full (*impeditis manibus*), are weighed down by their armor (*magno et gravi onere armorum oppressis*), and must jump into the shallow waters and fight the enemy at the same time (*simul et de navibus desiliendum et in fluctibus consistendum et cum hostibus erat pugnandum*).

2. What advantages do the Britons have (lines 5–7)? Cite the Latin that supports your answer and translate or accurately paraphrase.

   It is almost exactly the opposite to the Roman situation. The Britons fight from dry land (*ex arido*) or the shoreline (*paulum in aquam*), have free hands (*omnibus membris expeditis*), and are very familiar with the locale (*notissimis locis*).

3. What happens as a result of this situation (lines 7–9)? Cite the Latin that supports your answer and translate or accurately paraphrase.

   The Romans are panicked—*perterriti*—and inexperienced—*imperiti*—in this mode of combat, and thus do not fight with their customary eagerness and enthusiasm—*non eadem alacritate ac studio*—as they do in regular infantry battles—*quo in pedestribus uti proeliis consuerant.*

Essay *Suggested time: 20 minutes*

5

Atque nostris militibus cunctantibus, maxime propter altitudinem
maris, qui decimae legionis aquilam ferebat, contestatus deos, ut ea res
legioni feliciter eveniret, "Desilite," inquit, "milites, nisi vultis aquilam
hostibus prodere: ego certe meum rei publicae atque imperatori officium
praestitero." Hoc cum voce magna dixisset, se ex navi proiecit atque in
hostes aquilam ferre coepit. Tum nostri cohortati inter se, ne tantum
dedecus admitteretur, universi ex navi desiluerunt. Hos item ex proximis
primis navibus cum conspexissent, subsecuti hostibus appropinquarunt.

In this passage the narrator describes how decisive action on the part of one man emboldens the Roman army. In a short essay, discuss the importance of this one man's contribution to the success of the attack, first in terms of literary effect and the devices used to make the encounter more dramatic, and then in terms of historical effect.

Support your assertions with references to the Latin text throughout the passage above. All Latin words must be copied or their line numbers provided, AND they must be translated or paraphrased closely enough that it is clear that you understand the Latin. It is your responsibility to convince the reader that you are basing your conclusions on the Latin text and not merely on a general recollection of the passage. Direct your answer to the question; do not merely summarize the passage. Please write your essay on a separate piece of paper.

Teachers should review with students the Essay Scoring Guidelines given at the beginning of this manual.

Students should recognize the significance of the soldier's position in the legion: he is responsible for the legionary eagle—*qui decimae legionis aquilam ferebat* (line 2)—that was each legion's prized possession. He is thus a man entrusted with great responsibility, which he uses to good effect by spurring on the remaining, hesitant soldiers. Students should recognize the use of direct discourse here, which makes the episode much more vivid. Students should note that the man's appeal to the soldiers' sense of shame is effective in inciting them to action—*ne tantum dedecus admitteretur* (lines 6–7). Other possibilities for comment include the appeal to the gods for divine favor—*contestatus deos, ut ea res legioni feliciter eveniret* (lines 2–3)—as a marker of success; the effect of a brave leader on the morale of the men (comparisons to Caesar himself may be appropos); and, artistically, the direct and quick speed of narration, to mimic the action being described.

Notes

CHAPTER 6: BOOK 4.26–27
BATTLE ON THE SHORES OF BRITAIN

[26] Pugnatum est ab utrisque acriter. Nostri tamen, quod neque ordines
servare neque firmiter insistere neque signa subsequi poterant atque alius
alia ex navi quibuscumque signis occurrerat se aggregabat, magnopere
perturbabantur; hostes vero, notis omnibus vadis, ubi ex litore aliquos
5   singulares ex navi egredientes conspexerant, incitatis equis impeditos
adoriebantur, plures paucos circumsistebant, alii ab latere aperto in
universos tela coiciebant. Quod cum animadvertisset Caesar, scaphas
longarum navium, item speculatoria navigia militibus compleri iussit et,
quos laborantes conspexerat, his subsidia summittebat. Nostri, simul in
10   arido constiterunt, suis omnibus consecutis, in hostes impetum fecerunt
atque eos in fugam dederunt; neque longius prosequi potuerunt, quod
equites cursum tenere atque insulam capere non potuerunt. Hoc unum
ad pristinam fortunam Caesari defuit. [27] Hostes proelio superati, simul
atque se ex fuga receperunt, statim ad Caesarem legatos de pace miserunt;
15   obsides daturos quaeque imperasset sese facturos polliciti sunt. Una
cum his legatis Commius Atrebas venit, quem supra demonstraveram a
Caesare in Britanniam praemissum. Hunc illi e navi egressum, cum ad eos
oratoris modo Caesaris mandata deferret, comprehenderant atque in vincula
coiecerant: tum proelio facto remiserunt. In petenda pace eius rei culpam
20   in multitudinem contulerunt et propter imprudentiam ut ignosceretur
petiverunt. Caesar questus quod, cum ultro in continentem legatis
missis pacem ab se petissent, bellum sine causa intulissent, ignoscere
imprudentiae dixit obsidesque imperavit; quorum illi partem statim
dederunt, partem ex longinquioribus locis accersitam paucis diebus sese
25   daturos dixerunt. Interea suos remigrare in agros iusserunt, principesque
undique convenire et se civitatesque suas Caesari commendare coeperunt.

Preparatory Questions

Line 1   Identify the tense and voice of *pugnatum est*. **perfect passive**

What does *acriter* modify? **pugnatum est**

Line 2   Identify the tense and mood of *poterant*. **imperfect indicative**

Find two infinitives that are complementary to *poterant*. **servare, insistere** (also) **subsequi**

Line 3   What word does *alia* modify? **navi**

Identify the case and use of *navi*. **ablative of place from which/separation**

To what or whom does *se* refer? **the Roman soldiers**

What part of speech is *magnopere*? **adverb**

Line 5   Identify the form and syntax of *egredientes*. **present participle active, accusative, direct object of *conspexerant***

Identify the tense and voice of *conspexerant*. **pluperfect active**

What case is *impeditos*? **accusative**

What word does *impeditos* modify? ***aliquos* (line 4)**

Line 6   What words does *ab* govern? ***latere aperto***

Line 7   Find a *cum* clause. ***Quod cum animadvertisset Caesar***

Identify the tense and mood of *animadvertisset*. **pluperfect subjunctive**

Line 8   What case is *navigia*? **accusative**

Identify the form and use of *militibus*. **ablative of means with *compleri***

What does *compleri* depend on? ***iussit***

Line 9   What is the unexpressed antecedent of *quos*? ***milites***

Identify the tense and voice of *summittebat*. **imperfect active**

Line 10   Identify the form of *suis*. **third person (reflexive pronoun) ablative plural**

What is the direct object of *fecerunt*? ***impetum***

Line 11   To whom does *eos* refer? **the Britons**

Identify the form and syntax of *longius*. **comparative adverb, modifying *prosequi***

Lines 11–12   Find the main verb in the sentence *neque longius . . . potuerant*. ***potuerunt* (line 11)**

Line 12   Identify the case and use of *equites*. **nominative, subject of *potuerant***

Find two infinitives that are complementary to *potuerant*. ***tenere, capere***

Line 13   Identify the form and use of *superati*. **perfect passive participle (of *supero*) used circumstantially**

What word does *superati* modify? ***hostes***

Line 14   Identify the case and use of *se*. **accusative, direct object of *receperunt***

Line 15   Find the subject of an indirect statement. ***sese* (line 15)**

What word is needed to complete the verb form *daturos*? ***esse***

Identify the tense of the infinitives in the indirect statement. **future**

Identify the form and syntax of *imperasset*. **pluperfect subjunctive, relative clause in indirect statement**

Line 16	What is the antecedent of *quem*? **Commius**
	Identify the form and syntax of *demonstraveram*. **pluperfect indicative, main verb of the relative clause**
	What about this verb form is unusual in Caesar's prose? **it is in the first person**
Line 17	Who is meant by *Hunc*? **Commius**
	Who is meant by *illi*? **the Britons**
	Identify the case and number of *illi*. **nominative plural**
Lines 17–18	Find a *cum* clause. **cum ad eos oratoris modo Caesaris mandata deferret**
Line 18	What is the subject of *deferret*? **Commius (line 16)**
	What is the subject of *comprehendant*? **illi (line 17)**
Line 19	Identify the case and use of *proelio facto*. **ablative absolute**
	What is the syntax of *In petenda pace*? **prepositional phrase with a gerundive**
Lines 20–21	Find an indirect command. **ut ignosceretur**
	What verb governs it? **petiverunt**
Line 21	Identify the form of *questus*. **perfect participle active of deponent verb queror**
	What word does it modify? **Caesar**
Lines 21–23	What kind of clause is introduced by *quod*? **causal**
	Identify the form and syntax of *intulissent*. **third person plural pluperfect subjunctive active, main verb of the causal clause**
	Find a *cum* clause. **cum ultro in continentem . . . pacem ab se petissent**
	What kind of *cum* clause is it? **concessive**
Line 22	Identify the form and syntax of *ignoscere*. **present infinitive active, verb of the indirect statement**
Line 23	Identify the case and use of *imprudentiae*. **dative with the verb ignoscere**
	Find two verbs in the indicative mood. **dixit, imperavit (also dederunt, line 24)**
	Identify the case and use of *quorum*. **partitive genitive (with partem)**
	What is its antecedent? **obsides**
Lines 23–25	Find an indirect statement. **partem ex longinquioribus locis . . . sese daturos (esse)**
Line 24	Identify the case and use of *sese*. **accusative subject of the infinitive in indirect statement (daturos [esse], line 25)**
	Identify the case and use of *paucis diebus*. **ablative of time within which**

Line 25	Identify the form and syntax of *remigrare*. **present infinitive active, complementary with *iusserunt***
Lines 25–26	Find two infinitives that depend on *coeperunt*. **convenire (line 26), *commendare* (line 26)**
Line 26	Identify the case and use of *Caesari*. **dative with *commendare***

Multiple Choice Questions *Suggested time: 30 minutes*

1. In line 1 (*pugnatum . . . acriter*) we learn that
   a. the battle was easy
   c. the fighting lasted a long time
   b. the Romans were victorious
   d. the battle was fought fiercely

2. The word *navi* in line 3 is dependent on
   a. *signis* (line 3)
   c. *alius* (line 2)
   b. *ex* (line 3)
   d. *se* (line 3)

3. *Ubi* in line 4 is translated
   a. where
   c. because
   b. when
   d. since

4. The case of *singulares* (line 5) is
   a. ablative
   c. dative
   b. nominative
   d. accusative

5. The participle *impeditos* (line 5) modifies
   a. *incitatis* (line 5)
   c. *aliquos* (line 4)
   b. *equis* (line 5)
   d. *plures* (line 6)

6. In lines 4–7 (*hostes . . . coiciebant*) we learn that
   a. the Romans were at a disadvantage
   c. the weather was rainy
   b. the enemy was boarding the ships
   d. the shore could be seen from the ships

7. In line 7 *Quod* is translated
   a. When
   c. Because
   b. This
   d. Since

8. The case of *navium* (line 8) is
   a. nominative
   c. accusative
   b. genitive
   d. ablative

9. The case of *his* (line 9) is determined by
    a. *subsidia* (line 9)
    b. *quos* (line 9)
    c. *conspexerat* (line 9)
    d. *summittebat* (line 9)

10. The phrase *in hostes* (line 10) is translated
    a. within the enemy
    b. against the enemy
    c. into the enemy
    d. in the enemy

11. In line 11 *longius* is
    a. a participle
    b. an adjective
    c. an adverb
    d. a preposition

12. The tense and mood of *potuerant* in line 12 is
    a. pluperfect subjunctive
    b. imperfect indicative
    c. imperfect subjunctive
    d. pluperfect indicative

13. The case of *Caesari* (line 13) is determined by
    a. *defuit* (line 13)
    b. *ad* (line 13)
    c. *Hoc* (line 12)
    d. *pristinam* (line 13)

14. In lines 13–14 the phrase *simul atque* is translated
    a. just like
    b. and also
    c. as soon as
    d. at the same time as

15. The phrase *quaeque imperasset* (line 15) is an example of
    a. a relative clause
    b. an indirect question
    c. a purpose clause
    d. an indirect statement

16. In line 16 *cum* is translated
    a. with
    b. since
    c. when
    d. although

17. In lines 17–19 (*Hunc . . . coiecerant*) Caesar tells us that
    a. Commius gave a fine speech
    b. Commius was thrown off the ship
    c. Commius was taken prisoner
    d. the Britons understood Commius's speech

18. In line 19 the phrase *eius rei* refers to
    a. the battle
    b. Commius's speech
    c. the peace agreement
    d. Commius's capture

19. The mood of the verb *petissent* (line 22) is determined by
    a. **cum (line 21)**
    b. *Caesar* (line 21)
    c. *quod* (line 21)
    d. *questus* (line 21)

20. The function of *bellum* (line 22) is
    a. subject of the verb
    b. **direct object**
    c. noun in apposition to *pacem*
    d. adjective modifying *continentem*

21. Who or what is meant by *illi* (line 23)?
    a. the Gauls
    b. Commius's men
    c. the Romans
    d. **the Britons**

22. In line 24 the phrase *paucis diebus* is an ablative of
    a. means
    b. manner
    c. **time**
    d. characteristic

23. What word must be supplied to complete the sense of *daturos* (line 25)?
    a. *Caesar*
    b. **esse**
    c. *fuisse*
    d. *sunt*

24. In lines 25–26 we learn that the British leaders
    a. plan to rebel again
    b. seek peace from Caesar
    c. join Caesar's army
    d. **entrust their communities to Caesar**

Translation *Suggested time: 15 minutes*

Hunc illi e navi egressum, cum ad eos oratoris modo Caesaris mandata deferret, comprehenderant atque in vincula coiecerant: tum proelio facto remiserunt. In petenda pace eius rei culpam in multitudinem contulerunt et propter imprudentiam ut ignosceretur petiverunt.

20 chunks. 10 points, ½ point each.

Hunc	This man (*i.e.*, Commius)
e navi	out of the ship
egressum	having stepped
illi	they (*i.e.*, the Britons)
cum ad eos	when he to them
oratoris modo	in the manner of an envoy
Caesaris mandata	the orders of Caesar
deferret,	was delivering
comprehenderant	they had seized
atque in vincula	and into chains
coiecerant:	they had thrown
tum proelio facto	then, when the battle was over/then, the battle having been completed/then, when the battle was completed
remiserunt	they sent [him] back
In petenda pace	In seeking peace
eius rei culpam	the blame for that affair
in multitudinem	upon the crowd
coiecerunt	they placed
et propter imprudentiam	and on account of their lack of judgment
ut ignosceretur	that he pardon [them]
petiverunt	they sought

Short Analysis Questions

[26] Pugnatum est ab utrisque acriter. Nostri tamen, quod neque ordines servare neque firmiter insistere neque signa subsequi poterant atque alius alia ex navi quibuscumque signis occurrerat se aggregabat, magnopere perturbabantur; hostes vero, notis omnibus vadis, ubi ex litore aliquos
5 singulares ex navi egredientes conspexerant, incitatis equis impeditos adoriebantur, plures paucos circumsistebant, alii ab latere aperto in universos tela coiciebant. Quod cum animadvertisset Caesar, scaphas longarum navium, item speculatoria navigia militibus compleri iussit et, quos laborantes conspexerat, his subsidia summittebat. Nostri, simul in
10 arido constituerunt, suis omnibus consecutis, in hostes impetum fecerunt atque eos in fugam dederunt; neque longius prosequi potuerunt, quod equites cursum tenere atque insulam capere non potuerant. Hoc unum ad pristinam fortunam Caesari defuit.

1. How do the Roman soldiers behave as they disembark from the ships (lines 1–4)? Cite the Latin that supports your answer and translate or accurately paraphrase.

    They have difficulty maintaining proper battle formations—(*quod . . . poterant*, lines 2–3) and instead marshall themselves wherever they can, in great confusion—*magnopere perturbantur* (lines 3–4).

2. What obstacles do the Romans face as they arrive on the shore (lines 1–3)? Cite the Latin that supports your answer and translate or accurately paraphrase.

    They face difficulties in maintaining ranks—*neque ordines servare* (lines 1–2), in gaining a solid foothold—*neque firmiter insistere* (line 2), and in finding their proper position—*neque signa subsequi poterant* (line 2).

3. What advantages do the enemy have over the Roman soldiers (lines 4–6)? Cite the Latin that supports your answer and translate or accurately paraphrase.

    The Britons are familiar with the shoreline—*notis omnibus vadis* (line 4), and can gang up against the confused Roman soldiers by attacking them on horseback —*incitatis . . . adoriebantur*, (lines 5–6).

4. What is the decisive action that turns the tide of battle in favor of the Romans (lines 7–9)? Who is responsible for this action?

    Caesar changes the manner of disembarkation for his soldiers, grouping them into small boats instead of having them leave the war ships one by one. This fills the troops with confidence and allows them to focus on attacking the enemy instead of being on the defensive.

5. What is the outcome of the battle (lines 9–12)? Cite the Latin that supports your answer and translate or accurately paraphrase.

    The Romans quickly gain confidence and charge the enemy—*in hostes impetum fecerunt* (line 10), and rout them—*atque eos in fugam dederunt* (line 11).

6. What is the one thing missing from a complete victory (lines 11–13)? Cite the Latin that supports your answer and translate or accurately paraphrase.

    Caesar is unable to follow up this success by pursuing the Britons as they retreat because the ships carrying the cavalry did not reach the shore of the island—*quod equites cursum tenere atque insulam capere non poterant.*

Essay *Suggested time: 20 minutes*

Quod cum animadvertisset Caesar, scaphas longarum navium, item
speculatoria navigia militibus compleri iussit et, quos laborantes
conspexerat, his subsidia summittebat. Nostri, simul in arido
constiterunt, suis omnibus consecutis, in hostes impetum fecerunt
5   atque eos in fugam dederunt; neque longius prosequi potuerunt, quod
equites cursum tenere atque insulam capere non potuerant. Hoc unum
ad pristinam fortunam Caesari defuit. [27] Hostes proelio superati, simul
atque se ex fuga receperunt, statim ad Caesarem legatos de pace miserunt;
obsides daturos quaeque imperasset sese facturos polliciti sunt. Una
10 cum his legatis Commius Atrebas venit, quem supra demonstraveram a
Caesare in Britanniam praemissum. Hunc illi e navi egressum, cum ad eos
oratoris modo Caesaris mandata deferret, comprehenderant atque in vincula
coiecerant: tum proelio facto remiserunt. In petenda pace eius rei culpam
in multitudinem contulerunt et propter imprudentiam ut ignosceretur
15 petiverunt. Caesar questus quod, cum ultro in continentem legatis
missis pacem ab se petissent, bellum sine causa intulissent, ignoscere
imprudentiae dixit obsidesque imperavit; quorum illi partem statim
dederunt, partem ex longinquioribus locis accersitam paucis diebus sese
daturos dixerunt. Interea suos remigrare in agros iusserunt, principesque
20 undique convenire et se civitatesque suas Caesari commendare coeperunt.

In this passage Caesar's leadership skills are on display as he oversees the battle taking place before him, as well as in his dealings with the defeated enemy in the aftermath of the battle. In a short essay, discuss the presentation of Caesar as a leader. What qualities does he possess that enable him to be an effective leader during the battle itself? Does he also show effective leadership in dealing with the Britons after the battle?

Support your assertions with references to the Latin text throughout the passage above. All Latin words must be copied or their line numbers provided, AND they must be translated or paraphrased closely enough that it is clear that you understand the Latin. It is your responsibility to convince the reader that you are basing your conclusions on the Latin text and not merely on a general recollection of the passage. Direct your answer to the question; do not merely summarize the passage. Please write your essay on a separate piece of paper.

Teachers should review with students the Essay Scoring Guidelines given at the beginning of this manual.

Caesar's most obvious strength as a leader is his ability to see immediately what needs to be done to secure victory, and to take swift action as a result. Here the narrative makes clear that his understanding of the situation—*quod cum animadvertisset Caesar* (line 1)—and his revised plan—*his subsidia summittebat* (line 3)—are almost simultaneously undertaken. The effect on his troops is similiarly immediate—*simul in arido constiterunt . . . in hostes impetum fecerunt atque eos in fugam dederunt* (lines 3–5). Caesar's leadership in dealing with the Britons is evident in his ability to subordinate his outrage at the ill treatment of his envoy Commius to the greater, common good, in accepting the surrender and the proferred excuses of the British chieftains for their people's behavior against Commius—*Caesar questus quod, cum ultro in continentem legatis missis pacem ab se petissent, bellum sine causa intulissent, ignoscere imprudentiae dixit* (lines 15–17). Thus, although he could have held the British chiefs responsible for the arrest of an envoy (note: envoys and ambassadors were considered to be inviolable according to ancient diplomatic practice), he elected to forgive their lack of judgment and to proceed with their surrender as if nothing had happened.

CHAPTER 7: BOOK 4.28–30
A STORM AT SEA, AND AMONG
THE BRITISH CHIEFTAINS

[28] His rebus pace confirmata, post diem quartum quam est in
Britanniam ventum naves XVIII, de quibus supra demonstratum est,
quae equites sustulerant, ex superiore portu leni vento solverunt. Quae
cum appropinquarent Britanniae et ex castris viderentur, tanta tempestas
5   subito coorta est ut nulla earum cursum tenere posset, sed aliae eodem
unde erant profectae referrentur, aliae ad inferiorem partem insulae,
quae est proprius solis occasum, magno sui cum periculo deicerentur;
quae tamen, ancoris iactis, cum fluctibus complerentur, necessario
adversa nocte in altum provectae, continentem petierunt. [29] Eadem
10   nocte accidit ut esset luna plena, qui dies maritimos aestus maximos in
Oceano efficere consuevit, nostrisque id erat incognitum. Ita uno tempore
et longas naves, quibus Caesar exercitum transportandum curaverat
quasque in aridum subduxerat, aestus compleverat et onerarias, quae ad
ancoras erant deligatae, tempestas adflictabat, neque ulla nostris facultas
15   aut administrandi aut auxiliandi dabatur. Compluribus navibus fractis,
reliquae cum essent funibus, ancoris, reliquisque armamentis amissis
ad navigandum inutiles, magna, id quod necesse erat accidere, totius
exercitus perturbatio facta est. Neque enim naves erant aliae quibus
reportari possent, et omnia deerant quae ad reficiendas naves erant usui
20   et, quod omnibus constabat hiemare in Gallia oportere, frumentum his in
locis in hiemem provisum non erat. [30] Quibus rebus cognitis, principes
Britanniae, qui post proelium ad Caesarem convenerant, inter se collocuti,
cum equites et naves et frumentum Romanis deesse intellegerent et
paucitatem militum ex castrorum exiguitate cognoscerent, quae hoc erant
25   etiam angustiora quod sine impedimentis Caesar legiones transportaverat,
optimum factu esse duxerunt, rebellione facta, frumento commeatuque
nostros prohibere et rem in hiemem producere, quod eis superatis aut
reditu interclusis neminem postea belli inferendi causa in Britanniam
transiturum confidebant. Itaque, rursus coniuratione facta, paulatim ex
30   castris discedere ac suos clam ex agris deducere coeperunt.

Preparatory Questions

Line 1   Identify the case and use of *pace*. **ablative of means**

Line 3   What is the antecedent of *quae*? ***naves* (line 2)**

               Identify the case and use of *equites*. **accusative, direct object (of *sustulerant*)**

               What noun does *leni* modify? ***vento***

Line 4   Find two verbs in a *cum* clause. ***appropinquarent, viderentur***

               What kind of *cum* clause is it? **circumstantial**

Lines 4–5   Find a result clause. ***ut nulla earum cursum tenere posset***

Line 5   What part of speech is *subito*? **adverb**

               Identify the case and use of *earum*. **partitive genitive (with *nulla*)**

               To what noun does *earum* refer? ***naves* (line 2)**

Line 6   Identify the mood and syntax of *referrentur*. **subjunctive, verb in a result clause**

               What words does the preposition *ad* govern? ***inferiorem partem***

Line 7   Identify the form and syntax of *proprius*. **comparative adjective, modifies *quae***

               Identify the mood and syntax of *deicerentur*. **subjunctive, result clause**

               Identify the subject of *deicerentur*. ***aliae* (line 5)**

Line 8   Find an ablative absolute. ***ancoris iactis***

Line 9   What is the form and use of *provectae*? **perfect passive participle, modifies the relative pronoun *quae* (line 8), the subject of the relative clause**

               Identify the form and syntax of *petierunt*. **(syncopated) third person plural perfect active indicative, main verb of the relative clause**

Lines 9–10   Find a substantive clause of result. **(*accidit*) *ut esset luna plena***

Line 10   What does *maximos* modify? ***aestus***

Line 11   What is the subject of *erat*? ***id***

               Identify the case and use of *tempore*. **ablative of time when**

Line 12   What is the case and use of *quibus*? **ablative of means**

               Find a gerundive. ***transportandum***

Line 13   What is the antecedent of *quasque*? ***naves***

               What is the subject of *compleverat*? ***aestus***

Lines 13–14   Find a relative clause. ***quae ad ancoras erant deligatae***

	What is the antecedent of *quae*? **onerarias (naves)**
Line 15	Identify the tense and voice of *dabatur*. **imperfect passive**
	Identify the case and use of *administrandi*. **objective genitive (with *facultas*)**
	On what word does *administrandi* depend? **facultas**
	Find an ablative absolute. **compluribus navibus fractis**
Lines 16–17	Find a *cum* clause. **reliquae cum essent . . . ad navigandum inutiles**
	What kind of *cum* clause is it? **causal**
Line 16	Identify the form and syntax of *amissis*. **ablative plural, perfect passive participle (of *amitto*), ablative absolute**
	What words does *amissis* modify? **funibus, ancoris, reliquisque armamentis**
Line 17	Identify the syntax of *ad navigandum*. **gerund of purpose**
	What word does *inutiles* modify? **reliquae (naves)**
	What word does *magna* modify? **perturbatio**
Line 18	Identify the case and use of *exercitus*. **genitive of possession**
	What part of speech is *enim*? **(postpositive) conjunction**
	Identify the case and use of *quibus*. **ablative of means**
Lines 19–20	Find a relative clause. **quae ad reficiendas naves erant usui**
Line 19	What is the subject of *deerant*? **omnia**
	What is the case and use of *usui*? **dative of purpose**
Line 21	What is the subject of *provisum erat*? **frumentum**
Line 22	Identify the case and use of *Britanniae*. **genitive of possession**
	Identify the tense and mood of *convenerant*. **pluperfect indicative**
Lines 23–24	What two verbs are part of a *cum* clause? **intellegerent, cognoscerent**
Line 23	What is the subject of *intellegerent*? **principes**
Line 24	Identify the case and use of *militum*. **partitive genitive (with *paucitatem*)**
	What word is governed by *ex*? **exiguitate**
	What is the antecedent of *quae*? **castrorum**
	Identify the case and use of *hoc*. **ablative of cause**
Line 25	What degree is the adjective *angustiora*? **comparative**
	Find a causal clause. **quod sine impedimentis Caesar legiones transportaverat**

Line 26   Identify the subject of *duxerunt*. **principes (line 21)**

Identify the tense and mood of *duxerunt*. **perfect indicative**

What is the syntax of *factu*? **(supine of *facio*) ablative of respect**

Find an ablative absolute. **rebellione facta**

Identify the case and use of *frumento*. **ablative of separation**

Line 27   Identify the case and use of *nostros*. **accusative, direct object of *prohibere***

Find an indirect statement. **nostros prohibere et rem in hiemem producere**

Lines 27–29   Find a causal clause. **quod eis . . . confidebant**

What word introduces it? **quod**

Identify the case and use of *superatis*. **ablative, perfect passive participle of an ablative absolute**

Line 28   Identify the case and use of *reditu*. **ablative of separation**

What part of speech is *postea*? **adverb**

On what word does *inferendi* depend? **causa**

Line 29   Identify the form and syntax of *transiturum*. **future active infinitive (with understood *esse*) in indirect statement**

What word must be understood with *transiturum* to fit the syntax? **esse**

What part of speech is *paulatim*? **adverb**

Line 30   Identify the tense and mood of *discedere* and *deducere*. **present infinitive**

On what word do these verbs depend? **coeperunt**

To what or whom does *suos* refer? **the Britons**

What part of speech is *clam*? **adverb**

Multiple Choice Questions *Suggested time: 40 minutes*

1. In lines 1–3 (*post . . . sustulerant*) we learn that
   - **a. the cavalry arrived on ships**
   - b. the battle lasted for four days
   - c. the wind washed the cavalry ashore
   - d. there was a demonstration of force

2. The number XVIII (line 2) equals
   - a. thirteen
   - b. twenty-three
   - **c. eighteen**
   - d. twelve

3. In line 3 the adjective *superiore* modifies
    a. *vento* (line 3)
    b. *leni* (line 3)
    c. *equites* (line 3)
    d. *portu* (line 3)

4. In line 4 *cum* is translated
    a. when
    b. although
    c. since
    d. with

5. The subject of *viderentur* in line 4 is
    a. the Britons
    b. the ships
    c. the waves
    d. the cavalry

6. In lines 3–7 (*Quae . . . deicerentur*) we learn that
    a. all the ships arrived safely
    b. some ships were blown off course
    c. some of the ships were delayed
    d. all of the ships were destroyed

7. In line 4 *tanta* signals a
    a. purpose clause
    b. conditional clause
    c. relative clause
    d. result clause

8. In line 7 the phrase *solis occasum* is translated as
    a. the west
    b. the north
    c. the east
    d. the south

9. In line 7 *cum* is translated
    a. when
    b. although
    c. since
    d. with

10. In line 9, *adversa* modifies
    a. *necessario* (line 8)
    b. *nocte* (line 9)
    c. *altum* (line 9)
    d. *provectae* (line 9)

11. Lines 9–11 (*Eadem . . . incognitum*) tell us that
    a. the Ocean was very dark
    b. sailors feared the waves
    c. the full moon affected the tides
    d. the Ocean was very large

12. The case of *naves* in line 12 is
    a. nominative
    b. genitive
    c. dative
    d. accusative

13. The subject of *compleverat* in line 13 is
    a. *Caesar* (line 12)
    b. *aestus* (line 13)
    c. *naves* (line 12)
    d. *aridum* (line 13)

14. The tense and mood of *adflictabat* in line 14 is
    a. present subjunctive
    b. perfect indicative
    c. imperfect indicative
    d. future indicative

15. *Ulla* in line 14 modifies
    a. *nostris* (line 14)
    b. *facultas* (line 14)
    c. *tempestas* (line 14)
    d. *administrandi* (line 15)

16. In line 15 *administrandi* and *auxiliandi* are
    a. finite verbs
    b. gerunds
    c. adjectives
    d. gerundives

17. The phrase *compluribus navibus fractis* in line 15 is
    a. an ablative of time
    b. an ablative of means
    c. an ablative of manner
    d. an ablative absolute

18. In line 16 *cum* is translated
    a. since
    b. with
    c. although
    d. when

19. *inutiles* in line 17 modifies
    a. *reliquae* (line 16)
    b. *ancoris* (line 16)
    c. *amissis* (line 16)
    d. *reliquisque* (line 16)

20. In lines 17–18 (*magna . . . facta est*) we find an example of
    a. chiasmus
    b. tmesis
    c. anaphora
    d. hyperbaton

21. In line 18 *enim* is translated
    a. because
    b. for
    c. now
    d. moreover

22. The case of *quibus* in line 18 is
    a. nominative
    b. genitive
    c. dative
    d. ablative

23. The phrase *ad reficiendas naves* in line 19 is
    a. a genitive of purpose
    c. a gerundive of purpose
    b. a relative clause
    d. an accusative of extent

24. In line 19 *usui* is
    a. an ablative of means
    c. a dative of reference
    b. a dative of purpose
    d. a partitive genitive

25. Lines 18–21 tell us that the reason the army was frightened is because
    a. they truly fear the British army
    c. they may be stranded without food
    b. they are woefully seasick
    d. they especially fear the Gauls

26. In line 22 *collocuti* is
    a. a passive infinitive
    c. a future infinitive
    b. a genitive of value
    d. a deponent participle

27. The tense and mood of *intellegerent* in line 23 is
    a. present subjunctive
    c. pluperfect subjunctive
    b. imperfect subjunctive
    d. present infinitive

28. In line 24 *hoc* is translated
    a. for this reason
    c. here
    b. than this
    d. to this place

29. The subject of *transportaverat* (line 25) is
    a. *principes* (line 21)
    c. *quae* (line 24)
    b. *legiones* (line 25)
    d. Caesar (line 25)

30. In line 26 *factu* is
    a. a gerundive
    c. a gerund
    b. a supine
    d. an infinitive

31. In line 27 *nostros* is
    a. the direct object of prohibere
    c. the object of *commeatu(que)*
    b. the subject of an indirect statement
    d. an accusative of respect

32. The case of *causa* (line 28) is
    a. nominative
    c. ablative
    b. accusative
    d. locative

33. In line 30 *suos* refers to

   a.   the Britons   b.   the Romans
   c.   the ships   d.   the cavalry

Translation *Suggested time: 15 minutes*

> Ita uno tempore et longas naves, quibus Caesar exercitum transportandum curaverat quasque in aridum subduxerat, aestus compleverat et onerarias, quae ad ancoras erant deligatae, tempestas adflictabat, neque ulla nostris facultas aut administrandi aut auxiliandi dabatur.

20 chunks. 10 points, ½ point each.

Ita uno tempore	**And so at one time**
et longas naves	**both the war ships**
quibus	**by means of which**
Caesar . . . curaverat	**Caesar had seen to**
exercitum transportandum	**the carrying across of the army**
quasque	**and which (ships)**
in aridum	**onto the shore**
subduxerat	**he had drawn up**
aestus compleverat	**the waves had filled**
et onerarias	**and the cargo ships**
quae ad ancoras	**which at anchor**
erant deligatae	**had been tied up**
tempestas adflictabat	**the storm was damaging**
neque ulla . . . facultas	**and no opportunity**
nostris	**to/for our men**
aut administrandi	**either of controlling (them)**
aut auxiliandi	**or of assisting (them)**
dabatur	**was being granted/given**

Short Analysis Questions

[28] His rebus pace confirmata, post diem quartum quam est in
Britanniam ventum naves XVIII, de quibus supra demonstratum est, quae
equites sustulerant, ex superiore portu leni vento solverunt. Quae cum
appropinquarent Britanniae et ex castris viderentur, tanta tempestas subito
5   coorta est ut nulla earum cursum tenere posset, sed aliae eodem unde
erant profectae referrentur, aliae ad inferiorem partem insulae, quae est
proprius solis occasum, magno sui cum periculo deicerentur; quae tamen,
ancoris iactis, cum fluctibus complerentur, necessario adversa nocte in
altum provectae, continentem petierunt.

1.   Who is on the ships that arrive later (lines 1–3)? Cite the Latin that supports your answer and translate or accurately paraphrase.

    The Roman cavalry—*naves . . . quae equites sustulerant* (lines 2–3)—is on the ships that arrive later.

2.   What causes the ships to go off course? Cite the Latin that answers the question and translate or accurately paraphrase.

    A large and sudden storm arises that blows them away from their destination—*tanta tempestas subito coorta est ut nulla earum cursum tenere posset* (lines 4–5).

3.   Do these ships contribute actively to Caesar's forces off the coast of Britain? Cite the Latin that supports your answer and translate or accurately paraphrase.

    No. Some are blown back to their port of origin—*aliae eodem unde erant profectae referrentur* (lines 5–6), while others are driven to a more dangerous part of Britain's coastline—*aliae ad inferiorem partem insulae . . . magno sui cum periculo deicerentur* (lines 5–7) and are forced to head back to the mainland—*continentem petierunt* (line 9).

[30] Quibus rebus cognitis, principes Britanniae, qui post proelium
ad Caesarem convenerant, inter se collocuti, cum equites et naves et
frumentum Romanis deesse intellegerent et paucitatem militum ex
castrorum exiguitate cognoscerent, quae hoc erant etiam angustiora quod
5   sine impedimentis Caesar legiones transportaverat, optimum factu esse
duxerunt, rebellione facta, frumento commeatuque nostros prohibere
et rem in hiemem producere, quod eis superatis aut reditu interclusis
neminem postea belli inferendi causa in Britanniam transiturum
confidebant. Itaque, rursus coniuratione facta, paulatim ex castris
10   discedere ac suos clam ex agris deducere coeperunt.

4. What considerations cause the British leaders to renew their resistance (lines 1–6)? Cite the
Latin that supports your answer and translate or accurately paraphrase.

**They perceive that the Romans are lacking in cavalry, ships, and their food supply—*cum
equites et naves et frumentum Romanis deesse intellegerent et paucitatem militum ex
castrorum exiguitate cognoscerent* (lines 2–4); they also infer that the Roman force on the
island is smaller than usual, because the camp is smaller—*paucitatem militum ex castrorum
exiguitate cognoscerent* (lines 3–4).**

5. According to lines 4–6, how can the Britons tell that Caesar's camp contains relatively few
soldiers? Cite the Latin that supports your answer and translate or accurately paraphrase.

**They detect that the camp is smaller because the troops have not also brought along
their baggage/supplies when they crossed to the island—*[castra] quae hoc erant etiam
angustiora quod sine impedimentis Caesar legiones transportaverat* (lines 4–5).**

6. What long-term result do the Britons hope will happen if they defeat Caesar's troops now? Cite
the Latin that supports your answer and translate or accurately paraphrase.

**They hope that nobody will consider invading Britain after Caesar's army will have suffered
so much on account of their lack of supplies and the harsh weather—*quod eis superatis aut
reditu interclusis neminem postea belli inferendi causa in Britanniam transiturum confidebant*
(lines 7–9).**

Essay *Suggested time: 20 minutes*

[29] Eadem nocte accidit ut esset luna plena, qui dies maritimos aestus maximos in Oceano efficere consuevit, nostrisque id erat incognitum. Ita uno tempore et longas naves, quibus Caesar exercitum transportandum curaverat quasque in aridum subduxerat, aestus compleverat et onerarias,
5   quae ad ancoras erant deligatae, tempestas adflictabat, neque ulla nostris facultas aut administrandi aut auxiliandi dabatur. Compluribus navibus fractis, reliquae cum essent funibus, ancoris, reliquisque armamentis amissis ad navigandum inutiles, magna, id quod necesse erat accidere, totius exercitus perturbatio facta est. Neque enim naves erant aliae quibus
10   reportari possent, et omnia deerant quae ad reficiendas naves erant usui et, quod omnibus constabat hiemare in Gallia oportere, frumentum his in locis in hiemem provisum non erat.

In this passage Caesar narrates at some length the disastrous effect on his troops of their encounter with a storm at sea. In a short essay, discuss the portrayal of the natural environment in this passage. Since Caesar, as general, is ultimately responsible for his army, is he to blame for the loss of ships and life? How does Caesar, as narrator, attempt to mitigate blame for the destruction?

Support your assertions with references to the Latin text throughout the passage above. All Latin words must be copied or their line numbers provided, AND they must be translated or paraphrased closely enough that it is clear that you understand the Latin. It is your responsibility to convince the reader that you are basing your conclusions on the Latin text and not merely on a general recollection of the passage. Direct your answer to the question; do not merely summarize the passage. Please write your essay on a separate piece of paper.

Teachers should review with students the Essay Scoring Guidelines given at the beginning of this manual.

From the outset of this episode Caesar the narrator suggests that he and his men are not to blame for the damage to the ships and the loss of life, because they did not know about the effect that a full moon has on the tidal currents—*nostrisque id erat incognitum* (line 2). It is possible to read this passage as a clear attempt by Caesar (as author) to avoid blame for the disaster, by downplaying the role of the general in planning and foreseeing possible obstacles to completing the mission. Students might note that the passage is structured, grammatically, to emphasize that the natural environment here is more powerful—*aestus* (lines 1 and 4) and *tempestas* (line 5) are in the nominative case, thereby making them the active elements in the passage, while Caesar portrays his men via a passive construction—*neque ulla nostris facultas aut administrandi aut auxiliandi dabatur* (lines 5–6). In the next sentence as well the Latin syntax emphasizes the effect of the storm on the army (rather than the army taking an active role)—*magna, id quod necesse erat accidere, totius exercitus perturbatio facta est* (lines 8–9). In this sentence several elements reinforce this idea: hyperbaton of adjective and noun (*magna . . . perturbatio*) creates an image that literally "surrounds" the army; *perturbatio* acts as subject while the army "receives" the action; and finally, Caesar claims that the army's reaction was natural and necessary—*id quod necesse erat accidere* (line 8).

Notes

CHAPTER 8: BOOK 4.31–33
A SURPRISE ATTACK!

[31] At Caesar, etsi nondum eorum consilia cognoverat, tamen et ex eventu
navium suarum et ex eo quod obsides dare intermiserant fore id quod
accidit suspicabatur. Itaque ad omnes casus subsidia comparabat. Nam
et frumentum ex agris cotidie in castra conferebat et, quae gravissime
5   adflictae erant naves, earum materia atque aere ad reliquas reficiendas
utebatur et quae ad eas res erant usui ex continenti comportari iubebat.
Itaque, cum summo studio a militibus administraretur, XII navibus
amissis, reliquis ut navigari commode posset effecit. [32] Dum ea geruntur,
legione ex consuetudine una frumentatum missa quae appellabatur
10 septima, neque ulla ad id tempus belli suspicione interposita, cum pars
hominum in agris remaneret, pars etiam in castra ventitaret, ei qui
pro portis castrorum in statione erant Caesari nuntiaverunt pulverem
maiorem quam consuetudo ferret in ea parte videri quam in partem
legio iter fecisset. Caesar id quod erat suspicatus, aliquid novi a barbaris
15 initum consili, cohortes quae in stationibus erant secum in eam partem
proficisci, ex reliquis duas in stationem cohortes succedere, reliquas
armari et confestim sese subsequi iussit. Cum paulo longius a castris
processisset, suos ab hostibus premi atque aegre sustinere et conferta
legione ex omnibus partibus tela coici animadvertit. Nam quod omni
20 ex reliquis partibus demesso frumento pars una erat reliqua, suspicati
hostes huc nostros esse venturos noctu in silvis delituerant; tum dispersos,
depositis armis in metendo occupatos subito adorti, paucis interfectis
reliquos incertis ordinibus perturbaverant, simul equitatu atque essedis
circumdederant. [33] Genus hoc est ex essedis pugnae. Primo per omnes
25 partes perequitant et tela coiciunt atque ipso terrore equorum et strepitu
rotarum ordines plerumque perturbant et, cum se inter equitum turmas
insinuaverunt, ex essedis desiliunt et pedibus proeliantur. Aurigae
interim paulatim ex proelio excedunt atque ita currus collocant ut, si illi
a multitudine hostium premantur, expeditum ad suos receptum habeant.
30 Ita mobilitatem equitum, stabilitatem peditum in proeliis praestant, ac
tantum usu cotidiano et exercitatione efficiunt uti in declivi ac praecipiti
loco incitatos equos sustinere et brevi moderari ac flectere et per temonem
percurrere et in iugo insistere et se inde in currus citissime recipere
consuerint.

Preparatory Questions

Line 1   What part of speech is *etsi*? **conjunction**

           Identify the tense and mood of *cognoverat*. **pluperfect indicative**

Line 2   Identify the case and syntax of *obsides*. **accusative, direct object of *dare***

           What is an alternative form for *fore*? **futurum esse**

Line 3   What or who is the subject of *comparabat*? ***Caesar* (line 1)**

Line 4   What part of speech is *cotidie*? **adverb**

Lines 4–5   Find a relative clause. ***quae gravissime adflictae erant***

           What is the antecedent of *quae*? ***naves* (note that it follows the relative clause)**

Line 5   Identify the case and use of *earum*. **genitive of possession**

           What noun does it replace? ***naves***

Lines 5–6   What two nouns are the objects of *utebatur*? ***materia, aere***

           What is the subject of *utebatur*? **Caesar (unexpressed)**

Line 6   Identify the case and use of *usui*. **dative of purpose**

Lines 7–8   Find an ablative absolute. ***XII navibus amissis***

Line 8   What kind of clause is *ut . . . posset*? **substantive clause of result**

           Identify the tense and mood of *geruntur*. **present indicative**

Line 9   Identify the form of *missa*. **perfect passive participle, feminine ablative singular (from *mitto*)**

           What noun does it modify? ***legione***

Lines 10–11   Find a *cum* clause. ***cum pars hominum in agris remaneret***

           What kind of *cum* clause is it? **circumstantial**

Lines 11–12   Find a relative clause. ***qui pro portis castrorum in statione erant***

Line 11   What/who is the antecedent of *qui*? ***ei* (= the soldiers)**

           Identify the form and syntax of *hominum*. **partitive genitive (with *pars*)**

Lines 12–14   Find an indirect statement. ***pulverem maiorem quam consuetudo ferret in ea parte videri quam in partem legio iter fecisset***

           What verb introduces it? ***nuntiaverunt* (line 12)**

Line 13   What word does *maiorem* modify? ***pulverem* (line 12)**

           Identify the tense and mood of *ferret*. **imperfect subjunctive**

Line 14	What is the tense and mood of *fecisset*? **pluperfect subjunctive**
	Identify the case and use of *novi*. **partitive genitive (with *aliquid*)**
	What word does it modify? ***consili* (line 15)**
Lines 14–15	What must be supplied to complete the sense of *aliquid . . . initum*? ***esse***
Lines 15–17	Find four infinitives belonging to an indirect statement. ***proficisci* (line 16), *succedere* (line 16), *armari* (line 17), *subsequi* (line 17)**
Line 15	Find a relative clause. ***quae in stationibus erant***
	Identify the case and use of *cohortes*. **accusative, subject of infinitive in indirect statement**
Line 16	Identify the form and use of *proficisci*. **present deponent infinitive, verb in indirect statement**
Line 17	Who/what is the subject of *iussit*? ***Caesar* (line 14)**
	Identify the form and use of *longius*. **comparative adverb, modifies *processisset***
Lines 17–18	Find a *cum* clause. ***cum paulo longius a castris processisset* (line 18)**
	What type of *cum* clause is it? **circumstantial**
Line 18	Identify the tense and mood of *processisset*. **pluperfect subjunctive**
Lines 18–19	Find an indirect statement. ***suos ab hostibus premi atque aegre sustinere et conferta legione ex omnibus partibus tela coici***
	What is the subject of *premi*? ***suos***
Line 19	Who/what is the subject of *animadvertit*? ***Caesar* (implied)**
Lines 19–21	Find a causal clause. ***quod omni ex reliquis partibus demesso frumento pars una erat reliqua***
Line 20	Identify the case and use of *demesso*. **ablative absolute**
	What word(s) does *reliqua* modify? ***pars***
	Identify the form of *suspicati*. **perfect deponent participle, masculine nominative plural (from *suspicor*)**
	What word(s) does it modify? ***hostes* (line 21)**
Line 21	Identify the case and use of *noctu*. **ablative of time within which**
Line 22	What part of speech is *subito*? **adverb**
Line 23	What is the tense of *perturbaverant*? **pluperfect**
Line 24	Identify the case and use of *pugnae*. **genitive of description**
	What part of speech is *primo*? **adverb**

Line 25	What tense is *perequitant*? **present**
	Identify the case and use of *terrore*. **ablative of means**
Line 26	On what word does *rotarum* depend? ***strepitu* (line 25)**
Lines 26–27	Find a *cum* clause. ***cum se inter equitum turmas insinuaverunt***
	What type of *cum* clause is it? **temporal**
Line 27	Identify the mood of *insinuaverunt*. **indicative**
	Identify the form and use of *pedibus*. **ablative of means**
Line 28	What part of speech is *interim*? **adverb**
	Identify the form and use of *currus*. **accusative, direct object (of *collocant*)**
Lines 28–29	Find a conditional sentence. ***si illi a multitudine hostium premantur, expeditum ad suos receptum habeant***
	What type of condition is it? **future less vivid**
Line 29	Explain the mood of *habeant*. **subjunctive in the apodosis of a future less vivid condition**
Line 30	What is the case and use of *equitum*? **genitive of possession**
	Identify the subject of *praestant*. **(unexpressed) *essedarii***
	What is the object of *in*? ***proeliis***
Lines 31–34	Find a result clause. ***uti in declivi ac praecipiti loco . . . consuerint***
Line 32	What words modify *loco*? ***declivi ac praecipiti* (line 31)**
Lines 32–34	Find five infinitives that depend on *consuerint*. ***moderari* (line 32), *flectere* (line 32), *percurrere* (line 33), *insistere* (line 33), *recipere* (line 33)**
Line 33	What part of speech is *citissime*? **adverb**
Line 34	Identify the form and syntax of *consuerint*. **perfect subjunctive active, result clause**

Multiple Choice Questions *Suggested time: 43 minutes*

1. The mood and tense of *cognoverat* (line 1) is
   a. imperfect indicative
   c. pluperfect indicative
   b. imperfect subjunctive
   d. perfect subjunctive

2. To whom does the possessive adjective *suarum* (line 2) refer?
   a. the ships
   c. the hostages
   b. the Romans
   d. the Britons

3. The phrase *ex eo* (line 2) is translated
   a. on account of this reason
   c. from that man
   b. from that place
   d. out of here

4. In lines 1–3 (*tamen . . . suspicabatur*) the main verb of the clause is
   a. *intermiserant* (line 2)
   c. suspicabatur (line 3)
   b. *dare* (line 2)
   d. *fore* (line 2)

5. The verb *fore* (line 2) is
   a. perfect passive infinitive
   c. future active infinitive
   b. future passive infinitive
   d. present active infinitive

6. The gender and case of *subsidia* (line 3) is
   a. feminine nominative
   c. neuter nominative
   b. feminine ablative
   d. neuter accusative

7. In line 3 the phrase *ad omnes casus* is translated
   a. in all cases
   c. toward all causes
   b. for each failure
   d. for all events

8. In lines 4–6 we learn that
   a. all the ships were unfit to sail
   c. some ships were used to repair others
   b. new ships were being sent from Gaul
   d. troop morale was very low

9. The case of *materia atque aere* (line 5) is determined by
   a. *earum* (line 5)
   c. *reficiendas* (line 5)
   b. utebatur (line 6)
   d. *reliquas* (line 5)

10. In line 7 *cum* is translated
    a. although
    c. since
    b. with
    d. when

11. The phrase *ut navigari commode posset* (line 8) is a
    a. purpose clause
    c. temporal clause
    b. causal clause
    d. substantive clause of result

12. The word *frumentatum* (line 9) is a
    a. present participle
    c. gerundive of purpose
    b. supine expressing purpose
    d. perfect passive participle

13. The case of *hominum* (line 11) is
    a. nominative
    c. genitive
    b. accusative
    d. dative

14. In line 12, the object of the preposition *pro* is
    a. *portis* (line 12)
    c. *qui* (line 11)
    b. *castrorum* (line 12)
    d. *statione* (line 12)

15. In lines 12–14 we learn that
    a. Caesar is always alert
    c. an unusual dust cloud is visible
    b. the Roman legions are foraging for grain
    d. part of the legion was missing

16. In line 13 the <u>first</u> *quam* is a(n)
    a. relative pronoun
    c. adversative particle
    b. conjunction
    d. relative adjective

17. What noun does the <u>second</u> *quam* (line 13) modify?
    a. *partem* (line 13)
    c. *parte* (line 13)
    b. *maiorem* (line 13)
    d. *legio* (line 14)

18. The word *novi* (line 14) modifies
    a. *aliquid* (line 14)
    c. *initum* (line 15)
    b. *barbaris* (line 14)
    d. *consili* (line 15)

19. In line 16 *proficisci* is translated
    a. to set out
    c. to be about to set out
    b. having set out
    d. will have set out

20. The pronoun *sese* in line 17 refers to
    a. *reliquas* (line 16)
    c. *stationem* (line 16)
    b. *Caesar* (line 14)
    d. *cohortes* (line 16)

21. The tense and mood of *processisset* (line 18) is
    a. perfect subjunctive
    c. pluperfect subjunctive
    b. imperfect indicative
    d. future perfect indicative

22. *aegre* (line 18) modifies
    a. *sustinere* (line 18)
    c. *legione* (line 19)
    b. *conferta* (line 18)
    d. *premi* (line 18)

23. *omni* in line 19 modifies
   a. *partibus* (line 19)
   c. frumento (line 20)
   b. *ex* (line 19)
   d. *pars* (line 20)

24. In line 21 *noctu* is ablative of
   a. means
   c. manner
   b. time
   d. agent

25. *adorti* in line 22 modifies
   a. *nostros* (line 21)
   c. *subito* (line 22)
   b. *silvis* (line 21)
   d. hostes (line 21)

26. The case of *incertis* (line 23) is
   a. genitive
   c. accusative
   b. dative
   d. ablative

27. The phrase *primo per omnes partes perequitant* (lines 24–25) is an example of
   a. alliteration
   c. asyndeton
   b. metaphor
   d. hyperbole

28. In line 26 *cum* is translated
   a. with
   c. although
   b. since
   d. when

29. In line 27 *pedibus* is translated
   a. on foot
   c. without shoes
   b. by kicking
   d. on high ground

30. In line 28 *paulatim* is translated
   a. a little
   c. little by little
   b. on foot
   d. for the most part

31. The phrase *ita currus collocant ut* (line 28) introduces a
   a. purpose clause
   c. conditional sentence
   b. result clause
   d. relative clause

32. The condition in lines 28–29 is a
   a. present contrary to fact
   c. future more vivid
   b. simple condition
   d. future less vivid

33. In line 30 *peditum* is
    a. nominative
    b. **genitive**
    c. accusative
    d. ablative

34. In lines 30–34 we learn that the British charioteers
    a. **are highly skilled and trained**
    b. risk their lives in battle
    c. ride small horses
    d. run through the fields

35. The phrase *declivi ac precipitati* (line 31) modifies
    a. *equos* (line 32)
    b. *brevi* (line 32)
    c. *sustinere* (line 32)
    d. *loco* **(line 32)**

36. The case and number of *currus* (line 33) is
    a. **accusative plural**
    b. accusative singular
    c. nominative plural
    d. nominative singluar

Translation *Suggested time: 20 minutes*

At Caesar, etsi nondum eorum consilia cognoverat, tamen et ex eventu navium suarum et ex eo quod obsides dare intermiserant fore id quod accidit suspicabatur. Itaque ad omnes casus subsidia comparabat. Nam et frumentum ex agris cotidie in castra conferebat et, quae gravissime
5 adflictae erant naves, earum materia atque aere ad reliquas reficiendas utebatur et quae ad eas res erant usui ex continenti comportari iubebat.

24 chunks. 12 points, ½ point each.

At Caesar,	But Caesar
etsi nondum . . . cognoverat	although he did not yet know
eorum consilia	their plans
tamen et ex eventu	nevertheless, both on account of the fate
navium suarum	of his ships
et ex eo quod	and on account of the fact that
obsides dare	the giving of hostages
intermiserant	they had suspended
fore id	that it would be
quod accidit	what happened
suspicabatur	he began to suspect
Itaque ad omnes casus	Accordingly, for every outcome
subsidia comparabat	he began to prepare resources
Nam et frumentum . . . conferebat	For he was bringing grain
ex agris cotidie in castra	from the fields into the camp every day
et, quae . . . naves	and those ships which
gravissime adflictae erant	had been most heavily damaged
earum materia atque aere	their timber and bronze
ad reliquas reficiendas	for the restoration of the rest
utebatur	he used
et quae ad eas res	and what things for those activities
erant usui	were useful
ex continenti comportari	to be brought over from the mainland
iubebat	he ordered

Short Analysis Questions

[33] Genus hoc est ex essedis pugnae. Primo per omnes partes perequitant
et tela coiciunt atque ipso terrore equorum et strepitu rotarum ordines
plerumque perturbant et, cum se inter equitum turmas insinuaverunt,
ex essedis desiliunt et pedibus proeliantur. Aurigae interim paulatim
5 ex proelio excedunt atque ita currus collocant ut, si illi a multitudine
hostium premantur, expeditum ad suos receptum habeant. Ita mobilitatem
equitum, stabilitatem peditum in proeliis praestant, ac tantum usu
cotidiano et exercitatione efficiunt uti in declivi ac praecipiti loco incitatos
equos sustinere et brevi moderari ac flectere et per temonem percurrere et
10 in iugo insistere et se inde in currus citissime recipere consuerint.

1. What type of fighting does Caesar describe in this passage? Cite the Latin that supports your
answer and translate or accurately paraphrase.

   **Caesar is describing chariot fighting—*Genus hoc est ex essedis pugnae* (line 1), a unique
combination of infantry and cavalry elements, used by the British tribes.**

2. What is the initial effect of the arrival of these specialist fighters (lines 1–3)?

   **They throw the ranks of Roman infantry into confusion and panic—*ipso terrore equorum et
strepitu rotarum ordines plerumque perturbant* (lines 2–3).**

3. What role do the *aurigae* (line 4) play in this type of battle? Cite the Latin that supports your
answer and translate or accurately paraphrase.

   **They are responsible for the chariot itself, slowly withdrawing it to the edges of the battle
—*paulatim ex proelio excedunt* (lines 4–5). They serve as "getaway drivers" —*ita currus
collocant ut, si illi a multitudine hostium premantur, expeditum ad suos receptum habeant*
(lines 5–6).**

4. What is it about these fighters that makes them so skilled and adaptable (lines 6–10)? Cite the
Latin that supports your answer and translate or accurately paraphrase.

   **They combine the strengths of both cavalry and infantry, being both highly mobile and
at the same time steadfast fighters—*Ita mobilitatem equitum, stabilitatem peditum in
proeliis praestant* (lines 6–7). Also, they undergo rigorous training to develop their skill at
handling the horses and equipment—*tantum usu cotidiano et exercitatione efficiunt uti in
declivi ac praecipiti loco incitatos equos sustinere et brevi moderari ac flectere et per temonem
percurrere et in iugo insistere et se inde in currus citissime recipere consuerint* (lines 7–10).**

Essay *Suggested time: 20 minutes*

[32] Dum ea geruntur, legione ex consuetudine una frumentatum missa
quae appellabatur septima, neque ulla ad id tempus belli suspicione
interposita, cum pars hominum in agris remaneret, pars etiam in
castra ventitaret, ei qui pro portis castrorum in statione erant Caesari
5   nuntiaverunt pulverem maiorem quam consuetudo ferret in ea parte videri
quam in partem legio iter fecisset. Caesar id quod erat suspicatus, aliquid
novi a barbaris initum consili, cohortes quae in stationibus erant secum
in eam partem proficisci, ex reliquis duas in stationem cohortes succedere,
reliquas armari et confestim sese subsequi iussit.

This passage presents a description of the sudden attack on Caesar's troops by the reinvigorated British rebellion. In the brief space of two sentences, Caesar narrates both the events and his own reaction. In a short essay, discuss the literary techniques Caesar uses to create suspense and drama. How do these two sentences work together to craft a succinct narrative of the events described? What is the effect on the reader?

Support your assertions with references to the Latin text throughout the passage above. All Latin words must be copied or their line numbers provided, AND they must be translated or paraphrased closely enough that it is clear that you understand the Latin. It is your responsibility to convince the reader that you are basing your conclusions on the Latin text and not merely on a general recollection of the passage. Direct your answer to the question; do not merely summarize the passage. Please write your essay on a separate piece of paper.

Teachers should review with students the Essay Scoring Guidelines given at the beginning of this manual.

In responding to this essay question, students will need to pay careful attention to the structure of the two sentences in the passage given. Caesar creates a suspenseful narrative by piling up dependent clauses in the first sentence (e.g., by using temporal clauses, ablative absolutes, a *cum* clause, etc.) that are designed to give the reader all the relevant information that "Caesar" (the general) needs to make a decision. The second sentence shows, in a more concise and direct structure, the action taken to deal with the crisis. Students should note the preponderance of "action" verbs in the second part, especially the string of infinitives all dependent upon *iussit* (line 9), with Caesar (of course) as the nominative subject. Especially perceptive students may note the periodic nature of even the second part, with the nominative opening the sentence and the verb closing, with all the pertinent content neatly enclosed within it. The effect is to reinforce for the reader the idea that Caesar is prepared for each eventuality and that he has uncanny foresight (note the phrase *id quod erat suspicatus*, line 6). His leadership and intuitive military genius are here on display.

Notes

CHAPTER 9: BOOK 4.34–36.1
CAESAR DEFEATS THE BRITONS

[34] Quibus rebus perturbatis nostris novitate pugnae tempore
opportunissimo Caesar auxilium tulit: namque eius adventu hostes
constiterunt, nostri se ex timore receperunt. Quo facto, ad lacessendum
hostem et ad committendum proelium alienum esse tempus arbitratus suo se
5   loco continuit et, brevi tempore intermisso, in castra legiones reduxit.
Dum haec geruntur, nostris omnibus occupatis, qui erant in agris
reliqui discesserunt. Secutae sunt continuos complures dies tempestates
quae et nostros in castris continerent et hostem a pugna prohiberent.
Interim barbari nuntios in omnes partes dimiserunt paucitatemque
10   nostrorum militum suis praedicaverunt et quanta praedae faciendae
atque in perpetuum sui liberandi facultas daretur, si Romanos castris
expulissent, demonstraverunt. His rebus celeriter magna multitudine
peditatus equitatusque coacta ad castra venerunt. [35] Caesar etsi idem
quod superioribus diebus acciderat fore videbat, ut, si essent hostes pulsi,
15   celeritate periculum effugerent, tamen nactus equites circiter XXX, quos
Commius Atrebas, de quo ante dictum est, secum transportaverat, legiones
in acie pro castris constituit. Commisso proelio, diutius nostrorum
militum impetum hostes ferre non potuerunt ac terga verterunt. Quos
tanto spatio secuti quantum cursu et viribus efficere potuerunt, complures
20   ex eis occiderunt, deinde omnibus longe lateque aedificiis incensis se in
castra receperunt. [36] Eodem die legati ab hostibus missi ad Caesarem de
pace venerunt.

Preparatory Questions

Line 1   Identify the case and use of *rebus*. **ablative of means or cause**

Identify the case and use of *novitate*. **ablative of means**

Line 2   Who/what is the subject of *tulit*? *Caesar*

To whom/what does *eius* refer? **Caesar**

Line 4   What noun does the phrase *ad committendum* modify? *proelium*

Identify the form and syntax of *arbitratus*. **perfect deponent participle (of *arbitror*), modifies unexpressed subject of *continuit* (line 5)**

Who/what is the subject of *arbitratus*? **Caesar**

What word does *alienum* modify? *tempus*

Line 5   Find an ablative absolute. ***brevi tempore intermisso***

         What is the object of the preposition *in*? ***castra***

Lines 6–7   Find a temporal clause. ***Dum haec geruntur***

         Find a relative clause. ***qui erant in agris reliqui***

Line 7   Who is meant by *reliqui*? **other Britons**

         Who/what is the subject of *secutae sunt*? ***tempestates***

         Identify the case and use of *dies*. **accusative of duration of time**

Line 8   Identify the form and syntax of *continerent*. **imperfect subjunctive active, relative clause of characteristic**

         Identify the case and use of *pugna*. **ablative of separation**

Line 9   Identify the case and use of *nuntios*. **accusative, direct object of *dimiserunt***

Line 10   Identify the case and use of *militum*. **genitive of possession**

         Identify the form and syntax of *faciendae*. **feminine genitive singular gerundive**

         What word does it modify? ***praedae***

Lines 10–11   Find an indirect question. ***quanta praedae faciendae . . . facultas daretur***

Line 11   What is the subject of *daretur*? ***facultas***

Line 12   Identify the form and syntax of *expulissent*. **pluperfect subjunctive (stands in for future perfect indicative of a future more vivid condition) in the indirect question**

         Who/what is the subject of *demonstraverunt*? **the messengers (*nuntios*, line 9)**

Line 13   Identify the case and use of *peditatus*. **genitive of description**

         What is the object of the preposition *ad*? ***castra***

Lines 13–15   Find an indirect statement. ***idem . . . fore***

Line 14   Find a relative clause. ***quod superioribus diebus acciderat***

         What is the antecedent of *quod*? ***idem* (line 13)**

Lines 14–15   Find a conditional sentence. ***si essent hostes pulsi, celeritate periculum effugerent***

         Identify the tense and mood of *essent . . . pulsi*. **pluperfect subjunctive**

Line 15   Identify the tense and mood of *effugerent*. **imperfect subjunctive**

         What part of speech is *circiter*? **adverb**

Line 16   What/who is the subject of *transportaverat*? ***Commius***

         Identify the tense and mood of *transportaverat*. **pluperfect indicative**

Line 17	Find an ablative absolute. ***Commisso proelio***
	Identify the form and syntax of *diutius*. **(comparative) adverb, modifying *ferre* (line 18)**
Line 18	What is the subject of *potuerunt*? ***hostes***
	Identify the case and use of *terga*. **accusative, direct object of *verterunt***
Line 19	Identify the case and use of *complures*. **accusative, direct object of *occiderunt***
Line 20	What is the unexpressed subject of *occiderunt*? ***equites* (line 15)**
	What part of speech is *longe*? **adverb**
	What words does *omnibus* modify? ***aedificiis***
Line 21	What word modifies *legati*? ***missi***
	What is the object of *ad*? ***Caesarem***
	What is the object of *de*? ***pace* (line 22)**
Line 22	Identify the form and syntax of *venerunt*. **perfect indicative active (of *venio*), main verb of the sentence**

Multiple Choice Questions *Suggested time: 30 minutes*

1. The case of *novitate* (line 1) is
   a. nominative
   c. vocative
   b. genitive
   d. ablative

2. The case of *eius* in line 2 is
   a. nominative
   c. vocative
   b. genitive
   d. ablative

3. The tense of *receperunt* (line 3) is
   a. present
   c. perfect
   b. imperfect
   d. pluperfect

4. The syntax of the phrase *ad committendum proelium* (line 4) is
   a. relative purpose clause
   c. gerundive of purpose
   b. indirect command
   d. accusative of extent of space

5. In line 4 *arbitratus* introduces
   a. an indirect question
   c. a relative clause
   b. an indirect statement
   d. a purpose clause

6. In line 6 *dum* is translated
   a. provided that
   b. in order that
   c. since
   d. while

7. The subject of *secutae sunt* (line 7) is
   a. *continuos* (line 7)
   b. *complures* (line 7)
   c. tempestates (line 7)
   d. *dies* (line 7)

8. The syntactical explanation for *continerent* (line 8) is
   a. relative clause in indirect speech
   b. relative clause of result
   c. relative clause of characteristic
   d. relative temporal clause

9. In line 9 *omnes* modifies
   a. *barbari* (line 9)
   b. partes (line 9)
   c. *nuntios* (line 9)
   d. *dimiserunt* (line 9)

10. The phrase *quanta . . . daretur* (lines 10–11) is dependent upon
    a. *dimiserunt* (line 9)
    b. *expulissent* (line 12)
    c. *praedicaverunt* (line 10)
    d. demonstraverunt (line 12)

11. In line 11 *facultas* is translated
    a. faculty
    b. facility
    c. opportunity
    d. opprobrium

12. The phrase *his rebus* (line 12) refers to
    a. the promises made by the messengers
    b. the earlier battles
    c. the storm that ruined the ships
    d. Caesar's actions in Britain

13. In line 12 *celeriter* is translated
    a. swift
    b. famously
    c. swiftly
    d. celery

14. In line 14 *superioribus diebus* is an ablative of
    a. means
    b. time when
    c. manner
    d. accompaniment

15. In line 14 *ut* introduces
    a. a purpose clause
    b. a result clause
    c. a temporal clause
    d. an indirect command

16. The tense of *effugerent* (line 15) is

    a. imperfect
    b. pluperfect
    c. perfect
    d. present

17. The unexpressed noun in agreement with *nactus* (line 15) is

    a. Commius
    b. Caesar
    c. the cavalry
    d. Atrebas

18. The phrase *in acie* (line 17) is translated

    a. in battle formation
    b. on the ridge
    c. in the camp
    d. before the camp

19. In line 17 *diutius* is

    a. an adjective
    b. a perfect passive participle
    c. a noun
    d. an adverb

20. In lines 17–18 we learn that

    a. the enemy routed Caesar's troops
    b. the enemy fled
    c. reinforcements arrived from Gaul
    d. the ships were repaired

21. The word that joins *tanto* (line 19) to form a correlative pair is

    a. quantum (line 19)
    b. *spatio* (line 19)
    c. *secuti* (line 19)
    d. *cursu* (line 19)

22. The dictionary entry for *viribus* (line 19) is

    a. *vir*
    b. *viridus*
    c. vis
    d. *vix*

23. In line 19 *complures* refers to

    a. the Romans
    b. the Britons
    c. the horses
    d. the buildings

24. In line 20 *deinde* is translated

    a. when
    b. then
    c. but
    d. nevertheless

25. In lines 21–22 we learn that

    a. Caesar sent for reinforcements
    b. the legates all died
    c. the Britons asked for peace
    d. Caesar sent the legates away

Translation *Suggested time: 15 minutes*

[34] Quibus rebus perturbatis nostris novitate pugnae tempore
opportunissimo Caesar auxilium tulit: namque eius adventu hostes
constiterunt, nostri se ex timore receperunt. Quo facto, ad lacessendum
hostem et ad committendum proelium alienum esse tempus arbitratus suo
5 se loco continuit et, brevi tempore intermisso, in castra legiones reduxit.

20 chunks. 10 points, ½ point each.

Quibus rebus	**By these events**
perturbatis nostris	**our men having been thrown into confusion**
novitate pugnae	**(and) by/because of the unusualness of the battle**
tempore opportunissimo	**in the nick of time (at the most advantageous moment)**
Caesar auxilium tulit	**Caesar brought assistance**
namque eius adventu	**for at his arrival**
hostes constiterunt	**the enemy stopped**
nostri se . . . receperunt	**our men recovered themselves**
ex timore	**from panic**
Quo facto	**Which thing having been done**
ad lacessendum	**for attacking**
et ad committendum proelium	**and engaging in battle**
alienum esse tempus	**the time was not advantageous**
arbitratus	**having thought (that)**
suo se loco continuit et	**he remained in his location and**
brevi tempore intermisso	**a short time having passed/when a short time had passed**
in castra	**into the camp**
legiones reduxit	**he led the legions back**

Short Analysis Questions

Secutae sunt continuos complures dies tempestates quae et nostros
in castris continerent et hostem a pugna prohiberent. Interim barbari
nuntios in omnes partes dimiserunt paucitatemque nostrorum militum
suis praedicaverunt et quanta praedae faciendae atque in perpetuum
5 sui liberandi facultas daretur, si Romanos castris expulissent,
demonstraverunt. His rebus celeriter magna multitudine peditatus
equitatusque coacta ad castra venerunt.

1. How does the weather affect the situation here? Cite the Latin that supports your answer and
    translate or accurately paraphrase.

    **There are continual storms for several days—*Secutae sunt continuos complures dies
    tempestates* (line 1). These prevent any renewal of the fighting. As a result, the battle is at a
    stalemate.**

2. What three pieces of information do the messengers use to encourage their people to join the rebellion (lines 2–5)? Cite the Latin that supports your answer and translate or accurately paraphrase.

They claim that the Romans have few soldiers—*paucitatem nostrorum militum* (line 3]), that there was an excellent opportunity for plunder—*quanta praedae faciendae . . . facultas* (lines 4–5) and, perhaps most importantly, that it was a chance to free themselves forever— *atque in perpetuum sui liberandi* (lines 4–5).

3. What is the result of these embassies (lines 6–7)? Cite the Latin that supports your answer and translate or accurately paraphrase.

The embassies are hugely successful. A vast number of Britons flocks to their camp to prepare for battle and advance on the Roman camp—*His rebus celeriter magna multitudine peditatus equitatusque coacta ad castra venerunt.*

Essay *Suggested time: 20 minutes*

[34] Quibus rebus perturbatis nostris novitate pugnae tempore
opportunissimo Caesar auxilium tulit: namque eius adventu hostes
constiterunt, nostri se ex timore receperunt. Quo facto, ad lacessendum
hostem et ad committendum proelium alienum esse tempus arbitratus suo se
5   loco continuit et, brevi tempore intermisso, in castra legiones reduxit.
Dum haec geruntur, nostris omnibus occupatis, qui erant in agris
reliqui discesserunt. Secutae sunt continuos complures dies tempestates
quae et nostros in castris continerent et hostem a pugna prohiberent.
Interim barbari nuntios in omnes partes dimiserunt paucitatemque
10   nostrorum militum suis praedicaverunt et quanta praedae faciendae
atque in perpetuum sui liberandi facultas daretur, si Romanos castris
expulissent, demonstraverunt. His rebus celeriter magna multitudine
peditatus equitatusque coacta ad castra venerunt. [35] Caesar etsi idem
quod superioribus diebus acciderat fore videbat, ut, si essent hostes pulsi,
15   celeritate periculum effugerent, tamen nactus equites circiter XXX, quos
Commius Atrebas, de quo ante dictum est, secum transportaverat, legiones
in acie pro castris constituit. Commisso proelio, diutius nostrorum
militum impetum hostes ferre non potuerunt ac terga verterunt. Quos
tanto spatio secuti quantum cursu et viribus efficere potuerunt, complures
20   ex eis occiderunt, deinde omnibus longe lateque aedificiis incensis se in
castra receperunt. [36] Eodem die legati ab hostibus missi ad Caesarem de
pace venerunt.

The beginning and end of this passage describe roughly the same behavior on the part of Caesar and his troops, but with very different outcomes. In a short essay, discuss the significance of the repetition of this action and, more importantly, what the passage tells us about Caesar's use of experience in his leadership. That is, how does past experience in this passage inform Caesar's decisions in later circumstances? What key quality of generalship does Caesar display here?

Support your assertions with references to the Latin text throughout the passage above. All Latin words must be copied or their line numbers provided, AND they must be translated or paraphrased closely enough that it is clear that you understand the Latin. It is your responsibility to convince the reader that you are basing your conclusions on the Latin text and not merely on a general recollection of the passage. Direct your answer to the question; do not merely summarize the passage. Please write your essay on a separate piece of paper.

Teachers should review with students the Essay Scoring Guidelines given at the beginning of this manual.

At the beginning of this passage, Caesar's troops are panicked by the strange battle tactics employed by the British tribes—*Quibus rebus perturbatis nostris novitate pugnae* (line 1). Caesar's arrival both calms their panic and halts the British attack—*namque eius adventu hostes constiterunt, nostri se ex timore receperunt* (lines 2–3). Thus, by his very presence, Caesar is able to turn the situation to his advantage. Subsequently he uses the newly arrived cavalry under the command of Commius to bring about a victory. But more importantly, Caesar recognizes that the battle is at a stalemate given the current tactics he employs; he must adapt his own tactics and this is the key character trait that allows him to succeed so effectively—*etsi idem quod superioribus diebus acciderat fore videbat, ut, si essent hostes pulsi, celeritate periculum effugerent, tamen . . .* (lines 13–15). Students might also note the enormous impact of only a few cavalry riders (thirty) on the apparently huge multitude of British fighters. By using his cavalry to gain an advantage over the Britons, Caesar is able to shift from defense to offense and to bring the campaign to an end.

CHAPTER 10: BOOK 5.24–25
WINTER QUARTERS

[24] Subductis navibus, concilioque Gallorum Samarobrivae peracto, quod
eo anno frumentum in Gallia propter siccitates angustius provenerat,
coactus est aliter ac superioribus annis exercitum in hibernis collocare,
legionesque in plures civitates distribuere. Ex quibus unam in Morinos
5   ducendam Gaio Fabio legato dedit, alteram in Nervios Quinto Ciceroni,
tertiam in Esubios Lucio Roscio; quartam in Remis cum Tito Labieno
in confinio Treverorum hiemare iussit. Tres in Bellovacis collocavit: eis
Marcum Crassum quaestorem et Lucium Munatium Plancum et Gaium
Trebonium legatos praefecit. Unam legionem, quam proxime trans Padum
10 conscripserat, et cohortes V in Eburones, quorum pars maxima est inter
Mosam ac Rhenum, qui sub imperio Ambiorigis et Catuvolci erant, misit.
Eis militibus Quintum Titurium Sabinum et Lucium Aurunculeium
Cottam legatos praeesse iussit. Ad hunc modum distributis legionibus
facillime inopiae frumentariae sese mederi posse existimavit. Atque
15 harum tamen omnium legionum hiberna, praeter eam quam Lucio Roscio
in pacatissimam et quietissimam partem ducendam dederat, milibus
passuum centum continebantur. Ipse interea, quoad legiones collocatas
munitaque hiberna cognovisset, in Gallia morari constituit. [25] Erat in
Carnutibus summo loco natus Tasgetius, cuius maiores in sua civitate
20 regnum obtinuerant. Huic Caesar pro eius virtute atque in se benevolentia,
quod in omnibus bellis singulari eius opera fuerat usus, maiorum
locum restituerat. Tertium iam hunc annum regnantem †inimicis iam multis
palam ex civitate et eis auctoribus eum †interfecerunt. Defertur ea res
ad Caesarem. Ille veritus, quod ad plures pertinebat, ne civitas eorum
25 impulsu deficeret, Lucium Plancum cum legione ex Belgio celeriter in
Carnutes proficisci iubet ibique hiemare, quorumque opera cognoverat
Tasgetium interfectum, hos comprehensos ad se mittere. Interim ab
omnibus legatis quaestoribusque, quibus legiones tradiderat certior factus
est in hiberna perventum locumque hibernis esse munitum.

Preparatory Questions

Line 1   Identify the case and use of *Gallorum*. **partitive genitive (with *concilio*)**

Line 2   Identify the case and use of *anno*. **ablative of time when**

Line 3   Identify the subject of *coactus est*. **he (Caesar understood)**

What does *superioribus* modify? **annis**

Lines 3–4   What two infinitives are dependent on *coactus est*? **collocare, distribuere**

Lines 4–7   What are the objects of *dedit*? **unam (line 4), *alteram* (line 5), *tertiam* (line 6), and quartam (line 6)**

Lines 4–5   *Unam in Morinos ducendam* is the object of what verb? **dedit**

Line 5   *Ducendam* modifies the understood antecedent of what word? **unam**

Identify the case and use of *Quinto Ciceroni*. **dative indirect object (with *dedit*)**

Line 6   Identify the case and use of *Remis*. **ablative object of the preposition *in* (place where)**

Line 7   What does *Tres* modify? **understood *legiones***

Lines 8–9   *Crassum* and *Plancum* are objects of what verb? **praefecit (line 9)**

Line 9   What is the antecedent of *quam*? **legionem**

Line 10   Identify the tense and mood of *conscripserat*. **pluperfect indicative**

What is the antecedent of *quorum*? **Eburones**

What does *maxima* modify? **pars**

Line 13   Identify the form and use of *praeesse*. **infinitive complementing *iussit***

Line 14   Identify the form and use of *facillime*. **superlative adverb modifying *mederi***

Find an indirect statement. **facillime inopiae . . . posse**

Lines 16–17   *Milibus passuum centum* is translated **one hundred thousand paces, one hundred miles**

Line 18   Identify the tense and mood of *cognovisset*. **pluperfect subjunctive**

Line 20   Identify the tense and mood of *obtinuerant*. **pluperfect indicative**

Line 22   Identify the form and use of *regnantem*. **present participle active accusative modifying *hunc***

Line 24   What/whom does *veritus* modify? **ille**

Lines 24–25   Find a negative clause of fear. **ne . . . deficeret**

Line 26   Identify the form and use of *proficisci*. **present deponent infinitive, with *iubet***

Line 27   What does *comprehensos* modify? **hos**

Line 28   What is the antecedent of *quibus*? **legatis quaestoribusque**

Line 29   Name two participles completed by *esse*. **perventum, munitum**

Multiple Choice Questions *Suggested time: 36 minutes*

1. In line 1 the first six words constitute
   - a. a double gerundive phrase
   - **b. a double ablative absolute**
   - c. a double substantive clause
   - d. a double relative clause

2. In line 2 we learn that
   - a. Caesar does not trust the Gauls
   - b. the Gauls have plenty of supplies
   - **c. the crops have not been good in Gaul**
   - d. the Gauls are revolting

3. In line 3 *aliter ac* means
   - **a. differently than**
   - b. likewise
   - c. alternately
   - d. regularly

4. In line 3 *hibernis* is a(n)
   - a. adjective
   - b. verb
   - **c. noun**
   - d. participle

5. In lines 4–6 *unam, alteram,* and *tertiam* all modify the understood noun
   - a. *Galliam*
   - b. *Caesarem*
   - **c. *legionem***
   - d. *hiberniam*

6. In line 4 *in Morinos* is translated
   - a. on the island Morini
   - b. against the Morini
   - **c. into the land of the Morini**
   - d. with the Morini

7. In line 5 *ducendam* is
   - a. a gerund
   - **b. a gerundive**
   - c. a verb
   - d. a noun

8. In line 6 *in Remis* is translated
   - a. into the land of the Remi
   - b. in the land of the Remi
   - c. on the island Remi
   - **d. among the Remi**

9. In line 7 *hiemare* is
   - a. a noun
   - b. an adjective
   - **c. an infinitive**
   - d. a linking verb

10. In line 7 *eis* refers to
    - a. the quaestor
    - b. the Gauls
    - **c. the three legions**
    - d. hostages

11. In line 9 *praefecit* is
    a. an intransitive verb with no object
    c. a participle
    b. an irregular verb
    d. a compound verb taking accusative and dative

12. In line 9 *proxime* is translated
    a. rarely
    c. recently
    b. nearby
    d. as possible

13. In line 10 *in Eburones* is translated
    a. into the land of the Eburones
    c. on the island Eburones
    b. in the land of the Eburones
    d. over the Eburones

14. In line 11 *Mosam* and *Rhenum* are
    a. continents
    c. people
    b. rivers
    d. armies

15. In line 11 *Ambiorigis* and *Catuvolci* are names of
    a. continents
    c. commanders
    b. rivers
    d. places

16. The objects of *praeesse* (line 13) are
    a. *legatos* (line 13) and *militibus* (line 12)
    c. *iussit* (line 13) and *misit* (line 11)
    b. *Ambiorigis* and *Catuvolci* (line 11)
    d. *hunc* and *modum* (line 13)

17. In line 14 *mederi* is translated
    a. to be moderate
    c. to mediate
    b. to remedy
    d. to be made

18. In line 16 *pacatissimam* and *quietissimam* are
    a. gerunds
    c. superlative adjectives
    b. comparative adjectives
    d. participles

19. In lines 13–17 we learn that Caesar
    a. prefers to have his soldiers scattered widely
    c. doesn't trust anybody
    b. trusts one part of Gaul more than the rest
    d. wants to leave Gaul

20. In line 17 *quoad* is translated
    a. until
    c. where
    b. because
    d. why

21. In lines 18–20 we learn that Tasgetius
    a. knew nothing about Rome
    b. was descended from rulers
    c. was an able soldier
    d. disliked foreigners

22. In line 20 *virtute* and *benevolentia* are qualities attributed to
    a. Caesar
    b. the Roman soldiers
    c. Tasgetius
    d. the Gallic people

23. In lines 21–22 *maiorum locum* is translated
    a. greater glory
    b. a greater position
    c. the position of his ancestors
    d. wider lands

24. In lines 22–23 we learn that Tasgetius
    a. was killed by Caesar
    b. was killed by political enemies
    c. was killed by personal enemies
    d. died by accident

25. In line 23 *auctoribus* is translated
    a. authorities
    b. opponents
    c. students
    d. instigators

26. In line 23 the pronoun *eum* refers back to
    a. Caesar
    b. the Roman legate
    c. Tasgetius
    d. an anonymous Gaul

27. In line 24 Caesar is deeply concerned by
    a. the place in which this occurred
    b. the scarcity of soldiers
    c. the number of people involved
    d. the time of year

28. In line 26 *quorumque opera* is translated
    a. and in the work (deed)
    b. and by whose work (deed)
    c. and what work (deed)
    d. and when they worked

29. In line 27 the action of *hos comprehensos mittere* is dependent upon
    a. *hiemare* (line 26)
    b. *Tasgetium* (line 27)
    c. *cognoverat* (line 26)
    d. *interfectum* (line 27)

30. In lines 28–29 *certior factus est* is translated
    a. he informed
    b. he reassured
    c. he was informed
    d. he certified

Translation *Suggested time: 15 minutes*

unam (legionem) in Morinos ducendam Gaio Fabio legato dedit, alteram
in Nervios Quinto Ciceroni, tertiam in Esubios Lucio Roscio; quartam in
Remis cum Tito Labieno in confinio Treverorum hiemare iussit. Tres in
Bellovacis collocavit: eis Marcum Crassum quaestorem et Lucium
5   Munatium Plancum et Gaium Trebonium legatos praefecit.

18 chunks. 9 points, ½ point each.

unam (legionem) . . . ducendam	**one (legion) . . . to be led**
in Morinos	**into (the land of) the Morini**
Gaio Fabio legato	**to Gaius Fabius the legate**
dedit	**he gave/entrusted**
alteram in Nervios	**the second into (the land of) Nervii**
Quinto Ciceroni	**to Quintus Cicero,**
tertiam in Esubios	**the third into (the land of) Esubii**
Lucio Roscio	**to Lucius Roscius,**
quartam in Remis	**the fourth among the Remi**
cum Tito Labieno	**with Titus Labienus**
in confinio Treverorum	**in borders/territory of the Treveri**
hiemare iussit	**he ordered to winter**
Tres . . . collocavit	**Three . . . he collected**
in Belgis	**among the Belgae**
eis Marcum Crassum quaestorem	**for/of them Marcus Crassus the quaestor**
et Lucium Munatium Plancum	**and Lucius Munatius Plancus**
et Gaium Trebonium legatos	**and Gaius Trebonius the legates**
praefecit	**he put in charge**

Short Analysis Questions

Subductis navibus, concilioque Gallorum Samarobrivae peracto, quod
eo anno frumentum in Gallia propter siccitates angustius provenerat,
coactus est aliter ac superioribus annis exercitum in hibernis collocare,
legionesque in plures civitates distribuere.

1. When the ships have been taken care of for the season, what does Caesar do next? Cite the Latin that supports your answer or accurately paraphrase.

    He calls a council of Gauls at Samarobrivae—*concilio Gallorum Samarobrivae* (line 1).

2. What economic situation do the Gauls place before Caesar? Cite the Latin that supports your answer or accurately paraphrase.

    A drought has greatly reduced their grain harvest—*frumentum in Gallia propter siccitates angustius provenerat* (line 2).

3. As a result of this, what unusual measure does Caesar decide to take? Cite the Latin that supports your answer or accurately paraphrase.

    He decides, contrary to his usual custom—*aliter ac superioribus annis* (line 3)—to spread the legions out among various Gallic states—*legionesque in plures civitates distribuere* (line 4).

> Erat in Carnutibus summo loco natus Tasgetius, cuius maiores in sua
> civitate regnum obtinuerant. Huic Caesar pro eius virtute atque in
> se benevolentia, quod in omnibus bellis singulari eius opera fuerat
> usus, maiorum locum restituerat. Tertium iam hunc annum regnantem
> 5 †inimicis, multis palam ex civitate eius auctoribus, eum †interfecerunt.

4. What was the family background of Tasgetius? How did Caesar take this into account? Cite the Latin that supports your answer or accurately paraphrase.

    Tasgetius was of noble birth—*summo loco natus* (line 1); his ancestors had been rulers of his state—*maiores in sua civitate regnum obtinuerant* (lines 1–2). Caesar was well disposed toward Tasgetius both because of his family background, and because Tasgetius himself was a man of good character—*pro eius virtute atque in se benevolentia* (lines 2–3).

5. What was Tasgetius's attitude toward Caesar and the Romans? Cite the Latin that supports your answer or accurately paraphrase.

    Tasgetius had been of great use to the Romans in all their wars—*in omnibus bellis singulari eius opera fuerat usus* (lines 3–4).

6. Although Caesar says that Tasgetius's personal enemies killed him, what implications could this have for his nation's attitude toward Rome? Cite the Latin that supports your answer or accurately paraphrase.

    Since Caesar had restored him to power—*Caesar . . . maiorum locum restituerat* (lines 2–4)—he must have had the support of Rome. To destroy such a man did not show friendship for Rome.

Essay *Suggested time: 20 minutes*

A)   Ad hunc modum distributis legionibus facillime inopiae frumentariae
       sese mederi posse existimavit. Atque harum tamen omnium legionum
       hiberna, praeter eam quam Lucio Roscio in pacatissimam et quietissimam
       partem ducendam dederat, milibus passuum centum continebantur.

B)   (Tasgetio interfecto) Defertur ea res ad Caesarem. Ille veritus, quod ad
       plures pertinebat, ne civitas eorum impulsu deficeret, Lucium Plancum
       cum legione ex Belgio celeriter in Carnutes proficisci iubet ibique hiemare,
       quorumque opera cognoverat Tasgetium interfectum, hos comprehensos
5   ad se mittere.

In these two passages Caesar explains the arrangements he has made for wintering his troops. In a short essay, discuss his consideration for the economic problems of the Gauls, his careful disposition of his troops in case of trouble, and his method of exploring the problems in the land of the Carnutes. Explain how this careful planning helped him to avoid potential problems for his war effort.

Support your assertions with references to the Latin text throughout the passages above. All Latin words must be copied or their line numbers provided, AND they must be translated or paraphrased closely enough that it is clear that you understand the Latin. It is your responsibility to convince the reader that you are basing your conclusions on the Latin text and not merely on a general recollection of the passage. Direct your answer to the question; do not merely summarize the passage. Please write your essay on a separate piece of paper.

Teachers should review the Essay Scoring Guidelines given at the beginning of this manual with students.

Caesar takes into account the Gauls' lack of food—*inopiae frumentariae* (line 1A) and spreads the legions out among them—*distributis legionibus* (line 1A). However, he is careful to have all of them within one hundred miles of each other—*milibus passuum centum continebantur* (line 4A)—except for the ones quartered in the most peaceful parts of the country—*praeter eam quam . . . in pacatissimam et quietissimam partem* (lines 3–4A). When he learned of the death of Tasgetius, he quickly sent a legion under Lucius Plancus from the land of the Belgae into the land of the Carnutes—*Lucium Plancum cum legione ex Belgio celeriter in Carnutes proficisci iubet* (lines 2–3B). They were to spend the winter there, find out who had killed Tasgetius, and send the culprits to Caesar—*ibique hiemare, quorumque opera cognoverat Tasgetium interfectum, hos comprehensos ad se mittere* (lines 3–5B). Caesar's planning shows consideration for the Gauls in their food shortage, but he takes care to keep his soldiers within reach of each other in case of trouble. His willingness to make adjustments in order to spare the provincials further hardship should lessen resentment toward the Romans, and his keeping his soldiers within easy reach should show his determination to retain control of the situation. His quick establishment of a sizable Roman force in Tasgetius's homeland and his determination to bring the killers to justice should help forestall any uprising there.

CHAPTER 11: BOOK 5.26–27
TROUBLE ARISES

[26] Diebus circiter quindecim quibus in hiberna ventum est initium
repentini tumultus ac defectionis ortum est ab Ambiorige et Catuvolco;
qui, cum ad fines regni sui Sabino Cottaeque praesto fuissent
frumentumque in hiberna comportavissent, Indutiomari Treveri nuntiis
5   impulsi suos concitaverunt subitoque oppressis lignatoribus magna
manu ad castra oppugnatum venerunt. Cum celeriter nostri arma
cepissent vallumque ascendissent atque una ex parte Hispanis equitibus
emissis equestri proelio superiores fuissent, desperata re hostes suos
ab oppugnatione reduxerunt. Tum suo more conclamaverunt, uti aliqui ex
10 nostris ad colloquium prodiret: habere sese quae de re communi dicere
vellent, quibus rebus controversias minui posse sperarent. [27] Mittitur
ad eos colloquendi causa Gaius Arpineius, eques Romanus, familiaris
Quinti Tituri, et Quintus Iunius ex Hispania quidam, qui iam ante missu
Caesaris ad Ambiorigem ventitare consuerat; apud quos Ambiorix ad hunc
15 modum locutus est: sese pro Caesaris in se beneficiis plurimum ei confiteri
debere, quod eius opera stipendio liberatus esset, quod Aduatucis finitimis
suis pendere consuesset, quodque ei et filius et fratris filius ab Caesare
remissi essent, quos Aduatuci obsidum numero missos apud se in servitute
et catenis tenuissent; neque id quod fecerit de oppugnatione castrorum,
20 aut iudicio aut voluntate sua fecisse, sed coactu civitatis, suaque esse
eiusmodi imperia, ut non minus haberet iuris in se multitudo quam ipse
in multitudinem. Civitati porro hanc fuisse belli causam, quod repentinae
Gallorum coniurationi resistere non potuerit. Id se facile ex humilitate
sua probare posse, quod non adeo sit imperitus rerum ut suis copiis
25 populum Romanum superari posse confidat. Sed esse Galliae commune
consilium: omnibus hibernis Caesaris oppugnandis hunc esse dictum
diem, ne qua legio alterae legioni subsidio venire posset. Non facile Gallos
Gallis negare potuisse, praesertim cum de reciperanda communi libertate
consilium initum videretur. Quibus quoniam pro pietate satisfecerit,
30 habere nunc se rationem offici pro beneficiis Caesaris: monere, orare
Titurium pro hospitio ut suae ac militum saluti consulat. Magnam manum
Germanorum conductam Rhenum transisse: hanc adfore biduo. Ipsorum
esse consilium, velintne priusquam finitimi sentiant eductos ex hibernis
milites aut ad Ciceronem aut ad Labienum deducere, quorum alter milia
35 passuum circiter quinquaginta, alter paulo amplius ab eis absit. Illud se
polliceri et iure iurando confirmare tutum iter per fines daturum. Quod
cum faciat, et civitati sese consulere, quod hibernis levetur, et Caesari pro
eius meritis gratiam referre. Hac oratione habita discedit Ambiorix.

Preparatory Questions

Line 1   Find and translate an impersonal verb. ***ventum est;* "they arrived/it was arrived"**

Line 2   Identify the case and use of *tumultus.* **genitive of possession**

         What is the subject of *ortum est*? ***initium* (line 1)**

Line 3   What is the antecedent of *qui*? ***Ambiorige et Catuvolco* (line 2)**

Line 4   Explain the form and syntax of *comportavissent.* **pluperfect subjunctive verb of *cum* clause**

         Identify the case and use of *nuntiis.* **ablative of means**

Line 5   Explain the case and use of *oppressis lignatoribus.* **ablative absolute**

Lines 6–9   Of what three verbs is *nostri* the subject? ***cepissent* (line 7), *ascendissent* (line 7), *fuissent* (line 8)**

Line 8   Whose response does the phrase *desperata re* describe? ***hostes***

Lines 9–11   Find three subjunctive verbs. ***prodiret* (line 10), *vellent* (line 11), *sperarent* (line 11)**

Lines 10–11   Find an indirect statement. ***habere . . . vellent***

Line 14   *Ventitare* is a frequentive of what verb? ***venio***

Line 15   What is the tense and voice of *locutus est*? **perfect deponent**

Lines 15–16   What is the subject and verb of the indirect statement? ***sese confiteri debere***

Line 16   What part of speech is *stipendio*? **noun**

         What is the case and use of *Aduatucis*? **dative, indirect object (of *consuesset*—line 17)**

Lines 17–19   What relatives of Ambiorix have been mistreated? **his son and his nephew**

Lines 19–20   What verb form does *neque* make into a negative? **the infinitive *fecisse***

Line 20   What does *sua* modify? ***voluntate* (also *iudicio* although in agreement only with [*voluntate*])**

Lines 21–22   Find a negative clause of result. ***ut non . . . multitudinem***

Line 21   *Quam* is best translated as? **than**

Lines 22–23   Why is the clause *quod repentinae . . . potuerit* in the subjunctive? **It represents a cause stated by someone other than the speaker.**

         What is the subject of *potuerit*? ***civitas* (understood)**

Line 25   Identify the form and use of *superari posse*. **infinitive phrase (both in present tense, passive and active respectively), verb of indirect statement**

Line 26   Identify the form and use of *oppugnandis*. **gerundive in dative, expresses plan or purpose**

Line 27	What is the meaning of *qua*? **any**
	What does *non facile* modify? **negare (line 20)**
Line 28	Identify the form and use of *reciperanda*. **gerundive in ablative, modifying *libertate***
Line 31	Find a volitive substantive clause. ***ut . . . consulat***
Line 32	*Adfore* is a shortened form of what future infinitive? ***adfuturam esse***
Line 33	*Priusquam* introduces what anticipatory clause? ***finitimi sentiant***
Line 34	What is the antecedent of *quorum*? ***Ciceronem aut Labienum***
Line 36	*Tutum iter* is best translated as? **safe passage/journey**
Line 37	Identify the tense, voice, and use of *levetur*. **present passive, verb of *quod* clause**
Line 38	Find an ablative absolute. ***hac oratione habita***

Multiple Choice Questions *Suggested time: 32 minutes*

1. In lines 2–3 we learn that Ambiorix and Catuvolcus are
   a. regions of Gaul
   b. Roman soldiers
   c. chieftains of Gaul
   d. horsemen

2. In line 3 *cum* is best translated
   a. after
   b. although
   c. when
   d. with

3. In line 3 *praesto fuissent* is best translated
   a. they were absent
   b. they had been absent
   c. they had been helpful
   d. they had ignored

4. In line 5 *suos* refers to
   a. Indutiomarus and his forces
   b. Ambiorix and Catuvolcus
   c. the Roman forces
   d. the forces of Ambiorix and Catuvolcus

5. In line 5 *lignatoribus* is best translated
   a. trees
   b. wood
   c. wood-gatherers
   d. scouts

6. In line 6 *oppugnatum* is
   a. part of a compound verb
   b. a gerundive
   c. a supine expressing purpose
   d. an infinitive

7. In lines 6–9 we learn that
   a. **the Romans beat off the attack**
   b. the Roman camp was taken
   c. the cavalry was of little use
   d. the Gauls celebrated victory

8. In line 9 *conclamaverunt* governs
   a. a passive periphrastic
   b. **an *ut* clause and an indirect statement**
   c. a *cum* clause and an indirect statement
   d. two indirect statements

9. In line 10 *quae* is best translated
   a. whom
   b. **things which**
   c. places where
   d. what things?

10. In line 11 *minui* is best translated
    a. to threaten
    b. to be threatened
    c. to increase
    d. **to be settled**

11. In lines 13–14 we learn that Quintus Iunius
    a. was very untrustworthy
    b. **had often been sent on missions by Caesar**
    c. did not at all like the Treveri
    d. was a beloved friend of Arpineius

12. In line 15 *pro Caesaris in se beneficiis* is best translated
    a. he was kind to Caesar
    b. in spite of his kindly feelings
    c. **for Caesar's kindness toward him**
    d. in spite of Caesar's kindness

13. In lines 16–19, which of the following had the Aduatuci NOT done to Ambiorix's people?
    a. compelled them to pay tribute
    b. held Ambiorix's relatives as hostages
    c. **expelled them from their lands**
    d. kept their hostages in chains and slavery

14. In lines 19–22 Ambiorix indicates that
    a. he is supreme ruler
    b. **the tribe can influence his actions**
    c. he listens only to Caesar
    d. he is an enemy to Romans

15. In line 22 *porro* is best translated
    a. suddenly
    b. unfortunately
    c. **furthermore**
    d. recently

16. In line 23 *humilitate* is best translated
    a. **weakness**
    b. low rank
    c. sorrow
    d. power

17. In line 24 *suis copiis* is
    a. an ablative absolute
    b. an ablative of means
    c. an ablative of manner
    d. a dative of reference

18. In lines 26–27 *dictum diem* is best translated
    a. a sad day
    b. a holiday
    c. the appointed day
    d. the best day

19. In line 27 *ne qua . . . posset* is
    a. a negative clause of purpose
    b. a result
    c. a denial of what went before
    d. a comparison

20. In line 29 *videretur* is best translated
    a. he (it) saw
    b. he (it) was seen
    c. they were seen
    d. it seemed

21. In line 29 *quoniam* is best translated
    a. once
    b. regardless
    c. now that
    d. even if

22. The subject of *habere, monere,* and *orare* (line 30), the infinitives that serve as the main verbs of the sentence, is
    a. *Caesaris* (line 30)
    b. *Titurium* (line 31)
    c. *suae* (line 31)
    d. *se* (line 30)

23. In line 32 the historical infinitives that serve as main verbs in the sentence are
    a. *transisse* and *adfore* (line 32)
    b. *biduo* and *conductam* (line 32)
    c. *biduo* and *adfore* (line 32)
    d. *biduo* and *transisse* (line 32)

24. In lines 33 and 34 Ambiorix advises the Romans to leave before
    a. the Germans take every bit of grain
    b. the neighboring Gauls learn Germans are here
    c. he mounts yet another attack
    d. the Germans arrive

25. In line 36 *iure iurando confirmare* is best translated
    a. he said in writing
    b. he indicated
    c. he swore by an oath
    d. promised

26. In line 37 *levetur* is
    a. an impersonal verb
    b. a passive subjunctive
    c. a passive indicative
    d. an irregular verb

27. In line 38 *gratiam referre* is best translated

    a. to thank

    c. to do a return favor

    b. to forget

    d. to recall

Translation *Suggested time: 20 minutes*

> Cum celeriter nostri arma cepissent vallumque ascendissent atque una
> ex parte Hispanis equitibus emissis equestri proelio superiores fuissent,
> desperata re hostes suos ab oppugnatione reduxerunt. Tum suo more
> conclamaverunt, uti aliqui ex nostris ad colloquium prodiret: habere sese
> 5   quae de re communi dicere vellent, quibus rebus controversias minui
> posse sperarent.

20 chunks. 10 points, ½ point each.

Cum . . . nostri	**When our men**
celeriter	**swiftly**
arma cepissent	**had seized arms**
vallumque ascendissent	**and had ascended the wall**
atque una ex parte	**and from one side/part**
Hispanis equitibus emissis	**the Spanish cavalry (having been) sent out**
equestri proelio superiores fuissent	**had been superior in a cavalry battle**
desperata re	**the thing having been given up/despaired of**
hostes suos . . . reduxerunt	**the enemy led back its men/retreated**
ab oppugnatione	**from the attack**
Tum suo more	**Then according to their custom**
conclamaverunt	**they shouted**
uti aliqui ex nostris	**that some of our men**
ad colloquium prodiret	**should come forward to a conference;**
habere sese	**they themselves to have**
quae . . . dicere vellent	**things that they wanted to say**
de re communi	**about the common interest**
quibus rebus	**by which things**
controversias minui posse	**the dispute to be able/could be lessened**
sperarent	**they hoped**

Short Analysis Questions

> Ambiorix ad hunc modum locutus est: sese pro Caesaris in se beneficiis
> plurimum ei confiteri debere, quod eius opera stipendio liberatus esset,
> quod Aduatucis finitimis suis pendere consuesset, quodque ei et filius et
> fratris filius ab Caesare remissi essent, quos Aduatuci obsidum numero
> 5   missos apud se in servitute et catenis tenuissent; neque id quod fecerit de
> oppugnatione castrorum, aut iudicio aut voluntate sua fecisse.

1. In lines 2–5, what two kindnesses or benefits received from Caesar does Ambiorix mention?

   Caesar has freed them from paying tribute to the Aduatuci—*eius opera stipendio liberatus esset* (line 2)—and he had rescued Ambiorix's son and nephew from slavery to them—*filius et fratris filius ab Caesare remissi essent* (lines 3–4).

2. How does Ambiorix indicate his unwillingness to be ungrateful for these? Quote the Latin that supports your answer and translate or accurately paraphrase.

   He says that he was most reluctant to attack the Romans—*neque id quod fecerit de oppugnatione castrorum, aut iudicio aut voluntate sua fecisse* (lines 5–6).

> (id quod fecerit fecisse) coactu civitatis, suaque esse eiusmodi imperia,
> ut non minus haberet iuris in se multitudo quam ipse in multitudinem.
> Civitati porro hanc fuisse belli causam, quod repentinae Gallorum
> coniurationi resistere non potuerit.

3. What kind of balance of power does Ambiorix claim for his state? Quote the Latin that supports your answer and translate or accurately paraphrase.

   He said that the power of his people over him was equal to his power over them—*non minus haberet iuris in se multitudo quam ipse in multitudinem* (line 2).

4. Why does Ambiorix say his state attacked the Romans? Quote the Latin that supports your answer and translate or accurately paraphrase.

   He says that his state alone was not able to resist a sudden general conspiracy of the Gauls—*repentinae Gallorum coniurationi resistere non potuerit* (lines 3–4).

Essay *Suggested time: 20 minutes*

Non facile Gallos Gallis negare potuisse, praesertim cum de recuperanda
communi libertate consilium initum videretur. Quibus quoniam pro
pietate satisfecerit, habere nunc se rationem offici pro beneficiis Caesaris:
monere, orare Titurium pro hospitio ut suae ac militum saluti consulat.
5   Magnam manum Germanorum conductam Rhenum transisse: hanc adfore
biduo. Ipsorum esse consilium, velintne priusquam finitimi sentiant
eductos ex hibernis milites aut ad Ciceronem aut ad Labienum deducere,
quorum alter milia passuum circiter quinquaginta, alter paulo amplius
ab eis absit. Illud se polliceri et iure iurando confirmare tutum iter per
10   fines daturum. Quod cum faciat, et civitati sese consulere, quod hibernis
levetur, et Caesari pro eius meritis gratiam referre.

In this passage Ambiorix tries to balance his duty toward his country with his personal obligations
to Caesar. Explain how he reports he is satisfying each one.

Support your assertions with references to the Latin text throughout the passages above. All Latin
words must be copied or their line numbers provided, AND they must be translated or paraphrased
closely enough that it is clear that you understand the Latin. It is your responsibility to convince the
reader that you are basing your conclusions on the Latin text and not merely on a general recollection
of the passage. Direct your answer to the question; do not merely summarize the passage. Please write
your essay on a separate piece of paper.

**Teachers should review the Essay Scoring Guidelines given at the beginning of this manual with
students.**

**Ambiorix begins by claiming that he had acted from patriotism to his country first—*pro pietate
satisfecerit* (lines 2–3). Now, he says, he wishes to repay the kindness of Caesar—*habere nunc se
rationem offici pro beneficiis Caesaris* (line 2). He says he is doing this by urging the Romans to go
at once from their winter quarters and join the forces of Cicero and/or Labienus, neither of whom
is very far away—*ex hibernis milites aut ad Ciceronem aut ad Labienum deducere, quorum alter milia
passuum circiter quinquaginta, alter paulo amplius ab eis absit* (lines 7–9). He says that this should be
done at once, before a great reinforcement force of Germans comes in—*Magnam manum Germanorum conductam Rhenum transisse; hanc adfore biduo* (lines 5–6). He promised them safe conduct
through his lands—*Illud se polliceri et iure iurando confirmare tutum iter per fines daturum* (lines 9–10).
He said that this would be good for his people, by relieving them of the quartering of the Romans,
and repay Caesar at the same time—*civitati sese consulere, quod hibernis levetur, et Caesari pro eius
meritis gratiam referre* (lines 10–11).**

CHAPTER 12: BOOK 5.28–29
DELIBERATION

[28] Arpineius et Iunius quae audierunt ad legatos deferunt. Illi
repentina re perturbati, etsi ab hoste ea dicebantur, tamen non
neglegenda existimabant, maximeque hac re permovebantur, quod
civitatem ignobilem atque humilem Eburonum sua sponte populo
5   Romano bellum facere ausam vix erat credendum. Itaque ad consilium rem
deferunt magnaque inter eos exsistit controversia. Lucius Aurunculeius
compluresque tribuni militum et primorum ordinum centuriones nihil
temere agendum neque ex hibernis iniussu Caesaris discedendum
existimabant: quantasvis magnas etiam copias Germanorum sustineri
10 posse munitis hibernis docebant: rem esse testimonio, quod primum
hostium impetum multis ultro vulneribus inlatis fortissime sustinuerint;
re frumentaria non premi; interea et ex proximis hibernis et a Caesare
conventura subsidia; postremo quid esset levius aut turpius quam auctore
hoste de summis rebus capere consilium? [29] Contra ea Titurius sero
15 facturos clamitabat, cum maiores manus hostium adiunctis Germanis
convenissent aut cum aliquid calamitatis in proximis hibernis esset
acceptum. Brevem consulendi esse occasionem. Caesarem arbitrari
profectum in Italiam; neque aliter Carnutes interficiendi Tasgeti consilium
fuisse capturos neque Eburones, si ille adesset, tanta contemptione nostri
20 ad castra venturos esse. Non hostem auctorem sed rem spectare: subesse
Rhenum; magno esse Germanis dolori Ariovisti mortem et superiores
nostras victorias; ardere Galliam tot contumeliis acceptis sub populi
Romani imperium redactam, superiore gloria rei militaris exstincta.
Postremo quis hoc sibi persuaderet, sine certa re Ambiorigem ad eiusmodi
25 consilium descendisse? Suam sententiam in utramque partem esse
tutam: si nihil esset durius, nullo cum periculo ad proximam legionem
perventuros; si Gallia omnis cum Germanis consentiret, unam esse in
celeritate positam salutem. Cottae quidem atque eorum, qui dissentirent
consilium quem haberet exitum, in quo si praesens periculum non, at certe
30 longinqua obsidione fames esset timenda.

Preparatory Questions

Line 1   Give the number and gender of *quae*. **plural neuter**

Line 2   Give the case and use of *repentina re*. **ablative of means**

           What does *perturbati* modify? ***Illi* (line 1)**

Line 3   What is the syntax of *neglegenda*? **future passive participle**

	What tense and voice is *permovebantur*? **imperfect passive**
Line 4	Translate the phrase *sua sponte*. **of its own accord**
Line 5	What does *ausam* modify? *civitatem* **(line 4)**
Line 6	What is the subject of *deferunt*? *legati* **(implied) or, more simply, "they"**
	What is the subject of *exsistit*? *controversia*
Line 7	*Tribuni* and *centuriones* are the subjects of what verb? *existimabant* **(line 9)**
Line 8	Find two gerundives. *agendum, discedendum*
Line 9	Give the number, gender, and case of *quantasvis*. **plural feminine accusative**
Line 10	What is the meaning of *docebant* in this context? **they said/they explained**
	Identify the case and use of *testimonio*. **dative of purpose**
Line 11	Find an ablative absolute. *multis . . . inlatis*
Line 13	Identify the form and use of *levius* and *turpius*. **comparative nominative neuter singular adjectives modifying** *quid*
Lines 13–14	Identify the case and use of *auctore hoste*. **ablative absolute**
Line 15	Identify the case and use of *adiunctis Germanis*. **ablative absolute**
Lines 15–16	Find two *cum* clauses. *cum . . . convenissent, cum . . . acceptum*
	What kind of *cum* clauses are they? **circumstantial**
	Give the verb of each *cum* clause. *convenissent, esset acceptum*
	Give the tense, voice, and mood of each of these verbs. **pluperfect active subjunctive; pluperfect passive subjunctive**
Line 17	Find a gerund. *consulendi*
	Find a deponent infinitive. *arbitrari*
Lines 17–20	This sentence is given as whose indirect statement? **Titurius's**
Line 18	From what verb does *profectum* come? *proficiscor*
Lines 18–19	Give the meaning of the idiom represented by *consilium fuisse capturos*. **to have been about to form a plan**
Line 19	Give the case and use of *tanta contemptione*. **ablative of manner**
	Nostri modifies what understood noun? *exercitus/milites*
Line 21	Does *superiores* refer to quality or to time? **time**
Line 23	What does *redactam* modify? *Galliam* **(line 22)**
Lines 24–25	Find a rhetorical question. *quis hoc sibi persuaderet?*

Line 25	What is the base word of *utramque*? **uterque**
Line 26	Find a conditional clause. **si . . . durius**
Line 27	Find a conditional clause. **si . . . consentiret**
Lines 27–28	What word do *unam* and *positam* modify? **salutem (line 28)**
Line 29	What is the antecedent of *quo*? **consilium**
Line 30	Find a passive periphrastic. **fames esset timenda**

Multiple Choice Questions *Suggested time: 25 minutes*

1. In lines 1–2 the advice the Romans have received seems dubious because
   a. it is in a strange language
   b. it comes from the enemy
   c. Caesar did not send it
   d. the Romans already know what to do

2. In lines 2–3 *non neglegenda* is an example of
   a. metaphor
   b. hyperbole
   c. polysyndeton
   d. litotes

3. The Romans were surprised by this brief message partly because
   a. it was gently worded
   b. it was not delivered to Caesar
   c. the Eburones were an obscure tribe
   d. they respected the Eburones

4. In line 5 *ausam* is
   a. the perfect participle of *audeo*
   b. an adjective
   c. a main verb
   d. part of *audio*

5. *agendum* (line 8) modifies
   a. *complures* (line 7)
   b. *nihil* (line 7)
   c. *militum* (line 7)
   d. *temere* (line 8)

6. In line 8 *iniussu Caesaris* is best translated
   a. with Caesar's disapproval
   b. with Caesar's permission
   c. not ordered by Caesar
   d. in conjunction with Caesar

7. In lines 9–10 Aurunculeius and others argue that
   a. the Germans are not coming
   b. they are in no danger
   c. this is all a bluff
   d. they could hold off an attack

8. In line 11 *ultro* is best translated
   a. beyond
   b. besides
   c. over
   d. under

9. In line 12 *et . . . et* means
   a. now . . . then
   b. in addition
   c. both . . . and
   d. soon . . . later

10. In line 13 *quid esse levius aut turpius* is
    a. a rhetorical question
    b. a pledge
    c. a lament
    d. a dare

11. The phrase *auctore hoste* (lines 13–14) is best translated
    a. on the enemy's authority
    b. in defiance of the enemy
    c. with Caesar's advice
    d. without proper equipment

12. In line 14 *sero* is best translated
    a. sowing grain
    b. rashly
    c. earnestly
    d. too late

13. In line 16 *aliquid calamitatis* is best translated
    a. some disaster
    b. some shouting
    c. anyone comes
    d. everything is lost

14. In lines 17–20 what concern does Titurius NOT raise?
    a. Caesar is probably in Italy
    b. the time is short for deliberation
    c. they are short of weapons
    d. Carnutes and Eburones seem defiant

15. In line 20 *rem* refers to
    a. supplies
    b. personnel
    c. the situation
    d. sickness

16. In lines 21–22 the Germans are bitter because
    a. they did not get a grain supply
    b. Ariovistus has been killed
    c. Caesar has not consulted them
    d. they liked Tasgetius

17. In lines 22–23 the Gauls are bitter because
    a. Caesar has not consulted them
    b. they have Roman winter quarters in their land
    c. their military glory has been lost
    d. they like the Germans

18. In line 25 *in utramque partem* is best translated

    a. in both cases   b. in an alternate case

    c. on one hand   d. eventually

19. In line 27 *perventuros* modifies the understood word

    a. *Germanos*   **b. *Romanos***

    c. *Gallos*   d. *Carnutes*

20. In lines 27–28 Titurius says that in a worst case scenario

    a. they must fight   b. safety lies in negotiation

    c. safety lies in swiftness   d. there is no hope

21. In line 29 Titurius asks

    a. where the Germans are   b. where Cotta is

    c. what was Cotta's plan   **d. what would be the outcome of Cotta's plan**

Translation *Suggested time: 15 minutes*

> Arpineius et Iunius quae audierunt ad legatos deferunt. Illi repentina
> re perturbati, etsi ab hoste ea dicebantur, tamen non neglegenda
> existimabant, maximeque hac re permovebantur, quod civitatem
> ignobilem atque humilem Eburonum sua sponte populo Romano bellum
> 5   facere ausam vix erat credendum.

18 chunks. 9 points, ½ point each.

Arpineius et Iunius	**Arpineius and Junius**
quae audierunt	**that which they heard**
ad legatos deferunt	**they report to the legates**
Illi . . . perturbati	**They . . . greatly alarmed**
repentina re	**by the unexpected event/affair**
etsi	**although**
ab hoste	**by the enemy**
ea dicebantur	**these things were said**
tamen non neglegenda	**nevertheless not to be neglected**
existimabant	**they considered (them)**
maximeque . . . permovebantur	**and especially . . . they were moved**
hac re	**by this fact/thing**
quod civitatem ignobilem atque humilem	**that the obscure and humble state**
Eburonum	**of the Eburones**
sua sponte	**on their own accord**
populo Romano	**for/upon the Roman people**
bellum facere ausam	**having dared/to have dared to make war**
vix erat credendum	**was scarcely to be believed**

Short Analysis Questions

Lucius Aurunculeius compluresque tribuni militum et primorum ordinum centuriones nihil temere agendum neque ex hibernis iniussu Caesaris discedendum existimabant: quantasvis magnas etiam copias Germanorum sustineri posse munitis hibernis docebant: rem esse testimonio, quod
5   primum hostium impetum multis ultro vulneribus inlatis fortissime sustinuerint; re frumentaria non premi; interea et ex proximis hibernis et a Caesare conventura subsidia; postremo quid esset levius aut turpius quam auctore hoste de summis rebus capere consilium?

1. In lines 2–5, what three arguments do Aurunculeius and the others give against moving? Cite the Latin that supports your answer or accurately paraphrase.

    Nothing should be done hastily/rashly—*nihil temere agendum* (line 2). They have no orders from Caesar—*iniussu Caesaris* (line 2). They can hold off the Germans—*quantasvis [magnas] etiam copias Germanorum sustineri posse* (lines 3–4).

2. In lines 5–6 what proof do they offer of their ability to endure the threatened attack? Quote the Latin that supports your answer and translate or accurately paraphrase.

    They had held off the earlier attack even with many wounds inflicted—*primum hostium impetum multis ultro vulneribus inlatis fortissime sustinuerint.*

3. In lines 6–8 what three final arguments do they offer? Quote the Latin that supports your answer and translate or accurately paraphrase.

    They are not pressed for food—*re frumentaria non premi* (line 6). Help will come soon from other Romans—*ex proximis hibernis et a Caesare conventura subsidia* (lines 6–7). It is disgraceful to make plans on the advice of the enemy—*quid esset levius aut turpius quam auctore hoste de summis rebus capere consilium* (lines 7–8).

Essay *Suggested time: 20 minutes*

Contra ea Titurius sero facturos clamitabat, cum maiores manus hostium adiunctis Germanis convenissent aut cum aliquid calamitatis in proximis hibernis esset acceptum. Brevem consulendi esse occasionem . . . Suam sententiam in utramque partem esse tutam: si nihil esset durius, nullo
5   cum periculo ad proximam legionem perventuros; si Gallia omnis cum Germanis consentiret, unam esse in celeritate positam salutem. Cottae quidem atque eorum, qui dissentirent, consilium quem haberet exitum, in quo si praesens periculum non, at certe longinqua obsidione fames esset timenda.

In this passage Titurius offers strong arguments for leaving winter quarters quickly. How does he communicate that the situation may soon grow more dangerous? What arguments does he give for his opinion whether or not the situation grows more perilous?

Support your assertions with references to the Latin text throughout the passages above. All Latin words must be copied or their line numbers provided, AND they must be translated or paraphrased closely enough that it is clear that you understand the Latin. It is your responsibility to convince the reader that you are basing your conclusions on the Latin text and not merely on a general recollection of the passage. Direct your answer to the question; do not merely summarize the passage. Please write your essay on a separate piece of paper.

Teachers should review the Essay Scoring Guidelines given at the beginning of this manual with students.

The enemy will soon be augmented by the Germans—*maiores manus hostium adiunctis Germanis convenissent* (lines 1–2). Some disaster may happen in nearby winter quarters—*aliquid calamitatis in proximis hibernis esset acceptum* (lines 2–3). He says that his plan will be safe whether or not things grow worse, as joining the other Romans will not be a problem if there is no danger—*nullo cum periculo ad proximam legionem perventuros* (lines 4–5). If there was a major conspiracy, only haste would save them—*si Gallia omnis cum Germanis consentiret, unam esse in celeritate positam salutem* (lines 5–6). They must not discount the possibility of a long siege, in which they could not possibly sustain a food supply—*at certe longinqua obsidione fames esset timenda* (lines 8–9).

Notes

CHAPTER 13: BOOK 5.30–32
MOVING OUT

[30] Hac in utramque partem disputatione habita, cum a Cotta primisque
ordinibus acriter resisteretur, "Vincite," inquit, "si ita vultis," Sabinus, et
id clariore voce, ut magna pars militum exaudiret: "neque is sum," inquit,
"qui gravissime ex vobis mortis periculo terrear: hi sapient; si gravius
5   quid acciderit, abs te rationem reposcent qui, si per te liceat, perendino
die cum proximis hibernis coniuncti communem cum reliquis belli
casum sustineant, non reiecti et relegati longe ab ceteris aut ferro aut
fame intereant." [31] Consurgitur ex consilio; comprehendunt utrumque
et orant ne sua dissensione et pertinacia rem in summum periculum
10   deducant: facilem esse rem, seu maneant, seu proficiscantur, si modo
unum omnes sentiant ac probent; contra in dissensione nullam se salutem
perspicere. Res disputatione ad mediam noctem perducitur. Tandem dat
Cotta permotus manus: superat sententia Sabini. Pronuntiatur prima
luce ituros. Consumitur vigiliis reliqua pars noctis, cum sua quisque
15   miles circumspiceret, quid secum portare posset, quid ex instrumento
hibernorum relinquere cogeretur. Omnia excogitantur, quare nec sine
periculo maneatur, et languore militum et vigiliis periculum augeatur.
Prima luce sic ex castris proficiscuntur ut quibus esset persuasum non ab
hoste, sed ab homine amicissimo Ambiorige consilium datum, longissimo
20   agmine maximisque impedimentis. [32] At hostes, postea quam ex
nocturno fremitu vigiliisque de profectione eorum senserunt, collocatis
insidiis bipertito in silvis opportuno atque occulto loco a milibus passuum
circiter duobus Romanorum adventum exspectabant, et cum se maior pars
agminis in magnam convallem demisisset, ex utraque parte eius vallis
25   subito se ostenderunt novissimosque premere et primos prohibere ascensu
atque iniquissimo nostris loco proelium committere coeperunt.

Preparatory Questions

Line 1   Give the case and use of *disputatione habita*. **ablative absolute**

Lines 1–2   Find a *cum* clause. ***cum . . . resisteretur***

          What kind of *cum* clause is it? **circumstantial**

Line 2   What is the infinitive form of *vultis*? ***velle***

Line 3   Find an *ut* clause. ***ut . . . exaudiret***

          What kind of *ut* clause is it? **purpose**

	What is the understood subject of *sum*? **I (= Sabinus)**
	What is its subject complement? *is*
Line 4	Give the mood, tense, and voice of *terrear*. **subjunctive present passive**
	Why is *terrear* in that mood? **verb in relative clause of characteristic**
	To whom does *hi* refer? **the soldiers**
Line 5	Find an impersonal verb. *liceat*
Lines 5–7	Find a relative clause. *qui ... intereant*
	What kind of relative clause is it? **characteristic**
Lines 5–6	Identify the case and use of *perendino die*. **ablative of time when**
Line 6	What does *communem* modify? *casum* **(line 7)**
Lines 6–8	Find an example of alliteration. *coniuncti communem ... casum*
Line 7	What do *reiecti* and *relegati* modify? *qui* **(line 5)**
Line 8	Find an impersonal verb. *consurgitur*
Lines 9–10	Find a negative subjunctive clause. *ne ... deducant*
	What kind of subjunctive clause is it? **(substantive clause of) purpose**
Line 11	What does *nullam* modify? *salutem*
Line 12	Identify the case and use of *disputatione*. **ablative of means**
Line 13	What is the subject of *superat*? *sententia*
Line 14	What word is needed to complete the phrase represented by *ituros*? *esse*
	What is the understood subject of this phrase? *eos*
Lines 15–16	Find an indirect question. *quid ... posset*
Line 18	Give the case and use of *quibus*. **dative, object of *esset persuasum***
Lines 18–19	Find an *ut* clause. *ut ... persuasum*
	What kind of *ut* clause is it? **explanatory (the subjunctive *persuasum esset* is part of a relative clause of characteristic)**
Line 21	Give the case and use of *fremitu*. **ablative, prepositional phrase with *ex* (line 20)**
Line 22	What does *opportuno* modify? *loco*
Line 23	To whom does *se* refer? **the greater part (*maior pars*) of the marching column**
Line 25	To whom does *se* refer? *hostes* **(line 20)**
	Premere and *prohibere* complete what verb? *coeperunt* **(line 26)**

Multiple Choice Questions *Suggested time: 22 minutes*

1. In line 3 *clariore voce* is an example of
   a. ablative of time
   b. ablative of manner
   c. ablative absolute
   d. dative of reference

2. In lines 4–5 the phrase *si . . . quid* is best translated
   a. if which
   b. by which
   c. if anything
   d. if he

3. In line 5 *abs te rationem reposcent* is best translated
   a. they will demand a reckoning from you
   b. you will be sorry
   c. they will mock you
   d. they will not follow

4. In lines 5–6 *perendino die* indicates
   a. the urgency of time
   b. the distance to the next Roman camp
   c. the determination of the soldiers
   d. the rising habits of the Gauls

5. In lines 9–10 the other Roman leaders beg Cotta and Sabinus
   a. to fortify the camp
   b. to take a break
   c. not to endanger everyone by dissension
   d. to speak more clearly

6. In lines 10–11 the leaders say that the situation can be made easier by
   a. leaving
   b. staying
   c. agreeing
   d. contacting Caesar

7. In lines 12–13 around midnight
   a. the Gauls attacked
   b. Cotta won
   c. Sabinus won
   d. they agreed to talk again the next day

8. In lines 15–16 the two *quid* clauses indicate
   a. choices the soldiers are making
   b. the uncertainty of the leaders
   c. the fears of the soldiers
   d. the safety of the camp

9. In lines 16–17 what concern is NOT raised?
   a. they could not stay without danger
   b. fatigue might make soldiers weaker
   c. lack of sleep might make soldiers weaker
   d. food was in short supply

10. In line 18 *sic . . . ut* is best translated
    a. so . . . that
    b. so that . . . not
    c. in such a way . . . as
    d. thus . . . that

11. In lines 19–20 *longissimo agmine maximisque impedimentis* indicates that

    a. the Romans were making a show of confidence

    b. they were taking only necessities

    c. they wanted to scare the Gauls

    d. they were thoroughly frightened

12. In line 21 *profectione* is best translated

    a. departure

    b. perfection

    c. haste

    d. preparation

13. In line 21 *collocatis* refers to

    a. *silvis* (line 22)

    b. *insidiis* (line 22)

    c. *vigiliis* (line 21)

    d. *opportuno* (line 22)

14. In line 22 *bipertito* refers to the

    a. Roman army

    b. ambush

    c. forest

    d. distance

15. In line 24 *magnam convallem* is best translated

    a. into great confusion

    b. into a great valley

    c. far ahead

    d. in great haste

16. In line 25 *se* refers to

    a. the Roman leaders

    b. Cotta and Sabinus

    c. the enemy

    d. relief Roman soldiers

17. In line 25 *novissimos* and *primos* refer to

    a. the Gauls

    b. the geography of Gauls in this area

    c. marching locations of Roman soldiers

    d. the weapons of the Roman soldiers

18. In line 26 *iniquissimo* is best translated

    a. uncertain

    b. unfavorable

    c. questionable

    d. remarkable

Translation *Suggested time: 15 minutes*

Consurgitur ex consilio; comprehendunt utrumque et orant, ne sua
dissensione et pertinacia rem in summum periculum deducant: facilem
esse rem, seu maneant, seu proficiscantur, si modo unum omnes sentiant
ac probent; contra in dissensione nullam se salutem perspicere.

16 chunks. 8 points, ½ point each.

Consurgitur	**it was risen/they arose/there was a rising**
ex consilio	**from the council**
comprehendunt utrumque	**detain both**
et orant	**and beg**
ne	**that not**
sua dissensione et pertinacia	**by their disagreement and stubbornness**
rem in summum periculum	**the affair into the greatest danger**
deducant:	**they might bring**
facilem esse rem	**the affair to be (was) easy**
seu maneant	**whether they might remain**
seu proficiscantu,	**or set out**
si modo unum omnes	**if only one opinion all (of them)**
sentiant ac probent	**might agree upon and approve**
contra in dissensione	**on the other hand in disagreement**
nullam salutem	**no safety**
se . . . perspicere	**they could see**

Short Analysis Questions

"Vincite," inquit, "si ita vultis," Sabinus, et id clariore voce, ut magna
pars militum exaudiret: "neque is sum," inquit, "qui gravissime ex vobis
mortis periculo terrear: hi sapient; si gravius quid acciderit, abs te rationem
reposcent qui, si per te liceat, perendino die cum proximis hibernis
5   coniuncti communem cum reliquis belli casum sustineant, non reiecti et
relegati longe ab ceteris aut ferro aut fame intereant."

1. Thus far, the discussion of whether to stay or go has been carried on among the Roman leaders.
    In lines 1–2, how does Sabinus subtly extend the discussion? Quote the Latin that supports
    your answer and translate or accurately paraphrase.

    **He raises his voice and speaks so that most of the soldiers can hear—*clariore voce, ut magna
    pars militum exaudiret.***

2. If the decision made turns out to be an unfortunate one, what does Sabinus in lines 4–5 say that the soldiers will do? Quote the Latin that supports your answer and translate or accurately paraphrase.

He then says that the soldiers will demand a reckoning if some of them die by this decision *si per te liceat . . . aut ferro aut fame intereant.*

3. In lines 5–6 how does Sabinus contrast the two possibilities for the upcoming confrontation? Quote the Latin that supports your answer and translate or accurately paraphrase.

He says that in two days they can be in the nearest Roman winter camp reinforced for war by allies—*perendino die cum proximis hibernis coniuncti communem cum reliquis belli casum sustineant.* **Or they can die unassisted by sword and famine in their present location**—*longe ab ceteris aut ferro aut fame intereant.*

Essay *Suggested time: 20 minutes*

> At hostes, postea quam ex nocturno fremitu vigiliisque de profectione
> eorum senserunt, collocatis insidiis bipertito in silvis opportuno
> atque occulto loco a milibus passuum circiter duobus Romanorum
> adventum exspectabant, et cum se maior pars agminis in magnam
> 5   convallem demisisset, ex utraque parte eius vallis subito se ostenderunt
> novissimosque premere et primos prohibere ascensu atque iniquissimo
> nostris loco proelium committere coeperunt.

In this passage the enemy have been watching closely. Discuss how the enemy learns that the Romans are planning to leave. Discuss how and where they set up an ambush and what they expect the disadvantages of the Romans to be.

Support your assertions with references to the Latin text throughout the passage above. All Latin words must be copied or their line numbers provided, AND they must be translated or paraphrased closely enough that it is clear that you understand the Latin. It is your responsibility to convince the reader that you are basing your conclusions on the Latin text and not merely on a general recollection of the passage. Direct your answer to the question; do not merely summarize the passage. Please write your essay on a separate piece of paper.

Teachers should review the Essay Scoring Guidelines given at the beginning of this manual with students.

From the noises and their watches the enemy learned that the Romans were leaving and thus set up an ambush. About two miles away from the Roman camp the enemy sets up a two-pronged ambush in a hidden place in the forest—*collocatis insidiis bipertito in silvis opportuno atque occulto loco a milibus passuum circiter duobus* **(lines 2–3). At this point the Romans had to march across a steep valley, and the enemy intended both to hinder the front lines coming out of the valley and to harass the rear lines**—*maior pars agminis in magnam convallem demisisset, ex utraque parte eius vallis subito se ostenderunt novissimosque premere et primos prohibere ascensu* **(lines 4–6).**

CHAPTER 14: BOOK 5.33–34
A TRAP

[33] Tum demum Titurius, qui nihil ante providisset, trepidare et
concursare cohortesque disponere, haec tamen ipsa timide atque ut eum
omnia deficere viderentur; quod plerumque eis accidere consuevit qui
in ipso negotio consilium capere coguntur. At Cotta, qui cogitasset haec
5   posse in itinere accidere atque ob eam causam profectionis auctor non
fuisset, nulla in re communi saluti deerat et in appellandis cohortandisque
militibus imperatoris et in pugna militis officia praestabat. Cum propter
longitudinem agminis minus facile omnia per se obire et quid quoque loco
faciendum esset providere possent, iusserunt pronuntiare ut impedimenta
10   relinquerent atque in orbem consisterent. Quod consilium etsi in eiusmodi
casu reprehendendum non est, tamen incommode accidit: nam et nostris
militibus spem minuit et hostes ad pugnam alacriores effecit, quod non
sine summo timore et desperatione id factum videbatur. Praeterea accidit,
quod fieri necesse erat, ut vulgo milites ab signis discederent, quae
15   quisque eorum carissima haberet ab impedimentis petere atque arripere
properaret, clamore et fletu omnia complerentur. [34] At barbaris consilium
non defuit. Nam duces eorum tota acie pronuntiare iusserunt, ne quis ab
loco discederet, illorum esse praedam atque illis reservari quaecumque
Romani reliquissent: proinde omnia in victoria posita existimarent. Erant
20   et virtute et †numero pugnandi †pares. Nostri, tametsi ab duce et a fortuna
deserebantur, tamen omnem spem salutis in virtute ponebant, et quotiens
quaeque cohors procurrerat, ab ea parte magnus numerus hostium cadebat.
Qua re animadversa, Ambiorix pronuntiari iubet ut procul tela coiciant
neu propius accedant et quam in partem Romani impetum fecerint cedant:
25   levitate armorum et cotidiana exercitatione nihil his noceri posse: rursus
se ad signa recipientes insequantur.

Preparatory Questions

Line 1	Find a relative clause. ***qui nihil ante providisset***
	Identify the mood of *providisset*. **subjunctive**
Lines 1–2	Find three historical infinitives. ***trepidare, concursare, disponere***
Line 2	Identify the case and gender of *haec*. **accusative neuter**
Lines 2–3	Find a result clause. ***ut eum omnia deficere viderentur***

Line 4   Identify the case and use of *consilium*. **accusative, direct object of *capere***

Identify the antecedent of *qui*. **Cotta**

What kind of clause does *qui* introduce? **relative clause (of characteristic), expressing cause (relative causal clause)**

Line 5   Identify the case and use of *profectionis*. **genitive, objective genitive (with *auctor*)**

Line 6   Find two gerundives. ***appellandis, cohortandis***

Line 7   Identify the case and use of *militis*. **genitive of possession**

Lines 7–9   Find a *cum* clause. ***Cum propter longitudinem agminis minus facile omnia per se obire et quid quoque loco faciendum esset providere possent***

What type of *cum* clause is it? **causal**

What two infinitives are complementary to *possent*? ***obire* (line 8), *providere* (line 9)**

Line 9   Find an example of the passive periphrastic. ***quid . . . faciendum esset***

Line 11   Identify the case and use of *casu*. **ablative, object of the preposition *in* (line 10)**

Identify the form and use of *reprehendendum . . . est*. **passive periphrastic/gerundive of obligation**

What part of speech is *incommode*? **adverb**

Line 12   Identify the subject of *minuit*. ***consilium* (line 10)**

Identify the case and use of *hostes*. **accusative, direct object of *effecit***

Lines 12–13   Find a causal clause. ***quod non sine summo timore et desperatione id factum videbatur***

Line 13   What two words does *summo* modify? ***timore, desperatione***

Lines 13–14   Find a result clause. ***ut vulgo milites ab signis discederent***

What verb introduces this result clause? ***accidit* (line 13)**

Line 15   Identify the form and use of *haberet*. **imperfect subjunctive, relative clause of characteristic**

Line 16   What is the subject of *complerentur*? ***omnia***

Identify the case and use of *barbaris*. **dative of possession with *defuit* (line 17)**

Line 17   Identify the case and use of *tota acie*. **ablative of place where**

Identify the form and use of *quis*. **nominative singular masculine (of the indefinite pronoun *aliquis, aliquid*), subject (of *discedere*, line 18)**

Explain what has happened to the spelling of *quis*. **shortened from *aliquis*, after *ne***

Line 19   Explain the mood and use of *reliquissent*. **subjunctive, indirect command**

Line 20	Identify the case and use of *pares*. **nominative, predicate adjective with (the copulative verb)** *erant* **(line 19)**
Line 21	Identify the case and use of *salutis*. **objective genitive (with** *spem*)
	What part of speech is *quotiens*? **adverb**
Line 23	Identify the form and use of *pronuntiari*. **present passive infinitive with** *iubet*
Lines 23–24	Find a triple indirect command. ***ut procul tela coiciant, neu propius accedant, et quam in partem Romani impetum fecerint cedant***
Line 24	What verb does *neu* negate? ***accedant***
	Find an indirect question. ***quam in partem Romani impetum fecerint***
Line 25	What word does *cotidiana* modify? ***exercitatione***
Line 26	Explain the tense and mood of *insequantur*. **present subjunctive primary sequence in indirect command**
	Identify the tense of *recipientes*. **present**

Multiple Choice Questions *Suggested time: 30 minutes*

1. In line 1 the phrase *qui . . . providisset* is
   a. a relative clause of result
   b. a relative clause of characteristic
   c. an indirect statement
   d. a relative clause

2. *Eum* in line 2 refers to
   a. Caesar
   b. Cotta
   c. Titurius
   d. the army

3. What part of speech is *plerumque* (line 3)?
   a. adverb
   b. adjective
   c. interjection
   d. conjunction

4. What figure of speech is evident in the phrase *consilium capere coguntur* (line 4)?
   a. litotes
   b. onomatopoeia
   c. hyperbaton
   d. alliteration

5. In lines 4–5 we learn that the legate Cotta
   a. was slow to depart from the camp
   b. had an accident on the march
   c. expected that the Gauls might attack
   d. spoke at length about the situation

6. The subject of *deerat* in line 6 is
   a. **Cotta (line 4)**
   c. *saluti* (line 6)
   b. *communi* (line 6)
   d. *nulla* (line 6)

7. What is the use of *officia* (line 7)?
   a. subject
   c. adjective modifying *pugna*
   b. **direct object**
   d. indirect object

8. *Cum* (line 7) is translated as
   a. Although
   c. When
   b. **Since**
   d. With

9. Who or what is the implied subject of *iusserunt* (line 9)?
   a. the Gauls
   c. the narrator
   b. the Roman soldiers
   d. **the Roman commanders**

10. In line 10 *eiusmodi* is dependent upon
    a. *consilium* (line 10)
    c. *reprehendendum est* (line 11)
    b. **casu (line 11)**
    d. *etsi* (line 10)

11. The subject of *minuit* (line 12) and *effecit* (line 12) is
    a. **consilium (line 10)**
    c. *militibus* (line 12)
    b. *spem* (line 12)
    d. *pugnam* (line 12)

12. In line 13 *Praeterea* is translated
    a. except for the fact that
    c. the praetor
    b. **furthermore**
    d. on the other hand

13. The phrase *accidit . . . ut vulgo milites ab signis discederent* (lines 13–14) includes a
    a. purpose clause
    c. conditional clause
    b. relative clause
    d. **result clause**

14. *carissima* (line 15) modifies
    a. *quisque* (line 15)
    c. **quae (line 14)**
    b. *petere* (line 15)
    d. *eorum* (line 15)

15. The verbs *petere* and *arripere* (line 15) are dependent upon
    a. **properaret (line 16)**
    c. *haberet* (line 15)
    b. *quae* (line 14)
    d. *quisque* (line 15)

16. Who is meant by *duces eorum* (line 17)?

    a. Cotta and Sabinus
    b. Caesar's army
    c. the German tribes
    d. the Gallic chieftains

17. In line 17 *tota acie* is translated

    a. over the mountain ridge
    b. by means of a pincer movement
    c. all along the battle line
    d. over the whole day

18. In lines 17–18 the phrase *ne quis ab loco discederet* is

    a. a purpose clause
    b. an indirect command
    c. a result clause
    d. a passive periphrastic

19. In line 19 the word *proinde* signals

    a. a change in speaker
    b. a logical conclusion
    c. a temporal indicator
    d. a contradiction

20. What is the grammatical function of *virtute* (line 20)?

    a. ablative object of a preposition
    b. ablative of manner
    c. ablative of cause
    d. ablative of specification

21. The voice and mood of *deserebantur* (line 21) is

    a. active subjunctive
    b. active indicative
    c. passive indicative
    d. passive subjunctive

22. In line 21 *quotiens* is translated

    a. how much?
    b. as often as
    c. how often?
    d. as much as

23. The phrase *qua re animadversa* (line 23) is

    a. an ablative absolute
    b. an indirect question
    c. a relative clause of characteristic
    d. a direct question

24. The phrase *quam in partem Romani impetum fecerint* (line 24) is dependent upon

    a. *pronuntiari* (line 23)
    b. *iubet* (line 23)
    c. cedant (line 24)
    d. *accedant* (line 24)

25. In line 26 *recipientes* refers to

    a. Ambiorix
    b. the Gallic soldiers
    c. the Romans
    d. Caesar

Translation *Suggested time: 15 minutes*

Cum propter longitudinem agminis minus facile omnia per se obire
et quid quoque loco faciendum esset providere possent, iusserunt
pronuntiare ut impedimenta relinquerent atque in orbem consisterent.
Quod consilium etsi in eiusmodi casu reprehendendum non est, tamen
5   incommode accidit.

16 chunks. ½ point, each 8 points.

Cum	**Since**
propter longitudinem	**on account of the length**
agminis	**of the column**
minus facile . . . possent	**they were less easily able**
omnia per se obire	**to see to everything themselves**
et quid . . . faciendum esset	**and what had to be done**
quoque loco	**in each location**
providere	**to look after**
iusserunt pronuntiare	**they gave the order to announce**
ut impedimenta relinquerent	**that they abandon the baggage**
atque in orbem	**and (that) into a circle**
consisterent	**they take up a position**
Quod consilium	**This plan**
etsi in eiusmodi casu	**although in a situation of that sort**
reprehendendum non est	**ought not to be censured**
tamen incommode accidit	**nevertheless turned out unfortunately**

Short Analysis Questions

Quod consilium etsi in eiusmodi casu reprehendendum non est, tamen
incommode accidit: nam et nostris militibus spem minuit et hostes ad
pugnam alacriores effecit, quod non sine summo timore et desperatione
id factum videbatur. Praeterea accidit, quod fieri necesse erat, ut vulgo
5   milites ab signis discederent, quae quisque eorum carissima haberet ab
impedimentis petere atque arripere properaret, clamore et fletu omnia
complerentur.

1.   What are the consequences, for each side, of the Roman defensive maneuver? Cite the Latin
that supports your answer and translate or accurately paraphrase.

**For the Roman soldiers the maneuver only serves to lower their hope of escaping the
battle—*et nostris militibus spem minuit* (line 2), while for the Gauls the maneuver gives
them greater confidence that they will defeat the Roman troops—*et hostes ad pugnam
alacriores effecit* (lines 2–3).**

2. Does Caesar, as narrator, approve of this maneuver? Cite the Latin that supports your answer and translate or accurately paraphrase.

> **Caesar equivocates. On the one hand, he says that the maneuver in these circumstances was not to be blamed—***Quod consilium etsi in eiusmodi casu reprehendendum non est* **(line 1)—but he also comments on how badly it turned out for the Romans—***tamen incommode accidit . . .* **(lines 1–2).**

3. How do the Roman soldiers behave? Cite the Latin that supports your answer and translate or accurately paraphrase.

> **The Romans are thrown into confusion and run around trying to save their most precious belongings—***ut vulgo milites ab signis discederent, quae quisque eorum carissima haberet ab impedimentis petere atque arripere properaret* **(lines 4–6).**

4. Do the Roman soldiers perform their duty in this situation? Cite the Latin that supports your answer and translate or accurately paraphrase.

> **No, they do not. They abandon their posts at their appointed standards—***milites ab signis discederent* **(lines 4–5)—and place a higher value on their possessions than on their responsibilites as soldiers—***quae quisque eorum carissima haberet ab impedimentis petere atque arripere properaret* **(lines 5–6).**

>   Nostri, tametsi ab duce et a fortuna deserebantur, tamen omnem spem
>   salutis in virtute ponebant, et quotiens quaeque cohors procurrerat, ab ea
>   parte magnus numerus hostium cadebat. Qua re animadversa, Ambiorix
>   pronuntiari iubet ut procul tela coiciant neu propius accedant et quam in
> 5   partem Romani impetum fecerint cedant: levitate armorum et cotidiana
>   exercitatione nihil his noceri posse: rursus se ad signa recipientes
>   insequantur.

5. What two assets do the Roman soldiers lack in this battle? Cite the Latin that supports your answer and translate or accurately paraphrase.

> **They lack both a good leader and good fortune—***ab duce et a fortuna deserebantur* **(line 1).**

6. In what do the Romans place all their hope? Is it effective? Cite the Latin that supports your answer and translate or accurately paraphrase.

> **They put their hope in their** *virtus,* **which is effective in that they make inroads against the Gallic attack by charging from their defensive position—***quotiens quaeque cohors procurrerat, ab ea parte magnus numerus hostium cadebat* **(lines 2–3).**

7. How does Ambiorix react to the tactics of the Romans? Cite the Latin that supports your answer and translate or accurately paraphrase.

> **Ambiorix aims to wear out the Romans from a distance. He tells his men to shoot their missiles from a distance—***procul tela coiciant* **(line 4), to fall back when the Romans charge—***neu propius accedant et quam in partem Romani impetum fecerint cedant* **(lines 4–5), but to attack the Romans as they retreat to their position in the circular formation—***rursus se ad signa recipientes insequantur* **(lines 6–7).**

8. According to this passage, what two advantages do Ambiorix's soldiers have in this battle? Cite the Latin that supports your answer and translate or accurately paraphrase.

They are aided by the lightness of their armor—*levitate armorum* (line 5), which makes them more mobile, and by their daily training regimen—*cotidiana exercitatione* (lines 5–6), which gives them the stamina to endure the rigors of battle.

Essay *Suggested time: 20 minutes*

Tum demum Titurius, qui nihil ante providisset, trepidare et
concursare cohortesque disponere, haec tamen ipsa timide atque ut eum
omnia deficere viderentur; quod plerumque eis accidere consuevit qui
in ipso negotio consilium capere coguntur. At Cotta, qui cogitasset haec
5   posse in itinere accidere atque ob eam causam profectionis auctor non
fuisset, nulla in re communi saluti deerat et in appellandis cohortandisque
militibus imperatoris et in pugna militis officia praestabat.

Caesar here recounts the behavior of his two legates, Quintus Titurius Sabinus and Lucius Aurunculeius Cotta, who had quarreled in the previous chapters about whether the army should leave its camp in the face of a Gallic attack led by Ambiorix. In a short essay, discuss Caesar's characterization of the two men, based on their reaction to the realization that they have been led into a trap. Which of his officers, based on your assessment of the language and characterization of this passage, does Caesar favor?

Support your assertions with references to the Latin text throughout the passage above. All Latin words must be copied or their line numbers provided, AND they must be translated or paraphrased closely enough that it is clear that you understand the Latin. It is your responsibility to convince the reader that you are basing your conclusions on the Latin text and not merely on a general recollection of the passage. Direct your answer to the question; do not merely summarize the passage. Please write your essay on a separate piece of paper.

Teachers should review with students the Essay Scoring Guidelines given at the beginning of this manual.

Caesar presents two clearly delineated character sketches of his legates, and invites the reader to make a comparison by using similar phrases to introduce each legate's reaction to the crisis—*Titurius, qui nihil ante providisset . . .* (line 1ff.)/*Cotta, qui cogitasset . . .* (line 4ff.). Titurius is presented as a man who has lost his head and the confidence of his soldiers—*haec tamen ipsa timide atque ut eum omnia deficere viderentur* (lines 2–3)—whereas Cotta's actions show leadership and a willingness to do anything required to try to save his men. Cotta both performs his duty as a commander—*et . . . imperatoris . . . officia praestabat* (lines 6–7) —and is not afraid to do the fighting himself —*et in pugna militis officia praestabat* (line 7). Another key difference (and clue to Caesar's preference) between the two men is their ability to plan ahead and prepare for all eventualities (students may remember that Caesar presents his use of foresight as one of his strongest advantages over his enemies). Where Titurius *nihil ante providisset*, Cotta both recognized that the Gauls might be trying to trick them—*qui cogitasset haec posse in itinere accidere* (lines 4–5)—and argued against setting out on the march—*ob eam causam profectionis auctor non fuisset* (lines 5–6). Students might also compare the descriptors used of each man: Titurius acts *timide*, but for Cotta—*nulla in re communi saluti deerat* (line 6)—he placed the common safety of his men above his own.

CHAPTER 15: BOOK 5.35–36
ROMAN BRAVERY IN ADVERSITY

[35] Quo praecepto ab eis diligentissime observato, cum quaepiam cohors ex orbe excesserat atque impetum fecerat, hostes velocissime refugiebant. Interim eam partem nudari necesse erat et ab latere aperto tela recipi. Rursus cum in eum locum unde erant egressi reverti coeperant, et ab
5 eis qui cesserant et ab eis qui proximi steterant circumveniebantur. Sin autem locum tenere vellent, nec virtuti locus relinquebatur neque ab tanta multitudine coiecta tela conferti vitare poterant. Tamen tot incommodis conflictati, multis vulneribus acceptis resistebant et magna parte diei consumpta, cum a prima luce ad horam octavam pugnaretur, nihil quod
10 ipsis esset indignum committebant. Tum T. Balventio, qui superiore anno primum pilum duxerat, viro forti et magnae auctoritatis, utrumque femur tragula traicitur; Q. Lucanius eiusdem ordinis, fortissime pugnans, dum circumvento filio subvenit, interficitur; L. Cotta legatus omnes cohortes ordinesque adhortans in adversum os funda vulneratur. [36] His
15 rebus permotus Q. Titurius, cum procul Ambiorigem suos cohortantem conspexisset, interpretem suum Cn. Pompeium ad eum mittit rogatum ut sibi militibusque parcat. Ille appellatus respondit: si velit secum colloqui, licere; sperare a multitudine impetrari posse, quod ad militum salutem pertineat; ipsi vero nihil nocitum iri, inque eam rem se suam
20 fidem interponere. Ille cum Cotta saucio communicat, si videatur, pugna ut excedant et cum Ambiorige una colloquantur: sperare ab eo de sua ac militum salute impetrari posse. Cotta se ad armatum hostem iturum negat atque in eo perseverat.

Preparatory Questions

Line 1   Find an ablative absolute. **quo praecepto ab eis diligentissime observato**

               Identify the form and use of *diligentissime*. **superlative adverb, modifies *observato***

Lines 1–2   Find a *cum* clause. **cum quaepiam cohors ex orbe excesserat atque impetum fecerat**

               What type of *cum* clause is it? **temporal**

Line 2   Identify the tense and mood of *fecerat*. **pluperfect indicative**

Line 3   Find an impersonal verb construction. **necesse erat**

               Identify the tense and voice of *recipi*. **present passive (infinitive)**

Line 4   What part of speech is *reverti*? **(verbal) noun (infinitive)**

Line 5   Identify the tense and mood of *steterant*. **pluperfect indicative**

Lines 5–6   Find a conditional clause. ***sin autem locum tenere vellent***

        Identify the tense and mood of *vellent*. **imperfect subjunctive**

        What type of conditional is this? **past contrary to fact (with imperfect subjunctive denoting continued or repeated action)**

Line 6   What is the subject of *relinquebatur*? ***locus***

Line 7   Identify the form and use of *conferti*. **masculine plural adjective, nominative in agreement with the unexpressed subject of *poterant***

Line 8   Find an ablative absolute. ***multis vulneribus acceptis***

        Identify the case and use of *diei*. **partitive genitive (with *magna parte*)**

Line 9   What part of speech is *consumpta*? **(verbal) adjective (perfect passive participle)**

        Find a *cum* clause. ***cum a prima luce ad horam octavam pugnaretur***

        What type of *cum* clause is it? **causal**

        Find an impersonal verb. ***pugnaretur***

        What is its tense and mood? **imperfect subjunctive**

Lines 9–10   Find a relative clause. ***quod ipsis esset indignum***

Line 10   Identify the tense and mood of *esset*. **imperfect subjunctive**

Line 11   Identify the tense and mood of *duxerat*. **pluperfect indicative**

        Identify the case and use of *magnae auctoritatis*. **genitive of quality**

Line 12   Identify the tense and voice of *traicitur*. **present passive**

        What is its subject? ***femur***

        What part of speech is *pugnans*? **present active participle**

Line 13   Find a temporal clause. ***dum circumvento filio subvenit***

        Who/what is the subject of *interficitur*? ***Q. Lucanius* (line 12)**

Lines 13–14   What word(s) does *omnes* modify? ***cohortes ordinesque***

Line 14   Identify the case and use of *os*. **accusative, object of the preposition *in***

        What does *adversum* modify? ***os***

Lines 15–16   Find a *cum* clause. ***cum procul Ambiorigem suos cohortantem conspexisset***

        What type of *cum* clause is it? **circumstantial**

Line 15	To what/whom does *suos* refer? **the Gauls**
Line 16	Identify the case and use of *interpretem*. **accusative, direct object of *mittit***
	Who/what is the subject of *mittit*? **Q. Titurius (line 15)**
Line 17	Identify the mood and syntax of *parcat*. **subjunctive, indirect command**
	Identify the form and syntax of *appellatus*. **perfect passive participle, nominative; modifies *Ille***
	Identify the tense and mood of *velit*. **present subjunctive**
Lines 17–18	Find a conditional clause. ***si velit secum colloqui***
Line 18	What two infinitives are dependent upon *sperare*? ***impetrari posse***
	Identify the case and use of *multitudine*. **ablative of separation with *a***
Lines 18–19	Find an indirect question. ***quod ad militum salutem pertineat***
Line 19	Identify the tense and voice of *nocitum iri*. **future passive**
Line 20	What is the object of the preposition *cum*? ***Cotta***
	Identify the case and use of *pugna*. **ablative of separation (with *excedant*, line 21)**
Line 21	Identify the tense and mood of *excedant*. **present subjunctive**
Line 22	Identify the case and use of *militum*. **genitive of possession**
	Identify the form and syntax of *impetrari*. **present passive infinitive, complementary with *posse***
	What word(s) does *armatum* modify? ***hostem***
	Who/what is the subject of *negat*? ***Cotta***

Multiple Choice Questions *Suggested time: 30 minutes*

1. *diligentissime* (line 1) is
   a. **a superlative adjective**
   b. a comparative adverb
   c. a superlative adverb
   d. a comparative adjective

2. What word does *quaepiam* (line 1) modify?
   a. *impetum* (line 2)
   b. *orbe* (line 2)
   c. ***cohors* (line 1)**
   d. *cum* (line 1)

3. The phrase *ab latere aperto* (line 3) is translated
   a. **on its exposed flank**
   b. through opening the line
   c. by removing clothing
   d. from the distant troops

4. In lines 4–5 we learn that
   a. the Gauls are retreating
   c. the Romans become surrounded
   b. the trap is unsuccessful
   d. the Romans make a hasty retreat

5. What is the unexpressed subject of *circumveniebantur* (line 5)?
   a. the legates
   c. the forests
   b. the Roman soldiers
   d. the Gallic soldiers

6. The case and use of *virtuti* (line 6) is
   a. partitive genitive
   c. nominative subject
   b. dative of indirect object
   d. ablative of place where

7. What is the dictionary entry for *conflictati* (line 8)?
   a. *conflexo*
   c. *confligo*
   b. *conflicto*
   d. *conflictato*

8. In lines 7–9 we learn that
   a. the Romans were quickly defeated
   c. the battle went on all through the night
   b. the Romans persevered despite the odds
   d. the legates divided up the troops

9. In line 10 *ipsis* refers to
   a. the Roman soldiers
   c. the baggage train
   b. the Gallic troops
   d. Titus Balventius

10. *forti* (line 11) modifies
    a. *magnae* (line 11)
    c. *auctoritatis* (line 11)
    b. *anno* (line 11)
    d. *viro* (line 11)

11. The case of *tragula* (line 12) is
    a. nominative
    c. accusative
    b. dative
    d. ablative

12. The subject of *subvenit* (line 13) is
    a. *Q. Lucanius* (line 12)
    c. *pugnans* (line 12)
    b. *T. Balventio* (line 10)
    d. *filio* (line 13)

13. The phrase *omnes cohortes ordinesque* (lines 13–14) is the object of
    a. *legatus* (line 13)
    c. *adhortans* (line 14)
    b. *vulneratur* (line 14)
    d. *pugnans* (line 12)

14. *suos* in line 15 refers to
    a. the Romans
    b. the Gauls
    c. Ambiorix's family
    d. Titurius's cohort

15. The tense and mood of *conspexisset* (line 16) is
    a. perfect subjunctive
    b. present subjunctive
    c. imperfect indicative
    d. pluperfect subjunctive

16. In line 16 *rogatum* is translated
    a. having been asked
    b. in order to ask
    c. having asked
    d. to be asked

17. Who is meant by *Ille* in line 17?
    a. Caesar
    b. Titurius
    c. Ambiorix
    d. Pompeius

18. The form of *colloqui* (line 18) is
    a. present deponent infinitive
    b. perfect passive participle
    c. perfect active infinitive
    d. masculine nominative plural

19. The word *militum* (line 18) is dependent on
    a. *pertineat* (line 19)
    b. *ad* (line 18)
    c. salutem (line 19)
    d. *quod* (line 18)

20. What case is *ipsi* (line 19)?
    a. nominative
    b. genitive
    c. dative
    d. accusative

21. In the phrase *inque . . . interponere* (lines 19–20), what is the subject of *interponere*?
    a. *rem* (line 19)
    b. se (line 19)
    c. *suam* (line 19)
    d. *fidem* (line 20)

22. The word *saucio* (line 20) modifies
    a. *communicat* (line 20)
    b. *Ille* (line 20)
    c. Cotta (line 20)
    d. *pugna* (line 20)

23. In line 20 *cum* is translated
    a. when
    b. since
    c. although
    d. with

24. Who is meant by *eo* in line 21?

   a. Cotta

   b. Titurius

   c. Caesar

   d. Ambiorix

25. In the phrase *Cotta . . . perseverat* (lines 22–23) which word introduces the indirect statement?

   a. *negat* (line 22)

   b. *iturum* (line 22)

   c. *armatum* (line 22)

   d. *se* (line 22)

Translation *Suggested time: 15 minutes*

Rursus cum in eum locum unde erant egressi reverti coeperant, et ab eis qui cesserant et ab eis qui proximi steterant circumveniebantur. Sin autem locum tenere vellent, nec virtuti locus relinquebatur neque ab tanta multitudine coiecta tela conferti vitare poterant.

18 chunks. ½ point, each 9 points.

Rursus cum	When back again
in eum locum	into the same place
unde erant egressi	whence they had proceeded
reverti coeperant	they began to return
et ab eis	both by those
qui cesserant	who had retreated
et ab eis	and by those
qui proximi steterant	who had remained closest in position
circumveniebantur	they were surrounded
Sin autem	But if, however,
locum tenere	to hold their position
vellent,	they (*i.e.,* the Romans) wanted
nec virtuti	neither for their courage
locus relinquebatur	was there room left (to maneuver)
neque ab tanta multitudine	nor, by so large a force
coiecta tela	the weapons that had been hurled
conferti	being packed together
vitare poterant	were they able to avoid

Short Analysis Questions

> Tamen tot incommodis conflictati, multis vulneribus acceptis resistebant
> et magna parte diei consumpta, cum a prima luce ad horam octavam
> pugnaretur, nihil quod ipsis esset indignum committebant. Tum T.
> Balventio, qui superiore anno primum pilum duxerat, viro forti et magnae
> 5 auctoritatis, utrumque femur tragula traicitur; Q. Lucanius eiusdem
> ordinis, fortissime pugnans, dum circumvento filio subvenit, interficitur;
> L. Cotta legatus omnes cohortes ordinesque adhortans in adversum os
> funda vulneratur.

1. What two active verbs characterize the actions of the Roman troops (lines 1–3)? Cite the Latin that supports your answer and translate or accurately paraphrase.

   The two verbs are *resistebant* (line 1) and (*nihil . . . indignum*) *committebant* (line 3). They fight bravely even in the face of serious disadvantages.

2. How does Caesar judge their actions positively or negatively? Cite the Latin that supports your answer and translate or accurately paraphrase.

   Caesar gives the troops a positive portrayal, since they are courageous and perform their duty admirably, in contrast to at least one of their commanders. They continue to fight even though wounded—*multis vulneribus accepta* (line 1)—and at a disadvantage—*tot incommodis conflictati* (line 1).

3. What happens to Titus Balventius? Cite the Latin that supports your answer and translate or accurately paraphrase.

   Titus Balventius is pierced in both thighs by an enemy weapon—*T. Balventio, . . . utrumque femur tragula traicitur* (lines 3–5).

4. What happens to Quintus Lucanius? Cite the Latin that supports your answer and translate or accurately paraphrase.

   He is killed while trying to rescue his son—*Q. Lucanius . . . fortissime pugnans, dum circumvento filio subvenit, interficitur* (lines 5–6).

5. What is Lucius Cotta doing when he is wounded? Cite the Latin that supports your answer and translate or accurately paraphrase.

   Cotta is exhorting the troops—*omnes cohortes ordinesque adhortans in adversum os funda vulneratur* (lines 7–8).

6. Is there an implicit judgment of Lucius Cotta? Cite the Latin that supports your answer and translate or accurately paraphrase.

   The fact that Cotta is wounded full in the face testifies to his bravery—*omnes cohortes ordinesque adhortans in adversum os funda vulneratur* (lines 7–8). He was not retreating at the time of his wound (which would then have been in the back). It is also noteworthy that Cotta is portrayed as still performing the duties of a general, in that he continues to exhort his men to battle, even as their hopes of victory were dwindling. The fact that Caesar states this explicitly suggests that he approved of Cotta's actions.

Essay *Suggested time: 20 minutes*

L. Cotta legatus omnes cohortes ordinesque adhortans in adversum
os funda vulneratur. [36] His rebus permotus Q. Titurius, cum procul
Ambiorigem suos cohortantem conspexisset, interpretem suum Cn.
Pompeium ad eum mittit rogatum ut sibi militibusque parcat. Ille
5   appellatus respondit: si velit secum colloqui, licere; sperare a multitudine
impetrari posse, quod ad militum salutem pertineat; ipsi vero nihil
nocitum iri, inque eam rem se suam fidem interponere. Ille cum Cotta
saucio communicat, si videatur, pugna ut excedant et cum Ambiorige una
colloquantur: sperare ab eo de sua ac militum salute impetrari posse. Cotta
10   se ad armatum hostem iturum negat atque in eo perseverat.

In this passage Caesar continues to highlight the contrasting leadership styles of his legates Lucius
Cotta and Quintus Titurius Sabinus. Here he also adds the voice of the enemy in the speech offered
by Ambiorix in response to Titurius's proposal. In a short essay, assess Caesar's characterization of his
officers as they respond to the new situation. How does Ambiorix's response add to the characterization of Cotta and Sabinus?

Support your assertions with references to the Latin text throughout the passage above. All Latin
words must be copied or their line numbers provided, AND they must be translated or paraphrased
closely enough that it is clear that you understand the Latin. It is your responsibility to convince the
reader that you are basing your conclusions on the Latin text and not merely on a general recollection
of the passage. Direct your answer to the question; do not merely summarize the passage. Please write
your essay on a separate piece of paper.

**Teachers should review with students the Essay Scoring Guidelines given at the beginning of this
manual.**

**Students should easily see the difference in the portrayals of Lucius Cotta and Quintus Titurius
Sabinus. On the one hand Cotta is characterized by his hands-on fighting, in the trenches with the
troops, where he receives a serious wound—*L. Cotta legatus omnes cohortes ordinesque adhortans
in adversum os funda vulneratur* (lines 1–2). Titurius, by contrast, seeks to negotiate a surrender at
the very first opportunity, an act of cowardice for a Roman legate—*Titurius, cum procul Ambiorigem
suos cohortantem conspexisset . . . rogatum ut sibi militibusque parcat* (lines 2–4). Astute observers
may notice that of the three leaders, only one is not focused on encouraging his troops—*L. Cotta . . .
adhortans* (line 1); *Ambiorigem suos cohortantem* (line 3). As for the role of Ambiorix in characterizing
the two Roman commanders, readers should note that since Ambiorix has already gone back on his
word about not attacking the Romans at all, he is hardly trustworthy. Thus when Titurius is shown
to be so ready to accept the terms Ambiorix proposes, he is portrayed all the more clearly as a fool.
Cotta, on the other hand, recognizes both the trickery and his duty—*Cotta se ad armatum hostem
iturum negat atque in eo perseverat* (lines 9–10).**

CHAPTER 16: BOOK 5.37–39
SABINUS'S LAST STAND

[37] Sabinus quos in praesentia tribunos militum circum se habebat
et primorum ordinum centuriones se sequi iubet et, cum propius
Ambiorigem accessisset, iussus arma abicere imperatum facit suisque
ut idem faciant imperat. Interim, dum de condicionibus inter se
5   agunt longiorque consulto ab Ambiorige instituitur sermo, paulatim
circumventus interficitur. Tum vero suo more victoriam conclamant
atque ululatum tollunt impetuque in nostros facto ordines perturbant.
Ibi L. Cotta pugnans interficitur cum maxima parte militum. Reliqui
se in castra recipiunt unde erant egressi. Ex quibus L. Petrosidius
10   aquilifer, cum magna multitudine hostium premeretur, aquilam intra
vallum proiecit; ipse pro castris fortissime pugnans occiditur. Illi aegre
ad noctem oppugnationem sustinent: noctu ad unum omnes desperata
salute se ipsi interficiunt. Pauci ex proelio elapsi incertis itineribus per
silvas ad T. Labienum legatum in hiberna perveniunt atque eum de rebus
15   gestis certiorem faciunt. [38] Hac victoria sublatus Ambiorix statim cum
equitatu in Aduatucos, qui erant eius regno finitimi, proficiscitur; neque
noctem neque diem intermittit peditatumque sese subsequi iubet. Re
demonstrata Aduatucisque concitatis, postero die in Nervios pervenit
hortaturque ne sui in perpetuum liberandi atque ulciscendi Romanos pro
20   eis quas acceperint iniuriis occasionem dimittant; interfectos esse legatos
duos magnamque partem exercitus interisse demonstrat; nihil esse negoti
subito oppressam legionem quae cum Cicerone hiemet interfici; se ad eam
rem profitetur adiutorem. Facile hac oratione Nerviis persuadet. [39] Itaque
confestim dimissis nuntiis ad Ceutrones, Grudios, Levacos, Pleumoxios,
25   Geidumnos, qui omnes sub eorum imperio sunt, quam maximas manus
possunt cogunt et de improviso ad Ciceronis hiberna advolant, nondum
ad eum fama de Tituri morte perlata. Huic quoque accidit, quod fuit
necesse, ut non nulli milites qui lignationis munitionisque causa in
silvas discessissent repentino equitum adventu interciperentur. Eis
30   circumventis, magna manu Eburones, Nervii, Aduatuci atque horum
omnium socii et clientes legionem oppugnare incipiunt. Nostri celeriter
ad arma concurrunt, vallum conscendunt. Aegre is dies sustentatur, quod
omnem spem hostes in celeritate ponebant atque hanc adepti victoriam in
perpetuum se fore victores confidebant.

Preparatory Questions

Line 1	What is the antecedent of *quos*? **tribunos**
	Find a relative clause. **quos in praesentia tribunos militum circum se habebat**
Line 2	What is the direct object of *sequi*? **se**
Lines 2–3	Find a *cum* clause. **cum propius Ambiorigem accessisset**
Line 3	Identify the tense and mood of *accessisset*. **pluperfect subjunctive**
	Identify the form and syntax of *iussus*. **perfect passive participle, nominative singular masculine modifying Sabinus (line 1)**
Lines 3–4	Find an indirect command. **ut idem faciant**
	Who/what is the implied subject of *faciant*? **suis (i.e., Titurius's soldiers)**
Line 4	What word is governed by *de*? **condicionibus**
Lines 4–5	What two clauses are joined by *–que*? **dum de condicionibus inter se agunt** and **longior consulto ab Ambiorige instituitur sermo**
Line 5	What part of speech is *consulto*? **adverb**
	Identify the subject of *instituitur*. **sermo**
Line 6	Identify the subject of *interficitur*. **Sabinus (understood)**
Line 7	Identify the case and use of *ululatum*. **accusative, direct object of tollunt**
	Identify the case and use of *impetu(que)*. **ablative absolute**
Line 8	What does *pugnans* modify? **L. Cotta**
	Identify the case and use of *militum*. **partitive genitive (with maxima parte)**
Line 9	Identify the subject of *erant egressi*. **Reliqui (line 8)**
Line 10	What is the tense and mood of *premeretur*? **imperfect subjunctive**
	Identify the case and use of *aquilam*. **accusative, direct object of proiecit (line 11)**
	What is the object of the preposition *intra*? **vallum (line 11)**
Line 11	What part of speech is *fortissime*? **adverb**
	What does it modify? **pugnans**
Line 12	What is the tense and mood of *sustinent*? **present indicative**
	Identify the case and use of *noctu*. **ablative of time when**
Line 13	What part of speech is *elapsi*? **(verbal) adjective (perfect passive participle)**
	What does it modify? **Pauci**

Identify the case and use of *itineribus*. **ablative of means**

Line 14   Identify the case and use of *hiberna*. **accusative, object of the preposition** *in*

Line 15   What does *certiorem* modify? *T. Labienum* **(line 14)**

Identify the case and use of *victoria*. **ablative of means**

What is the object of *cum*? *equitatu* **(line 16)**

Line 16   Find a relative clause. *qui erant eius regno finitimi*

What is the antecedent of *qui*? *Aduatucos*

Line 17   Identify the case and use of *peditatum(que)*. **accusative subject of infinitive (*subsequi*) in indirect statement**

On what word does *subsequi* depend? *iubet*

Line 18   Who/what is the subject of *pervenit*? **Ambiorix**

Lines 19–20   Find an indirect command. *ne sui in perpetuum liberandi . . . occasionem dimittant*

Line 19   Explain the form and use of *ulciscendi*. **genitive gerund, objective genitive with** *occasionem* **(line 20)**

Line 20   What is the antecedent of *quas*? *eis . . . iniuriis*

Line 21   What does *duos* modify? *legatos* **(line 20)**

Explain the form and use of *interisse*. **perfect active infinitive, indirect statement**

Identify the case and use of *negoti*. **partitive genitive (with** *nihil*)

Line 22   Explain the tense and mood of *hiemet*. **present subjunctive, subordinate clause in indirect statement**

Line 23   Identify the case and use of *Nerviis*. **dative object of** *persuadet*

Line 24   Find an ablative absolute. *dimissis nuntiis*

Line 25   Find a relative clause. *qui omnes sub eorum imperio sunt*

What is the object of the preposition *sub*? *imperio*

Line 26   Identify the case and use of *hiberna*. **accusative, object of the preposition** *ad*

Line 27   What word(s) does *perlata* modify? *fama*

Identify the case and use of *Tituri*. **genitive of possession**

To what does *huic* refer? *Ciceronis* **(line 26)**

Lines 27–28   Find a relative clause. *qui lignationis munitionisque causa in silvas discessissent*

Line 28   Identify the case and use of *lignationis*. **objective genitive with** *causa*

Line 29   Explain the tense and mood of *discessissent*. **pluperfect subjunctive, relative clause of characteristic**

What part of speech is *repentino*? **adverb**

Lines 30–31   Find five words that serve as subjects of *incipiunt*. ***Eburones, Nervii, Aduatuci, socii, clientes***

Line 31   Identify the form and use of *oppugnare*. **present active infinitive, complementary with *incipiunt***

Line 32   Identify the case and use of *vallum*. **accusative, direct object of *conscendunt***

What is the subject of *sustentatur*? ***dies***

Lines 32–34   Find a causal clause. ***quod omnem spem hostes in celeritate ponebant***

What word introduces it? ***quod***

Line 34   Explain the form and use of *fore*. **equals *futurum esse*, the future infinitive of *sum*. Used in indirect statement.**

What is the subject of *confidebant*? ***hostes* (line 33)**

Multiple Choice Questions *Suggested time: 40 minutes*

1. In line 1 the phrase *in praesentia* is translated
   a. in front of him
   b. at hand
   c. in the commander's tent
   d. for the present

2. What word serves as a complement to *iubet* (line 2)?
   a. *sequi* (line 2)
   b. *centuriones* (line 2)
   c. *Sabinus* (line 1)
   d. *habebat* (line 1)

3. In line 3 *Ambiorigem* is the
   a. subject
   b. object of a preposition
   c. direct object
   d. accusative subject of an infinitive

4. Who/what is the subject of *accessisset* (line 3)?
   a. Ambiorix
   b. the military tribunes
   c. the centurions
   d. Sabinus

5. In line 5 *consulto* is translated
   a. on purpose
   b. by the consul
   c. in the command tent
   d. after consultation

6. Who is the understood subject of *interficitur* (line 6)?
   a. Ambiorix
   b. Sabinus
   c. the surrounded army
   d. the interpreter

7. In lines 8–9 we learn that
   a. Ambiorix was killed while negotiating
   c. Cotta was killed, some soldiers escaped
   b. Cotta barely escaped with his life
   d. Ambiorix forced Cotta to kill most of his army

8. Who/what is meant by *quibus* (line 9)?
   a. the camp
   c. Ambiorix and his men
   b. the escaping soldiers
   d. those who were killed with Cotta

9. What is the fate of the remaining Roman soldiers in the camp (lines 11–13)?
   a. they all fight in front of the camp
   c. they are rescued
   b. they settle down to sleep at night
   d. they commit mass suicide

10. The phrase *incertis itineribus* (line 13) is an example of
    a. an ablative of means
    c. an indirect object
    b. a conditional phrase
    d. an ablative absolute

11. The phrase *certiorem faciunt* (line 15) is translated
    a. they make certain
    c. they act with certainty
    b. they inform
    d. they are informed

12. The case of *victoria* (line 15) is
    a. nominative
    c. accusative
    b. genitive
    d. ablative

13. What is the antecedent of *qui* (line 16)?
    a. *Ambiorix* (line 15)
    c. Aduatucos (line 16)
    b. *victoria* (line 15)
    d. *equitatu* (line 16)

14. What is the direct object of *subsequi* (line 17)?
    a. *iubet* (line 17)
    c. *peditatumque* (line 17)
    b. sese (line 17)
    d. *neque noctem neque diem* (lines 16–17)

15. The phrase *postero die* (line 18) is an ablative of
    a. means
    c. duration of time
    b. time when
    d. manner

16. The verb *hortaturque* (line 19) introduces
    a. a relative clause
    c. a result clause
    b. an indirect statement
    d. an indirect command

17. In line 20 *eis* modifies
    a. *Romanos* (line 19)
    b. *quas* (line 20)
    c. ***iniuriis* (line 20)**
    d. *ulciscendi* (line 19)

18. The case of *exercitus* (line 21) is
    a. nominative
    b. **genitive**
    c. accusative
    d. ablative

19. The phrase *nihil . . . negoti* (line 21) is an example of
    a. genitive of value
    b. time within which
    c. **partitive genitive**
    d. hyperbole

20. In line 23 *profitetur* is translated
    a. he will profit
    b. **he proposes**
    c. he is offered
    d. he has confessed

21. What is the object of *persuadet* (line 23)?
    a. ***Nerviis* (line 23)**
    b. *hac* (line 23)
    c. *oratione* (line 23)
    d. *facile* (line 23)

22. What part of speech is *itaque* (line 23)?
    a. preposition
    b. adverb
    c. **conjunction**
    d. adjective

23. The names mentioned in lines 24–25 (*Ceutrones . . . Geidumnos*) are all
    a. rivers
    b. towns
    c. **peoples**
    d. chieftains

24. *eorum* in line 25 refers to
    a. **the Nervii**
    b. the Aduatuci
    c. Ambiorix
    d. the Romans

25. The phrase *de improviso* (line 26) is translated
    a. unseen
    b. unproven
    c. unheard
    d. **unexpectedly**

26. The word *eum* (line 27) refers to
    a. **Cicero**
    b. Titurius
    c. Ambiorix
    d. Caesar

27. In line 27 the word *accidit* is translated
    - a. accident
    - **b. occurs**
    - c. receives
    - d. adds

28. In lines 28–29 the phrase *ut . . . interciperentur* is a
    - **a. result clause**
    - b. purpose clause
    - c. relative clause
    - d. conditional clause

29. In line 31 the verb *oppugnare* governs
    - a. *incipiunt* (line 31)
    - b. *clientes* (line 31)
    - **c. *legionem* (line 31)**
    - d. *magna manu* (line 30)

30. What part of speech is *celeriter* (line 31)?
    - **a. adverb**
    - b. conjunction
    - c. adjective
    - d. verb

31. In line 32 *quod* is translated
    - a. which
    - b. that
    - **c. because**
    - d. when

32. What is the dictionary entry for *adepti* (line 33)?
    - a. *adcipio*
    - b. *adimo*
    - c. *adpeto*
    - **d. *adipiscor***

33. What does *hanc* (line 33) modify?
    - a. *adepti* (line 33)
    - **b. *victoriam* (line 33)**
    - c. *perpetuum* (line 34)
    - d. *victores* (line 34)

Translation *Suggested time: 15 minutes*

Eis circumventis, magna manu Eburones, Nervii, Aduatuci atque horum omnium socii et clientes legionem oppugnare incipiunt. Nostri celeriter ad arma concurrunt, vallum conscendunt. Aegre is dies sustentatur, quod omnem spem hostes in celeritate ponebant atque hanc adepti victoriam in perpetuum se fore victores confidebant.

5

20 chunks. 10 points, ½ point each.

Eis circumventis	Those men having been surrounded
magna manu	with/by a large band [of men]
Eburones, Nervii, Aduatuci	the Eburones, the Nervii, and the Aduatuci
atque horum omnium	and of all these
socii et clientes	the allies and clients
legionem oppugnare	to besiege the legion
incipiunt	begin
Nostri celeriter . . . concurrunt	Our men swiftly run
ad arma	to their weapons
vallum conscendunt	[and] climb up the rampart
Aegre is dies	With difficulty this day
sustentatur	is endured
quod omnem spem	because [their] whole hope
hostes . . . ponebant	the enemy placed
in celeritate	in speed
atque	and
hanc adepti victoriam	having achieved this victory
in perpetuum	forever
se fore victores	[that] they would be conquerors
confidebant	they were sure

Short Analysis Questions

Sabinus quos in praesentia tribunos militum circum se habebat
et primorum ordinum centuriones se sequi iubet et, cum propius
Ambiorigem accessisset, iussus arma abicere imperatum facit suisque
ut idem faciant imperat. Interim, dum de condicionibus inter se
5   agunt longiorque consulto ab Ambiorige instituitur sermo, paulatim
circumventus interficitur. Tum vero suo more victoriam conclamant
atque ululatum tollunt impetuque in nostros facto ordines perturbant.
Ibi L. Cotta pugnans interficitur cum maxima parte militum. Reliqui se
in castra recipiunt unde erant egressi. Ex quibus L. Petrosidius aquilifer,
10   cum magna multitudine hostium premeretur, aquilam intra vallum
proiecit; ipse pro castris fortissime pugnans occiditur. Illi aegre ad noctem
oppugnationem sustinent: noctu ad unum omnes desperata salute se ipsi
interficiunt.

1. Which officers does Sabinus have with him? What orders does he issue to them? Cite the Latin that supports your answer and translate or accurately paraphrase.

   He has tribunes of the soldiers—*quos . . . tribunos militum* (line 1)—and centurions of the first ranks—*primorum ordinum centuriones* (line 2). He tells them to follow him—*se sequi iubet* (line 2).

2. In the meeting for negotiations (lines 2–4), who approaches whom? Who gives the orders? Cite the Latin that supports your answer and translate or accurately paraphrase.

   Sabinus approaches Ambiorix, who is in control of the meeting. Ambiorix orders Sabinus to lay down his weapons—*iussus arma abicere* (line 3)—and Sabinus tells his men to do the same—*imperatum facit suisque ut idem faciant imperat* (lines 3–4).

3. What tactics does Ambiorix use to distract the Romans? What happens to Sabinus? Cite the Latin that supports your answer and translate or accurately paraphrase.

   Ambiorix distracts the Romans by engaging in a long speech—*longiorque consulto ab Ambiorige instituitur sermo* (line 5). While he is speaking his troops sneak up on the Romans and kill Sabinus—*paulatim circumventus [Sabinus] interficitur* (lines 5–6).

4. What verbs are used to refer to the deaths of Sabinus (line 6) and Cotta (line 8)? How do the modifiers applied to these verbs distinguish their deaths? Cite the Latin that supports your answer and translate or accurately paraphrase.

   Caesar describes both legates' death using *interficitur*, but Sabinus dies *circumventus* while Cotta dies *pugnans*, indicating that he has a more honorable death.

5. With what heroic action is L. Petrosidius credited? Cite the Latin that supports your answer and translate or accurately paraphrase.

> **Petrosidius saves the legionary eagle, which was sacred to the legion. Although he is engaged in heavy fighting, he manages to hurl the eagle into the Roman camp, thereby saving it from capture, which would have been a tremendous disgrace—*L. Petrosidius aquilifer, cum magna multitudine hostium premeretur, aquilam intra vallum proiecit* (lines 9–11).**

6. For how long do the remaining Roman troops withstand the attack? What is their fate? Cite the Latin that supports your answer and translate or accurately paraphrase.

> **They hold out, with difficulty, for the rest of the daytime. But that night they commit suicide to a man, in order to save themselves from being captured—*illi aegre ad noctem oppugnationem sustinent: noctu ad unum omnes desperata salute se ipsi interficiunt* (lines 11–13).**

Essay *Suggested time: 20 minutes*

Hac victoria sublatus Ambiorix statim cum equitatu in Aduatucos,
qui erant eius regno finitimi, proficiscitur; neque noctem neque
diem intermittit peditatumque sese subsequi iubet. Re demonstrata
Aduatucisque concitatis, postero die in Nervios pervenit hortaturque
5   ne sui in perpetuum liberandi atque ulciscendi Romanos pro eis quas
acceperint iniuriis occasionem dimittant; interfectos esse legatos duos
magnamque partem exercitus interisse demonstrat; nihil esse negoti
subito oppressam legionem quae cum Cicerone hiemet interfici; se ad eam
rem profitetur adiutorem. Facile hac oratione Nerviis persuadet. [39] Itaque
10   confestim dimissis nuntiis ad Ceutrones, Grudios, Levacos, Pleumoxios,
Geidumnos, qui omnes sub eorum imperio sunt, quam maximas manus
possunt cogunt et de improviso ad Ciceronis hiberna advolant, nondum ad
eum fama de Tituri morte perlata.

In this passage the Gallic chieftain Ambiorix aims to build upon his victory over the Roman troops led by Sabinus and Cotta, which Caesar has described at length in the preceding chapters. In a short essay, discuss the ways that Caesar sets up the reader for the next episode involving Ambiorix and Quintus Cicero. What clues does Caesar give about Ambiorix's character and actions that may lead him into an additional victory, or perhaps defeat?

Support your assertions with references to the Latin text throughout the passage above. All Latin words must be copied or their line numbers provided, AND they must be translated or paraphrased closely enough that it is clear that you understand the Latin. It is your responsibility to convince the reader that you are basing your conclusions on the Latin text and not merely on a general recollection of the passage. Direct your answer to the question; do not merely summarize the passage. Please write your essay on a separate piece of paper.

Teachers should review with students the Essay Scoring Guidelines given at the beginning of this manual.

The key to understanding Caesar's portrayal of Ambiorix's character is given in the first sentence of this passage, where the Gaul is described as elated by his victory—*victoria sublatus* (line 1). Because Ambiorix's confidence stems entirely from his recent victory over Cotta and Sabinus (though this is of course no small accomplishment), it can last only as long as the Roman response to his deceptive stratagem continues to fail to be informed by traditional Roman good sense and training, that is, the kind that Caesar himself displays throughout the work. Students should note that Ambiorix rushes into action—cf. *statim* (line 1), *neque noctem neque diem intermittit* (lines 2–3); this could be interpreted positively, in that he is trying to follow up on his success before the Romans have a chance to regroup, or, more negatively, as a signal to the reader that his rash action will lead him into danger (speed, in the *De bello Gallico*, is normally only a positive characteristic for Caesar himself). Furthermore, Ambiorix in his speech to the Nervii is made to underestimate potential Roman opposition—*nihil esse negoti* (line 7)—and the Nervii are too easily swayed by his boastfulness—*facile hac oratione Nerviis persuadet* (line 9). A careful reader, aware of Roman military excellence, should suspect that Quintus Cicero's training and leadership will serve him better than that of the ill-fated legates whom Ambiorix has just defeated. The main question in the reader's mind, from the author's point of view, is whether Q. Cicero will follow the model of Titurius Sabinus or Cotta in the episode that follows. Ambiorix's fate will depend on the outcome of that question.

Notes

CHAPTER 17: BOOK 5.40–41
QUINTUS CICERO UNDER ATTACK

[40] Mittuntur ad Caesarem confestim ab Cicerone litterae, magnis
propositis praemiis, si pertulissent: obsessis omnibus viis missi
intercipiuntur. Noctu ex materia quam munitionis causa comportaverant
turres admodum centum XX excitantur incredibili celeritate; quae deesse
5   operi videbantur perficiuntur. Hostes postero die multo maioribus coactis
copiis castra oppugnant, fossam complent. Eadem ratione, qua pridie,
ab nostris resistitur. Hoc idem reliquis deinceps fit diebus. Nulla pars
nocturni temporis ad laborem intermittitur; non aegris, non vulneratis
facultas quietis datur. Quaecumque ad proximi diei oppugnationem
10   opus sunt noctu comparantur: multae praeustae sudes, magnus muralium
pilorum numerus instituitur; turres contabulantur, pinnae loricaeque
ex cratibus attexuntur. Ipse Cicero, cum tenuissima valetudine esset, ne
nocturnum quidem sibi tempus ad quietem relinquebat, ut ultro militum
concursu ac vocibus sibi parcere cogeretur. [41] Tunc duces principesque
15   Nerviorum qui aliquem sermonis aditum causamque amicitiae cum
Cicerone habebant colloqui sese velle dicunt. Facta potestate eadem
quae Ambiorix cum Titurio egerat commemorant: omnem esse in armis
Galliam; Germanos Rhenum transisse; Caesaris reliquorumque hiberna
oppugnari. Addunt etiam de Sabini morte; Ambiorigem ostentant fidei
20   faciendae causa. Errare eos dicunt, si quicquam ab eis praesidi sperent
qui suis rebus diffidant; sese tamen hoc esse in Ciceronem populumque
Romanum animo ut nihil nisi hiberna recusent atque hanc inveterascere
consuetudinem nolint: licere illis incolumibus per se ex hibernis discedere
et quascumque in partes velint sine metu proficisci. Cicero ad haec unum
25   modo respondit: non esse consuetudinem populi Romani accipere ab hoste
armato condicionem: si ab armis discedere velint, se adiutore utantur
legatosque ad Caesarem mittant; sperare pro eius iustitia quae petierint
impetraturos.

Preparatory Questions

Line 1	What is the subject of *mittuntur*? **litterae**
	What part of speech is *confestim*? **adverb**
Lines 1–2	Find a conditional clause. **si pertulissent**
	Identify the tense and mood of *pertulissent*. **pluperfect subjunctive**
Line 3	Identify the case and use of *materia*. **ablative, object of the preposition *ex***

Find a relative clause. ***quam munitionis causa comportaverant***

Line 4   Identify the tense and voice of *excitantur*. **present passive**

Line 5   What is the subject of *perficiuntur*? ***quae* (line 4)**

Explain the form and use of *coactis*. **perfect passive participle in an ablative absolute**

Line 6   Identify the case and use of *castra*. **accusative, direct object of *oppugnant***

What is the antecedent of *qua*? ***ratione***

Line 7   Identify the case and use of *nostris*. **ablative of agent**

Line 8   Identify the case and use of *temporis*. **partitive genitive (with *pars*, line 7)**

Line 9   What is the subject of *datur*? ***facultas***

Explain the case and use of *quietis*. **dative of indirect object**

Line 10   Explain the form and use of *sunt*. **third person plural present indicative active, used with *opus* in the idiom "there is need," main verb of the clause**

What two words modify *sudes*? ***multae praeustae***

Line 11   Identify the subject of *instituitur*. ***numerus***

What words does *–que* connect? ***pinnae, loricae***

Line 12   Find a *cum* clause. ***cum tenuissima valetudine esset***

What type of *cum* clause is it? **adversative**

Lines 12–13   What word(s)/phrase indicate(s) that *nocturnum* is emphasized? ***ne . . . quidem***

Lines 13–14   Find a result clause. ***ut ultro militum concursu ac vocibus sibi parcere cogeretur***

Line 14   What is the function of *parcere*? **complementary with *cogeretur***

Identify the case and use of *sibi*. **dative object with the verb *parcere***

Line 15   What is the antecedent of *qui*? ***duces principesque* (line 14)**

What words does *–que* connect? ***duces, principes***

Line 16   Identify the tense and mood of *habebant*. **imperfect indicative**

Identify the case and use of *sese*. **accusative, subject of *velle* in indirect statement**

What is the function of *velle*? **infinitive of the indirect statement**

Identify the case and use of *eadem*. **accusative plural, direct object of *commemorant***

Line 17   Find a relative clause. ***quae Ambiorix cum Titurio egerat***

What is the antecedent of *quae*? ***eadem* (line 16)**

Who/what is the subject of *commemorant*? ***duces principesque Nerviorum* (lines 14–15)**

Explain the case and use of *omnem*. **accusative, modifies *Galliam*, the subject of the infinitive in indirect statement**

Lines 17–19   Find three infinitives and explain their tenses. ***esse* (line 17), *transisse* (line 18), *oppugnari* (line 19); the first and last are present indicating time contemporaneous with the statement, while *transisse* is perfect to indicate an action already completed (before the action of the main verb)**

Line 18   On what word does *reliquorumque* depend? ***hiberna***

Explain the case and use of *Caesaris*. **genitive of possession**

Line 19   Identify the case and use of *morte*. **ablative object of the preposition *de***

Line 20   What word(s) does *causa* govern? ***fidei faciendae* (lines 19–20)**

Lines 20–21   Find an indirect statement. ***errare eos . . . , si quicquam ab eis praesidi sperent qui suis rebus diffidant***

What verb introduces it? ***dicunt***

Find a conditional clause. ***si quicquam ab eis praesidi sperent***

Explain the case and use of *quicquam*. **accusative, direct object of *sperent***

Line 21   What is the antecedent of *qui*? ***eis* (line 20)**

Identify the case and use of *rebus*. **dative with the intransitive verb *diffidant***

What word does *hoc* modify? ***animo* (line 22)**

Line 22   Identify the function of *nihil*. **direct object of *recusent***

Explain the tense and mood of *recusent*. **present subjunctive primary sequence in a result clause**

Line 23   Identify the verb that complements *nolint*. ***inveterascere* (line 22)**

Identify the form and use of *licere*. **present infinitive active, indirect statement**

Identify the case and use of *illis*. **ablative absolute**

Line 24   Find an indirect question. ***quascumque in partes velint***

Explain the form and function of *proficisci*. **present deponent infinitive, complementary with *licere* (line 23)**

What words are governed by *in*? ***quascumque partes***

Line 25   Explain the form and use of *esse*. **present infinitive active, indirect statement**

Identify the case and use of *populi Romani*. **genitive of possession**

Line 26   Identify the case and use of *armato*. **ablative modifying *hoste* (line 25)**

Identify the case and use of *adiutore*. **ablative, predicate noun, complement of *utor***

Lines 26–27   Find a conditional sentence. ***si ab armis discedere velint, se adiutore utantur legatosque ad Caesarem mittant***

Identify the protasis. ***si ab armis discedere velint***

Identify the apodosis. ***se adiutore utantur legatosque ad Caesarem mittant***

Line 27   Identify the tense and mood of *mittant*. **present subjunctive**

Explain the mood of *mittant*. **future less vivid condition**

Identify the case and use of *iustitia*. **ablative with the preposition** *pro*

Identify the tense and mood of *petierint*. **perfect subjunctive**

Line 28   Identify the form and function of *impetraturos*. **future participle masculine plural nominative (= infinitive with understood** *esse***) in indirect statement**

Multiple Choice Questions *Suggested time: 30 minutes*

1. In line 1 *confestim* is translated
    a. secretly
    c. slowly
    b. immediately
    d. carefully

2. What is the subject of *pertulissent* (line 2)?
    a. *litterae* (line 1)
    c. *Cicerone* (line 1)
    b. *praemiis* (line 2)
    d. *si* (line 2)

3. In line 3 the word *noctu* is an ablative of
    a. means
    c. accompaniment
    b. manner
    d. time when

4. What is the case and number of *turres* (line 4)?
    a. nominative singular
    c. nominative plural
    b. accusative plural
    d. accusative singular

5. What part of speech is *admodum* (line 4)?
    a. adjective
    c. preposition
    b. adverb
    d. conjunction

6. The form and use of *celeritate* (line 4) is
    a. adverbial accusative
    c. ablative of manner
    b. dative of purpose
    d. ablative of cause

7. In line 5 *multo* is an ablative of
   a. time when
   b. degree of difference
   c. means
   d. separation

8. The word *deinceps* (line 7) is translated
   a. thereafter
   b. then
   c. from the beginning
   d. one after another

9. In lines 8–9 we find an example of
   a. simile
   b. tmesis
   c. anaphora
   d. polysyndeton

10. In lines 8–10 we learn that
    a. the Romans prepared their defenses
    b. an attack was made by night
    c. the farm animals were brought in
    d. the Romans surrendered

11. The word *cum* in line 12 is translated
    a. when
    b. with
    c. since
    d. although

12. The gender and case of *tempus* (line 13) is
    a. neuter nominative
    b. masculine nominative
    c. neuter accusative
    d. masculine accusative

13. The pronoun *sibi* (line 13) refers to
    a. the soldiers
    b. Cicero
    c. the defenses
    d. the voices

14. In line 14 *tunc* is translated
    a. at that time
    b. however
    c. from that place
    d. indeed

15. In line 16 *velle* is
    a. imperfect subjunctive
    b. present indicative
    c. present infinitive
    d. imperfect infinitive

16. The case and number of *eadem* (line 16) is
    a. ablative singular
    b. nominative singular
    c. nominative plural
    d. accusative plural

17. In line 17 *commemorant* is translated
    a. they honor
    b. they mention
    c. they accompany
    d. they think

18. The subject of *transisse* (line 18) is
    a. *Germanos* (line 18)
    b. *omnem* (line 17)
    c. *Rhenum* (line 18)
    d. *Galliam* (line 18)

19. In line 20 *faciendae* is dependent upon
    a. *Ambiorigem* (line 19)
    b. *causa* (line 20)
    c. *ostentant* (line 19)
    d. *fidei* (line 19)

20. The tense and mood of *sperent* (line 20) is
    a. present indicative
    b. imperfect subjunctive
    c. perfect indicative
    d. present subjunctive

21. In line 21 *in* is translated
    a. against
    b. in
    c. towards
    d. into

22. In lines 22–23 *ut . . . nolint* is a
    a. purpose clause
    b. result clause
    c. explanatory clause
    d. jussive clause

23. On what word do *discedere* (line 23) and *proficisci* (line 24) depend?
    a. *licere* (line 23)
    b. *quascumque* (line 24)
    c. *velint* (line 24)
    d. *incolumibus* (line 23)

24. What grammatical construction do we find in lines 25–26 (*non esse . . . condicionem*)?
    a. purpose clause
    b. gerundive of obligation
    c. indirect statement
    d. ablative absolute

25. Who is meant by *eius* in line 27?
    a. Ambiorix
    b. Cicero
    c. the legates
    d. Caesar

Translation *Suggested time: 15 minutes*

Mittuntur ad Caesarem confestim ab Cicerone litterae, magnis propositis
praemiis, si pertulissent: obsessis omnibus viis missi intercipiuntur.
Noctu ex materia quam munitionis causa comportaverant turres admodum
centum XX excitantur incredibili celeritate; quae deesse operi videbantur
5   perficiuntur.

20 chunks. 10 points, ½ point each.

Mittuntur	are being sent
ad Caesarem	to Caesar
confestim	immediately
ab Cicerone	from Cicero
litterae,	letters
magnis propositis praemiis,	with great rewards having been promised
si pertulissent	if they should reach (him)
obsessis omnibus viis	since all the roads were being watched
missi intercipiuntur	those which had been sent are being intercepted
Noctu	At night
ex materia	from the lumber
quam	which
munitionis causa	for the sake of fortifications
comportaverant	they had carried in
turres . . . excitantur	towers are built
admodum centum XX	a full 120
incredibili celeritate	with unbelievable speed
quae . . . videbantur	what (things) seemed
deesse operi	to be lacking for the works
perficiuntur	are completed

Short Analysis Questions

> Hostes postero die multo maioribus coactis copiis castra oppugnant, fossam
> complent. Eadem ratione, qua pridie, ab nostris resistitur. Hoc idem reliquis
> deinceps fit diebus. Nulla pars nocturni temporis ad laborem intermittitur;
> non aegris, non vulneratis facultas quietis datur. Quaecumque ad proximi
> 5 diei oppugnationem opus sunt noctu comparantur: multae praeustae sudes,
> magnus muralium pilorum numerus instituitur; turres contabulantur,
> pinnae loricaeque ex cratibus attexuntur. Ipse Cicero, cum tenuissima
> valetudine esset, ne nocturnum quidem sibi tempus ad quietem relinquebat,
> ut ultro militum concursu ac vocibus sibi parcere cogeretur.

1. What actions are taken by the Gauls to attack the camp (lines 1–3)? Cite the Latin that supports your answer and translate or accurately paraphrase.

   They gather together many more troops for besieging the camp—*multo maioribus coactis copiis castra oppugnant* (line 1), and they fill in the ditch—*fossam complent* (lines 1–2) that protected the Roman camp (to enable them to advance on its fortifications).

2. When do the Romans undertake their preparations? Cite the Latin that supports your answer and translate or accurately paraphrase.

   They work all night each night to strengthen the fortifications—*nulla pars nocturni temporis ad laborem intermittitur* (line 3).

3. In lines 5–7, how does Caesar's sentence structure enhance the image created by the content of the sentences? Cite the Latin that supports your answer and translate or accurately paraphrase.

   Caesar uses a number of coordinate sentences, each with the same basic word order, namely subject + passive verb, to build up the structure, both literally and metaphorically: *multae praeustae sudes . . . instituitur; turres contabulantur, pinnae loricaeque ex cratibus attexuntur.*

4. How is Cicero's leadership characterized in lines 7–9? Cite the Latin that supports your answer and translate or accurately paraphrase.

   Q. Cicero is portrayed here as a leader who puts the safety and welfare of his troops before his own, and who toils in the trenches with them rather than using his superior position to escape such labor: his men voluntarily come to him and compel him to look after himself, given his weakened state—*Ipse Cicero, cum tenuissima valetudine esset, ne nocturnum quidem sibi tempus ad quietem relinquebat, ut ultro militum concursu ac vocibus sibi parcere cogeretur.*

Essay Suggested time: 20 minutes

Tunc duces principesque Nerviorum qui aliquem sermonis aditum
causamque amicitiae cum Cicerone habebant colloqui sese velle dicunt.
Facta potestate eadem quae Ambiorix cum Titurio egerat commemorant:
omnem esse in armis Galliam; Germanos Rhenum transisse; Caesaris
5   reliquorumque hiberna oppugnari. Addunt etiam de Sabini morte;
Ambiorigem ostentant fidei faciendae causa. Errare eos dicunt, si
quicquam ab eis praesidi sperent qui suis rebus diffidant; sese tamen hoc
esse in Ciceronem populumque Romanum animo ut nihil nisi hiberna
recusent atque hanc inveterascere consuetudinem nolint: licere illis
10   incolumibus per se ex hibernis discedere et quascumque in partes velint
sine metu proficisci. Cicero ad haec unum modo respondit: non esse
consuetudinem populi Romani accipere ab hoste armato condicionem:
si ab armis discedere velint, se adiutore utantur legatosque ad Caesarem
mittant; sperare pro eius iustitia quae petierint impetraturos.

As the leaders of the Nervii begin to negotiate with Cicero they explicitly bring up the example of Ambiorix and Quintus Titurius Sabinus, which Caesar narrated in the chapters immediately preceding these. Caesar thus sets up the attack on Cicero's camp as a parallel to the earlier one.

In a short essay, discuss the arguments undertaken by the Nervii and Cicero in this passage. Do the Nervii present a persuasive argument for Cicero's surrender? Is Cicero's response reasonable, especially in light of the fate of Sabinus and Cotta?

Support your assertions with references to the Latin text throughout the passage above. All Latin words must be copied or their line numbers provided, AND they must be translated or paraphrased closely enough that it is clear that you understand the Latin. It is your responsibility to convince the reader that you are basing your conclusions on the Latin text and not merely on a general recollection of the passage. Direct your answer to the question; do not merely summarize the passage. Please write your essay on a separate piece of paper.

Teachers should review with students the Essay Scoring Guidelines given at the beginning of this manual.

Students should recognize that Caesar sets up the possibility of a parallel outcome as in the episode with Cotta and Sabinus: the Gallic leaders seek an opportunity to negotiate with Quintus Cicero— *Tunc duces principesque Nerviorum . . . colloqui sese velle dicunt* **(lines 1–2), which reminds the reader of Ambiorix's initial overtures to Sabinus and Cotta. The arguments employed are designed to cause the same panic as had happened earlier. They claim that the whole of Gaul is in revolt—** *omnem esse in armis Galliam* **(line 4), that the Germans pose an additional threat—** *Germanos Rhenum transisse* **(line 4)—and that there is no hope of receiving aid from any of the other Roman winter camps—** *Caesaris reliquorumque hiberna oppugnari* **(lines 4–5). In short, they prey on the fear that this legion is left on its own to defend itself. And indeed, it is precisely because the legion is isolated that their claims cannot be verified: if the camp is surrounded by the Gallic siege, news of the situation elsewhere cannot be ascertained. The further mention of the death of Sabinus (note that Cotta is not explicitly mentioned) is designed to provoke Cicero into a rash action such as that which Sabinus had undertaken. But Cicero**

proves to be made of sterner stuff than Sabinus. He gives almost the same response to the Nervii's overtures that marked Cotta's last interaction with Sabinus—*non esse consuetudinem populi Romani accipere ab hoste armato condicionem* (lines 11–12). Thus Cicero places his duty to his commanding officer and his loyalty to Rome above his self-preservation. The parallel with Cotta's position in a similar situation is good evidence that Caesar also approved of Cicero's actions here.

CHAPTER 18: BOOK 5.42–43
THE NERVII ATTACK

Ab hac spe repulsi Nervii vallo pedum IX et fossa pedum XV hiberna
cingunt. Haec et superiorum annorum consuetudine ab nobis cognoverant
et quos clam de exercitu habebant captivos ab eis docebantur; sed nulla
ferramentorum copia quae esset ad hunc usum idonea, gladiis caespites
5   circumcidere, manibus sagulisque terram exhaurire videbantur. Qua
quidem ex re hominum multitudo cognosci potuit: nam minus horis tribus
milium in circuitu III munitionem perfecerunt reliquisque diebus turres
ad altitudinem valli, falces testudinesque, quas idem captivi docuerant,
parare ac facere coeperunt. [43] Septimo oppugnationis die maximo coorto
10   vento ferventes fusili ex argilla glandes fundis et fervefacta iacula in casas,
quae more Gallico stramentis erant tectae, iacere coeperunt. Hae celeriter
ignem comprehenderunt et venti magnitudine in omnem locum castrorum
distulerunt. Hostes maximo clamore sicuti parta iam atque explorata
victoria turres testudinesque agere et scalis vallum ascendere coeperunt.
15   At tanta militum virtus atque ea praesentia animi fuit ut, cum undique
flamma torrerentur maximaque telorum multitudine premerentur suaque
omnia impedimenta atque omnes fortunas conflagrare intellegerent, non
modo demigrandi causa de vallo decederet nemo sed paene ne respiceret
quidem quisquam, ac tum omnes acerrime fortissimeque pugnarent. Hic
20   dies nostris longe gravissimus fuit, sed tamen hunc habuit eventum, ut eo
die maximus numerus hostium vulneraretur atque interficeretur, ut se sub
ipso vallo constipaverant recessumque primis ultimi non dabant. Paulum
quidem intermissa flamma et quodam loco turri adacta et contingente
vallum, tertiae cohortis centuriones ex eo, quo stabant, loco recesserunt
25   suosque omnes removerunt, nutu vocibusque hostes, si introire vellent,
vocare coeperunt: quorum progredi ausus est nemo. Tum ex omni parte
lapidibus coiectis deturbati, turrisque succensa est.

Preparatory Questions

Line 1   Identify the case and use of *repulsi*. **nominative case, modifies *Nervii***

                Identify the case and use of *pedum*. **genitive of measure**

Line 2   What part of speech is *nobis*? **pronoun**

Lines 2–3   What part of speech is *et . . . et*? **(correlative) conjunction**

Line 3   What is the antecedent of *quos*? ***captivos***

	Identify and explain the tense and voice of *docebantur*. **imperfect passive, main verb of clause**
Line 4	Identify the case and use of *gladiis*. **ablative of means**
Line 6	What part of speech is *quidem*? **adverb**
	What is the form of *cognosci*? **passive infinitive**
	Explain what *minus tribus horis* measures. **time**
Line 7	Identify the case and use of *circuitu*. **ablative of specification**
Lines 7–9	Find three objects of *parare ac facere*. **turres (line 7), falces, testudines (both, line 8)**
Line 8	What are the antecedents of *quas*? **turres, falces, testudines**
	Give the case, number, and use of *idem*. **nominative plural, modifies captivi**
Line 9	Identify the case and use of *Septimo die*. **ablative of time when**
Lines 9–10	Find an ablative absolute. **maximo coorto vento**
Line 10	Identify the form and use of *fervefacta*. **perfect participle passive, nominative plural neuter modifies iacula**
Line 11	Identify the case and use of *more Gallico*. **ablative of specification**
	To what or whom does *Hae* refer? **casas (line 10)**
Line 12	Identify the case and use of *magnitudine*. **ablative of means or cause**
Line 13	What part of speech is *sicuti*? **conjunction**
Lines 13–14	Find an ablative absolute. **parta iam atque explorata victoria**
Line 15	What kind of clause does *ut* introduce? **result clause**
Lines 15–17	Find a *cum* clause. **cum . . . intellegerent**
	What kind of *cum* clause is it? **adversative**
Line 18	What word goes with *ne* to form a phrase? **quidem (line 19)**
Line 19	Identify the form and use of *acerrime fortissimeque*. **superlative adverbs, modify pugnarent**
Line 20	What is the subject of *habuit*? **dies**
Lines 20–21	Find a substantive clause of result. **ut . . . interficeretur**
Lines 21–22	Find an *ut* clause of explanation. **ut . . . dabant**
Lines 25–26	Find a conditional clause. **si . . . vellent**
	Find a semi-deponent verb. **ausus est**
Line 27	What helping verb needs to be added to complete *deturbati*? **sunt**

Multiple Choice Questions *Suggested time: 20 minutes*

1. In lines 1–2 what typical Roman tactic are the Nervii adopting?
   a. dividing the army in two parts
   b. a frontal assault
   c. building a wall and trench
   d. using digging tools

2. In lines 2–3 where had they learned this technique?
   a. from the Germans
   b. from their ancestors
   c. from the Aedui
   d. from the Romans

3. In lines 3–4 we learn that the Nervii lack
   a. courage
   b. fighting men
   c. iron tools
   d. military skill

4. In line 5 how are they moving soil?
   a. in their hands and military cloaks
   b. in wheelbarrows and buckets
   c. forcing prisoners to do it
   d. using relay lines

5. In lines 5–7 the Romans judge the number of enemy soldiers by
   a. organized battle lines
   b. number of commanders
   c. time it takes to build the wall
   d. reports from captives

6. *falces testudinesque* (line 8) are
   a. geographical features
   b. instruments for fortress attack
   c. military formations
   d. beasts of burden

7. In lines 9–11 the rising wind brought great danger because
   a. the Romans could not see the enemy
   b. the weather grew cold
   c. the spears flew further
   d. firebrands could burn straw roofs

8. In lines 13–14 the enemy behaves as if
   a. they are afraid of fire
   b. they fear the Romans
   c. they have a victory
   d. they are giving up hope

9. In lines 15–19 which of these statements is NOT true?
   a. the camp was burning
   b. Romans were surrounded by the enemy
   c. Roman possessions were being lost
   d. the Romans retreated from the wall

10. In lines 21–22 a major outcome of this day was that
    a. the Gauls gave up
    b. many Gauls were killed
    c. the weather improved
    d. reinforcements arrived

11. In line 22 *primis* and *ultimi* modify the understood noun
    a. days
    c. soldiers
    b. winds
    d. houses

12. In line 23 *turri adacta et contingente* is
    a. an ablative absolute
    c. a gerund
    b. the subject of *stabant* (line 24)
    d. a pair of present participles

13. In line 25 *suosque omnes removerunt* is best translated
    a. they dispatched the enemy
    c. they hid
    b. they moved soldiers back
    d. they moved alone

14. In line 25 *nutu vocibusque* is best translated
    a. with gestures and words
    c. angrily
    b. silently
    d. with feet and words

15. The understood subject of *deturbati* (line 27) is
    a. *turris*
    c. *Romani*
    b. *hostes*
    d. *centuriones*

16. In line 27 the understood verb is
    a. *sunt*
    c. *voluerunt*
    b. *est*
    d. *succendit*

Translation *Suggested time: 15 minutes*

Ab hac spe repulsi Nervii vallo pedum IX et fossa pedum XV hiberna cingunt. Haec et superiorum annorum consuetudine ab nobis cognoverant et, quos clam de exercitu habebant captivos, ab eis docebantur; sed nulla ferramentorum copia quae esset ad hunc usum idonea, gladiis caespites circumcidere, manibus sagulisque terram exhaurire videbantur.

5

20 chunks. 10 points, ½ point each.

Ab hac spe	By/in this hope
repulsi	disappointed
Nervii	the Nervii
vallo pedum IX et fossa pedum XV	by a 9 foot wall and a 15 foot ditch
hiberna cingunt	surround the winter quarters
Haec	These (techniques)
et . . . consuetudine	both by association
superiorum annorum	in former years
ab nobis	from us
cognoverant	they had learned
et, . . . ab eis docebantur	and they were taught by those
quos clam de exercitu habebant captivos	whom from our army as captives they held
sed nulla . . . copia	but as (they had) no supply
ferramentorum	of iron tools
quae esset . . . idonea	which might be suitable
ad hunc usum	for this use
gladiis caespites circumcidere	with swords to cut the turf/turfs/pieces of turf
manibus sagulisque	and with hands and cloaks
terram exhaurire	to remove the earth
videbantur	they were seen

Short Analysis Questions

Qua quidem ex re hominum multitudo cognosci potuit: nam minus
horis tribus milium in circuitu III munitionem perfecerunt; reliquisque
diebus turres ad altitudinem valli, falces testudinesque, quas idem captivi
docuerant, parare ac facere coeperunt.

1. We have learned that the Gauls have no tools for digging or moving earthworks. What does
    their speed of construction under such circumstances say about their determination? About
    their numbers? Cite the Latin that supports your answer or accurately paraphrase.

    **They work diligently and shortly achieve their purpose—*minus horis tribus milium in
    circuitu III munitionem perfecerunt* (lines 1–2). They built the fortification in only three hours
    and started constructing siege equipment, so their numbers must have been great—*Qua
    quidem ex re hominum multitudo cognosci potuit* (line 1).**

Septimo oppugnationis die maximo coorto vento ferventes fusili ex argilla
glandes fundis et fervefacta iacula in casas, quae more Gallico stramentis
erant tectae, iacere coeperunt. Hae celeriter ignem comprehenderunt
et venti magnitudine in omnem locum castrorum distulerunt. Hostes
5   maximo clamore sicuti parta iam atque explorata victoria turres
testudinesque agere et scalis vallum ascendere coeperunt.

2. How does the rising wind pose a special danger to the Roman camp? Cite the Latin that
    supports your answer or accurately paraphrase.

    **The Gauls have heated missiles and javelins to throw into camp, where the huts are roofed
    with straw—*ferventes . . . glandes . . . in casas, quae more Gallico stramentis erant tectae,
    iacere coeperunt* (lines 1–3).**

3. How is this danger realized in lines 3–4? Cite the Latin that supports your answer or accurately
    paraphrase.

    **Fire is quickly started and the wind carries it throughout the camp—*Hae celeriter ignem
    comprehenderunt et venti magnitudine in omnem locum castrorum distulerunt.***

4. In lines 4–6, how does the enemy seize upon this advantage? Cite the Latin that supports your
    answer or accurately paraphrase.

    **The enemy bring up the siege engines and begin to scale the walls—*Hostes . . . turres
    testudinesque agere et scalis vallum ascendere coeperunt.***

Essay *Suggested time: 20 minutes*

> At tanta militum virtus atque ea praesentia animi fuit, ut, cum undique
> flamma torrerentur maximaque telorum multitudine premerentur suaque
> omnia impedimenta atque omnes fortunas conflagrare intellegerent, non
> modo demigrandi causa de vallo decederet nemo, sed paene ne respiceret
> 5   quidem quisquam, ac tum omnes acerrime fortissimeque pugnarent
> . . . Paulum quidem intermissa flamma et quodam loco turri adacta et
> contingente vallum tertiae cohortis centuriones ex eo, quo stabant, loco
> recesserunt suosque omnes removerunt, nutu vocibusque hostes, si
> introire vellent, vocare coeperunt; quorum progredi ausus est nemo. Tum
> 10   ex omni parte lapidibus coniectis deturbati, turrisque succensa est.

In this passage the qualities of Roman soldiers that made them so often victorious are evident. Discuss their ability to focus on the primary task in the face of danger and destruction, their attitude toward enemies who appear to have them at a great disadvantage, and the effects both concrete and abstract that these qualities had on their opponents.

Support your assertions with references to the Latin text throughout the passages above. All Latin words must be copied or their line numbers provided, AND they must be translated or paraphrased closely enough that it is clear that you understand the Latin. It is your responsibility to convince the reader that you are basing your conclusions on the Latin text and not merely on a general recollection of the passage. Direct your answer to the question; do not merely summarize the passage. Please write your essay on a separate piece of paper.

Teachers should review the Essay Scoring Guidelines given at the beginning of this manual with students.

Caesar mentions their bravery—*tanta militum virtus* (line 1)—first. But immediately following that and really more important in this instance is presence of mind—*praestantia animi* (line 1). They are not distracted by roaring flames—*flamma torrerentur* (line 2)—or the thought that their supplies and possessions are likely being lost—*omnia impedimenta atque omnes fortunas conflagrare* (line 3). They know that the first order of business is to stop the influx of enemy or they will be dead and in no need of possessions. Thus they fight fiercely and do not look back—*de vallo decederet nemo sed paene ne respiceret quidem quisquam* (lines 4–5). Their activities bring death to many enemies, and when they step back from the wall and invite the enemy in, no one comes—*loco recesserunt suosque omnes removerunt, nutu vocibusque hostes, si introire vellent, vocare coeperunt; quorum progredi ausus est nemo* (lines 7–9). Both in numbers killed and in attitude, they have surpassed the enemy who has such obvious advantages over them.

Notes

CHAPTER 19: BOOK 5.44–46
BRAVERY AND LETTERS TO CAESAR

[44] Erant in ea legione fortissimi viri, centuriones, qui primis ordinibus
appropinquarent, Titus Pullo et Lucius Vorenus. Hi perpetuas inter se
controversias habebant, quinam anteferretur, omnibusque annis de
locis summis simultatibus contendebant. Ex his Pullo, cum acerrime ad
5   munitiones pugnaretur, "Quid dubitas," inquit, "Vorene? Aut quem locum
tuae pro laude virtutis spectas? Hic dies de nostris controversiis iudicabit."
Haec cum dixisset, procedit extra munitiones, quaeque pars hostium
confertissima est visa irrumpit. Ne Vorenus quidem tum sese vallo
continet sed omnium veritus existimationem subsequitur. Tum mediocri
10   spatio relicto Pullo pilum in hostes immittit atque unum ex multitudine
procurrentem traicit; quo percusso et exanimato hunc scutis protegunt,
in hostem tela universi coniciunt neque dant regrediendi facultatem.
Transfigitur scutum Pulloni et verutum in balteo defigitur. Avertit hic
casus vaginam et gladium educere conanti dextram moratur manum,
15   impeditumque hostes circumsistunt. Succurrit inimicus illi Vorenus et
laboranti subvenit. Ad hunc se confestim a Pullone omnis multitudo
convertit; illum veruto arbitrantur occisum. Gladio comminus rem gerit
Vorenus, atque uno interfecto reliquos paulum propellit: dum cupidius
instat, in locum deiectus inferiorem concidit. Huic rursus circumvento fert
20   subsidium Pullo, atque ambo incolumes compluribus interfectis summa
cum laude sese intra munitiones recipiunt. Sic fortuna in contentione et
certamine utrumque versavit, ut alter alteri inimicus auxilio salutique
esset neque diiudicari posset, uter utri virtute anteferendus videretur. [45]
Quanto erat in dies gravior atque asperior oppugnatio, et maxime quod
25   magna parte militum confecta vulneribus res ad paucitatem defensorum
pervenerat, tanto crebriores litterae nuntiique ad Caesarem mittebantur;
quorum pars deprehensa in conspectu nostrorum militum cum cruciatu
necabatur. Erat unus intus Nervius, nomine Vertico, loco natus honesto,
qui a prima obsidione ad Ciceronem perfugerat, suamque ei fidem
30   praestiterat. Hic servo spe libertatis magnisque persuadet praemiis ut
litteras ad Caesarem deferat. Has ille in iaculo inligatas effert, et Gallus
inter Gallos sine ulla suspicione versatus ad Caesarem pervenit. Ab eo de
periculis Ciceronis legionisque cognoscitur. [46] Caesar, acceptis litteris
hora circiter undecima diei, statim nuntium in Bellovacos ad Marcum
35   Crassum quaestorem mittit, cuius hiberna aberant ab eo milia passuum

XXV; iubet media nocte legionem proficisci celeriterque ad se venire. Exit
cum nuntio Crassus. Alterum ad Gaium Fabium legatum mittit, ut in
Atrebatum fines legionem adducat, qua sibi iter faciendum sciebat. Scribit
Labieno, si rei publicae commodo facere posset, cum legione ad fines
40   Nerviorum veniat. Reliquam partem exercitus, quod paulo aberat longius,
non putat exspectandam; equites circiter quadringentos ex proximis
hibernis colligit.

Preparatory Questions

Line 1   With what word is *centuriones* in apposition? ***viri***

Line 2   To whom does *inter se* refer? ***Hi***

Line 3   Give the case and use of *omnibusque annis.* **ablative of time when**

Line 4   Identify and explain the tense of *contendebant.* **imperfect (indicative), habitual action**

Lines 4–5   Identify the type of *cum* clause. **circumstantial/temporal (it sets up the narrative circumstances under which the episode takes place)**

Line 5   Identify the case and use of *Vorene.* **vocative, direct address**

Line 6   What is the subject of *iudicabit?* ***dies***

Line 7   Identify the type of *cum* clause. **circumstantial (referring to the past)**

Line 8   What word joins with *quidem* to form a phrase? ***ne***

Line 9   *Veritus* is a part of what verb? ***vereor***

Line 11   Identify the subject of *protegunt.* **they (the enemy)**

Line 12   Explain the case and use of *regrediendi.* **objective genitive (with *facultatem*)**

Lines 13–14   What is the subject of *avertit?* ***casus* (line 14)**

Line 15   What pronoun should be supplied with *impeditum?* ***eum/hunc***

Line 16   Identify the form and use of *laboranti.* **present participle active, dative modifies *illi* (line 15)**

Line 21   Translate the phrase *sese recipiunt.* **escape/withdraw**

Lines 22–23   Find a double dative of purpose and reference. ***alteri, auxilio salutique***

Line 25   Find an ablative absolute. ***magna parte confecta***

Line 26   Give the tense and voice of *mittebantur.* **imperfect passive**

Line 28   Find an ablative of specification. ***nomine Vertico***

               Find an ablative of source. ***loco honesto***

Line 30	Give the case and use of *servo*. **dative with *persuadet***
Line 35	Identify the direct object of *mittit*. **nuntium**
Lines 35–36	Find an accusative of distance or extent of space. ***milia passuum XXV***
Line 36	Identify the form and use of *proficisci*. **present infinitive deponent, indirect statement**
Line 38	What word must be understood with *faciendum*? ***esse***
Lines 38–39	Find a conditional clause. ***si ... posset***

Multiple Choice Questions *Suggested time: 30 minutes*

1. In line 3 *quinam* is best translated
   a. a certain man
   b. as to which
   c. with whom
   d. from which

2. In line 4 *simultatibus* is best translated
   a. similarity
   b. rivalry
   c. simultaneous
   d. unique

3. In line 5 *quem* is
   a. an interrogative adverb
   b. a relative pronoun
   c. a demonstrative adjective
   d. an interrogative adjective

4. The tense and mood of *dixisset* (line 7) is
   a. perfect indicative
   b. perfect subjunctive
   c. pluperfect indicative
   d. pluperfect subjunctive

5. In line 8 *est visa* is best translated
   a. seemed
   b. he saw
   c. he was seen
   d. sight was

6. Vorenus rushed against the enemy because he
   a. had lost a friend
   b. wanted to defend a friend
   c. feared the soldiers' opinion
   d. enjoyed fighting

7. *Hostem* (line 12) refers to
   a. the Gauls
   b. Vorenus
   c. the Romans
   d. Pullo

8. In lines 14–15 Pullo cannot easily use his sword because
   - a. he had dropped it
   - **b. a javelin had turned his sword belt**
   - c. the enemy was too thick around him
   - d. it was broken

9. In line 15 Vorenus is called *inimicus* rather than *hostis* because
   - a. *inimicus* is masculine
   - b. he is the subject of the sentence
   - **c. his enmity is personal**
   - d. he is acquainted with Pullo

10. The enemy all turned against Vorenus (lines 15–16) because
    - a. he was a Roman
    - b. he had just arrived
    - c. he was an officer
    - **d. they thought Pullo was dead**

11. *inferiorem* (line 19) modifies
    - **a. *locum* (line 19)**
    - b. *paulum* (line 18)
    - c. *Vorenus* (line 18)
    - d. *cupidius* (line 18)

12. *circumvento* (line 19) modifies
    - a. *Pullo* (line 20)
    - **b. *huic* (line 19)**
    - c. *subsidium* (line 20)
    - d. *ambo* (line 20)

13. In line 20 *incolumes* refers to
    - a. the Gauls
    - b. the Romans
    - c. sword and spear
    - **d. Pullo and Vorenus**

14. *Alter . . . alteri* (line 22) is best translated
    - a. both . . . and
    - **b. one . . . to the other**
    - c. sometimes . . . sometimes
    - d. one side . . . another side

15. In line 23 *anteferendus* is a(n)
    - **a. gerundive**
    - b. verb
    - c. adjective
    - d. gerund

16. In lines 24–26 *quanto . . . tanto* is best translated as
    - a. when . . . where
    - **b. as . . . so**
    - c. wherever . . . there
    - d. great . . . greater

17. In line 27 *quorum* is a
    - **a. partitive genitive**
    - b. adverb
    - c. adjective
    - d. indefinite pronoun

18. In line 28 we learn that Vertico is
    a. a Roman nobleman
    b. one of the Nervii
    c. a Roman soldier
    d. a slave

19. The antecedent of *has* (line 31) is
    a. *Caesarem* (line 31)
    b. *inligatas* (line 31)
    c. litteras (line 31)
    d. *Gallus* (line 31)

20. *Hora circiter undecima diei* (line 34) tells us that Caesar learned of the situation
    a. in the early morning
    b. an hour before midnight
    c. at lunchtime
    d. toward evening

21. *Media nocte* (line 36) is a(n)
    a. accusative of extent
    b. ablative absolute
    c. ablative of time
    d. ablative of respect

22. In line 36 *legionem* is a(n)
    a. direct object
    b. object of preposition
    c. subject of infinitive
    d. appositive

23. *Sibi iter faciendum* (line 38) is
    a. a passive periphrastic
    b. an independent clause
    c. a gerund phrase
    d. an ablative absolute

24. *Quadringentos* (line 41) modifies
    a. *hibernis* (line 42)
    b. equites (line 41)
    c. *exercitus* (line 40)
    d. *exspectandam* (line 41)

Translation *Suggested time: 15 minutes*

Huic rursus circumvento fert subsidium Pullo, atque ambo incolumes
compluribus interfectis summa cum laude sese intra munitiones recipiunt.
Sic fortuna in contentione et certamine utrumque versavit, ut alter alteri
inimicus auxilio salutique esset neque diiudicari posset, uter utri virtute
5 anteferendus videretur.

18 chunks. 9 points, ½ point each.

Huic rursus circumvento	**to this one surrounded**
fert subsidium Pullo	**Pullo brought aid**
atque ambo incolumes	**and both unharmed**
compluribus interfectis	**many (enemies) having been killed**
summa cum laude	**with great praise**
sese ... recipiunt	**withdrew**
intra munitiones	**within the fortifications**
Sic fortuna ... versavit	**So fortune turned/turned out**
in contentione et certamine	**in the rivalry and conflict**
utrumque	**on each side**
ut alter. . . inimicus	**that one ... enemy**
alteri	**to the other**
auxilio salutique esset	**was an aid and a safety**
neque diiudicari posset	**nor could it be decided**
uter	**which**
utri	**to the other**
virtute	**in courage**
anteferendus videretur	**seemed to be preferred**

Short Analysis Questions

Quanto erat in dies gravior atque asperior oppugnatio, et maxime quod
magna parte militum confecta vulneribus res ad paucitatem defensorum
pervenerat, tanto crebriores litterae nuntiique ad Caesarem mittebantur;
quorum pars deprehensa in conspectu nostrorum militum cum cruciatu
5 necabatur.

1. In lines 1–3, in what ways is the situation growing more desperate for the Romans? Cite the
   Latin that supports your answer or accurately paraphrase.

   **A great many of the soldiers are wounded and there is a scarcity of defenders—*maxime
   quod magna parte militum confecta vulneribus res ad paucitatem defensorum* (lines 1–2).**

2. In lines 4–5, how are the Gauls making a bad situation worse for the Romans? Cite the Latin that supports your answer or accurately paraphrase.

   The Gauls were torturing and killing the messengers who attempted to carry a message to Caesar in the sight of the Romans—*deprehensa in conspectu nostrorum militum cum cruciatu necabatur.*

   Erat unus intus Nervius, nomine Vertico, loco natus honesto, qui a prima
   obsidione ad Ciceronem perfugerat, suamque ei fidem praestiterat. Hic
   servo spe libertatis magnisque persuadet praemiis ut litteras ad Caesarem
   deferat. Has ille in iaculo inligatas effert et Gallus inter Gallos sine ulla
   5   suspicione versatus ad Caesarem pervenit. Ab eo de periculis Ciceronis
   legionisque cognoscitur.

3. In lines 1–3, what do we learn about Vertico that makes him trustworthy? Cite the Latin that supports your answer or accurately paraphrase.

   Vertico had defected to Cicero at the beginning of the blockade and had shown loyalty to him—*a prima obsidione ad Ciceronem perfugerat suamque ei fidem praestiterat* (lines 1–2).

4. How does Vertico win his slave's help (lines 3–4)? Cite the Latin that supports your answer or accurately paraphrase.

   He persuaded the slave with the promise of freedom and great rewards to carry a message to Caesar—*servo spe libertatis magnisque persuadet praemiis, ut litteras ad Caesarem deferat.*

5. How does the slave succeed in his mission (lines 4–6)? Cite the Latin that supports your answer or accurately paraphrase.

   As a Gaul the slave passed the enemy lines without any suspicion and carried the letter to Caesar—*Gallus inter Gallos sine ulla suspicione versatus ad Caesarem pervenit* (lines 4–5).

Essay *Suggested time: 20 minutes*

> Caesar acceptis litteris hora circiter undecima diei statim nuntium
> in Bellovacos ad Marcum Crassum quaestorem mittit, cuius hiberna
> aberant ab eo milia passuum XXV; iubet media nocte legionem proficisci
> celeriterque ad se venire. Exit cum nuntio Crassus. Alterum ad Gaium
> 5   Fabium legatum mittit, ut in Atrebatum fines legionem adducat, qua sibi
> iter faciendum sciebat. Scribit Labieno, si rei publicae commodo facere
> posset, cum legione ad fines Nerviorum veniat. Reliquam partem exercitus,
> quod paulo aberat longius, non putat exspectandam.

Caesar is famous for his quick but carefully planned responses to situations. In a brief essay discuss the rapidity of his reactions to this crisis, the limitations of his choices, and the careful selection of available resources that he makes.

All Latin words must be copied or their line numbers provided, AND they must be translated or paraphrased closely enough that it is clear that you understand the Latin. It is your responsibility to convince the reader that you are basing your conclusions on the Latin text and not merely on a general recollection of the passage. Direct your answer to the question; do not merely summarize the passage. Please write your essay on a separate piece of paper.

Teachers should review the Essay Scoring Guidelines given at the beginning of this manual with students.

When Caesar received the message about the Romans' peril late in the day he immediately sent a messenger to Marcus Crassus, whose winter quarters were some twenty-five miles away, that he should set out in the middle of the night and come to him—*ad Marcum Crassum quaestorem mittit, cuius hiberna aberant ab eo milia passuum XXV; iubet media nocte legionem proficisci celeriterque ad se venire* (lines 2–4). He sent another to Gaius Fabius, directing him to move a legion into the Atrebates' territory, to which he must go on his way to help—*Gaium Fabium legatum mittit, ut in Atrebatum fines legionem adducat, qua sibi iter faciendum sciebat* (lines 4–6). He sent a third message to Labienus, asking him to bring a legion if it were feasible—*Scribit Labieno, si rei publicae commodo facere posset, cum legione ad fines Nerviorum veniat* (lines 6–7). He discounts using the rest of the army, which is too far away, but assembles a cavalry—*equites colligit* (lines 7–8). Thus we see Caesar coolly appraising what portions of his army can be used in this rescue effort and very quickly sending for them—some to meet him on his way, some to go with him, some to be left *in situ* if that is the most sensible approach to make.

CHAPTER 20: BOOK 5.47–48
HELP IS COLLECTED

Hora circiter tertia ab antecursoribus de Crassi adventu certior factus,
eo die milia passuum XX procedit. Crassum Samarobrivae praeficit
legionemque attribuit, quod ibi impedimenta exercitus, obsides civitatum,
litteras publicas, frumentumque omne quod eo tolerandae hiemis
5   causa devexerat relinquebat. Fabius, ut imperatum erat, non ita multum
moratus in itinere cum legione occurrit. Labienus interitu Sabini et caede
cohortium cognita, cum omnes ad eum Treverorum copiae venissent
veritus ne, si ex hibernis fugae similem profectionem fecisset, hostium
impetum sustinere non posset praesertim quos recenti victoria efferri
10 sciret, litteras Caesari remittit, quanto cum periculo legionem ex hibernis
educturus esset; rem gestam in Eburonibus perscribit; docet omnes
equitatus peditatusque copias Treverorum tria milia passuum longe ab
suis castris consedisse. [48] Caesar, consilio eius probato, etsi opinione
trium legionum deiectus ad duas redierat, tamen unum communis
15 salutis auxilium in celeritate ponebat. Venit magnis itineribus in
Nerviorum fines. Ibi ex captivis cognoscit quae apud Ciceronem gerantur
quantoque in periculo res sit. Tum cuidam ex equitibus Gallis magnis
praemiis persuadet uti ad Ciceronem epistolam deferat. Hanc Graecis
conscriptam litteris mittit, ne intercepta epistola nostra ab hostibus
20 consilia cognoscantur. Si adire non possit, monet ut tragulam cum epistola
ad ammentum deligata intra munitionem castrorum abiciat. In litteris
scribit se cum legionibus profectum celeriter adfore; hortatur ut pristinam
virtutem retineat. Gallus periculum veritus, ut erat praeceptum, tragulam
mittit. Haec casu ad turrim adhaesit neque ab nostris biduo animadversa
25 tertio die a quodam milite conspicitur, dempta ad Ciceronem defertur. Ille
perlectam in conventu militum recitat maximaque omnes laetitia adficit.
Tum fumi incendiorum procul videbantur; quae res omnem dubitationem
adventus legionum expulit.

Preparatory Questions

Line 1   Identify the case and use of *hora circiter tertia*. **ablative of time when**

Who is the implied subject of *certior factus*? **understood he (Caesar)**

Line 2   Identify the case and use of *milia passuum XX*. **accusative of extent**

Identify the case and use of *Samarobrivae*. **dative, used with *praeficit***

Line 3   What indirect object must be supplied with *attribuit*? **ei**

Lines 3–5   Find four direct objects of *relinquebat*. **impedimenta (line 3), obsides (line 3), litteras (line 4), frumentum (line 4)**

Line 4   What part of speech is *eo*? **adverb**

Line 5   Identify the form and use of *devexerat*. **pluperfect indicative, verb of relative clause**

                What part of speech is *non*? **adverb**

                What does it modify? **moratus (line 6)**

Lines 6–7   Find the two nouns of the ablative absolute. **interitu, caede**

Lines 7–8   Identify the type of *cum* clause. **circumstantial**

Lines 8–9   Find a conditional clause. **si . . . fecisset**

Line 8   Identify the case and use of *fugae*. **dative with similem**

Line 9   What is the antecedent of *quos*? **hostium (line 8)**

                Identify the case and use of *victoria*. **ablative of means**

Lines 10–11   What verb from line 11 may be used with *quanto . . . esset*? **perscribit**

Line 13   What is the antecedent of *suis*? **he in docet (i.e., Labienus, line 11)**

                Find an ablative absolute. **consilio probato**

Lines 13–15   Find a conditional clause. **etsi . . . deiectus**

Line 16   Identify the gender, case, and use of *quae*. **neuter nominative, subject (of relative clause)**

Line 17   Identify and explain the mood of *sit*. **subjunctive in an indirect question**

                Identify the case and use of *cuidam*. **dative, object of persuadet (line 18)**

Line 18   What is the antecedent of *hanc*? **epistolam**

Line 19   Find an ablative absolute. **intercepta epistola nostra**

Line 20   Find a conditional clause. **Si . . . possit**

Line 22   Identify the subject of *adfore*. **se**

Line 24   What is the antecedent of *haec*? **tragulam (line 23)**

Line 25   Identify the case and use of *tertio die*. **ablative of time when**

                To what does *dempta* refer? **tragulam (line 23)**

Line 27   Identify the subject of *videbantur*. **fumi**

Multiple Choice Questions *Suggested time: 26 minutes*

1. In line 1 Caesar is notified of the approach of Crassus by
   a. the smoke of his fires
   b. Crassus's arrival
   c. his advance guard
   d. a smuggled letter

2. In line 3 *quod* is best translated
   a. which
   b. where
   c. because
   d. why

3. *Tolerandae hiemis causa* (lines 4–5) is best translated
   a. a tolerable winter
   b. for enduring the winter
   c. because of the winter
   d. during the winter

4. In lines 5–6 *non multum moratus* is an example of
   a. anaphora
   b. hyperbole
   c. chiasmus
   d. litotes

5. Labienus (line 6) is cautious because
   a. that is his nature
   b. he distrusts Caesar
   c. there has been a Roman disaster
   d. the weather is bad

6. In line 7 *ad* is best translated
   a. near
   b. for
   c. over
   d. to

7. In line 8 Labienus does not want a departure that will appear to be
   a. ill-planned
   b. sneaky
   c. like a flight
   d. like an attack

8. *Praesertim* (line 9) is best translated
   a. especially
   b. extra
   c. first
   d. recent

9. *Educturus* (line 11) is a
   a. simple verb
   b. future participle within verb
   c. gerund
   d. infinitive

10. *Rem gestam* (line 11) refers to
    a. military achievement
    b. plot foiled
    c. new plan
    d. future hope

11. In line 11 *docet* is best translated
    a. he reenacts
    b. he explains
    c. he acts
    d. he reasons

12. In line 12 *equitatus peditatusque* is a(n)
    a. nominative appositive
    b. genitive of possession
    c. genitive of description
    d. accusative of content

13. In line 12 *longe* is best translated
    a. far
    b. long
    c. away
    d. by far

14. In line 13 *opinione* is best translated
    a. idea
    b. expectation
    c. belief
    d. argument

15. *Magnis itineribus* (line 15) underscores Caesar's dependence upon
    a. *fines*
    b. *consilia*
    c. *celeritas*
    d. *Nervii*

16. *Magnis praemiis* (lines 17–18) is
    a. an ablative of means
    b. an ablative absolute
    c. a dative of possession
    d. an indirect object

17. In line 21 *abiciat* is subjunctive because it is the verb of
    a. a clause of result
    b. a condition contrary to fact
    c. an indirect command
    d. a clause of purpose

18. *Veritus* (line 23) comes from a verb meaning
    a. to verify
    b. to fear
    c. to avoid
    d. to come

19. In lines 24–25 we learn that two days pass before the message is read because
    a. it is in Greek
    b. it is mangled
    c. it is stuck to a tower
    d. the soldiers conceal it

20. *Perlectam* (line 26) refers to the
    a. *tragulam* (line 23)
    b. *tertio die* (line 25)
    c. *epistola* (line 20)
    d. *periculum* (line 23)

21. In line 27, the entrapped Romans rejoice to see

    a. Caesar's soldiers   **b. fires in the distance**

    c. the enemy retreating   d. Caesar's letter

22. In lines 27–28 doubt about the arrival of more legions

    a. grows   b. decreases somewhat

    c. is removed   d. remains

Translation *Suggested time: 15 minutes*

Tum cuidam ex equitibus Gallis magnis praemiis persuadet uti ad
Ciceronem epistolam deferat. Hanc Graecis conscriptam litteris mittit,
ne intercepta epistola nostra ab hostibus consilia cognoscantur. Si adire
non possit, monet ut tragulam cum epistola ad ammentum deligata intra
5   munitionem castrorum abiciat.

20 chunks. 10 points, ½ point each.

Tum cuidam	then a certain man
ex equitibus Gallis	from the Gallic cavalry
magnis praemiis persuadet	he persuades by great rewards
uti . . . deferat	that he might carry
ad Ciceronem	to Cicero
epistolam	a letter
Hanc . . . conscriptam	this, written
Graecis litteris	in Greek letters
mittit	he sends
ne intercepta epistola nostra	so that . . . not, our letter having been intercepted
ab hostibus	by the enemy
consilia cognoscantur	the plans may be learned
Si adire non possit	If he could not approach
monet	he advised
ut tragulam	that a spear
cum epistola . . . deligata	with the letter tied
ad ammentum	to a strap
intra munitionem	within the fortification
castrorum	of the camp
abiciat	he throw

Short Analysis Questions

> Crassum Samarobrivae praeficit legionemque attribuit, quod ibi
> impedimenta exercitus, obsides civitatum, litteras publicas, frumentumque
> omne quod eo tolerandae hiemis causa devexerat relinquebat.

1. Why in this emergency does Caesar leave an entire legion and an experienced commander behind? What does this tell you about Caesar's estimation of his and his rescue party's danger? Cite the Latin that supports your answer or accurately paraphrase.

   He leaves Crassus and his legion behind to care for the army's baggage, the hostages, public records, and the food supply—*quod ibi impedimenta exercitus, obsides civitatum, litteras publicas, frumentumque omne quod eo tolerandae hiemis causa devexerat relinquebat* (lines 1–3). Since he is leaving all these important possessions behind with an experienced commander and a legion, he indicates that there is a possibility that he and the rescue force will not return.

> Labienus interitu Sabini et caede cohortium cognita, cum omnes ad eum
> Treverorum copiae venissent veritus ne, si ex hibernis fugae similem
> profectionem fecisset, hostium impetum sustinere non posset, praesertim
> quos recenti victoria efferri sciret, litteras Caesari remittit: quanto cum
> 5 periculo legionem ex hibernis educturus esset; rem gestam in Eburonibus
> perscribit; docet omnes equitatus peditatusque copias Treverorum tria
> milia passuum longe ab suis castris consedisse.

2. What two factors does Labienus tell Caesar pose great dangers to his legion if he moves? Cite the Latin that supports your answer or accurately paraphrase.

   There has been a recent disaster to the Romans, and all the Treveri are encamped very close to Labienus—*interitu Sabini et caede cohortium cognita, cum omnes ad eum Treverorum copiae venissent* (lines 1–2).

3. What effect has the disaster that befell Sabinus and his troops had on the Gauls? Cite the Latin that supports your answer or accurately paraphrase.

   The Gauls were elated by their victory and expectant of further success—*quos recenti victoria efferri sciret* (line 4).

4. What facts about the number and position of Treveran troops does Labienus give? What does he hint may be their purpose? Cite the Latin that supports your answer or accurately paraphrase.

   All the Treveri troops both horse and foot are encamped very near Labienus—*omnes equitatus peditatusque copias Treverorum tria milia passuum longe ab suis castris consedisse* (lines 6–7). He hints that their purpose may be a full attack on him at the first opportunity.

Essay *Suggested time: 20 minutes*

Hora circiter tertia ab antecursoribus de Crassi adventu certior factus, eo
die milia passuum XX procedit . . .

Fabius, ut imperatum erat, non ita multum moratus in itinere cum legione
occurrit . . .

5   Caesar, consilio eius probato, etsi opinione trium legionum deiectus
ad duas redierat, tamen unum communis salutis auxilium in celeritate
ponebat. Venit magnis itineribus in Nerviorum fines.

[Lines in excerpts correspond to lines 1–2, 4–5, and 15–16 of the chapter Latin passage.]

In these excerpts we see the rapidity with which all Caesar's forces responded to crises. Discuss the
use of main verbs, times of day, and distances, as well as the use of descriptive words and phrases,
which indicate very rapid movement and culminate in the phrase that might well be considered one
of Caesar's basic principles, "*unum communis salutis auxilium in celeritate ponebat.*" How does Caesar's
narration of events add to the feeling that speed is the of the essence in these situations?

Support your assertions with references to the Latin text throughout the passages above. All Latin
words must be copied or their line numbers provided, AND they must be translated or paraphrased
closely enough that it is clear that you understand the Latin. It is your responsibility to convince the
reader that you are basing your conclusions on the Latin text and not merely on a general recollection
of the passage. Direct your answer to the question; do not merely summarize the passage. Please write
your essay on a separate piece of paper.

**Teachers should review the Essay Scoring Guidelines given at the beginning of this manual with
students.**

**"One aid to communal safety is in swiftness." In this passage Caesar has proved once again that he
lives by this principle, and he has obviously taught it to his commanders, as he learns at the third hour
that Crassus has arrived, and Caesar advances twenty miles in that one day to meet him—*Hora circiter
tertia ab antecursoribus de Crassi adventu certior factus, eo die milia passuum XX procedit* (lines 1–2).**

**Crassus's early arrival and Caesar's twenty-mile march both indicate decisive action that takes
very little time for deliberation.**

**Fabius has not delayed and meets him—*Fabius, ut imperatum erat, non ita multum moratus in iti-
nere cum legione occurrit . . .* (lines 3–4). Caesar, with all the troops he has so quickly raised, comes by
forced marches into the land of the Nervii—*Venit magnis itineribus in Nerviorum fines* (line 7).**

**The time of Fabius's arrival is not mentioned, but we are assured that he has not delayed. Caesar
goes forward by forced marches, which may make an even greater speed than that very impressive
twenty miles in one day.**

Notes

CHAPTER 21: BOOK 6.13
DRUIDS

[13] In omni Gallia eorum hominum qui aliquo sunt numero atque honore,
genera sunt duo. Nam plebes paene servorum habetur loco, quae nihil
audet per se, nullo adhibetur consilio. Plerique, cum aut aere alieno aut
magnitudine tributorum aut iniuria potentiorum premuntur, sese in
servitutem dicant nobilibus, quibus in hos eadem omnia sunt iura quae
dominis in servos. Sed de his duobus generibus alterum est Druidum,
alterum equitum. Illi rebus divinis intersunt, sacrificia publica ac privata
procurant, religiones interpretantur: ad hos magnus adulescentium
numerus disciplinae causa concurrit, magnoque hi sunt apud eos honore.
Nam fere de omnibus controversiis publicis privatisque constituunt et,
si quod est admissum facinus, si caedes facta, si de hereditate, de finibus
controversia est, idem decernunt, praemia poenasque constituunt; si qui
aut privatus aut populus eorum decreto non stetit, sacrificiis interdicunt.
Haec poena apud eos est gravissima. Quibus ita est interdictum, hi
numero impiorum ac sceleratorum habentur, his omnes decedunt, aditum
sermonemque defugiunt, ne quid ex contagione incommodi accipiant,
neque his petentibus ius redditur neque honos ullus communicatur. His
autem omnibus Druidibus praeest unus, qui summam inter eos habet
auctoritatem. Hoc mortuo, aut si qui ex reliquis excellit dignitate succedit,
aut, si sunt plures pares, suffragio Druidum, non numquam etiam armis
de principatu contendunt. Hi certo anni tempore in finibus Carnutum,
quae regio totius Galliae media habetur, considunt in loco consecrato. Huc
omnes undique, qui controversias habent conveniunt eorumque decretis
iudiciisque parent. Disciplina in Britannia reperta atque inde in Galliam
translata esse existimatur, et nunc qui diligentius eam rem cognoscere
volunt plerumque illo discendi causa proficiscuntur.

Preparatory Questions

Line 1   What is the antecedent of *qui*? **hominum**

Line 2   What does *duo* modify? **genera**

            Identify the subject of *habetur*. **plebes**

Line 3   Give the infinitive form of *audet*. **audere**

            Identify the subject of *audet* and *adhibetur*. **quae (line 2)**

Line 4	Find a genitive of possession. **tributorum/potentiorum**
	Find a reflexive pronoun. **sese**
Line 5	What is the antecedent of *hos*? **plerique (line 3)**
Line 6	What verb must be understood? **sunt (as verb of relative clause)**
Line 7	*Illi* refers to what group? **Druids**
Lines 7–8	Find three verbs whose subject is *illi*. **intersunt, procurant, interpretantur**
Line 9	Identify the case and use of *disciplinae*. **genitive after *causa***
	Find the antecedent of *eos*. **illi (line 7)**
Lines 11–12	Find a conditional clause. **si . . . facinus or si caedes facta [est] or si de hereditate, . . . controversia est**
	What is the tense and voice of *est admissum*? **perfect passive**
Line 12	Find the direct objects of *constituunt*. **praemia poenasque**
	Find the subject of a conditional clause. **qui**
Lines 14–15	Find the antecedent of *quibus*. **eos**
Line 15	Give the case and use of *his*. **ablative of separation**
Line 16	What is the subject of *defugiunt*? **omnes (line 15)**
Line 17	Identify the form, case, and use of *petentibus*. **present participle active, dative, modifies *his***
Line 18	What is the subject of *praeest*? **unus**
Lines 19–20	Find an ablative absolute. **hoc mortuo**
	Find two conditional clauses. **si . . . succedit; si . . . pares**
Line 21	What does *certo* modify? **tempore**
Line 22	What does *totius* modify? **Galliae**
Line 23	What part of speech is *undique*? **adverb**
Lines 23–24	Give the case and use of *decretis iudiciisque*. **dative object with *parent***
Line 24	What word must be supplied with *reperta*? **est**
Line 25	Identify the form and use of *diligentius*. **comparative adverb, modifies *cognoscere***
Line 26	Identify the form and use of *discendi*. **objective genitive gerund after *causa***

Multiple Choice Questions *Suggested time: 25 minutes*

1. *Numero* (line 1) is best translated

   a. number

   c. count

   b. multitude

   d. rank

2. In line 2 *genera* is in the

   a. nominative plural

   c. ablative singular

   b. nominative singular

   d. dative singular

3. *Plerique* (line 3) refers to

   a. *genera* (line 2)

   c. *consilio* (line 3)

   b. *plebes* (line 2)

   d. *servorum* (line 2)

4. Lines 3–4 contain three

   a. ablatives of agent

   c. ablatives of means

   b. ablatives of manner

   d. ablatives of time

5. In line 5 *dicant* is best translated

   a. they predict

   c. they give . . . up

   b. they say

   d. they teach

6. *Generibus* (line 6) governs the understood noun

   a. *servorum*

   c. *equitum*

   b. *hominum*

   d. *Druidum*

7. In lines 6–7 *alterum . . . alterum* is best translated

   a. to . . . from

   c. one . . . the other

   b. some . . . others

   d. ours . . . yours

8. In lines 7–8 we learn that the Druids are in charge of matters of

   a. money

   c. war

   b. religion

   d. the economy

9. In line 10 *constituunt* is best translated

   a. they stand

   c. they decide

   b. they travel

   d. they ignore

10. In line 12 *idem* refers to

    a. the common people

    c. the decisions

    b. the Druids

    d. the knights

11. *Stetit* (line 13) is best translated
    a. **has abided by**
    b. stood under
    c. saw
    d. built

12. In line 16 *ne . . . accipiant* is a(n)
    a. clause of result
    b. ablative of means
    c. **clause of purpose**
    d. relative clause

13. In lines 16–17 we learn that
    a. Druids have little power
    b. decisions are arbitrated
    c. Druids are merciful
    d. **interdiction is irreversible**

14. In line 18 *omnibus* modifies
    a. *his* (line 17)
    b. *honos* (line 17)
    c. ***Druidibus* (line 18)**
    d. *ullus* (line 17)

15. In line 19 *dignitate* is best translated
    a. good manners
    b. influence
    c. grace
    d. **worthiness**

16. In line 20 *non numquam* is best translated
    a. **sometimes**
    b. never
    c. immediately
    d. at length

17. In line 21 *anni* is in the
    a. nominative
    b. **genitive**
    c. dative
    d. ablative

18. In line 22 we learn that the meeting place is considered
    a. very pleasant
    b. **the center of all Gaul**
    c. cool in summer
    d. defensible

19. In line 23 *qui . . . habent* is a
    a. **relative clause**
    b. conditional statement
    c. purpose clause
    d. result clause

20. In line 24 *disciplina* is best translated
    a. behavior correction
    b. **teaching**
    c. good manners
    d. punishment

21. In lines 24–26 we learn that

    a. the most serious students go to Britain
    c. British ideas are different

    b. Britain and Gaul are at war
    d. the Druids do not respect Britain

Translation *Suggested time: 15 minutes*

Haec poena apud eos est gravissima. Quibus ita est interdictum, hi numero impiorum ac sceleratorum habentur, his omnes decedunt, aditum sermonemque defugiunt, ne quid ex contagione incommodi accipiant, neque his petentibus ius redditur neque honos ullus communicatur.

16 chunks. 8 points, ½ point each.

Haec poena	**this punishment**
apud eos	**among them**
est gravissima	**is very serious**
Quibus	**(for) whom/those**
ita est interdictum	**it is so forbidden**
hi ... habentur	**these ... are held/considered**
numero impiorum ac sceleratorum	**in the number of impious and criminal**
his omnes decedunt	**all depart from them**
aditum sermonemque defugiunt	**they flee their approach and talk**
ne ... accipiant	**lest ... they receive**
quid ex contagione incommodi	**any harm/disaster from the contact**
neque	**neither**
his petentibus	**to those asking**
ius redditur	**it the right restored**
neque	**nor**
honos ullus communicatur	**is any honor shared/communicated**

Short Analysis Questions

Nam plebes paene servorum habetur loco, quae nihil audet per se, nullo adhibetur consilio. Plerique, cum aut aere alieno aut magnitudine tributorum aut iniuria potentiorum premuntur, sese in servitutem dicant nobilibus, quibus in hos eadem omnia sunt iura quae dominis in servos.

1. What place in the power structure do the common people have? Cite the Latin that supports your answer or accurately paraphrase.

    The common people have no place in the power structure; they are held almost as slaves who dare do nothing and who are never included in consultation—*plebes paene servorum habetur loco, quae nihil audet per se, nullo adhibetur consilio* (lines 1–2).

2. What are the three major factors that bring the common people to financial ruin? Cite the Latin that supports your answer or accurately paraphrase.

The common people are ruined by debt, taxes, and deliberate injustice—*cum aut aere alieno aut magnitudine tributorum aut iniuria potentiorum premuntur* (lines 2–3).

3. What happens to them then? Cite the Latin that supports your answer or accurately paraphrase.

They sell themselves into slavery to some noble—*sese in servitutem dicant nobilibus* (lines 3–4).

> His autem omnibus Druidibus praeest unus, qui summam inter eos habet auctoritatem. Hoc mortuo, aut si qui ex reliquis excellit dignitate succedit, aut, si sunt plures pares, suffragio Druidum, non numquam etiam armis de principatu contendunt.

4. How are the Druids themselves ruled? Cite the Latin that supports your answer or accurately paraphrase.

One supreme Druid rules them completely—*His autem omnibus Druidibus praeest unus, qui summam inter eos habet auctoritatem* (lines 1–2).

5. Explain the three ways by which new rulership is chosen. Cite the Latin that supports your answer or accurately paraphrase.

If there is one man obviously outstanding, he succeeds the dead leader—*Hoc mortuo aut si qui ex reliquis excellit dignitate succedit* (line 2). If there are several strong candidates, a vote is taken among the Druids—*si sunt plures pares, suffragio Druidum* (line 3). If neither of these conditions prevail, the Druids may decide by armed conflict—*non numquam etiam armis de principatu contendunt* (lines 3–4).

Essay *Suggested time: 20 minutes*

Illi rebus divinis intersunt, sacrificia publica ac privata procurant,
religiones interpretantur: ad hos magnus adulescentium numerus
disciplinae causa concurrit, magnoque hi sunt apud eos honore. Nam fere
de omnibus controversiis publicis privatisque constituunt et, si quod est
5   admissum facinus, si caedes facta, si de hereditate, de finibus controversia
est, idem decernunt, praemia poenasque constituunt; si qui aut privatus
aut populus eorum decreto non stetit, sacrificiis interdicunt. Haec poena
apud eos est gravissima.

The Druids held great power in Gallic life. In a short essay, discuss the broad range of their power over religious and secular life and their means of enforcing their will.

Support your assertions with references to the Latin text throughout the passages above. All Latin words must be copied or their line numbers provided, AND they must be translated or paraphrased closely enough that it is clear that you understand the Latin. It is your responsibility to convince the reader that you are basing your conclusions on the Latin text and not merely on a general recollection of the passage. Direct your answer to the question; do not merely summarize the passage. Please write your essay on a separate piece of paper.

Teachers should review the Essay Scoring Guidelines given at the beginning of this manual with students.

Since the Druids preside over religious matters, carry out public and private sacrifices, and interpret religious questions and signs from the gods, they control religion completely—*Illi rebus divinis intersunt, sacrificia publica ac privata procurant, religiones interpretantur* (lines 1–2). Because of their great power youngsters come to learn from them, so they can perpetuate their system—*magnus adulescentium numerus disciplinae causa concurrit* (lines 2–3). They settle disputes both public and private, make decrees about criminal matters, and set up both rewards and punishments—*controversiis publicis privatisque constituunt et, si quod est admissum facinus, si caedes facta, si de hereditate, de finibus controversia est, idem decernunt, praemia poenasque constituunt* (lines 4–6). Thus they control both civil and criminal law. If any of their decrees are not carried out, they fall back on their religious powers and forbid the dissidents from the sacrifices—*si qui aut privatus aut populus eorum decreto non stetit, sacrificiis interdicunt* (lines 6–7). Thus the dissident has not been cleansed by attending sacrifices.

Such a system was not likely to be overthrown from within, as the control was so absolute. If the Romans had not gone and conquered Gaul, the Druids might still be in power.

Notes

CHAPTER 22: BOOK 6.14–16
POWER AND PRIVILEGE AMONG THE GAULS

[14] Druides a bello abesse consuerunt, neque tributa una cum reliquis
pendunt; militiae vacationem omniumque rerum habent immunitatem.
Tantis excitati praemiis et sua sponte multi in disciplinam conveniunt et
a parentibus propinquisque mittuntur. Magnum ibi numerum versuum
5   ediscere dicuntur. Itaque annos non nulli XX in disciplina permanent.
Neque fas esse existimant ea litteris mandare, cum in reliquis fere rebus,
publicis privatisque rationibus, Graecis litteris utantur. Id mihi duabus
de causis instituisse videntur, quod neque in vulgum disciplinam
efferri velint neque eos qui discunt litteris confisos minus memoriae
10   studere; quod fere plerisque accidit ut praesidio litterarum diligentiam
in perdiscendo ac memoriam remittant. In primis hoc volunt persuadere,
non interire animas sed ab aliis post mortem transire ad alios, atque hoc
maxime ad virtutem excitari putant, metu mortis neglecto. Multa praeterea
de sideribus atque eorum motu, de mundi ac terrarum magnitudine,
15   de rerum natura, de deorum immortalium vi ac potestate disputant et
iuventuti tradunt. [15] Alterum genus est equitum. Hi, cum est usus atque
aliquod bellum incidit (quod fere ante Caesaris adventum quot annis
accidere solebat, uti aut ipsi iniurias inferrent aut inlatas propulsarent),
omnes in bello versantur; atque eorum ut quisque est genere copiisque
20   amplissimus, ita plurimos circum se ambactos clientesque habet. Hanc
unam gratiam potentiamque noverunt. [16] Natio est omnium Gallorum
admodum dedita religionibus, atque ob eam causam qui sunt adfecti
gravioribus morbis quique in proeliis periculisque versantur aut pro
victimis homines immolant aut se immolaturos vovent, administrisque
25   ad ea sacrificia Druidibus utuntur; quod, pro vita hominis nisi hominis
vita reddatur, non posse deorum immortalium numen placari arbitrantur,
publiceque eiusdem generis habent instituta sacrificia. Alii immani
magnitudine simulacra habent, quorum contexta viminibus membra vivis
hominibus complent; quibus succensis circumventi flamma exanimantur
30   homines. Supplicia eorum qui in furto aut in latrocinio aut aliqua noxia
sint comprehensi gratiora dis immortalibus esse arbitrantur, sed, cum eius
generis copia deficit, etiam ad innocentium supplicia descendunt.

Preparatory Questions

Line 1	Identify the tense and mood of *consuerunt*. **perfect indicative**
	Identify the case and use of *tributa*. **accusative, direct object of *pendunt* (line 2)**
Line 3	Identify the case and use of *tantis*. **ablative of means**
	What word does it modify? ***praemiis***
Line 4	Identify the tense and voice of *mittuntur*. **present passive**
	Identify the case and use of *versuum*. **partitive genitive (with *magnum numerum*)**
Line 5	On what word does *ediscere* depend? ***dicuntur***
Lines 6–7	Find a *cum* clause. ***cum in reliquis fere rebus, publicis privatisque rationibus, Graecis litteris utantur***
	What type of *cum* clause is it? **concessive**
Line 7	Explain the case and use of *litteris*. **ablative, object of *utantur***
Lines 8–9	What kind of clause does *quod* introduce? **causal**
Line 9	Explain the tense and mood of *velint*. **present subjunctive, subjunctive used where the explanation given is on the authority of someone other than the speaker/narrator**
	Identify the tense and voice of *efferri*. **present passive**
Line 11	Identify the form and use of *perdiscendo*. **gerund, in ablative, after the preposition *in***
Line 12	Explain the case and use of *mortem*. **accusative, object of the preposition *post***
Line 13	What degree and part of speech is *maxime*? **superlative adverb**
	What is the subject of *excitari*? **the subject is unexpressed; the implied subject is "people" or "men"**
Line 14	To what does *eorum* refer? ***sideribus***
Line 16	Identify the case and use of *iuventuti*. **dative with the intransitive verb *tradunt***
	Identify the case and use of *equitum*. **genitive of description**
	Find a *cum* clause. ***cum est usus atque aliquod bellum incidit***
Line 17	What is the antecedent of *quod*? ***bellum***
	What does *quot annis* (usually *quotannis*) modify? ***accidere* (line 18)**
Line 18	What does *inlatas* modify? ***iniurias***
Line 19	Explain the form and use of *versantur*. **third person plural present passive indicative, main verb in its clause**

Identify the case and use of *genere*. **ablative of specification**

Line 20   What is the object of *habet*? **plurimos . . . ambactos clientesque**

Line 21   Identify the case and use of *gratiam*. **accusative, direct object of *noverunt***

Line 22   What does *dedita* modify? **natio (line 21)**

What word(s) does *ob* govern? **eam causam**

Line 23   Explain the case and use of *morbis*. **ablative of means**

Line 24   Identify the tense and mood of *immolant*. **present indicative**

What is its subject? **the whole relative clause (*qui sunt adfecti . . . versantur* [lines 22–23])**

Line 25   Identify the case and use of *Druidibus*. **ablative object with *utuntur***

Line 26   Identify the case and use of *vita*. **nominative, subject of *reddatur***

Identify the form and use of *placari*. **present passive infinitive, complementary with *posse***

Line 28   Identify the case and use of *magnitudine*. **ablative of description**

Identify the case and use of *quorum*. **genitive of possession**

Identify the form and use of *contexta*. **perfect passive participle, accusative modifying *membra***

Line 29   What is the subject of *complent*? **Alii (line 27)**

Identify the subject of *exanimantur*. **homines (line 30)**

Line 30   What three prepositional phrases are connected by *aut*? **in furto, in latrocinio, [in] aliqua noxia**

Line 31   Identify the form and syntax of *sint comprehensi*. **third person plural perfect passive subjunctive, relative clause of characteristic**

Identify the form and use of *gratiora*. **comparative adjective, accusative plural neuter, modifying *supplicia* (line 32)**

Line 32   Identify the tense and mood of *deficit*. **present indicative**

Identify the case and use of *supplicia*. **accusative, object of the preposition *ad***

What is the subject of *descendunt*? **subject is unexpressed, "they/the Gauls" understood**

Multiple Choice Questions *Suggested time: 34 minutes*

1. In line 2 *pendunt* is translated
    a. they hang
    b. they pay
    c. they are paid
    d. they discuss

2. In line 2 the phrase *omniumque rerum* is dependent upon
    a. *militiae* (line 2)
    b. *vacationem* (line 2)
    c. *immunitatem* (line 2)
    d. *habent* (line 2)

3. The phrase *sua sponte* (line 3) is translated
    a. with their wives
    b. via a bridge
    c. openly
    d. voluntarily

4. The grammatical explanation for *annos* (line 5) is
    a. time within which
    b. duration of time
    c. direct object
    d. accusative with numerals

5. In line 6 *cum* is translated
    a. although
    b. with
    c. because
    d. when

6. From lines 6–7 we learn that the Druids
    a. were taught by Greeks
    b. use writing only for religious purposes
    c. render their financial accounts orally
    d. do not entrust their teachings to writing

7. In line 9 *eos* refers to
    a. the letters
    b. the students
    c. the teachers
    d. the training

8. The case of *litteris* (line 9) is
    a. nominative
    b. ablative
    c. dative
    d. accusative

9. In lines 10–11 (*ut praesidio . . . remittant*) we find an example of a
    a. result clause
    b. passive periphrastic
    c. purpose clause
    d. jussive subjunctive

10. The subject of *non interire* (line 12) is
    a. *persuadere* (line 11)
    b. *animas* (line 12)
    c. *primis* (line 11)
    d. *volunt* (line 11)

11. In line 13 *metu . . . neglecto* is an ablative
    a. of cause
    b. of means
    c. of manner
    d. absolute

12. In lines 13–16 we find an example of
    a. hyperbole
    b. apostrophe
    c. chiasmus
    d. anaphora

13. In line 16 *cum* is translated
    a. although
    b. with
    c. because
    d. when

14. In line 17 *aliquod* is translated
    a. some
    b. which
    c. anyone at all
    d. whichever

15. In line 18 *inlatas* is a form derived from
    a. *intollere*
    b. *inferre*
    c. *inlatare*
    d. *inlare*

16. In line 19 *genere copiisque* is ablative of
    a. source
    b. manner
    c. specification
    d. separation

17. The degree of the adjective *plurimos* (line 20) is
    a. positive
    b. comparative
    c. superlative
    d. exponential

18. In line 22 *admodum* is a(n)
    a. adjective
    b. adverb
    c. preposition
    d. conjunction

19. The tense and voice of *sunt adfecti* (line 22) are
    a. present passive
    b. perfect active
    c. present active
    d. perfect passive

20. In line 23 (*quique in proeliis periculisque*) we find an example of
    a. metonymy
    b. alliteration
    c. chiasmus
    d. anaphora

21. From lines 21–25 (*Natio . . . utuntur*) we learn that the Gauls
    a. **engage in human sacrifice**
    b. were often afflicted by disease
    c. are not religious at all
    d. throw themselves on the pyre as offerings

22. The main verb of the causal clause in lines 25–26 (*quod . . . arbitrantur*) is
    a. *reddatur* (line 26)
    b. *posse* (line 26)
    c. *placari* (line 26)
    d. **arbitrantur (line 26)**

23. On what word does *deorum immortalium* (line 26) depend?
    a. *posse* (line 26)
    b. **numen (line 26)**
    c. *arbitrantur* (line 26)
    d. *placari* (line 26)

24. The antecedent of *quorum* (line 28) is
    a. *magnitudine* (line 28)
    b. *contexta* (line 28)
    c. **simulacra (line 28)**
    d. *membra* (line 28)

25. *Circumventi* (line 29) modifies
    a. **homines (line 30)**
    b. *flamma* (line 29)
    c. *succensis* (line 29)
    d. *exanimantur* (line 29)

26. The case of *dis* (line 31) is
    a. nominative
    b. accusative
    c. **dative**
    d. ablative

27. In line 31 *cum* is translated
    a. although
    b. with
    c. because
    d. **when**

28. The object of the preposition *ad* (line 32) is
    a. *gratiora* (line 31)
    b. **supplicia (line 32)**
    c. *innocentium* (line 32)
    d. *descendunt* (line 32)

Translation *Suggested time: 20 minutes*

Alterum genus est equitum. Hi, cum est usus atque aliquod bellum incidit
(quod fere ante Caesaris adventum quot annis accidere solebat, uti aut
ipsi iniurias inferrent aut inlatas propulsarent), omnes in bello versantur;
atque eorum ut quisque est genere copiisque amplissimus, ita plurimos
5 circum se ambactos clientesque habet. Hanc unam gratiam potentiamque
noverunt.

24 chunks. 12 points, ½ point each.

Alterum genus	The other class
est equitum	is of knights
Hi	These men
cum est usus	when there is a need
atque aliquod bellum	and some war
incidit	occurs
(quod fere	(which generally just about
ante Caesaris adventum	before Caesar's arrival
quot annis	every year
accidere solebat	used to happen
uti aut ipsi iniurias inferrent	with the result that either they engage in assaults
aut inlatas propulsarent)	or they ward off assaults that have been launched)
omnes in bello versantur	they are all engaged in warfare
atque eorum	and of those
ut quisque est	as each man is
genere copiisque	in class and resources
amplissimus	most distinguished
ita plurimos	so the greatest number (of)
circum se	around him
ambactos clientesque	retainers and clients
habet	he has
Hanc unam	This (is the) one (form of)
gratiam potentiamque	influence and power
noverunt	they know

Short Analysis Questions

Druides a bello abesse consuerunt, neque tributa una cum reliquis
pendunt; militiae vacationem omniumque rerum habent immunitatem.
Tantis excitati praemiis et sua sponte multi in disciplinam conveniunt et
a parentibus propinquisque mittuntur. Magnum ibi numerum versuum
5 ediscere dicuntur. Itaque annos non nulli XX in disciplina permanent.

1. In terms of military service and political life, what distinguishes the Druids from the rest of the tribe? Cite the Latin that supports your answer and translate or accurately paraphrase.

The Druids abstain from warfare—*a bello abesse consuerunt* (line 1)—and they are not required to pay tribute (taxes) —*neque tributa una cum reliquis pendunt* (lines 1–2). In fact, they are free from military service and civic obligations altogether—*militiae vacationem omniumque rerum habent immunitatem* (line 2).

2. Were Gallic families eager to send their sons to be taught by the Druids? Cite the Latin that supports your answer and translate or accurately paraphrase.

Yes. The families were spurred on to send their young men to study with them because of the financial and personal rewards that becoming a Druid offered: *tantis excitati praemiis . . . multi . . . et a parentibus propinquisque mittuntur* (lines 3–4).

3. How long was the training period among the Druids? Cite the Latin that supports your answer and translate or accurately paraphrase.

Several Druids-in-training stayed for as long as twenty years—*annos non nulli XX in disciplina permanent* (line 5).

Neque fas esse existimant ea litteris mandare, cum in reliquis fere rebus,
publicis privatisque rationibus, Graecis litteris utantur. Id mihi duabus
de causis instituisse videntur, quod neque in vulgum disciplinam
efferri velint neque eos qui discunt litteris confisos minus memoriae
5   studere; quod fere plerisque accidit ut praesidio litterarum diligentiam
in perdiscendo ac memoriam remittant. In primis hoc volunt persuadere,
non interire animas sed ab aliis post mortem transire ad alios, atque hoc
maxime ad virtutem excitari putant, metu mortis neglecto. Multa praeterea
de sideribus atque eorum motu, de mundi ac terrarum magnitudine,
10   de rerum natura, de deorum immortalium vi ac potestate disputant et
iuventuti tradunt.

4. In lines 1–2, what does Caesar tell us about the use of writing among the Druids? Cite the Latin that supports your answer and translate or accurately paraphrase.

The Druids did not permit their teachings to be written down—*neque fas esse existimant ea litteris mandare*—but in other aspects of life, Greek characters were used for written records—*cum in reliquis fere rebus, publicis privatisque rationibus, Graecis litteris utantur*.

5. What two explanations does Caesar offer for cases where writing is not used? Cite the Latin that supports your answer and translate or accurately paraphrase.

The first reason is that the Druids wanted their teachings to remain exclusively within their purview—*quod neque in vulgum disciplinam efferri velint* (lines 3–4); secondly, they felt that if students relied on written words it would weaken their skills in remembering—*eos qui discunt litteris confisos minus memoriae studere* (lines 4–5).

6. What are the the views of the Druids about the afterlife? What practical effects does this belief have? Cite the Latin that supports your answer and translate or accurately paraphrase.

The Druids believe that souls migrate from one life to another after death—*non interire animas sed ab aliis post mortem transire ad alios* (line 7). As a result men are roused to strive for maximum greatness (in battle), since death need not be feared—*hoc maxime ad virtutem excitari putant, metu mortis neglecto* (lines 7–8).

7. What four subjects are discussed by the Druids with their students? Cite the Latin that supports your answer and translate or accurately paraphrase.

The Druids engage in discussions about astronomy—*de sideribus atque eorum motu* (line 9), geography—*de mundi ac terrarum magnitudine* (line 9), philosophy—*de rerum natura* (line 10), and religion—*de deorum immortalium vi ac potestate* (line 10).

Essay *Suggested time: 20 minutes*

Natio est omnium Gallorum admodum dedita religionibus, atque ob
eam causam qui sunt adfecti gravioribus morbis quique in proeliis
periculisque versantur aut pro victimis homines immolant aut se
immolaturos vovent, administrisque ad ea sacrificia Druidibus utuntur;
5   quod, pro vita hominis nisi hominis vita reddatur, non posse deorum
immortalium numen placari arbitrantur, publiceque eiusdem generis
habent instituta sacrificia. Alii immani magnitudine simulacra habent,
quorum contexta viminibus membra vivis hominibus complent; quibus
succensis circumventi flamma exanimantur homines. Supplicia eorum qui
10   in furto aut in latrocinio aut aliqua noxia sint comprehensi gratiora dis
immortalibus esse arbitrantur, sed, cum eius generis copia deficit, etiam ad
innocentium supplicia descendunt.

In this passage we are given Caesar's observations about the religious customs of the Gauls. In a short essay, discuss the principles that guide Gallic religious behavior, focusing on the Gallic understanding of their relationship with the gods. Does Caesar present this material objectively, or does he color the information in a way that suggests his attitude toward these practices?

Support your assertions with references to the Latin text throughout the passage above. All Latin words must be copied or their line numbers provided, AND they must be translated or paraphrased closely enough that it is clear that you understand the Latin. It is your responsibility to convince the reader that you are basing your conclusions on the Latin text and not merely on a general recollection of the passage. Direct your answer to the question; do not merely summarize the passage. Please write your essay on a separate piece of paper.

Teachers should review with students the Essay Scoring Guidelines given at the beginning of this manual.

The Gauls, according to Caesar, are wholly devoted to maintaining religious scruples and to preserving their relationship with their gods—*Natio est omnium Gallorum admodum dedita religionibus* (line 1). This relationship is largely based on a quid pro quo structure: those who are in danger of losing their lives seek the favor of the gods by sacrificing the life of another in return for having the gods preserve their own lives—*qui sunt adfecti gravioribus morbis quique in proeliis periculisque versantur aut pro victimis homines immolant aut se immolaturos vovent* (lines 2–4); cf. *quod, pro vita hominis nisi hominis vita reddatur, non posse deorum immortalium numen placari arbitrantur* (lines 5–6). Students should observe that Caesar seems to focus overmuch on the barbarity of the practice of human sacrifice, perhaps for added "shock value" among his Roman readership. The passage focuses only on the most lurid and unfamiliar aspects of Gallic religious practice (although we know only what he tells us), and uses language that conveys Caesar's attitude quite clearly: though a Roman would not blink at punishing criminals in a violent manner, the use of *innocentes* in human sacrifice is not acceptable to the Romans. Caesar's attitude is further revealed in his choice of diction, since he says that they "sink" to this practice—*etiam ad innocentium supplicia descendunt* (lines 11–12).

CHAPTER 23: BOOK 6.17–18
THE GAULS AND THEIR GODS

[17] Deum maxime Mercurium colunt. Huius sunt plurima simulacra,
hunc omnium inventorem artium ferunt, hunc viarum atque itinerum
ducem, hunc ad quaestus pecuniae mercaturasque habere vim maximam
arbitrantur. Post hunc Apollinem et Martem et Iovem et Minervam. De
5   his eandem fere quam reliquae gentes habent opinionem: Apollinem
morbos depellere, Minervam operum atque artificiorum initia tradere,
Iovem imperium caelestium tenere, Martem bella regere. Huic, cum
proelio dimicare constituerunt, ea quae bello ceperint plerumque
devovent: quae superaverint, animalia capta immolant, reliquasque res
10   in unum locum conferunt. Multis in civitatibus harum rerum exstructos
tumulos locis consecratis conspicari licet, neque saepe accidit ut neglecta
quispiam religione aut capta apud se occultare aut posita tollere auderet,
gravissimumque ei rei supplicium cum cruciatu constitutum est. [18]
Galli se omnes ab Dite patre prognatos praedicant, idque ab Druidibus
15   proditum dicunt. Ob eam causam spatia omnis temporis non numero
dierum sed noctium finiunt; dies natalis et mensum et annorum initia sic
observant ut noctem dies subsequatur. In reliquis vitae institutis hoc fere
ab reliquis differunt quod suos liberos, nisi cum adoleverunt ut munus
militiae sustinere possint, palam ad se adire non patiuntur filiumque
20   puerili aetate in publico in conspectu patris adsistere turpe ducunt.

Preparatory Questions

Line 1   Identify the case and use of *deum*. **accusative, direct object or genitive, partitive**
(***Mercurium* is the "part" for which *deorum* "the gods" are the "whole.")**

Identify the case and use of *simulacra*. **nominative, predicate noun with *sunt***

Line 2   Identify the person and number of *ferunt*. **third plural**

Lines 2–3   Find an example of indirect statement. ***hunc ad quaestus pecuniae mercaturasque habere vim maximam***

Line 3   What two words does *ducem* govern? ***viarum atque itinerum* (line 2)**

Who is meant by *hunc*? **Mercury**

Line 5   What does *eandem* modify? ***opinionem***

Line 6   Identify the case and use of *morbos*. **accusative, direct object of *depellere***

Identify the case and use of *operum*. **genitive of possession**

Line 7   Explain the form and use of *regere*. **present infinitive active, used in implied indirect statement**

            Identify the case and use of *huic*. **dative of indirect object**

Line 8   Identify the tense and mood of *ceperint*. **perfect subjunctive, relative clause of characteristic**

            What part of speech is *plerumque*? **adverb**

Line 9   Identify the form and use of *capta*. **perfect passive participle, accusative modifying *animalia***

Line 10   What does *multis* modify? ***civitatibus***

Line 11   Find an impersonal verb. ***licet***

            What part of speech is *saepe*? **adverb**

Line 12   Explain the form and use of *auderet*. **imperfect subjunctive active, result clause**

Line 13   What degree is the adjective *gravissimum(que)*? **superlative**

            What does it modify? ***supplicium***

            Identify the case and use of *cruciatu*. **ablative of accompaniment with *cum***

Line 14   Identify the case and use of *patre*. **ablative of source**

            Find a word in apposition to *patre*. ***Dite***

Line 15   What must be supplied with *proditum* to fit the syntax? ***esse***

            Identify the case and use of *omnis*. **partitive genitive (with *spatia*)**

            Identify the case and use of *numero*. **ablative of means**

Line 16   Explain the form and function of *initia*. **accusative plural, direct object of *observant* (line 17)**

Line 17   Find a result clause. ***ut noctem dies subsequatur***

Line 18   What type of clause is introduced by *quod*? **causal**

Line 19   What is the complement of the verb *possint*? ***sustinere***

Line 20   Identify the case and use of *puerili*. **ablative of specification**

            What does it modify? ***aetate***

            Identify the case and use of *conspectu*. **ablative, object of the preposition *in***

            Explain the tense and use of *adsistere*. **present (infinitive), used in indirect statement to express contemporaneous time**

Multiple Choice Questions *Suggested time: 31 minutes*

1. In line 1 *colunt* is translated
   a. **they worship**
   b. they sacrifice to
   c. they contemplate
   d. they speak with

2. The positive degree form of *plurima* (line 1) is
   a. **multa**
   b. *magna*
   c. *parva*
   d. *plura*

3. In lines 2–4 (*hunc . . . arbitrantur*) we find an example of
   a. alliteration
   b. **anaphora**
   c. hyperbaton
   d. apostrophe

4. In line 2 *ferunt* is translated
   a. they carry
   b. they are reported
   c. **they consider**
   d. they bear

5. The object of *habere* (line 3) is
   a. *mercaturas* (line 3)
   b. *quaestus* (line 3)
   c. *simulacra* (line 1)
   d. **vim (line 3)**

6. In line 3 (*Post . . . Minervam*) what verb must be supplied from earlier in the passage?
   a. *ferunt*
   b. **colunt**
   c. *arbitrantur*
   d. *sunt*

7. In line 5 *his* refers to
   a. sacrifices
   b. **gods**
   c. Gauls
   d. roads and journeys

8. In line 5 *quam* is translated
   a. **which**
   b. as
   c. whom
   d. than

9. The subject of *tradere* (line 6) is
   a. *operum* (line 6)
   b. *gentes* (line 5)
   c. **Minervam (line 6)**
   d. *artificiorum* (line 6)

10. In line 7 the gender and case of *caelestium* are
    a. neuter nominative
    b. feminine genitive
    c. masculine accusative
    d. **neuter accusative**

11. In line 8 *proelio* is ablative of
    a. means
    c. manner
    b. description
    d. accompaniment

12. The clause *quae bello ceperint* (line 8) is a(n)
    a. descriptive relative clause
    c. indirect question
    b. relative clause of characteristic
    d. relative clause of result

13. The subject of *superaverint* (line 9) is
    a. *animalia* (line 9)
    c. *plerumque* (line 8)
    b. *capta* (line 9)
    d. *quae* (line 9)

14. In line 10 *harum rerum* refers to
    a. soldiers
    c. plunder
    b. temples
    d. warfare

15. *Locis* in line 11 is
    a. nominative
    c. dative
    b. genitive
    d. ablative

16. The word on which *conspicari* (line 11) depends is
    a. *tumulos* (line 11)
    c. *consecratis* (line 11)
    b. *licet* (line 11)
    d. *rerum* (line 10)

17. From lines 11–13 we learn that
    a. religious scruple was not respected
    c. the plunder was distributed equally
    b. those who took religious property were severely punished
    d. captives were often hidden away

18. In line 13 *ei rei* refers to
    a. religious sacrifice
    c. theft of divine property
    b. worship of the gods
    d. setting up piles of plunder

19. In line 14 the verb *praedicant* introduces a(n)
    a. indirect statement
    c. purpose clause
    b. ablative absolute
    d. relative clause of characteristic

20. The phrase *ob eam causam* (line 15) is translated
    a. after seeing this
    c. from this purpose
    b. for this reason
    d. towards a new cause

21. In line 15 the case of *numero* is
    a. nominative
    c. ablative
    b. dative
    d. locative

22. In line 16 *sic* is translated
    a. for this reason
    c. at this time
    b. here
    d. in this way

23. In lines 17–20 we learn that
    a. boys grow up to be warriors
    c. boys are not to be seen with their fathers
    b. children are sent away to school
    d. children can only be seen in public

24. In line 19 *palam* is a(n)
    a. adverb
    c. participle
    b. adjective
    d. verb

25. In line 20 *puerili aetate* is
    a. ablative of time within which
    c. ablative of manner
    b. ablative absolute
    d. ablative of description

26. In line 20 *ducunt* is translated
    a. they consider
    c. they march
    b. they lead
    d. they report

Translation *Suggested time: 15 minutes*

Deum maxime Mercurium colunt. Huius sunt plurima simulacra,
hunc omnium inventorem artium ferunt, hunc viarum atque itinerum
ducem, hunc ad quaestus pecuniae mercaturasque habere vim maximam
arbitrantur. Post hunc Apollinem et Martem et Iovem et Minervam. De his
5   eandem fere quam reliquae gentes habent opinionem.

20 chunks. 10 points, ½ point each.

Deum maxime . . . colunt	**Of the gods they especially worship/they worship the god Mercury the most**
Mercurium	**Mercury**
Huius sunt	**Of him there are**
plurima simulacra,	**very many images**
hunc . . . inventorem . . . ferunt	**him they consider the founder**
omnium . . . artium	**of all skills**
hunc . . . ducem	**him [they consider] the guide**
viarum atque itinerum	**of roads and journeys**
hunc . . . habere	**[that] he has**
ad quaestus pecuniae	**for the pursuit of money**
mercaturasque	**and commerce**
vim maximam	**the greatest power**
arbitrantur	**they believe**
Post hunc	**After this [god]**
Apollinem et Martem	**Apollo and Mars**
et Iovem et Minervam	**and Jupiter and Minerva**
De his	**Concerning these [divinities]**
eandem fere . . . opinionem	**pretty much the same opinion**
quam reliquae gentes	**as other peoples**
habent	**they hold**

Short Analysis Questions

> Galli se omnes ab Dite patre prognatos praedicant, idque ab Druidibus
> proditum dicunt. Ob eam causam spatia omnis temporis non numero
> dierum sed noctium finiunt; dies natalis et mensum et annorum initia sic
> observant ut noctem dies subsequatur. In reliquis vitae institutis hoc fere
> 5   ab reliquis differunt quod suos liberos, nisi cum adoleverunt ut munus
> militiae sustinere possint, palam ad se adire non patiuntur filiumque
> puerili aetate in publico in conspectu patris adsistere turpe ducunt.

1. From which god do the Gauls claim that they descend? Cite the Latin that supports your answer or accurately paraphrase.

   They claim that they are descended from *Dis*—*Galli se omnes ab Dite patre prognatos praedicant* (line 1).

2. From whom do they get this belief?

   The Druids—*idque ab Druidibus proditum dicunt* (lines 1–2).

3. What distinctive elements are there in the Gallic system of time reckoning? Cite the Latin that supports your answer or accurately paraphrase.

   They mark the divisions of time by nights, not by days—*spatia omnis temporis non numero dierum sed noctium finiunt* (lines 2–3). According to their system of time reckoning, days follow nights—*sic observant ut noctem dies subsequatur* (lines 3–4).

4. Does Caesar consider the Gauls to be generally similar to other peoples? Cite the Latin that supports your answer or accurately paraphrase.

   By implication, yes: his phrasing suggests that the major difference is in what follows [see next question], and by implication they are similar—*in reliquis vitae institutis* (line 4).

5. In what significant way do they differ? Cite the Latin that supports your answer or accurately paraphrase.

   They do not allow their sons to be seen in public or to approach their fathers openly until they have reached adulthood—*nisi cum adoleverunt . . . palam ad se adire non patiuntur . . .* (lines 5–6).

6. What are the distinguishing markers of adulthood among Gallic youths? Cite the Latin that supports your answer or accurately paraphrase.

   Young men must reach an age where they can bear military service—*cum adoleverunt ut munus militiae sustinere possint* (lines 5–6).

7. Do young Gallic boys often appear in the company of their fathers? Briefly explain.

   No. It is considered disgraceful—*filiumque puerili aetate in publico in conspectu patris adsistere turpe ducunt* (lines 6–7).

Essay *Suggested time: 20 minutes*

> Post [Mercurium] Apollinem et Martem et Iovem et Minervam. De
> his eandem fere quam reliquae gentes habent opinionem: Apollinem
> morbos depellere, Minervam operum atque artificiorum initia tradere,
> Iovem imperium caelestium tenere, Martem bella regere. Huic, cum
> 5 proelio dimicare constituerunt, ea quae bello ceperint plerumque
> devovent: quae superaverint, animalia capta immolant, reliquasque res
> in unum locum conferunt. Multis in civitatibus harum rerum exstructos
> tumulos locis consecratis conspicari licet, neque saepe accidit ut neglecta
> quispiam religione aut capta apud se occultare aut posita tollere auderet,
> 10 gravissimumque ei rei supplicium cum cruciatu constitutum est.

In this excerpt Caesar continues to explain the social, moral and religious customs of the Gauls, offering observations about the attributes assigned to each deity and the behavior expected by the community in worshipping these gods. In a short essay, discuss the ways that Caesar makes the elements of Gallic religion recognizable and understandable to his audience. For what purpose does he include such details about Gallic religious customs? What conclusions can we draw about the Gauls, as a people, from their religious values?

 Support your assertions with references to the Latin text throughout the passage above. All Latin words must be copied or their line numbers provided, AND they must be translated or paraphrased closely enough that it is clear that you understand the Latin. It is your responsibility to convince the reader that you are basing your conclusions on the Latin text and not merely on a general recollection of the passage. Direct your answer to the question; do not merely summarize the passage. Please write your essay on a separate piece of paper.

Teachers should review with students the Essay Scoring Guidelines given at the beginning of this manual.

Students will immediately recognize that Caesar uses Roman names to refer to the gods of the Gauls (who probably had different names for them in their own languages). Caesar does so because in this passage, which is part of his ethnographical essay on the customs of the Gauls and the Germans, he is trying to make the Gauls more readily understandable to his Roman audience. Thus, he tells us, they worship gods whose functions are similar to Roman gods, and they recognize and venerate the same major divinities as the Romans do, although Gallic religion emphasizes a different hierarchy. They worship Mercury first among the gods—*Post [Mercurium] Apollinem et Martem et Iovem et Minervam* (line 1). Students might note that the gods Caesar singles out among the Gallic pantheon reveal what qualities are important to their society: commerce and trade, travel, health, heavenly power, arts and craftsmanship, and warfare. Note that of these, Caesar only elaborates on Gallic religious worship of Mars—*Huic, cum proelio dimicare constituerunt . . . constitutum est* (lines 4–10). One explanation for this is that this would be the type of ritual that Caesar might have been able to learn of more readily than others. It may also serve to emphasize the great prominence of warfare among the Gallic tribes, which in turn serves to reinforce the greatness of Caesar's ultimate victory over them.

CHAPTER 24: BOOK 6.19–20
LIFE AMONG THE GAULS

[19] Viri quantas pecunias ab uxoribus dotis nomine acceperunt tantas
ex suis bonis aestimatione facta cum dotibus communicant. Huius
omnis pecuniae coniunctim ratio habetur fructusque servantur: uter
eorum vita superarit, ad eum pars utriusque cum fructibus superiorum
5   temporum pervenit. Viri in uxores, sicuti in liberos, vitae necisque
habent potestatem; et cum pater familiae inlustriore loco natus decessit,
eius propinqui conveniunt et, de morte si res in suspicionem venit, de
uxoribus in servilem modum quaestionem habent et, si compertum est,
igni atque omnibus tormentis excruciatas interficiunt. Funera sunt pro
10   cultu Gallorum magnifica et sumptuosa; omniaque quae vivis cordi
fuisse arbitrantur in ignem inferunt, etiam animalia; ac paulo supra
hanc memoriam servi et clientes quos ab eis dilectos esse constabat iustis
funeribus confectis una cremabantur. [20] Quae civitates commodius
suam rem publicam administrare existimantur habent legibus sanctum,
15   si quis quid de re publica a finitimis rumore aut fama acceperit, uti ad
magistratum deferat neve cum quo alio communicet: quod saepe homines
temerarios atque imperitos falsis rumoribus terreri et ad facinus impelli
et de summis rebus consilium capere cognitum est. Magistratus quae visa
sunt occultant, quaeque esse ex usu iudicaverunt multitudini produnt. De
20   re publica nisi per concilium loqui non conceditur.

Preparatory Questions

Line 1   Find two correlatives. **quantas . . . tantas**

               Identify the case and use of *dotis*. **genitive of description**

Line 2   Find an ablative absolute. **aestimatione facta**

Line 3   Identify the case and use of *omnis*. **objective genitive (with *ratio*)**

               Identify the subject of *habetur*. **ratio**

               Identify the form and use of *servantur*. **third person plural present passive indicative, main verb of its clause**

Line 4   Identify the case and use of *eorum*. **partitive genitive (with *pars*)**

Line 5   Identify the tense and mood of *pervenit*. **present indicative**

               Identify the case and use of *uxores*. **accusative, object of the preposition *in***

Line 6   What word(s) does *potestatem* govern? **vitae necisque (both line 5)**

             Find a *cum* clause. **cum pater familiae inlustriore loco natus decessit**

             What is the mood of the verb in the *cum* clause? **indicative**

             Explain the use of that mood. **indicative is used in temporal *cum* clauses**

Line 7   Identify the case and use of *propinqui*. **nominative, subject of *conveniunt***

             What is the subject of *venit*? **res**

Lines 7–8   Find two prepositional phrases containing *de*. **morte, uxoribus**

Line 8   What does *servilem* modify? **modum**

             Find a conditional sentence. **si compertum est, igni atque omnibus tormentis excruciatas interficiunt**

             Identify the protasis of the condition. **si compertum est**

             Identify the apodosis of the condition. **igni atque omnibus tormentis excruciatas interficiunt**

Line 9   Identify the form and use of *excruciatas*. **perfect passive participle, feminine accusative, used to describe action taking place prior to the main verb**

             What does it modify? **the understood noun *uxores***

             What words modify *funera*? **magnifica et sumptuosa (line 10)**

Lines 9–10   Identify the object of *pro*. **cultu (line 10)**

Lines 10–11   Find a relative clause. **quae vivis cordi fuisse arbitrantur**

             Find an example of indirect statement. **quae vivis cordi fuisse**

Line 11   Explain the tense of *fuisse*. **perfect, indicates action prior to that of the verb introducing the indirect statement**

             Who/what is the subject of *inferunt*? **unexpressed: the Gauls (or the relatives)**

Line 12   Identify the case and use of *hanc memoriam*. **accusative, object of the preposition *supra* (line 11)**

             Explain the form and use of *dilectos esse*. **accusative, perfect passive infinitive in indirect statement**

Line 13   Identify the tense and voice of *cremabantur*. **imperfect passive**

             What part of speech is *una*? **adverb**

Lines 14–15   Find a conditional clause. **si quis quid de re publica a finitimis rumore aut fama acceperit**

Line 14   Identify the voice and mood of *existimantur*. **passive indicative**

             What part of speech is *legibus*? **noun**

Line 15	Identify the tense and mood of *acceperit*. **future perfect indicative**
	What type of clause is introduced by *uti*? **indirect command**
Line 16	Identify the case and use of *magistratum*. **accusative, object of the preposition *ad* (line 15)**
	Identify the tense and mood of *communicet*. **present subjunctive**
Lines 16–17	Find a causal clause. ***quod saepe homines temerarios ... cognitum est***
	What word introduces it? ***quod***
	What is the main verb of the causal clause? ***cognitum est* (line 18)**
Line 17	What does *temerarios* modify? ***homines* (line 16)**
	Identify the case and use of *rumoribus*. **ablative of means**
Line 18	Identify the case and use of *magistratus*. **nominative, subject of *occultant* (line 19)**
	Find a relative clause. ***quae visa sunt***
Line 19	Who/what is the subject of *produnt*? **the relative clause: *quaeque esse ex usu iudicaverunt***
	Explain the tense and mood of *iudicaverunt*. **perfect indicative, factual relative clause**
Line 20	Identify the case and use of *re publica*. **ablative, object of the preposition *de* (line 19)**
	Explain the form and use of *loqui*. **present deponent infinitive, complementary with *conceditur***

Multiple Choice Questions *Suggested time: 35 minutes*

1. The object of *acceperunt* (line 1) is
   a. *uxoribus* (line 1)   **b. *pecunias* (line 1)**
   c. *tantas* (line 1)   d. *dotis* (line 1)

2. *Communicant* (line 2) is translated
   a. they communicate   b. they meditate with
   c. they share   d. they spread via disease

3. In line 3 *coniunctim* is a(n)
   a. adverb   b. preposition
   c. indeclinable noun   d. adjective

4. The case of *vita* (line 4) is
   a. nominative
   b. genitive
   c. accusative
   d. ablative

5. The words *superiorum temporum* (lines 4–5) are translated
   a. of better times
   b. of previous times
   c. of a higher power
   d. of higher value

6. In line 5 *sicuti* is translated
   a. just as
   b. in order that
   c. whenever
   d. in contrast with

7. From lines 5–6 (*Viri . . . potestatem*) we learn that Gallic husbands
   a. love all their children equally
   b. live with their wives and children
   c. are empowered to kill family members
   d. set aside money for the family

8. In line 6 *cum* is translated
   a. although
   b. since
   c. when
   d. with

9. The form of *natus* (line 6) is
   a. fourth declension noun
   b. adjective
   c. perfect active participle
   d. adverb

10. To whom does *eius* (line 7) refer?
    a. *pater* (line 6)
    b. *loco* (line 6)
    c. *propinqui* (line 7)
    d. *inlustriore* (line 6)

11. The subject of *venit* (line 7) is
    a. *morte* (line 7)
    b. *res* (line 7)
    c. *suspicionem* (line 7)
    d. *pater* (line 6)

12. The tense and voice of *compertum est* (line 8) is
    a. present active
    b. perfect active
    c. pluperfect passive
    d. perfect passive

13. The case of *igni* (line 9) is
    a. nominative
    b. accusative
    c. ablative
    d. genitive

14. In line 9 *pro* is translated
    a. **in proportion to**
       b. in front of
    c. in return for
       d. in the place of

15. The antecedent of *quae* (line 10) is
    a. *sumptuosa* (line 10)
       b. ***omnia(que)* (line 10)**
    c. *animalia* (line 11)
       d. *cordi* (line 10)

16. The phrase *quae vivis cordi fuisse* (lines 10–11) is an example of
    a. **a relative purpose clause**
       b. an indirect question
    c. a double dative
       d. an ablative absolute

17. The phrase *paulo supra hanc memoriam* (lines 11–12) is translated
    a. a little after this memorial
       b. a little while in the future
    c. **a little before our time**
       d. a small gap in memory

18. To whom does *eis* (line 12) refer?
    a. the relatives of the dead person
       b. **the deceased**
    c. the animals
       d. the slaves and clients

19. In line 12 *iustis* is translated
    a. with justice
       b. **rites**
    c. official
       d. recent

20. In line 13 *commodius* is a(n)
    a. **adverb in the comparative degree**
       b. adverb in the positive degree
    c. adjective in the superlative degree
       d. adjective in the comparative degree

21. *Legibus* (line 14) is an ablative of
    a. manner
       b. separation
    c. **means**
       d. personal agent

22. In line 15 *quis* is translated
    a. whom
       b. what
    c. **anyone**
       d. anything

23. The tense and mood of *deferat* (line 16) is
    a. **present subjunctive**
       b. imperfect indicative
    c. future indicative
       d. perfect subjunctive

24. The phrase *cum quo alio* (line 16) is translated
    a. without another
    b. within the tribe alone
    c. since another person knows
    d. with anyone else

25. The gender and case of *facinus* (line 17) is
    a. masculine nominative
    b. neuter accusative
    c. masculine genitive
    d. neuter nominative

26. The subject of *occultant* (line 19) is
    a. *magistratus* (line 18)
    b. *quae* (line 18)
    c. *facinus* (line 17)
    d. *quaeque* (line 19)

27. In line 19 the phrase *ex usu* is translated
    a. from experience
    b. out of use
    c. advantageous
    d. out of necessity

28. The case of *multitudini* (line 19) is
    a. ablative
    b. dative
    c. genitive
    d. accusative

29. The phrase *nisi per concilium* (line 20) is translated
    a. unless each councilor agrees
    b. in exceptional circumstances
    c. except through the council
    d. if the council is present

Translation *Suggested time: 15 minutes*

Funera sunt pro cultu Gallorum magnifica et sumptuosa; omniaque quae vivis cordi fuisse arbitrantur in ignem inferunt, etiam animalia; ac paulo supra hanc memoriam servi et clientes quos ab eis dilectos esse constabat iustis funeribus confectis una cremabantur.

18 chunks. 9 points, ½ point each.

Funera sunt	**The funerals are**
pro cultu Gallorum	**in proportion to their civilization**
magnifica et sumptuosa	**splendid and lavish**
omniaque quae	**and all the things that**
vivis cordi fuisse	**to have been (were) dear to (the deceased) while alive**
arbitrantur	**they believe**
in ignem inferunt	**they put into the fire**
etiam animalia	**even animals**
ac paulo	**and (by) a little**
supra hanc memoriam	**before this memory (=before our time)**
servi et clientes	**the slaves and retainers**
quos	**whom**
ab eis	**by them**
dilectos esse	**to have been loved/cherished**
constabat	**it was known**
iustis funeribus confectis	**the funeral rites having been completed**
una cremabantur	**were burned together (with the deceased)**

Short Analysis Questions

Quae civitates commodius suam rem publicam administrare existimantur habent legibus sanctum, si quis quid de re publica a finitimis rumore aut fama acceperit, uti ad magistratum deferat neve cum quo alio communicet: quod saepe homines temerarios atque imperitos falsis rumoribus terreri et ad facinus impelli et de summis rebus consilium capere cognitum est. Magistratus quae visa sunt occultant, quaeque esse ex usu iudicaverunt multitudini produnt. De re publica nisi per concilium loqui non conceditur.

5

1. What does Caesar mean when he says that some communities are managed *commodius*? Cite the Latin that supports your answer or accurately paraphrase.

    He is referring to those that have laws designed to manage society and maintain public order—*quae civitates... habent legibus sanctum...* (lines 1–2)—through controlling rumor and hearsay about political affairs.

2. What is the substance of the directive sanctioned by law (lines 2–3)? Cite the Latin that supports your answer or accurately paraphrase.

    Anyone who hears any political rumors must report this only to the magistrates and not spread it about—*si quis quid de re publica a finitimis rumore aut fama acceperit, uti ad magistratum deferat neve cum quo alio communicet* (lines 2–3).

3. What type of information is covered by this law? Cite the Latin that supports your answer or accurately paraphrase.

    The information is that which concerns the state—*de re publica* (line 2), is heard—*acceperit* (line 3) from neighboring peoples—*a finitimis* (line 2) or by rumor—*fama* (line 3).

4. What two things must someone who has this information do? Cite the Latin that supports your answer or accurately paraphrase.

    Anyone who hears such information must report it directly to the magistrate, and not share it with anyone else—*uti ad magistratum deferat neve cum quo alio communicet* (line 3).

5. What characteristics does Caesar ascribe to the Gauls here (lines 4–5)? Cite the Latin that supports your answer or accurately paraphrase.

    Caesar describes them as rash—*temerarios* (line 4), inexperienced—*imperitos* (line 4), and prone to panic—*falsis rumoribus terreri* (line 4). They also are prone to taking rash action without considering all the evidence—*et ad facinus impelli et de summis rebus consilium capere cognitum est* (line 5).

6. What is the role of the magistrates? Cite the Latin that supports your answer or accurately paraphrase.

    The magistrates assess the information and determine what can be advantageously shared with the people as a whole—*Magistratus quae visa sunt occultant, quaeque esse ex usu iudicaverunt multitudini produnt* (lines 6–7).

Essay *Suggested time: 20 minutes*

Viri quantas pecunias ab uxoribus dotis nomine acceperunt tantas ex
suis bonis aestimatione facta cum dotibus communicant. Huius omnis
pecuniae coniunctim ratio habetur fructusque servantur: uter eorum vita
superarit, ad eum pars utriusque cum fructibus superiorum temporum
5   pervenit. Viri in uxores, sicuti in liberos, vitae necisque habent potestatem;
et cum pater familiae inlustriore loco natus decessit, eius propinqui
conveniunt et, de morte si res in suspicionem venit, de uxoribus in
servilem modum quaestionem habent et, si compertum est, igni atque
omnibus tormentis excruciatas interficiunt.

In this excerpt Caesar turns to an account of Gallic family hierarchy and funeral customs. In a short essay, assess the position of wives among the Gallic tribes, as reported by Caesar. What benefits and disadvantages, whether financial or legal, do they have?

Support your assertions with references to the Latin text throughout the passage above. All Latin words must be copied or their line numbers provided, AND they must be translated or paraphrased closely enough that it is clear that you understand the Latin. It is your responsibility to convince the reader that you are basing your conclusions on the Latin text and not merely on a general recollection of the passage. Direct your answer to the question; do not merely summarize the passage. Please write your essay on a separate piece of paper.

Teachers should review with students the Essay Scoring Guidelines given at the beginning of this manual.

The portrait of social customs and family hierarchy among the Gauls has elements that suggest a paradoxical position for wives among the German tribes. On the one hand they are treated as equals when it comes to the financial components of the relationship, for the sums of money brought to the marriage by each party are treated equally—*Viri quantas pecunias ab uxoribus dotis nomine acceperunt tantas ex suis bonis aestimatione facta cum dotibus communicant* (lines 1–2)—and managed in such a way that the wife does not hand over control of the finances to her husband—*Huius omnis pecuniae coniunctim ratio habetur fructusque servantur* (lines 2–3). Indeed, after the death of one party, Gallic custom dictates that the shared portion, along with any profits, is transferred to the survivor—*uter eorum vita superarit, ad eum pars utriusque cum fructibus superiorum temporum pervenit* (lines 3–5).

On the other hand, wives are at the mercy of their husbands in that the head of the household, the *pater familias*, has complete legal power over the members of his household—*viri in uxores, sicuti in liberos, vitae necisque habent potestatem* (line 5). Indeed, in higher-status households the wife is at an even more serious disadvantage, since she is subjected to a rigorous investigation if her husband should die before her; if there is any evidence that the death occurred under suspicious circumstances, the man's relatives are empowered to subject his wife to torture to obtain evidence about the manner of death—*et cum pater familiae inlustriore loco natus decessit, eius propinqui conveniunt et, de morte si res in suspicionem venit, de uxoribus in servilem modum quaestionem habent* (lines 6–8). The Gauls were evidently very much concerned about murder and/or assassination within the household, for the penalty for any wife found guilty of such an act was extreme—*si compertum est, igni atque omnibus tormentis excruciatas interficiunt* (lines 8–9).

PAIRED PASSAGE ESSAYS
VERGIL AND CAESAR

Nam fere de omnibus controversiis publicis privatisque [Druides]
constituunt, et, si quod est admissum facinus, si caedes facta, si de
hereditate, de finibus controversia est, idem decernunt, praemia poenasque
constituunt; si qui aut privatus aut populus eorum decreto non stetit,
5   sacrificiis interdicunt. Haec poena apud eos est gravissima. Quibus ita est
interdictum, hi numero impiorum ac sceleratorum habentur, his omnes
decedunt, aditum sermonemque defugiunt, ne quid ex contagione
incommodi accipiant, neque his petentibus ius redditur neque honos ullus
communicatur.

Caesar De Bello Gallico 6.13.6–9

Tum foribus divae, media testudine templi,
saepta armis, solioque alte subnixa Dido resedit.
Iura dabat legesque viris, operumque laborem
partibus aequabat iustis, aut sorte trahebat:

Vergil Aeneid 1.505–508

Essay

In a short essay, compare and contrast the official dispensers of justice Vergil describes for the city of
Carthage with those Caesar describes for the Gallic tribes. Include the bearing, if any, that religion
has on each.

Support your assertions with references to the Latin text in the passages above. All Latin words
must be copied or their line numbers provided, AND they must be translated or paraphrased closely
enough that it is clear that you understand the Latin. It is your responsibility to convince the reader
that you are basing your conclusions on the Latin text and not merely on a general recollection of the
passage. Direct your answer to the question; do not merely summarize the passage. Please write your
essay on a separate piece of paper.

Teachers should review with students the Essay Scoring Guidelines given at the beginning of this manual.

Among the Gauls the priestly class of Druids decides all matters between citizens and also dispenses judgment and sentence in criminal matters—*de omnibus controversiis publicis privatisque [Druides] constituunt, et, si quod est admissum facinus, si caedes facta, si de hereditate, de finibus controversia est, idem decernunt* (lines 1–3). Their decrees are absolute, and they, being the religious leaders, evidently speak for the gods, in so doing, they use religious power to compel obedience to their decrees—*si qui aut privatus aut populus eorum decreto non stetit, sacrificiis interdicunt* (lines 4–5). This punishment works very well because of the evident strong belief and regard in which the people hold the Druids—*Quibus ita est interdictum, hi numero impiorum ac sceleratorum habentur, his omnes decedunt, aditum sermonemque defugiunt, ne quid ex contagione incommodi accipiant, neque his petentibus ius redditur neque honos ullus communicatur* (lines 5–9). Thus, these societies are ruled by a theocratic oligarchy.

Vergil presents Dido's Carthage, on the other hand, as an absolute monarchy drawing authority partly from her military might, as she comes to her throne of judgment surrounded by armed guards—*saepta armis* (line 506). Her authority is partly derived from religion as this judgment throne is located in a temple (the temple of Juno; that specific identification appears in the lines just prior to the AP lines but students may recall that it is Juno's temple from their English reading and from class discussion about Juno favoring the Carthaginians)—*foribus divae, media testudine templi* (line 505). She gives laws and judgments, and also assigns tasks, using lots—*sorte* (line 508)—to determine assignments if some tasks are more burdensome than others. As lots drawn were seen as the will of the gods, she evidently has, if not a theocratic monarchy, something very close to one.

Caesar and Vergil are of course writing from widely differing perspectives. Vergil is presenting a poetic picture of an orderly society whose leader is interested in impartial justice—*partibus aequabat iustis* (line 508)—and who is using the gods or chance—*aut sorte trahebat* (line 508)—to address disparities. Caesar's Druids simply make absolute decrees—*idem decernunt* (line 3) and inflict isolation on any who dare rebel.

Yet, for both the Gauls and the Carthaginians, political power is closely allied to religious power.

[29] Eadem

nocte accidit ut esset luna plena, qui dies maritimos aestus maximos in
Oceano efficere consuevit, nostrisque id erat incognitum. Ita uno tempore
et longas naves, quibus Caesar exercitum transportandum curaverat
5   quasque in aridum subduxerat, aestus compleverat et onerarias, quae ad
ancoras erant deligatae, tempestas adflictabat, neque ulla nostris facultas
aut administrandi aut auxiliandi dabatur. Compluribus navibus fractis,
reliquae cum essent funibus, ancoris, reliquisque armamentis amissis
ad navigandum inutiles, magna, id quod necesse erat accidere, totius
10   exercitus perturbatio facta est. Neque enim naves erant aliae quibus
reportari possent, et omnia deerant quae ad reficiendas naves erant usui
et, quod omnibus constabat hiemare in Gallia oportere, frumentum his in
locis in hiemem provisum non erat.

Caesar De Bello Gallico 4.29

Aeolus haec contra: 'tuus, o regina, quid optes
explorare labor; mihi iussa capessere fas est.
tu mihi quodcumque hoc regni, tu sceptra Iovemque
concilias, tu das epulis accumbere divum
80   nimborumque facis tempestatumque potentem'
    Haec ubi dicta, cavum conversa cuspide montem
impulit in latus; ac venti velut agmine facto,
qua data porta, ruunt et terras turbine perflant.
incubuere mari totumque a sedibus imis
85   una Eurusque Notusque ruunt creberque procellis
Africus, et vastos volvunt ad litora fluctus.
insequitur clamorque virum stridorque rudentum;
eripiunt subito nubes caelumque diemque
Teucrorum ex oculis; ponto nox incubat atra;
90   intonuere poli et crebris micat ignibus aether
praesentemque viris intentant omnia mortem.

Vergil Aeneid 1.76–91

Essay

These two passages narrate the sudden onset of a storm at sea. In a short essay, discuss the ways in
which the conventions of each genre affect the way the storms are depicted. In what ways are the two
passages similar? How do they differ?

Support your assertions with references to the text in the passages above. All Latin words must be
copied or their line numbers provided, AND they must be translated or paraphrased closely enough
that it is clear that you understand the Latin. It is your responsibility to convince the reader that you
are basing your conclusions on the Latin text and not merely on a general recollection of the passage.
Direct your answer to the question; do not merely summarize the passage. Please write your essay on
a separate piece of paper.

Teachers should review with students the Essay Scoring Guidelines given at the beginning of this manual.

Both passages depict the storms from the vantage point of an omniscient narrator. In the Caesar passage, the narrator reports the storm with additional knowledge after the fact —*nostrisque id erat incognitum* (line 3) and with a superior understanding of the nature of these types of events—*id quod necesse erat accidere* (line 9). In the *Aeneid* passage, the narrator reports the onset of the storm as if watching from afar, recounting the sights and sounds of the storm, both on the sea—*et vastos volvunt ad litora fluctus* (line 86); *intonuere poli* (line 90) and in the sky—*eripiunt subito nubes caelumque diemque / Teucrorum ex oculis* (line 88–89): this is a narrator who sees the whole scene before him. A second similarity can be found in the structure of the two scenes: both set up the episode with background information for the first two-thirds of the passage but then switch to focus on the effect of the storm on the men. In the Caesar passage this pivotal point is marked by hyperbaton and a parenthetical statement—*magna, id quod necesse era taccidere, totius exercitus perturbatio facta est* (line x), while in the Vergil excerpt the Trojans come into focus more gradually, first via their shouts—*insequitur clamorque virum* (line 87), then through emphasis on the threat of imminent death that seems to await them—*praestentemque viris intentant omnia mortem* (line 91), again with a slight hyperbaton framing the line. Both passages use highly literary methods for heightening the drama: Caesar's sentences are periodic—for example, *Ita uno tempore . . . dabatur* (lines 3–7) and relatively complex, joined by a number of conjunctions and subordinate clauses—*Neque enim naves erant aliae . . . provisum non erat* (line 10–13). Vergil seems to go out of his way to join phrases and clauses with *-que*, especially in his description of the stormy seas and skies, perhaps to mimic the rolling waves and the movement of the clouds in the sky.

The two passages also show differences that reflect their genres. As is typical in epic poetry, it is the gods who are responsible for meteorological phenomena, thus it is Aeolus, god of the winds, who rouses the storm at Juno's request (lines 76–80). In historical prose such as Caesar's, however, the gods have no place and thus the focus is instead on an almost scientific explanation, that the full moon caused the tides to be higher than normal—*accidit ut esset luna plena, qui dies maritimos aestus maximos in Oceano efficere consuevit* (lines 2–3). In Vergil, the narrator's focus is on the description of the storm itself, allowing the poet room to show off his artistic skill. By contrast, Caesar focuses on the practical effect of the storm—that the ships are damaged and the men possibly stranded—as one would expect in a military narrative. In Vergil the storm is used as a plot point to drive the Trojans ashore in Africa, whereas in Caesar the storm is narrated in a way that serves to exonerate Caesar from blame for the failure of the expedition (note especially the repetition of impersonal verbs—*accidit* (line 1) and *constabat* (line 12)—and the fact that the elements themselves are subjects of other verbs—*aestus compleverat* (line 5); *tempestas adflictabat* (line 6)).

PAIRED PASSAGE ESSAYS
TWO EXCERPTS FROM CAESAR

Apud Helvetios longe nobilissimus fuit et ditissimus Orgetorix. Is
M. Messala et M. Pupio Pisone consulibus, regni cupiditate inductus,
coniurationem nobilitatis fecit et civitati persuasit ut de finibus suis cum
omnibus copiis exirent . . .

5 Ad eas res conficiendas Orgetorix deligitur. Is sibi legationem ad civitates
suscepit. In eo itinere persuadet Castico, Catamantaloedis filio,
Sequano, cuius pater regnum in Sequanis multos annos obtinuerat et a
senatu populi Romani amicus appellatus erat, ut regnum in civitate sua
occuparet, quod pater ante habuerat; itemque Dumnorigi Aeduo, fratri
10 Diviciaci, qui eo tempore principatum in civitate obtinebat ac maxime
plebi acceptus erat, ut idem conaretur persuadet eique filiam suam
in matrimonium dat. Perfacile factu esse illis probat conata perficere,
propterea quod ipse suae civitatis imperium obtenturus esset: non
esse dubium quin totius Galliae plurimum Helvetii possent; se suis
15 copiis suoque exercitu illis regna conciliaturum confirmat. Hac oratione
adducti inter se fidem et ius iurandum dant et regno occupato per tres
potentissimos ac firmissimos populos totius Galliae sese potiri posse
sperant. . . .

Caesar De Bello Gallico 1.2–3

        . . . Ambiorix ad hunc
modum locutus est: sese pro Caesaris in se beneficiis plurimum ei confiteri
debere, quod eius opera stipendio liberatus esset, quod Aduatucis finitimis
suis pendere consuesset, quodque ei et filius et fratris filius ab Caesare
5 remissi essent, quos Aduatuci obsidum numero missos apud se in servitute
et catenis tenuissent; neque id quod fecerit de oppugnatione castrorum,
aut iudicio aut voluntate sua fecisse, sed coactu civitatis, suaque esse
eiusmodi imperia, ut non minus haberet iuris in se multitudo quam ipse
in multitudinem. Civitati porro hanc fuisse belli causam, quod repentinae
10 Gallorum coniurationi resistere non potuerit. Id se facile ex humilitate
sua probare posse, quod non adeo sit imperitus rerum ut suis copiis

populum Romanum superari posse confidat. Sed esse Galliae commune
consilium: omnibus hibernis Caesaris oppugnandis hunc esse dictum
diem, ne qua legio alterae legioni subsidio venire posset. Non facile Gallos
15 Gallis negare potuisse, praesertim cum de reciperanda communi libertate
consilium initum videretur. Quibus quoniam pro pietate satisfecerit,
habere nunc se rationem offici pro beneficiis Caesaris: monere, orare
Titurium pro hospitio ut suae ac militum saluti consulat.

Caesar *De Bello Gallico* 5.27

In a short essay, compare and contrast Orgetorix *DBG* 1.2–3 and Ambiorix *DBG* 5.27 in the above passages
as to their status within their states, their application of powers of persuasion, and their evident aims.

Support your assertions with references to the Latin text in the passages above. All Latin words
must be copied or their line numbers provided, AND they must be translated or paraphrased closely
enough that it is clear that you understand the Latin. It is your responsibility to convince the reader
that you are basing your conclusions on the Latin text and not merely on a general recollection of the
passage. Direct your answer to the question; do not merely summarize the passage. Please write your
essay on a separate piece of paper.

Teachers should review with students the Essay Scoring Guidelines given at the beginning of this manual.

Each of these leaders is powerful and has an eye to expanding or holding his power by persuading others of things that are doubtful or actually inaccurate. Thus both men are playing dangerous games in the struggle for supremacy and power.

Orgetorix is a very powerful man—*Apud Helvetios longe nobilissimus fuit et ditissimus Orgetorix* (line 1). He is trying to create a coalition with two other powerful tribes to rule all the Gallic nations— *per tres potentissimos ac firmissimos populos totius Galliae sese potiri posse sperant* (lines 16–18). To bring about this difficult achievement, he promises to take power in the Helvetian state—*ipse suae civitatis imperium obtenturus esset* (line 13), and he urges two men who are near to power and who may feel they are not enough regarded to do the same. Casticus the Sequanian was the son of a former leader—*Castico Sequano, . . . ut regnum in civitate sua occuparet, quod pater ante habuerat* (lines 6–9). Dumnorix the Aeduan might well envy the power that his brother held. *Dumnorigi Haeduo, fratri Diviciaci, qui eo tempore principatum in civitate obtinebat ac maxime plebi acceptus erat, ut idem conaretur persuadet* (lines 9–11).

Ambiorix has a different set of circumstances. He is the acknowledged leader of his people, but he tries to convince Caesar that he cannot go against them—*suaque esse eiusmodi imperia ut haberet iuris in se multitudo quam ipse in multitudinem* (lines 7–9). Such explanation would hardly be necessary if his power were not very evident. While Orgetorix is trying to persuade two men in neighboring states to take hold of a power they do not presently have, Ambiorix is trying to maintain his balance between two forces already powerful: Caesar and the Gallic coalition determined to destroy the Romans. He tells Caesar that he has taken part in the conspiracy against the Romans out of pietas and is now trying to repay the kindness of Caesar by warning the Roman soldiers to leave before the coming of German reinforcements—*Quibus quoniam pro pietate satisfecerit, habere nunc se rationem offici pro beneficiis Caesaris: monere, orare Titurium pro hospitio, ut suae ac militum saluti consulat* (lines 17–18).

Orgetorix obviously intends to become a power player in a large federation while Ambiorix is trying to lead the Romans into a risky move by proclaiming friendship.

Atque nostris militibus
cunctantibus, maxime propter altitudinem maris, qui decimae legionis
aquilam ferebat, contestatus deos, ut ea res legioni feliciter eveniret,
"Desilite," inquit, "milites, nisi vultis aquilam hostibus prodere: ego
5   certe meum rei publicae atque imperatori officium praestitero." Hoc cum
voce magna dixisset, se ex navi proiecit atque in hostes aquilam ferre
coepit. Tum nostri cohortati inter se, ne tantum dedecus admitteretur,
universi ex navi desiluerunt. Hos item ex proximis primis navibus cum
conspexissent, subsecuti hostibus appropinquarunt.

Caesar *De Bello Gallico* 4.25

Erant in ea legione fortissimi viri, centuriones, qui primis ordinibus
appropinquarent, Titus Pullo et Lucius Vorenus. Hi perpetuas inter se
controversias habebant, quinam anteferretur, omnibusque annis de
locis summis simultatibus contendebant. Ex his Pullo, cum acerrime ad
5   munitiones pugnaretur, "Quid dubitas," inquit, "Vorene? Aut quem locum
tuae pro laude virtutis spectas? Hic dies de nostris controversiis iudicabit."
Haec cum dixisset, procedit extra munitiones, quaeque pars hostium
confertissima est visa irrumpit. Ne Vorenus quidem tum sese vallo
continet sed omnium veritus existimationem subsequitur. Tum mediocri
10   spatio relicto Pullo pilum in hostes immittit atque unum ex multitudine
procurrentem traicit; quo percusso et exanimato hunc scutis protegunt,
in hostem tela universi coniciunt neque dant regrediendi facultatem.
Transfigitur scutum Pulloni et verutum in balteo defigitur. Avertit hic
casus vaginam et gladium educere conanti dextram moratur manum,
15   impeditumque hostes circumsistunt. Succurrit inimicus illi Vorenus et
laboranti subvenit.

Caesar *De Bello Gallico* 5.44

Essay

Caesar has in these two passages created a lively narrative focused on the actions of individual Roman soldiers. In a short essay compare and contrast the actions of the *aquilifer* (the eagle-bearer of the tenth legion in the first passage) and Titus Pullo, as described here. What motivates each man's action? How does Caesar, as author, emphasize the importance of their actions? What is the outcome of each action?

   Support your assertions with references to the text in the passages above. All Latin words must be copied or their line numbers provided, AND they must be translated or paraphrased closely enough that it is clear that you understand the Latin. It is your responsibility to convince the reader that you are basing your conclusions on the Latin text and not merely on a general recollection of the passage. Direct your answer to the question; do not merely summarize the passage. Please write your essay on a separate piece of paper.

Teachers should review with students the Essay Scoring Guidelines given at the beginning of this manual.

Students should immediately recognize that *oratio recta* (direct speech) is used here to punctuate the episode and to add dramatic intensity. Because this mode of speech is used so rarely in Caesar, it stands out from the surrounding narrative. Moreover, Caesar uses both episodes as vehicles for revealing his own assessment of the qualities Roman soldiers should possess. That is, by recounting these vignettes about the *aquilifer* and Pullo and Vorenus, Caesar can describe in an individual way the characteristics common to—or at least expected of—Roman military men.

In the passage from Book 4 the *aquilifer* is motivated by his awareness of the desperate situation faced by the Romans as they try to disembark from the ships—*nostris militibus cunctantibus, maxime propter altitudinem maris* (lines 1–2). Furthermore, he recognizes the importance of the eagle to the Roman soldiers—*nisi vultis aquilam hostibus prodere* (line 3), namely that it must be protected at all costs, and uses this to urge his comrades forward. Although the eagle-bearer takes individual action, he is shown to do so for all the right reasons, namely to do his duty to the republic and to his commander—*ego certe meum rei publicae atque imperatori officium praestitero* (lines 4–5). His action spurs the men to follow in order that they not be tainted with dishonor—*tum nostri cohortati inter se, ne tantum dedecus admitteretur* (line 7)—and their hesitation dissolves: they leap forward—*universi ex navi desiluerunt* (line 8), in turn encouraging other men on nearby ships as well—*hos item ex †proximis primis† navibus cum conspexissent, subsecuti hostibus approprinquarunt* (lines 8–9). In this way, the eagle-bearer's bravery is singled out for emphasis in the narrative both because it serves as a catalyst for the outcome of the larger battle episode, and because it highlights the appropriate and praiseworthy action of a Roman legionary.

In the Pullo and Vorenus episode, individual action is used to illustrate a different kind of bravery. The centurions' rivalry is the good kind of strife—that which spurs a man to excel—but it is clear from the description of the episode that it is only through the cooperative efforts of both men that they are able to escape death. Titus Pullo's actions are motivated by his desire to surpass Vorenus in glory; this could be interpreted as a selfish act, unlike that of the *aquilifer* in the first passage. Indeed, Vorenus's motivation is his fear of what the others would think—*sed omnium veritus existimationem subsequitur* (line 9). On the other hand, Caesar emphasizes the importance of cooperative effort here, since although Pullo believes that their longstanding quarrel will be decided in that moment—*hic dies de nostris controversiis iudicabit* (line 6), the episode shows that the centurions' reciprocal efforts saves them both—*succurrit inimicus illi Vorenus et laboranti subvenit* (lines 15–16). Vorenus is described by Caesar as Pullo's personal enemy (*inimicus*), but this does not stop Vorenus either from fighting off the external enemy (*hostem*), or from risking his own life to save Pullo. The actions of each centurion are motivated by personal pride, which could be detrimental to the army as a whole, but the end result of their rivalry is cooperation, another hallmark of Roman legionary excellence.

VOCABULARY*

In this vocabulary, the numbers 1, 2, and 4 indicate for regular verbs the conjugation to which the verb belongs, and that their principal parts are formed according to the patterns of the model verbs **laudō**, **moneō**, and **audiō**, respectively; or, if the verb is deponent, according to the patterns of **hortor**, **vereor**, and **partior**.

Words in *italics* are explanatory and are not part of the definition. Words in square brackets are the root(s) from which a word is derived or another closely related word.

The symbol • follows the last letter of the base or stem of the word. To this base, subsequent syllables are added, e.g., **abic•iō, -ere = abiciō, abicere** or **āc•er, -ris, -re = ācer, ācris, ācre.** (NB: In Caesar's day, nouns that ended in **-ius** and **-ium** regularly had a genitive **-ī**, rather than **-iī**, e.g., **auxil•ium, -ī.**)

References such as § = section refer to the Grammatical Appendix for *Caesar: Selections from his* COMMENTARII DE BELLO GALLICO by Hans-Friedrich Mueller, which can be found at www.bolchazy.com/extras/caesarappendix.pdf.

The following signs and abbreviations are used in this glossary.

§ = section
abl. = ablative
acc. = accusative
adj. = adjective
adv. = adverb
card. = cardinal
cf. = *cōnfer* (*i.e.,* compare)
comp. = comparative
conj. = conjunction
dat. = dative
def. = defective
dim. = diminutive
etc. = *et cētera* (*i.e.,* and so on)
f. = feminine
freq. = frequentative
gen. = genitive
i.e., id est (*i.e.,* that is)
impers. = impersonal
indecl. = indeclinable
indef. = indefinite
inf. = infinitive

interrog. = interrogative
m. = masculine
n. = neuter
nom. = nominative
num. = numeral
obs. = obsolete
ord. = ordinal
part. = participle
pass. = passive
pers. = personal
pl. = plural
poss. = possessive
prep. = preposition
pres. = present
pron. = pronoun
rel. = relative
reflex. = reflexive
sc. = *scīlicet* (*i.e.,* supply)
sing. = singular
superl. = superlative

* The glossary in this volume, with some minor variation, is taken with permission from *Caesar: Selections from his* COMMENTARII DE BELLO GALLICO by Hans-Friedrich Mueller (Bolchazy-Carducci Publishers 2012).

A.

ā (*before consonants*), **ab** (*before vowels and some consonants*), **abs** (*before tē, and in some compounds*), *prep. with abl., originally denoting separation;* (1) *of place, persons, time, etc.,* from, away from, from the vicinity of; (2) *denoting position, in some phrases,* at, in, on, on the side of; **ā tergō**, in the rear; (3) *with expressions of measure,* away, off; **ab mīlibus passuum duōbus,** two miles away; (4) *with the pass. voice often expressing agent (the person by whom the action is performed),* by; (5) *variously translated in other expressions,* from, by, in respect to, after.

a. = **ante** *adv.,* (1) before, above, previously; (2) *prep. with acc.,* before, in front of, in advance of.

A., *abbr. for* **Aulus**, *a Roman praenomen.*

abic•iō, -ere, abiēcī, abiectum [**iaciō**, throw. App. §7], throw away *or* down; hurl.

abs, *see* **ā.**

absum, abesse, āfuī, — [**sum**, be. App. §78], be away, be absent *or* distant, be lacking *or* free from.

ac, *see* **atque.**

ac•cēdō, -cēdere, -cessī, -cessum [**ad + cēdō**, go], approach, come near to, arrive at, come to; to be added.

accersō see **arcessō**

ac•cidō, -cidere, -cidī, — [**ad + cadō**, fall], fall to *or* upon; befall; happen, fall to the lot of, occur.

ac•cipiō, -cipere, -cēpī, -ceptum [**ad + capiō**, take], take *or* receive to oneself, accept; experience, suffer; learn, hear, take.

āc•er, -ris, -re, *adj.,* sharp [App. §36].

aci•ēs, -ēī (*old gen.* **aciē**), *f.,* sharp point *or* edge *of a weapon;* sharp *or* keen sight, glance; a line (*as forming an edge*), battle line; **prīma,** the vanguard; **media,** the center; **novissima,** the rear (guard).

ad, *prep. with acc., originally expressing motion toward:* (1) *expressing motion,* toward, against, to the vicinity of; (2) *expressing position,* at, by, near; (3) *expressing purpose, with the gerund and gerundive,* to, for (the purpose of); (4) *with numbers,* up to, about; (5) *of time,* up to, until; at, on; (6) *variously translated in other relations,* at, after, for, to, according to, in the eyes of, among.

adāctus, *see* **adigō.**

ad•dō, -dere, -didī, -ditum [**dō**, put], place on, add.

ad•dūcō, -dūcere, -dūxī, -ductum [**dūcō**, lead], lead to, draw to, bring to; induce, influence.

adeō, *adv.,* to such an extent, so much, so very, so; in fact.

ad•eō, -īre, -iī, -itum [**eō**, go. App. §84], go to, approach, visit, assail, attack.

ad•ficiō, -ficere, -fēcī, -fectum [**ad + faciō**, do], affect, inspire; **magnō dolōre afficere,** to annoy greatly.

ad•flīgō, -flīgere, -flīxī, -flīctum, strike against; overthrow; damage, injure.

adgregō see **aggregō**

ad•haereō, -haerēre, -haesī, -haesum [**haereō**, stick], cling to, stick to.

adhib•eō, -ēre, -uī, -itum [**habeō**, have], bring to, bring in, summon; employ, use.

adhortor, 1 [**hortor,** encourage], encourage, incite.

ad•igō, -igere, -ēgī, -āctum [**ad + agō**, move], drive *or* bring by force, move; thrust, plunge, hurl (*of weapons*); bind (*by an oath*).

ad•ipīscor, -ipīscī, -eptus sum, attain to, gain.

adit•us, -ūs, *m.* [**adeō**, go to], approach, means of approach, right to approach, access.

ad•iungō, -iungere, -iūnxī, -iūnctum [**iungō**, join], attach, join to, unite, add.

adiūt•or, -ōris, *m.* [**adiuvō**, aid], helper, assistant, abettor.

adminis•ter, -trī, *m.* [**minister,** servant], attendant, priest.

administrō, 1 [**minister,** servant], serve, attend, wait upon; manage, guide.

ad•mittō, -mittere, -mīsī, -missum [**mittō**, send], admit; commit; incur; let go; give reins (*to a horse*).

admodum, *adv.* [**modus,** measure], *literally: up to the measure;* very much, very; *with numbers,* fully; *with negative,* at all.

ad•olēscō, -olēre, -olēvī, -ultum, grow up.

ad•orior, -orīrī, -ortus sum [**orior,** arise], rise against, assail, attack.

ad•scīscō, -scīscere, -scīvī, -scītum [**ad + scīscō**, approve], approve, admit *or* receive (*as allies*).

adsistō see **assistō**

adsum, adesse, adfuī [**sum**, be, App. §77], be near, be present, be at hand, appear.

Aduātic•ī, -ōrum, *m., a people in Belgic Gaul,* the Aduatici.

advent•us, -ūs, *m.* [**veniō,** come], arrival, approach, coming.

adversus, *prep. with acc.* [**adversus,** turned against], opposite to, against.

advers•us, -a, -um, *adv.* [perf. part. of **advertō,** turn to], turned to, turned against; opposite, fronting; adverse, unfavorable; unsuccessful; **adversō flūmine,** up the river; **in adversum ōs,** full in the face.

advolō, 1 [**volō,** fly], fly to or against, rush on or at.

aedifi•cium, -cī, n. [**aedificiō,** build], building, house.

Aedu•us, -a, -um, adj., of the Aedui; as a noun: an Aeduan; pl. as a noun: the Aedui or Aeduans, one of the most powerful Gallic tribes.

ae•ger, -gra, -grum, adj., sick, ill.

aes, aeris, n., copper; anything made of copper, coin, money; **aes aliēnum,** someone else's money: debt.

aes•tās, -tātis, f., summer.

aestimāti•ō, -ōnis, f. [**aestimō,** value], valuation, appraisal.

aest•us, -ūs, m., heat, boiling, surging, tide; **minuente aestū,** at ebb tide.

af•ficiō, -ficere, -fēcī, -fectum [**ad + faciō,** do], do to, treat, affect; **magnō dolōre afficere,** to annoy greatly.

ag•er, -rī, m., field, land; district, territory.

aggreg•ō, 1 [**ad + grex,** flock] unite in a flock; assemble; join, attach.

agm•en, -inis, n. [**agō,** move], a moving body; a marching column; army; **in agmine,** on the march; **prīmum agmen,** the vanguard (those in front); **novissimum** or **extrēmum agmen,** the rear (guard) (those in back).

ag•ō, -ere, ēgī, actum, set in motion, drive (animals); move forward, advance (military works); do, transact, carry on (business); discuss, speak; hold (**conventum,** a meeting); give, render (**grātiās,** thanks); plead (**causam,** a case); **quod agitur,** the matter in hand; **rēs agitur,** something is at stake.

ala•cer, -cris, -cre, adj., lively, eager, active, ready, joyous, "fired up."

alacri•tās, -tātis, f. [**alacer,** lively], enthusiasm, eagerness.

Alesi•a, -ae, f., Alesia; main city of the Mandubii; now called Alise-Sainte-Reine.

aliās, adv. [**alius,** another], at another place, elsewhere; at another time; **aliās . . . aliās,** at one time . . . at another.

aliēn•us, -a, -um, adj. [**alius,** other], of or belonging to another, another's; strange, alien, unfamiliar; unfavorable; foreign to the purpose; **aes aliēnum,** debt; **aliēnissimī,** complete strangers.

aliō, adv. [**alius,** other], to another place, person, or thing; elsewhere.

ali•quis, -quid and **ali•quī, -qua, -quod,** indef. pron. [**quis,** who. App. §62, a], someone, something; anyone, anything, any.

aliter, adv. [**alius,** other], otherwise; **aliter . . . ac,** otherwise . . . than.

ali•us, -a, -ud, gen. **alīus** (App. §32), another, other; **alius . . . alius . . . ,** one . . . another . . . ; in pl., some . . . others . . .

Allobrog•ēs, -um, m., the Allobroges, a Gallic people in the Roman Province.

Alp•ēs, -ium, f., Alps; the mountains that separate northern Italy from Germany and Transalpine Gaul.

alt•er, -era, -erum (App. §32), the other (of two); second; the one; **alter . . . alter,** the one . . . the other; **alterī . . . alterī,** the one party . . . the other.

altitūd•ō, -inis, f. [**altus,** high, deep], height, depth; thickness (of timber).

alt•us, -a, -um, adj., high, deep; n. as noun: the deep, the sea.

ambact•us, -ī, m., vassal.

Ambarr•ī, -ōrum, m., Ambarri; a tribe living to the east of the Arar river.

Ambior•īx, -īgis, m., Ambiorix, king of the Eburones.

amb•ō, -ae, -a, adj., both.

amīciti•a, -ae, f. [**amīcus,** friend], friendship.

amīc•us, -a, -um, adj. [**amō,** love], friendly, well-disposed; devoted.

amīc•us, -ī, m. [**amō,** love], friend, ally.

ā•mittō, -mittere, -mīsī, -missum [**mittō,** send], send away, dismiss; let go; lose.

āmment•um, -ī, n., strap or thong, fastened to the shaft of a javelin to aid its propulsion.

amplē, adv. [**amplus,** large], largely; comp., **amplius,** more, farther.

ampl•us, -a, -um, adj., of large extent, spacious, large; illustrious, splendid, noble; generous, magnificent; **amplius,** comparative as noun, more, a greater number, a greater distance.

an, conj., used to introduce the second element of alternative questions, or, or rather.

ancor•a, -ae, f., anchor; **in ancorīs,** at anchor.

angustē, adv. [**angustus,** narrow], narrowly; in close quarters.

angusti•ae, -ārum, f. pl. [**angustus,** narrow], narrowness; a narrow place or pass, strait, defile; straits, difficulties, perplexities.

angust•us, -a, -um, adj. [**angō,** squeeze], compressed, confined, narrow; **in angustō,** in a critical condition.

anim•a, -ae, f., breath, life, soul.

animad•vertō, -vertere, -vertī, -versum [**animus,** mind + **ad** + **vertō,** turn], turn the mind to; notice; **animadvertere in,** punish.

anim•al, -ālis, *n.* [**anima,** breath], animal, living (*and* breathing) creature.

anim•us, -ī, *m.,* mind, intellect; feelings; character; spirit, soul; resolution, courage; **animī causā,** for amusement; **in animō habēre,** intend.

ann•us, -ī, *m.,* year.

ante (1) *adv.,* before, above, previously; (2) *prep. with acc.,* before, in front of, in advance of.

antecurs•or, -ōris, *m.* [**currō,** run], forerunner; *pl.,* vanguard.

ante•ferō, -ferre, -tulī, -lātum [**ferō,** carry. App. §81], carry *or* bear before; prefer.

aper•iō, -īre, -uī, -tum, open, expose.

Apoll•ō, -inis, *m., the god* Apollo.

appellō, 1, call, name, call by name, accost.

appropinquō, 1 [**ad + propinquus,** near], come near, come close, approach.

Apr. = Aprīl•is, -e, *adj.,* of (*the month of*) April.

Aprīl•is, -e, *adj.,* of (*the month of*) April.

apud, *prep. with acc.,* at, among, near, with; (*with persons*) at the house of, in the presence of.

aqua, -ae, *f.,* water.

aquil•a, -ae, *f.,* an eagle; a military standard (*the* aquila *was the main* standard *of the legion*).

aquili•fer, -ferī, *m.* [**aquila,** eagle + **ferō,** carry], standard-bearer.

Aquītān•ī, -ōrum, *m.,* the Aquitani *or* Aquitanians (*a people located on the Atlantic coast above the Pyrenees, the mountains that separate the Iberian peninsula from Gaul*).

Aquītān•us, -a, -um, *adj.,* Aquitanian, of Aquitania.

Arar, -is, *m.* (*acc.:* **-im**), Arar (*river*); *now called* Saône.

arbitror, 1, decide, think, believe.

arcess•ō, -ere, -īvī, -ītum, summon, send for, invite.

ārd•eō, -ēre, ārsī, ārsum, burn, blaze, be inflamed, be eager.

argill•a, -ae, *f.,* white clay.

ārid•us, -a, -um, *adj.* [**āreō,** be dry], dry; *n. as noun:* dry land.

Ariovist•us, -ī, *m.,* Ariovistus, a Germanic king.

arm•a, -ōrum, *n. pl.,* arms, equipment, weapons; *by metonymy:* battle, war.

armāment•a, -ōrum, *n. pl.* [**armō,** arm], implements, gear; tackle *or* rigging (*of a ship*).

Arpīnē•ius, -ī, *m.,* Gaius Arpineius, *an equestrian in Caesar's army.*

arrip•iō, -ere, -uī, arreptum [**ad + rapiō,** seize], take *or* seize hurriedly.

ars, artis, *f.,* skill, art; *pl.* the arts.

arti•ficium, -ficī, *n.* [**ars,** art + **faciō,** make], a trade, handicraft; artifice, trick.

a•scendō, -scendere, -scendī, -scēnsum [**ad + scandō,** climb], climb up, ascend, mount, climb.

a•scīscō, -scīscere, -scīvī, -scītum [**ad + scīscō,** approve], approve, admit *or* receive (*as allies*).

assistō, assistere, astitī, — [**ad + sistō,** stand], stand by, stand near.

ascēns•us, -ūs, *m.* [**ascendō,** climb up], ascent, approach, climbing up.

asp•er, -era, -erum, *adj.,* rough, violent.

at, *conj.,* but, at least.

atque, ac (**ac** *only before consonants,* **atque** *before vowels and consonants*), *usually adds something especially important, while* **et** *usually adds things of equal importance; and also, and even, and; after words expressing a comparison or difference: than, as, from.*

Atre•bās, -bātis, *m.,* an Atrebatian; *pl.* the Atrebates.

at•texō, -texere, -texuī, -textum [**ad + texō,** weave], weave on.

atting•ō, -ere, attigī, attactum [**ad + tangō,** touch], touch *or* border on, reach, extend to, arrive at, attain.

at•tribuō, -tribuere, -tribuī, -tribūtum [**ad + tribuō,** assign], assign, allot.

auctor, -is, *m.* [**augeō,** increase], one who produces, creates, *or* originates; promoter, instigator, advisor, author.

auctōri•tās, -tātis, *f.* [**auctor,** producer], influence, character, authority, reputation.

audācter, *adv.* [**audāx,** bold], boldly, fearlessly, daringly. *Comp.* **audācius;** *superl.* **audācissimē.**

aud•eō, -ēre, ausus sum (App. §74), dare, risk, venture.

audiō, 4, hear, hear of; **dictō audiēns,** obedient.

auge•ō, -ēre, auxī, auctum, increase, augment, enhance, add to.

aurīg•a, -ae, *m.,* charioteer.

Aurunculēi•us, -ī, *m.,* Lucius Aurunculeius Cotta, *one of Caesar's lieutenants.*

aut, *conj., used where the difference is important or exclusive,* or; **aut . . . aut,** either . . . or.

autem, *conj.,* but (*a weak adversative*); however, on the other hand; now; moreover.

auxilior, 1 [**auxilium,** help], help, give aid, assist, render assistance.

auxil•ium, -ī, *n.* [**augeō,** increase], help, assistance, aid; *pl.,* auxiliary troops; reinforcements.

āvert•ō, -ere, -ī, āversum [ab + vertō, turn], turn away from *or* away, turn aside; turn back, repulse; *perf. part. as adj.:* with back turned.

B.

balte•us, -ī, *m.,* sword belt.

Balven•tius, -tī, *m.,* Titus Balventius, *one of Caesar's centurions.*

barbar•us, -a, -um, *adj.,* foreign (*to Romans and Greeks*), uncivilized; *pl. as noun:* barbarians.

Belg•ae, -ārum, *m.,* the Belgians *or* Belgae (*a people located in northern Gaul along the English Channel*).

Belg•ium, -ī, *n.,* the territory belonging to the Belgae.

bellō, 1, make war, carry on war, wage war.

bellovac•ī, -ōrum, *m.,* the Bellovaci (*a Belgic people*).

bell•um, -ī, *n.,* war.

benefi•cium, -cī, *n.* [**bene,** well + **faciō,** do], benefit, favor, kindness, good deed.

benevolenti•a, -ae, *f.* [**bene,** well + **volō,** wish], goodwill, kindness.

Bibract•e, -is, *n.,* Bibracte; *capital of the Aedui.*

bīdu•um, -ī, *n.* [**bis,** twice + **diēs,** day], space *or* period of two days.

bienn•ium, -ī, *n.* [**bis,** twice + **annus,** year], two years.

bipertītō, *adv.* [**bis,** twice + **partior,** divide], in two parts *or* divisions, in two ways.

Bōi•ī, -ōrum, *m.,* the Boii, *a Celtic tribe in southern Germany and Cisalpine Gaul who had once been powerful.*

bon•us, -a, -um, *adj.,* good, beneficial, profitable, well-disposed; (*with* **animō**) friendly; *as noun,* **bon•um, -ī,** *n.,* profit, advantage; **bon•a, -ōrum,** *n. pl.,* goods, property, estate; **bon•ī, -ōrum,** *m. pl.,* the good (people), good men, good citizens. *Comp.:* **melior;** *superl.:* **optimus** (App. §42).

brev•is, -e, *adv.,* short, brief, transitory.

Britanni•a, -ae, *f.,* Britannia, Britain.

C.

C., *abbr. for praenomen* **Gāius.**

C., *sign for* **centum,** one hundred.

cad•ō, -ere, cecidī, cāsum, fall; fall in battle, be killed, die.

caed•ēs, -is, *f.* [**caedō,** cut], slaughter, massacre, murder.

caelest•is, -e, *adj.* [**caelum,** sky], *what is in the sky,* heavenly, celestial; *pl. as noun:* the gods (*who live in the sky*).

Caes•ar, -aris, *m.,* (1) Gaius Julius Caesar, *general in Gaul and author of the Commentaries;* (2) Lucius Julius Caesar, *Caesar's relative and one of his lieutenants.*

caesp•es, -itis, *m.,* sod, turf.

calami•tās, -tātis, *f.,* disaster, misfortune, defeat.

cap•iō, -ere, cēpī, captum, take, capture, seize, catch; take in, beguile, induce; take up (*arms*); choose, select (*a place*); form; adopt (*a plan*); reach; arrive at (*a place*); make (*a beginning*); **collem capere,** take a position on a hill; **fugam capere,** take to flight.

captīv•us, -a, -um, *adj.* [**capiō,** take], prisoner, captive.

Carnut•ēs, -um, *m.,* the Carnutes (*a people in central Gaul*).

carr•us, -ī, *m.,* cart, wagon.

car•us, -a, -um, *adj.,* dear, precious.

cas•a, -ae, *f.,* hut, barrack.

Cass•ius, -ī, *m.,* Lucius Cassius Longinus, *consul in 107 BCE, defeated and slain in battle by the Tigurini.*

Castic•us, -ī, *m.,* Casticus, *an important man among the Sequani.*

castr•a, -ōrum, *n. pl.* [**castrum,** fortress], camp, fortified camp; **castra facere** *or* **pōnere,** pitch camp; **castra movēre,** break camp.

cās•us, -ūs, *m.* [**cadō,** fall], *what befalls:* accident, chance, misfortune, fate; crisis; **cāsū,** by chance.

Catamantaloed•is, -is, *m.,* Catamantaloedis, *a leader among the Sequani before Caesar's day.*

catēn•a, -ae, *f.,* chain, fetter.

Catuvolc•us, -ī, *m.,* Catuvolcus, *a leader among the Eburones who eventually poisons himself when things go badly for him.*

caus•a, -ae, *f.,* cause, reason, grounds, motive; situation, condition; a (*legal*) case, cause; **causam dīcere,** to plead a case; **causā,** *following a gen.,* for the sake of, for the purpose of, for.

cēd•ō, -ere, cessī, cessum, go, go away; give way, yield, retreat.

celeri•tās, -tātis, *f.* [**celer,** swift], quickness, speed, swiftness.

celeriter, *adv.* [**celer,** swift], quickly, rapidly, speedily.

Celt•ae, -ārum, *m.,* the Celts *or* Kelts, the Celtae.

centum (C.), *indecl. card. number,* one hundred.

centuri•ō, -ōnis, *m.* [**centum,** hundred], centurion, *the commander of the century, a unit corresponding to one-sixtieth of a legion.*

certām•en, -inis, *n.* [**certō,** struggle], strife, struggle, contest, combat.

certē, *adv.* [**certus,** certain], certainly, at least, at all events.

cert•us, -a, -um, *adj.,* decided, certain, sure, fixed; **certiōrem facere,** inform *(with acc. and inf.)*; order *(with* **ut** *or* **nē** *and the subjunctive);* **certior fierī,** be informed.

cēter•ī, -ae, -a, *adj.,* the rest of, the remainder; *as noun:* the rest, the remaining, the others.

Ceutron•ēs, -um, *m.,* the Ceutrones: (1) *a Belgic people subject to the Nervii or* (2) *a people living in the eastern part of the Roman Province.*

cibāri•us, -a, -um, *adj.* [**cibus,** food], pertaining to food; *n. pl. as noun:* provisions; **molita cibāria,** flour, meal.

Cicer•ō, -ōnis, *m.,* Quintus Tullius Cicero, *brother of the more famous orator and consul of 63 BCE, Marcus Tullius Cicero. He served as one of Caesar's legates.*

cing•ō, -ere, cīnxī, cīnctum, encircle, surround, invest, encompass; man *(a wall).*

circiter, *adv.,* about, around, near.

circuit•us, -ūs, *m.* [**circumeō,** go around], a going around; a winding path; circumference, circuit.

circum, *prep. with acc.* [**circus,** circle], around, about, near.

circumcīd•ō, -ere, -ī, circumcīsum [**circum,** around + **caedō,** cut], cut around, cut off, cut; isolate.

circum•dō, -dare, -dedī, -datum [**dō,** put], put around, encompass, surround.

circum•sistō, -sistere, -stitī, — [**sistō,** stand], stand, flock *or* rally around, surround, hem in.

circum•spiciō, -spicere, -spexī, -spectum [**speciō,** look], look *(around)* for *or* at, consider, examine.

circum•veniō, -venīre, -vēnī, -ventum [**veniō,** come], come *or* get around, surround, cut off, beset; betray, defraud.

citō, *adv.,* quickly, speedily. *Comp.* **citius;** *superl.* **citissimē.**

cīvi•tās, -tātis, *f.* [**cīvis,** citizen], citizenship; the citizens *(as forming a community),* state, city.

clam, *adv.,* secretly.

clāmitō, 1 [*frequentative of* **clāmō,** cry out], cry out repeatedly, exclaim.

clām•or, -ōris, *m.* [**clāmō,** cry out], outcry, noise, shouting, clamor.

clār•us, -a, -um, *adj.,* clear, loud.

clēmenti•a, -ae, *f.* [**clēmēns,** gentle], gentleness, kindness, mercy, clemency.

cliēns, clientis, *m., f.* [**clueō,** hear, obey], client, vassal, dependent, retainer.

co•emō, -emere, -ēmī, -ēmptum [**emō,** buy], buy, buy up.

coepī, coepisse (App. §86), began, commenced, undertook; **coeptus,** *perf. part.,* begun, commenced.

cōgitō, 1 [**co + agitō,** consider], consider thoroughly *or* carefully, ponder, reflect; think, purpose, plan.

cog•nōscō, -nōscere, -nōvī, -nitum [**co + (g)nōscō,** learn], learn, ascertain; study, investigate; *perf.,* I *have learned, and thus:* I know (App. §193, I, *a.*).

cōgō, cōgere, coēgī, coāctum [**co + agō,** drive], drive *or* bring together, collect, draw together, assemble, force, compel.

cohor•s, -tis, *f.,* cohort.

cohortor, 1 [**co + hortor,** encourage], encourage greatly, cheer, animate.

co•iciō, -icere, -iēci, -iectum [**co + iaciō,** throw. App. §7], hurl, throw, cast.

commentāri•us, -ī, *m.* [**commentor,** consider], notebook, sketchbook, memorandum, journal; sketch, memorandum, report; explanation, commentary.

con•iciō, -icere, -iēcī, -iectum [**co + iaciō,** throw. App. §7], hurl, throw, cast; put; put together *(logically),* conjecture; **in fugam conicere,** put to flight.

colligō, 1 [**con + ligō,** bind], bind *or* fasten together.

col•ligō, -ligere, -lēgī, -lēctum [**con + legō,** gather], gather together, collect; acquire; **sē colligere,** *collect oneself:* rally, recover.

collocō, 1 [**con + locō,** place], place, set, station; arrange; **nūptum collocāre,** to give in marriage.

collo•quium, -quī, *n.* [**colloquor,** talk together], talking together; conference, parley, interview.

col•loquor, -loquī, -locūtus sum [**con + loquor,** talk], speak with, converse, confer, have a conference.

colō, colere, coluī, cultum, cultivate, dwell in; honor, worship.

comb•ūrō, -ūrere, -ussī, -ustum [**con + ūrō,** burn], burn up.

commeāt•us, -ūs, *m.* [**commeō,** go back and forth], trip, voyage; supplies, provisions.

commemorō, 1 [**memorō,** call to mind], remind one of; state, mention.

commendō, 1 [**mandō,** entrust], entrust, surrender.

commeō, 1 [meō, go], go back and forth; *with* ad, resort to, visit.

comminus, *adv.* [manus, hand], hand to hand, in close combat.

com•mittō, -mittere, -mīsī, -missum [mittō, send], join, splice; commit (*a crime*), do; allow, permit; entrust; **proelium committere**, join *or* begin battle.

Com•mius, -mī, *m.*, Commius, *a leader of the Atrebates. He was loyal to Caesar until 52 BCE when he led troops in support of the general Gallic revolt.*

commodē, *adv.* [commodus, convenient], conveniently; readily, easily, fitly; **satis commodē**, to great advantage, very easily.

commod•us, -a, -um, *adj.* [modus, measure], *in full measure:* convenient, suitable, satisfactory.

commod•um, -ī, *n.* [commodus, convenient], convenience, interest, advantage.

commūnicō, 1 [commūnis, common], make common, communicate, impart, share.

commūn•is, -e, *adj.*, common, general; **rēs commūnis**, the common interest.

comparō, 1 [parō, prepare], prepare, get ready; acquire, gain, secure, prepare for.

com•periō, -perīre, -perī, -pertum [pariō, procure], find out with certainty, discover, ascertain.

com•pleō, -plēre, -plēvī, -plētum [*obs.*: pleō, fill], fill up *or* completely; complete; cover.

complūr•ēs, -a, *adj.* [plūs, more], several, many; a great many.

comportō, 1 [portō, carry], carry together, collect, bring.

com•prehendō, -prehendere, -prehendī, -prehēnsum [prehendō (=prendō), seize], grasp *or* lay hold of, seize, catch, arrest, take, catch (*fire*).

con•cēdō, -cēdere, -cessī, -cessum [cēdō, go], go away, depart, withdraw; grant, yield; allow, permit.

con•cīdō, -cīdere, -cīsī, -cīsum [caedō, cut], cut down, kill, slay, cut off.

con•cidō, -ere, -cidī, —, [cadō, fall], fall down, fall.

conciliō, 1 [concilium, assembly], bring together; gain *or* win over, secure; reconcile, conciliate.

concil•ium, -ī, *n.*, assembly, gathering, council.

concitō, 1 [citō, put in motion], stir up, rouse, instigate, incite.

conclāmō, 1 [clāmō, shout], shout out, call aloud, yell.

con•currō, -currere, -cursī, -cursum [currō, run], run *or* rush together; hurry, run, rush; run to the rescue; come, gather.

concursō, 1 [*frequentative of* concurrō, run], run about.

concurs•us, -ūs, *m.* [concurrō, run], a running together, attack, onset; collision.

condici•ō, -ōnis, *f.*, condition, state; agreement, stipulation, terms.

con•dūcō, -dūcere, -dūxī, -ductum [dūcō, lead], lead *or* bring together, assemble, conduct; hire.

cōnfectus, *see* **cōnficiō**.

cōn•ferō, -ferre, contulī, collātus [ferō, bring. App. §81], bring *or* get together, collect, gather, carry, bring; crowd together; ascribe to; put off, defer; compare; **sē cōnferre**, betake oneself, take refuge.

cōnfert•us, -a, -um, *adj.* [*perf. part. of* cōnferciō, crowd together], dense, thick, compact, stuffed.

cōnfestim, *adv.*, hastily, at once, immediately.

cōn•ficiō, -ficere, -fēcī, -fectum [faciō, make], make *or* do thoroughly, complete, accomplish, finish; finish up, exhaust, weaken; furnish; dress *or* treat (*leather*).

cōn•fīdō, -fīdere, -fīsī, -fīsum [fīdō, trust. App. §74], trust completely, rely on, feel confident, hope; **cōnfīsus**, *perf. part. with pres. meaning:* relying on.

cōnfīn•ium, -ī, *n.* [fīnis, boundary], common boundary, neighborhood.

cōnfīrmō, 1 [fīrmō, strengthen], establish, strengthen, encourage, console; declare, assert.

cōn•fiteor, -fitērī, -fessus sum [fateor, confess], acknowledge, confess.

cōnflagrō, 1 [flagrō, burn], burn, be on fire.

cōnflīctō, 1 [*freq. of* cōnflīgō], strike together; *in the pass.:* be distressed.

cōn•flīgō, -flīgere, -flīxī, -flīctum [flīgō, strike], strike against; contend, fight.

coniūnctim, *adv.* [coniungō, join], jointly.

con•iungō, -iungere, -iūnxī, -iūnctum [coniungō, join], join with *or* together, connect, unite, bind.

coniūrāti•ō, -ōnis, *f.* [coniūrō, swear], a swearing together; plot, conspiracy; secret organization; confederacy; gang.

cōnor, 1, try, attempt, endeavor.

cōn•scendō, -scendere, -scendī, -scēnsum [scandō, climb], climb, mount; go on board, embark.

cōn•scīscō, -scīscere, -scīvī, -scītum [scīscō, resolve], resolve upon; **sibi mortem cōnscīscere**, commit suicide.

cōn•scrībō, -scrībere, -scrīpsī, -scrīptum [scrībō, write], *write together in a list:* levy, enroll, enlist; write.

cōnsecrō, 1 [sacrō, dedicate], dedicate, consecrate.

cōnsecūtus, *see* cōnsequor.

cōn•sentiō, -sentīre, -sēnsī, -sēnsum [sentiō, feel], *think together*: agree, combine.

cōn•sequor, -sequī, -secūtus sum [sequor, follow], follow up; go after, pursue; reach, overtake; gain, attain, accomplish; ensue, succeed.

cōn•sīdō, -sīdere, -sēdī, -sessum [sīdō, sit down], sit down together, settle; take a position.

cōnsili•um, -ī, *n.*, consultation, deliberation; counsel, advice; plan, design; measure, course of action; judgement; prudence, wisdom; an assembly for deliberation, council, council of war; **commūnī cōnsiliō**, by, *or* in accordance with, general action; **pūblicō cōnsiliō**, by action of the state; **cōnsilium capere** *or* **inīre**, form *or* adopt a plan; **cōnsilium habēre**, think, consider.

cōn•sistō, -sistere, -stitī, — [sistō, stand], take a stand *or* position, keep one's position, stand, form (*when soldiers make a formation*); stop, halt, remain, stay; (*of ships*) lie at anchor; consist in, depend *or* rest on.

cōnspect•us, -ūs, *m.* [conspiciō, look at], sight, view; presence.

cōn•spiciō, -spicere, -spexī, -spectum [speciō, look], look at, observe, discern, perceive.

cōnspicor, 1 [speciō, look], observe, discern, perceive.

cōnstipō, 1, press *or* crowd closely.

cōn•stituō, -stituere, -stituī, -stitūtum [statuō, set up], set up, erect, construct, appoint, decide, decree, determine, establish, set, settle; (*of troops*) draw up (*in formation*); (*of ships*) anchor, station; raise (*a legion*).

cōn•stō, -stāre, -stitī, -statum [stō, stand], stand firm; depend on; be complete; cost; *impers.*: it is agreed, certain, evident, *or* known.

cōn•suēscō, -suēscere, -suēvī, -suētum [suēscō, become used to], become accustomed *or* used to; *perf.* (App. §193, I, *a.*), be accustomed; **cōnsuētus**, *perf. part. as adj.*: accustomed, usual.

cōnsuētūd•ō, -inis, *f.* [cōnsuēscō, become accustomed], habit, custom, practice; mode of life, "lifestyle."

cōn•sul, -sulis, *m.*, consul, *one of the two chief magistrates elected annually at Rome.*

cōnsul•ō, -ere, -uī, -tum, take counsel, consult, consider; *with dat.*: take counsel for, consider the interests of, take care for; spare.

cōn•sūmō, -sūmere, -sūmpsī, -sūmptum [sūmō, take], *take together or all at once*: devour, consume, destroy; use up, waste, pass.

cōn•surgō, -surgere, -surrēxī, -surrectum [surgō, rise], arise together, arise in a body, arise.

contabulō, 1 [tabula, board], floor over, build in multiple stories, build up.

contāgi•ō, -ōnis, *f.* [contingō, touch], contact.

contempti•ō, -ōnis, *f.* [contemnō, despise], disdain, contempt.

con•tendō, -tendere, -tendī, -tentum [tendō, stretch], push forward, hasten; march; strive, contend, fight; be anxious for; maintain, insist.

contenti•ō, -ōnis, *f.* [contendō, strive], striving, struggle, contest, dispute.

con•testor, -ārī, -ātum [con + testor, witness], to call to witness.

con•texō, -texere, -texuī, -textum [texō, weave], weave *or* bind together, connect.

contigī, *see* contingō.

contin•ēns, -entis, *adj.* [contineō, hold together], *holding together*; continuous, unbroken; neighboring; *as noun*, mainland, continent.

continenter, *adv.* [continēns, continuous], without interruption, continually, continuously.

con•tineō, -tinēre, -tinuī, -tentum [teneō, hold], hold together; hold, keep, restrain; bound, shut up, contain; **sē continēre**, *with abl.*, remain in, on, *or* within.

con•tingō, -tingere, -tigī, -tāctum [tangō, touch], touch, reach; extend to; befall, happen, to.

continu•us, -a, -um, *adj.* [contineō, hold together], holding together, unbroken, uninterrupted, continuous.

contrā, *adv. and prep. with acc.*: (1) *as adv.*: against him *or* them; on the other hand; **contrā atque**, contrary to what; (2) *as prep.*, against, contrary to; opposite, facing.

contrōversi•a, -ae, *f.* [contrā, against + versus, turned], dispute, argument, quarrel, controversy.

contumēli•a, -ae, *f.*, affront, indignity, insult; injury, violence.

convall•is, -is, *f.* [vallis, valley], enclosed valley, defile.

con•veniō, -venīre, -vēnī, -ventum [veniō, come], come together, assemble; convene, meet; come to, arrive; to be agreed upon; *impers.*: be convenient, suitable, *or* necessary.

convent•us, -ūs, *m.* [conveniō, come together], a coming together, meeting, assembly; court.

con•vertō, -vertere, -vertī, -versum [verto, turn], turn completely, turn around, wheel around; turn, change; **signa convertere**, (turn) about face.

co•orior, -orīrī, -ortus sum [orior, rise], arise, spring up, break out.

cōpi•a, -ae, *f.,* supply, plenty, abundance, number; *pl.:* resources; forces, troops.

cor, cordis, *n.,* heart.

cotīdiān•us, -a, -um, *adj.* [**cotīdiē,** daily], every day, daily; usual, customary.

cotīdiē, *adv.* [**quot,** how many + **diēs,** day], daily, every day.

Cott•a, -ae, *m.,* Lucius Aurunculeius Cotta, *one of Caesar's lieutenants.*

Crass•us, -ī, *m.,* Marcus Licinius Crassus, *(together with Pompey) political ally and supporter of Caesar, consul in 55 BCE, is killed while leading the Parthian expedition of 53 BCE; (2) his younger son,* Publius Licinius Crassus, *who served as one of Caesar's lieutenants 58–56 BCE; died in battle with his father in Parthia in 53 BCE; and (3) an elder son,* Marcus Licinius Crassus, *who served as one of Caesar's quaestors after his brother left Gaul.*

crāt•es, -is, *f.,* wickerwork; fascine *(a bundle of sticks used for filling trenches).*

crēb•er, -ra, -rum, *adj.,* thick, close, repeated, numerous, frequent, at short intervals. *Comp.:* **crēbrior;** *superl.:* **crēberrimus** (App. §40).

crēd•ō, -ere, -idī, -itum, believe, suppose; entrust.

cremō, 1, burn.

cruciāt•us, -ūs, *m.* [**cruciō,** torture; **crux,** cross *(used for crucifixion)*], torture, torment.

culp•a, -ae, *f.,* blame, fault, guilt.

cult•us, -ūs, *m.* [**colō,** cultivate], cultivation, civilization; mode of life, lifestyle; dress; religious worship.

cum, *conj.,* when, as, while; after, as soon as; whenever; since, because; although; **cum . . . tum,** not only . . . but also, both . . . and; **cum prīmum,** as soon as. *See* App. §§238–242.

cum, *prep. with abl.,* with, along with, together with.

cūnctor, 1, delay, hesitate, be reluctant.

cupidē, *adv.* [**cupidus,** desirous], desirously, eagerly.

cupidi•tās, -tātis, *f.* [**cupidus,** eager], eagerness, desire, greed, avarice.

cupid•us, -a, -um, *adj.* [**cupiō,** desire], eager, desirous, zealous, fond.

cūrō, 1 [**cūra,** care], care for, take care of, provide for; *with gerundive* (App. §285, II, *b.*): have, order.

curr•us, -ūs, *m.,* chariot.

curs•us, -ūs, *m.* [**currō,** run], running, speed; course, career; pasage, voyage.

D.

D., *sign for* **quīngentī,** five hundred.

d. = diem.

damnō, 1 [**damnum,** damage], declare guilty, sentence, condemn.

dē, *prep. with abl., originally expressing motion from;* (1) *of place,* from, down from, away from, out of; (2) *of time,* just after, about; (3) *variously translated in other relations,* about, concerning, of, from, in accordance with, for.

dēbeō, 2 [**dē + habeō,** have], have, *or* keep from *someone:* owe; *with inf.:* ought, must, have to; *pass.:* be due.

dē•cēdō, -cēdere, -cessī, -cessum [**cēdō,** go], go from *or* away, depart, withdraw, leave, forsake; die.

decem (X), *indecl. card. number,* ten.

dē•cernō, -cernere, -crēvī, -crētum [**cernō,** separate; decide], decide, vote, decree.

dēclīv•is, -e, *adj.* [**clīvus,** a slope], sloping downward, declining; *n. pl. as noun:* slopes.

dē•decus, -oris, *n.* [**decus,** honor], dishonor, disgrace.

dēditus, *see* **dēdō.**

dē•dō, -dere, -didī, -ditum [**dō,** give], give up, give over, yield, surrender; devote; **sē dēdere,** submit, surrender.

dē•dūcō, -dūcere, -dūxī, -ductum [**dūcō,** lead], lead down, lead away, withdraw; bring, conduct, lead; influence; launch *(ships)*; give in marriage.

dēfecti•ō, -ōnis, *f.* [**dēficiō,** fail], falling away, desertion, revolt.

dēfēnsor, -is, *m.* [**dēfendō,** defend], defender, protector; *(means of)* defense.

dē•ferō, -ferre, -tulī, -lātum [**ferō,** carry. App. §81], bring from, bring down, carry, take; report, disclose; bring before, refer; bestow, confer; **dēlātus** *(sometimes),* falling; coming by chance.

dē•ficiō, -ficere, -fēcī, -fectum [**faciō,** make], fail, desert, fall away, revolt.

dē•fīgō, -fīgere, -fīxī, -fīxum [**fīgō,** fix], fix *or* fasten down, drive in, plant.

dē•fugiō, -fugere, -fūgī, -fugitum [**fugiō,** flee], flee from, run away, shun.

dē•iciō, -icere, -iēcī, -iectum [**iaciō,** throw. App. §7], hurl *or* cast down; dislodge; kill; foil, disappoint.

deinceps, *adv.,* one after the other, in turn, successively.

deinde, *adv.* [**dē + inde,** from there, thence], then, next, after this, thereupon.

dēlīberō, 1 [lībra, balance], weigh well; consider, deliberate.

dēligō, 1 [ligō, bind], bind or tie down, fasten, moor.

dē•ligō, -ligere, -lēgī, -lēctum [legō, choose], pick out, select, choose.

dē•litēscō, -tēscere, -lituī, — [latēscō, inceptive of lateō, lie hidden], hide oneself, lurk.

dē•metō, -metere, -messuī, -messum [metō, reap], mow, reap.

dē•migrō, 1 [migrō, move, migrate], move from, move away, emigrate, remove.

dē•mittō, -mittere, -mīsī, -missum [mittō, send], send, thrust, or let down; sink; bow (one's head); sē dēmittere, come or get down, descend; sē animō dēmittere, lose courage; dēmissus, perf. part. as adj.: low.

dēmō, dēmere, dēmpsī, dēmptum [dē + emō, take], take down, remove.

dēmōnstrō, 1 [mōnstrō, show], point out, show, explain, describe; declare, state, say.

dēmum, adv., at length, at last, finally.

dē•pellō, -pellere, -pulī, -pulsum [pellō, drive], drive from or away, ward off.

dē•pōnō, -pōnere, -posuī, -positum [pōnō, put], lay down, put aside, put away, give up; place, station, deposit.

dē•prehendō, -prehendere, -prehendī, -prehēnsum [prehendō (=prendō), seize], seize, capture, catch.

dē•scendō, -scendere, -scendī, -scēnsum [scandō, climb], climb down, go down, descend; have recourse (to), resort.

dē•serō, -serere, -seruī, -sertum [serō, entwine, join], disjoin; abandon, desert, forsake; dēsertus, perf. part. as adj.: deserted, solitary.

dē•siliō, -silīre, -siluī, -sultum [saliō, jump], jump from, leap down, alight, dismount.

dēspērāti•ō, -ōnis, f. [dēspērō, despair], despair, hopelessness.

dēspērō, 1 [spērō, hope], despair, be hopeless, lack confidence; dēspērātus, perf. part.: despaired of; as adj.: desperate.

de•sum, -esse, -fuī, — [sum, be. App. §66], be lacking, be absent from, fail.

dēturbō, 1 [turbō, disturb], drive off, dislodge.

de•us, -ī (nom. pl.: diī; dat. pl.: dīs), m., god.

dē•vehō, -vehere, -vexī, -vectum [vehō, carry], carry away, bring.

dē•voveō, -vovēre, -vōvī, -vōtum [voveō, vow], consecrate, devote; dēvōtus, perf. part. as noun: a sworn follower.

dext•er, -ra, -rum, adj., on the right, right.

dextra, -ae, f. [dexter, right; sc. manus, hand], the right hand.

dīcō, dīcere, dīxī, dictum, say, tell, speak, express, mention; name, appoint; causam dīcere, plead a case; iūs dīcere, administer justice.

d. = diem.

diēs, diēī, m. and f., day; time; in diēs, from day to day; diem ex diē, day after day.

differō, differre, distulī, dīlātum [ferō, carry. App. §81], scatter, spread; put off, defer; be different, differ.

difficil•is, -e, adj. [facilis, easy], not easy, hard, troublesome, difficult.

difficul•tās, -tātis, f. [difficilis, difficult], difficulty, trouble, embarrassment.

dif•fīdō, -fīdere, -fīsī, -fīsum [fīdō, trust. App. §74], distrust, lack confidence, despair.

digni•tās, -tātis, f. [dignus, worthy], worthiness, dignity, (personal) merit or worth, status, rank.

dīiūdicō, 1 [iūdicō, judge], decide.

dīligenter, adv. [dīligēns, careful], carefully; with exactness, pains, or care.

dīligenti•a, -ae, f. [dīligēns, careful], carefulness, painstaking care.

dī•ligō, -ligere, -lēgī, -lēctum [legō, choose], choose or single out, esteem highly, love.

dīmicō, 1 [micō, brandish], fight, struggle, contend.

dī•mittō, -mittere, -mīsī, -missum [mittō, send], send in different directions, send away, send off, dismiss; break up; let go, let slip, let pass, give up, lose.

Dīs, Dītis, m., Dis, the god Pluto, god of the underworld.

dīs, see deus.

dis- (dī-, dif-, dir-), inseparable prefix, apart, asunder, in different directions; negative: equivalent to English un-, not.

dis•cēdō, -cēdere, -cessī, -cessum [cēdō, go], go away, depart, retire; leave (especially with ab or ex).

disciplīn•a, -ae, f. [discō, learn], learning, discipline; instruction, teaching; system.

discō, discere, didicī, —, learn, be taught.

di•spergō, -spergere, -spersī, -spersum [spargō, scatter], scatter, disperse.

dis•pōnō, -pōnere, -posuī, -positum [pōnō, put], place apart; distribute, arrange, station.

disputāti•ō, -ōnis, f. [disputō, discuss], argument, discussion.

disputō, 1 [putō, reckon], discuss, debate about.

dissensi•ō, -ōnis, f. [dissentiō, think differently], disagreement, dissension.

dis•sentiō, -sentīre, -sēnsī, -sēnsum [sentiō, feel], differ, disagree.

dis•tribuō, -tribuere, -tribuī, -tribūtum [tribuō, assign], assign, divide, distribute.

distulī, see differō.

dītissimus, superl. of dīves.

diū, adv., for a long time, long; quam diū, as long as; comp.: diūtius, longer, too long, any longer; superl.: diūtissimē, for the longest time.

dīves, dīvitis, adj., rich, wealthy; superl.: dītissimus.

Dīviciāc•us, -ī, m., Diviciacus, a leader of the Aedui, friendly to the Romans. Caesar pardons Dumnorix at his request.

dī•vidō, -videre, dīvīsī, dīvīsum, divide, distribute, separate; dīvīsus, perf. part. as adj.: divided, distributed, separated.

dīvīn•us, -a, -um, adj. [dīvus, divine], of the gods, divine, sacred.

dō, dare, dedī, datum (App. §85), give, bestow, present, grant, furnish; offer; yield, give up; in fugam dare, put to flight; dare manūs, yield; dare negōtium, with dat.: employ, engage, direct. (Some compounds of dō are derived from an obs. verb, dō, put.)

doceō, docēre, docuī, docitum, show, teach, instruct, inform.

dol•or, -ōris, m. [doleō, grieve], grief, distress, pain (physical or mental), anguish, annoyance.

domin•us, -ī, m., master.

dom•us, -ūs (App. §29, d.), f., house; home; native country.

dōs, dōtis, f. [dō, give], a marriage present, dowry.

Druid•ēs, -um, m., the Druids, the priests of the Celts in Gaul and Britain.

dubitāti•ō, -ōnis, f. [dubitō, doubt], doubt, uncertainty; hesitation.

dubitō, 1 [dubius, doubtful], be uncertain, doubt; hesitate, delay.

dubi•us, -a, -um, adj., uncertain, doubtful.

dūcō, dūcere, dūxī, ductum, lead, conduct, guide, draw; bring, fetch; trace, construct; extend; deem, consider, judge; protract, defer.

dum, conj., while, as long as; till, until.

Dumnor•ix, -īgis, m., Dumnorix, a leader of the Aeduans, brother of Diviciacus, son-in-law of Orgetorix, enemy of Caesar, and leader of the anti-Roman party. Caesar orders his execution in 54 BCE when he tries to escape.

du•o, -ae, -a (App. §49), card. num. and adj., two.

duodecim, card. number and adj. [duo, two + decem, ten], twelve.

dūr•us, -a, -um, adj., hard, rough, harsh, difficult, dangerous; severe, inclement.

dux, ducis, m. [dūcō, lead], leader, commander, general; guide.

E.

ē (only before consonants), ex (before vowels and some consonants), prep. with abl., originally expressing motion out of; (1) of place, out of, from, away from; expressing position, in some phrases, on; ūnā ex parte, on one side; (2) of time, from, after, since; ex itinere, immediately after the march; (3) variously translated in other relations: from, out of, of, because of, in accordance with; ē regiōne, opposite.

eā, adv. [= eā viā], by that way, there.

Eburōn•ēs, -um, m., the Eburones, a Belgic people who in 54 BCE destroyed troops under the command of Sabinus and Cotta. Afterwards, Caesar almost exterminated them.

ē•discō, -discere, -didicī, — [discō, learn], learn thoroughly, learn by heart.

ē•dūcō, -dūcere, -dūxī, -ductum [dūcō, lead], lead out, lead forth; draw (a sword).

effēminō, 1 [ex + fēmina, woman], make effeminate, weaken.

efferō, efferre, extulī, ēlātum [ex + ferō, carry. App. §81], bring or carry out, carry or take away; raise; spread around, publish widely, make known; elate, puff up.

ef•ficiō, -ficere, -fēcī, -fectum [faciō, make], make or do completely, complete, accomplish, construct; make, cause, bring about, render.

ef•fugiō, -fugere, -fūgī, — [fugiō, flee], flee from, run away, escape.

ēgī, see agō.

egō, meī (App. §51), first pers. pron., I, me; pl. nōs, we, us, etc.

ē•gredior, -gredī, -gressus sum [gradior, step], step out, go out, come forth, depart; march out, make a sortie; land (from a ship), disembark.

eiusmodī, of such a sort *or* kind, such.

ē•mittō, -mittere, -mīsī, -missum [mittō, send], let go, send out *or* forth, release; hurl, discharge; drop.

enim, *conj.*, in fact, really; for; **sed enim**, but in fact, however.

ē•nūntiō, 1 [nūntiō, announce], report, declare, disclose.

eō, īre, iī (īvī), itum (App. §84), go, proceed, march, pass.

eō, *abl.* of **is**.

eō, *adv.* [*old dat. of* **is**], to that place, there (*in the sense of* thither), to the place (*where, etc.*), to them (it, him, etc.).

eōdem, *adv.* [*old dat. of* **īdem**], to the same place, to the same point (result, purpose, etc.).

epistol•a, -ae, *f.*, letter, epistle.

equ•es, -itis, *m.* [equus, horse], a horseman, a rider; *pl.*: cavalry. *Roman society was organized by class or income levels. Originally, those who could afford their own horse were assigned to the cavalry. In Caesar's day, rich men who belonged to this class, even if they did not serve in the cavalry, were called* equestrians. *Rich Gauls were also called* equestrians.

equitāt•us, -ūs, *m.* [equus, horse], cavalry, horseman.

equ•us, -ī, *m.*, horse.

ē•ripiō, -ripere, -ripuī, -reptum [rapiō, seize], take away, wrest from, extort, deprive; rescue, relieve, save.

errō, 1, wander; err, be mistaken.

essedāri•us, -a, -um, *adj.* [essedum, war chariot], a soldier who fought from a two-wheeled British war chariot.

essed•um, -ī, *n.*, a two-wheeled war chariot used by the Britons.

Esuvi•ī, -ōrum, *m.*, the Esuvii, *a people in northwestern Gaul.*

et, *conj.*, and; also, too, even; **et . . . et**, both . . . and.

etiam, *conj.*, and also, also, even, yet.

etsī, *conj.* [et + sī, if], even if, although.

ē•veniō, -venīre, -vēnī, -ventum [veniō, come], turn out, result.

ēvent•us, -ūs, *m.* [ēveniō, turn out], outcome, issue, result, consequence.

ex, *see* **ē**.

ex•animō, 1 [anima, breath], deprive of breath, render breathless, exhaust; kill.

ex•audiō, 4 [audiō, hear], hear (*from a distance*).

ex•cēdō, -cēdere, -cessī, -cessum [cēdō, go], go out, go away, withdraw, retire.

ex•cellō, -cellere, —, —, excel, surpass.

excitō, 1 [citō, rouse], call forth, excite, animate, arouse; erect, construct (*towers*); kindle (*fires*).

excōgitō, 1 [cōgitō, think], think out, contrive, devise, invent.

excruciō, 1 [cruciō, torture; crux, cross (*used for crucifixion*)], torture severely, torment.

ex•eō, -īre, -iī, -ītum [eō, go. App. §84], go from, go out, depart from, leave.

exercitāti•ō, -ōnis, *f.* [*frequentative of* **exercitō**, *from* **exerceō**, exercise], exercise, training, practice, experience.

exercit•us, -ūs, *m.* [exerceō, exercise], *a trained or disciplined body of men*, an army.

ex•hauriō, -haurīre, -hausī, -haustum [hauriō, drain], draw out, empty.

exigui•tās, -tātis, *f.* [exiguus, scanty], scantiness, meagerness, shortness, dearth, want.

exīstimāti•ō, -ōnis, *f.* [exīstimō, estimate], judgement, opinion.

exīstimō, 1 [aestimō, reckon], estimate, reckon, think, consider.

exit•us, -ūs, *m.* [exeō, go out], a going out, exit, passage; issue, result, end.

expediō, 4 [pēs, foot], set free; arrange, prepare.

expedīt•us, -a, -um, *adj.* [*perf. part. of* expediō, set free], unimpeded, free, unobstructed; without baggage; light armed; *as noun*: a light-armed soldier.

ex•pellō, -pellere, -pulī, -pulsum [pellō, drive], drive out, drive forth, expel.

explōrō, 1, search *or* find out, investigate, spy out, reconnoiter.

ex•sequor, -sequī, -secūtus sum [sequor, follow], follow out, enforce.

ex•sistō, -sistere, stitī, — [sistō, stand], stand *or* come forth, appear, arise; ensue.

exspectō, 1 [spectō, look at], look out for, await, expect; wait to see; anticipate, apprehend.

ex•stinguō, -stinguere, -stīnxī, -stīnctum, put out, quench; destroy.

ex•struō, -struere, -strūxī, -strūctum [struō, build], build *or* pile up; construct, build.

extrā, *adv. and prep. with acc.*, out of, outside of, beyond, without.

extrēm•us, -a, -um, *adj.* [*superl. of* **exterus**. App. §44], outermost, utmost, farthest, extreme; the farthest part of; **extrēmī** (*as noun*), the rear ("the ones at the back"); **ad extrēmum,** at last, at the end; as a last resort.

ex•ūrō, -ūrere, -ussī, -ustum [ex + **ūro,** burn], burn up.

F.

Fab•ius, -ī, *m.* (1) Quintus Fabius Maximus, *victor over the Gallic Allobroges, Arverni, and Ruteni, in 121 BCE, after which he was also called* Allobricus. (2) Gaius Fabius, *one of Caesar's lieutenants.* (3) Lucius Fabius, *a centurion of the 8th legion; killed at Gergovia.*

facile, *adv.* [**facilis,** easy], easily, readily. *Comp.:* **facilius;** *superl.:* **facillimē** (App. §41).

facil•is, -e, *adj.* [**faciō,** do], easy.

fac•iō, -ere, fēcī, factum, make, construct, form, do, execute (*commands, etc.*); give (*opportunity, etc.*); *with* **ut,** bring about, cause; *intransitive:* do, act. *Pass.:* **fīō, fierī, factus sum** (App. §83), *with pass. meanings, and, used impers.,* result, happen, come to pass.

facin•us, -oris, *n.* [**faciō,** do] deed; misdeed, outrage, crime.

facul•tās, -tātis, *f.* [**facilis,** easy], power; opportunity, chance; resources, supply.

fals•us, -a, -um, *adj.* [*perf. part. of* **fallō,** deceive], false.

falx, falcis, *f.*, sickle, pruning hook; hook (*for pulling down walls*).

fām•a, -ae, *f.* [**fārī,** to speak], common talk, rumor, report, reputation, fame.

fam•ēs, -is, *f.*, starvation, hunger.

famili•a, -ae, *f.*, household (*including slaves*); retinue (*including all dependents*); family.

familiār•is, -e, *adj.* [**familia,** household], personal, private; *as noun:* intimate friend; **rēs familiāris,** personal property, estate.

fās, *n.*, *indeclin.*, divine law, religiously correct, right, proper, permissable. *Compare:* **iūs,** human law.

fem•ur, -oris *or* **-inis,** *n.*, the thigh.

ferē, *adv.*, almost, nearly, about, for the most part.

ferō, ferre, tulī, lātum (App. §81), carry, bear, bring; endure, suffer, support, withstand; receive; tell, report, give, render (*aid*); offer, propose (*terms*); **graviter** *or* **molestē ferre,** be annoyed *or* angry at; *passive (sometimes)* rush. *In the intransitive, almost =* *verb* to be.

ferrāment•um, -ī, *n.* [**ferrum,** iron], an iron tool *or* implement.

ferr•um, -ī, *n.*, iron; tool; sword.

ferve•faciō, -facere, -fēcī, -factum [**ferveō,** be red hot + **faciō,** make], heat, melt.

ferv•ēns, -entis, *adj.* [*pres. part. of* **ferveō,** be red hot], heated, glowing, hot.

fid•ēs, -eī, *f.* [**fīdō,** confide], faith, confidence; faithfulness, loyalty, trustworthiness; allegiance, protection, dependence; pledge, assurance; **fidem facere,** convince *or* give a pledge; **fīdem sequī,** surrender.

figūr•a, -ae, *f.* [**fingō,** form], form, shape, figure.

fīli•a, -ae, *f.*, daughter.

fīl•ius, -ī, *m.*, son.

fīniō, 4 [**fīnis,** limit], limit, bound; determine, measure.

fīn•is, -is, *m.*, boundary, limit, border, end; *pl.* boundaries; territory, country.

fīnitim•us, -a, -um, *adj.* [**fīnis,** limit], bordering on, adjoining, neighboring.

fīō, fierī, factus sum, *see* **faciō.**

firmiter, *adv.* [**firmus,** firm], firmly.

firm•us, -a, -um, *adj.*, strong, stable, vigorous, firm.

flamm•a, -ae, *f.*, fire, blaze.

flectō, flectere, flexī, flectum, bend, turn, direct.

flēt•us, -ūs, *m.* [**fleō,** weep], weeping, lamentation.

flūct•us, -ūs, *m.* [**fluō,** flow], flood, billow, wave.

flūm•en, -inis, *n.* [**fluō,** flow], river, stream.

fluō, fluere, flūxī, —, flow, run.

fore = futūrum esse, *see* **sum.**

fort•is, -e, *adj.*, strong, brave.

fortitūd•ō, -inis, *f.* [**fortis,** brave], bravery, courage.

fortūn•a, -ae, *f.* [**fors,** chance], fortune, luck, chance, opportunity, lot, condition; good fortune, success, property, estate. *All* fortuna *was the domain of the goddess* Fortuna, *a deity Caesar and his troops cultivated with great devotion.*

foss•a, -ae, *f.* [*perf. part. of* **fodiō,** dig], trench, ditch.

frangō, frangere, frēgī, frāctum, break, wreck; crush, discourage.

frāt•er, -ris, *m.*, brother.

fremit•us, -ūs, *m.*, confusion, noise, uproar.

frūct•us, -ūs, *m.* [**fruor,** enjoy], fruit; profit, reward.

frūmentāri•us, -a, -um, *adj.* [**frūmentum,** grain], of *or* pertaining to grain; *of places,* fruitful, productive of grain; **rēs frūmentāria,** grain supply, provisions.

frūmentor, 1 [frūmentum, grain], get grain, forage.

frūment•um, -ī, n., grain; pl.: crops.

fug•a, -ae, f., flight; in fugam conicere or dare, put to flight.

fūm•us, -ī, m., smoke.

fund•a, -ae, f., sling.

fūn•is, -is, m., rope, cable.

fūn•us, -eris, n., funeral.

fūrt•um, -ī, n., theft.

fūsil•is, -e, adj. [fundō, pour], liquid, molten.

G.

Gabin•ius, -ī, m., Aulus Gabinius, consul with Lucius Calpurnius Piso in 58 BCE.

Ga•ius, -ī, m., a Roman first name, abbreviated C.

Galli•a, -ae, f., Gaul.

Gallic•us, -a, -um, adj. [Gallia, Gaul], pertaining to Gaul or the Gauls, Gallic.

Gall•us, -a, -um, adj., of Gaul, Gallic; pl. as noun: the Gauls, inhabiting Gaul, Northern Italy, etc.

Garumn•a, -ae, m., the Garumna or Garonne, a river that formed the boundary between Aquitania and Celtic Gaul.

Geidumn•ī, -ōrum, m., the Geidumni, a people of Belgic Gaul, clients of the Nervii.

Genav•a, -ae, f., Genava, a city belonging to the Allobroges on the shores of Lacus Lemanus; now called Geneva.

gen•us, -eris, n., descent, origin, race, class, tribe, family; kind, nature.

Germān•ī, -ōrum, m., the Germani or the Germans.

ger•ō, -ere, gessī, gestum, carry, bear, wield; (of war) carry on, perform, wage, conduct; pass.: be done, go on, occur.

glad•ius, -ī, m., sword.

glān•s, -dis, f., acorn; ball, slug of lead.

glōri•a, -ae, f., glory, renown, honor, fame, reputation.

Gnae•us, -ī, m., a Roman first name, abbreviated Cn.

Graec•us, -a, -um, adj., of or belonging to the Greeks, Greek; pl. as noun: the Greeks.

grāti•a, -ae, f. [grātus, pleasing], favor, goodwill, gratitude, esteem, influence, popularity; grātiās agere, thank; grātiam habēre, to feel grateful; grātiam referre, to return a favor; hanc grātiam referre, to return a favor in this way; grātiam inīre, to gain favor; grātiā, following a gen.: for the purpose of, in order to.

grav•is, -e, adj., heavy, oppressive, hard, severe, serious; advanced (in years).

Grudi•ī, -ōrum, m., the Grudii, a Belgic people near the Nervii.

H.

hab•eō, -ēre, -uī, -itum, have, hold, possess; think, consider, regard; deliver (with ōrātiōnem); in animō habēre, intend; ratiōnem habēre, have regard for; take care or see that (followed by an ut clause); cōnsilium habēre, form a plan; in numerō hostium habēre, consider as enemies; aliter sē habēre, be otherwise or be different; for habēre with the perf. pass. part., e.g., vectīgālia redempta habēre, see App. §286, b.

Helvēti•us, -a, -um, adj., of the Helvetii, Helvetians; as noun: one of the Helvetii, a Helvetian; pl.: the Helvetii or Helvetians.

heredi•tās, -tātis, f. [hērēs, heir], inheritance.

hībern•a, -ōrum, n. [deriving from the adj. that modified castra, fortified camp], winter camp, winter quarters.

hic, haec, hoc, demonstrative pron. (App. §54), used for what is close in space, time, or thought: this, this man, this woman, this thing; he, she, it (more emphatic than is, ea, id); abl. sing. hōc, on this account, in this respect; the (with comparatives); hic . . . ille, the latter . . . the former. See App. §170, a.

hiemō, 1 [hiems, winter], pass the winter, winter.

hiem•s, -is, f., wintertime, winter.

hinc, adv., from that point or place, hence.

Hispāni•a, -ae, f., Hispania, Spain.

Hispān•us, -a, -um, adj., Spanish.

hom•ō, -inis, m., human being, person (as opposed to animals); pl.: humankind, humanity.

honest•us, -a, -um, adj. [honōs, honor], honorable, worthy, distinguished, eminent.

hon•ōs, -ōris, m., honor, regard, glory, distinction; honorable position, office.

hōr•a, -ae, f., hour. There were twenty-four hours in the Roman day, but they divided those hours into twelve hours of light and twelve hours of darkness (between sunrise and sunset). Except at the equinoxes, the hours were thus not of equal length, and varied according to the season.

hortor, 1, exhort, encourage, incite, urge strongly.

hospit•ium, -ī, n. [hospes, host or guest], the reciprocal relationship that exists between a host and a guest; friendship, hospitality.

host•is, -is, *m. or f., (public)* enemy, enemy combatant (*as opposed to* **inimīcus,** a personal enemy); *pl.:* the enemy.

hūc, *adv.* [*from* **hic,** this], to this place, hither, here; against these, to these.

hūmāni•tās, -tātis, *f.* [**hūmānus,** human], humanity, culture, refinement.

hūmān•us, -a, -um, *adj.,* human; civilized, cultured, refined, cultivated.

humil•is, -e, *adj.* [**humus,** the ground], *on the ground;* low, humble, abject, weak.

humili•tās, -tātis, *f.* [**humilis,** low], humility, lowness; weakness.

I.

iac•eō, -ēre, iacuī, —, lie; lie slain *or* slaughtered.

iaciō, iacere, iēcī, iactum, throw, cast, hurl; (*of an* **agger,** rampart), throw up *or* together, construct.

iacul•um, -ī, *n.* [**iaciō,** throw], javelin, spear, dart.

iam, *adv.,* now, at this time; already, by this time, at last; really, indeed, even; **neque iam** *or* **iam nōn,** no longer; **ubi iam,** as soon as.

ibi, *adv.,* there, in that place.

Īd., *abbr. of* **Īdūs.**

īdem, eadem, idem (App. §58), *demon. pron.* [**is,** this, that], the same; this very; **īdem atque,** the same as.

idōne•us, -a, -um, *adj.,* fit, suitable, adapted.

Īd•ūs, -uum, *f. pl.,* the Ides: *the 15th of March, May, July, and October, and the 13th of other months.*

ign•is, -is, *m.,* fire.

ignōbil•is, -e, *adj.* [**in** + (**g)nōbilis,** well-known], unknown, undistinguished, obscure.

ig•nōscō, -nōscere, -nōvī, -nōtum [**in** + (**g)nōscēns,** knowing (*from* **nōscō,** know)], forgive, pardon.

ignōt•us, -a, -um, *adv.* [**in** + (**g)nōtus,** known (**nōscō,** know)], unknown, unfamiliar.

illātus, *see* **īnferō.**

ille, illa, illud, *gen.* **illīus,** *dat.* **illī** (App. §56), *demon. pron.* (*of what is remote in time, place, thought, etc.; compare* **hic**), that, that man, that woman, that thing; he, she, it; **hic . . . ille,** the latter . . . the former, *see* App. §170, *a.*

illigō, 1 [**ligō,** bind], attach, hold together, bind together.

illūstr•is, -e, *adj.,* distinguished, illustrious.

immān•is, -e, *adj.,* huge, immense.

im•mittō, -mittere, -mīsī, -missum [**mittō,** send], send *or* let into, insert; send against, direct toward *or* against; **trabibus immissīs,** beams placed between.

immolō, 1, sacrifice.

immortāl•is, -e, *adj.* [**in** + **mortālis,** mortal], not mortal, immortal, deathless.

immūni•tās, -tātis, *f.* [**in** + **mūnis,** burden], freedom from public burdens, duties, *or* taxes; exemption.

impedīment•um, -ī, *n.* [**impediō,** hinder], hindrance, obstacle, impediment; *pl.:* baggage, luggage (*of an army*), baggage-train (*including pack animals*).

impediō, 4 [**in** + **pēs,** foot], *entangle the feet,* hamper, obstruct, hinder, impede, delay.

im•pellō, -pellere, -pulī, -pulsum [**pellō,** drive], drive *or* urge on, incite, instigate, impel.

im•pendeō, -pendēre, —, — [**in** + **pendeō,** hang], overhang, impend.

imperāt•or, -ōris, *m.* [**imperō,** order], commander-in-chief, general.

imperīt•us, -a, -um, *adj.* [**in** + **perītus,** experienced], inexperienced, unskilled, ignorant.

imper•ium, -ī, *n.* [**imperō,** order], right to command; authority, supreme power; jurisdiction, dominion, sovereignty; supreme military command, highest official power; command, order.

imperō, 1 [**in** + **parō,** procure], demand from, requisition; command, order, instruct, rule.

impetrō, 1, obtain (*by request*), accomplish, succeed in obtaining (*one's request*); **impetrāre ā (ab)**, gain permission from, persuade.

impet•us, -ūs, *m.,* attack, onset, charge; impetuosity, force, vehemence.

impi•us, -a, -um, *adj.* [**in** + **pius,** loyal], *without reverence for gods, parents, country:* ungodly, unrespectful, unpatriotic, wicked.

importō, 1 [**in** + **portō,** carry], carry *or* bring in, import.

imprōvīsō, *adv.* [**imprōvīsus,** unforeseen], unexpectedly, without warning.

imprōvīs•us, -a, -um, *adj.* [**in** + **prōvīsus,** foreseen], unforeseen, unexpected; **dē imprōvīsō,** unexpectedly, suddenly.

imprudenti•a, -ae, *f.* [**imprūdens,** imprudent], imprudence, lack of foresight *or* forethought, ignorance, indiscretion.

impuls•us, -ūs, *m.* [**impellō,** impel], impulse, instigation.

in, *prep. with acc. and abl.* With acc.: (1) *of motion, from one place into or toward another place,* into, to; in, among; toward, for, against; at; upon; (2) *of time,* till, into; for; on, at; and (3) *other uses,* in, in respect to, for, under, over, on; **in diēs,** from day to day; **in fugam conicere,** to put to flight; **in Caesarem incidere,** meet with Caesar; **summum in cruciātum venīre,** be punished with the severest torture. With abl.: (1) *of place where or motion within a place,* in, among, over, within, throughout, on, upon; (2) *of time,* in, during, in the course of; on; and (3) *other uses,* in, in the case of; in consequence of, in view of; on, upon; **in Ararī,** over the Arar; **in eō,** in his case; **in ancorīs,** at anchor; **in opere esse,** be engaged in the work.

incend•ium, -ī, *n.* [**incendō,** burn], fire, burning, conflagration.

in•cendō, -cendere, -cendī, -cēnsum, set fire to, burn; inflame, excite.

incert•us, -a, -um, *adj.* [**in + certus,** decided], undecided, uncertain, untrustworthy; indefinite, vague; disordered.

in•cidō, -cidere, -cidī, — [**ad + cadō,** fall], fall into *or* upon; fall in with, meet; happen, arise.

in•cīdō, -cīdere, -cīsī, -cīsum [**caedō,** cut], cut into.

in•cipiō, -cipere, -cēpī, -ceptum [**ad + capiō,** take], undertake; begin, commence.

incitō, 1 [**citō,** put in motion], set in motion; excite, arouse, urge on, stimulate; exasperate; **cursū incitātō,** at full speed.

incognit•us, -a, -um, *adj.* [**in + cognitus,** known], unknown.

incol•ō, -ere, -uī, — [**colō,** cultivate], inhabit, dwell in, live in.

incolum•is, -e, *adj.,* unhurt, uninjured, safe and sound, unimpaired.

incommodē, *adv.* [**incommodus,** inconvenient], inconveniently.

incommod•um, -ī, *n.* [**incommodus,** inconvenient], inconvenience, disadvantage, trouble; disaster, defeat, loss, injury.

incrēdibil•is, -e, *adj.* [**in + crēdibilis,** believable], unbelievable, incredible, unlikely; extraordinary.

inde, *adv.,* from that place, thence; then, thereupon.

indic•ium, -ī, *n.* [**indicō,** disclose], disclosure, information; **per indicium,** through informers.

indign•us, -a, -um, *adj.* [**in + dignus,** worthy], unworthy, disgraceful.

in•dūcō, -dūcere, -dūxī, -ductum [**dūcō,** lead], lead *or* draw on; induce; influence, instigate; cover.

Indutiomār•us, -ī, *m.,* Indutiomarus, *a leader of the Treveri, rival to Cingetorix, and hostile to Caesar.*

in•eō, -īre, -iī, -itum [**eō,** go. App. §84], go into; enter upon, begin; **inīre cōnsilium,** form; **inīre ratiōnem,** make an estimate, decide; **inīre grātiam,** gain favor; **inīre numerum,** enumerate.

īnfer•ior, -ius, *comp. of* **īnferus.**

īn•ferō, īnferre, intulī, inlātum [**ferō,** carry. App. §81], carry into, import, inflict, cause, produce; cast into; **in equum īnferre,** mount on a horse; **causā illātā,** making an excuse; **signa īnferre,** advance the standards, attack.

īnfer•us, -a, -um, *adj.,* low, below; *comp.:* **īnferior,** lower, inferior; **ab īnferiōre parte,** below, downstream; *superl.:* **īnfimus** *or* **īmus,** lowest, last; *with* **collis** (hill), the base of; **ad īnfimum, ab īnfimō,** at the bottom.

inimīc•us, -a, -um, *adj.* [**in + amīcus,** friendly], unfriendly, hostile; *as a noun: personal* enemy, rival; *as opposed to* **hostis,** *public* enemy.

inīqu•us, -a, -um, *adj.* [**in + aequus,** even, just], uneven; unjust, unfair; unfavorable, disadvantageous.

init•ium, -ī, *n.* [**ineō,** go into], beginning, commencement, origin; edge *of a country,* borders.

iniūri•a, -ae, *f.* [**in + iūs,** right], wrong, injustice; outrage, injury, harm, damage, violence.

iniussū, *abl. of* **iniussus, -ūs,** *m.* [**iubeō,** order], without command *or* order.

inligō see **illigō**

inlūstris see **illūstris**

innoc•ēns, -entis, *adj.* [**in + nocēns,** harmful], not harmful, innocent.

inopi•a, -ae, *f.* [**inops,** needy], need, lack, poverty; lack of provisions, hunger.

inqu•am, -is, -it, *def. verb used only with direct quotations and following one or more of the words in the quotation,* say.

īn•sequor, -sequī, -secūtus sum [**sequor,** follow], follow up, follow after, follow close behind, pursue.

īnsidi•ae, -ārum, *f. pl.* [**sedeō,** sit], a sitting *or* lying in wait; ambush; treachery; artifice, trick, crafty device.

īnsinuō, 1 [**sinuō,** wind], wind into; make one's way into, penetrate.

īn•sistō, -sistere, -stitī, — [**sistō,** stand], stand upon; stand firm, take a stand; press on, pursue; *with* **ratiōnem,** adopt, use.

īn•stituō, -stituere, -stituī, -stitūtum [**statuō,** set up], set up *or* put in order, draw up; train, educate; procure; prepare; build, construct;

begin, determine, decide upon, adopt; **īnstitūtus,**
perf. part. as adj. (*in addition to the definitions above*):
usual, customary; finished.

īnstitūt•um, -ī, *n.,* established plan *or* principle;
custom, institution, habit.

īn•stō, -stāre, -stitī, -stātum [stō, stand], stand upon
or near, be at hand, press on; threaten.

īnstrūment•um, -ī, *n.* [īnstruō, build], build upon,
build, construct; form, draw up *in battle array;*
equip, furnish.

īnsuēfact•us, -a, -um, *adj.* [suēscō, become
accustomed, **faciō,** make], accustomed, trained.

īnsul•a, -ae, *f.,* island.

intel•legō, -legere, -lēgī, -lēctum [inter + legō,
choose, select], select *or* distinguish between;
understand; know; see, perceive, realize; find out,
learn.

inter, *prep. with acc.* (*sometimes follows its noun*), (1) *of
place,* among, between; (2) *of time,* during, within,
for; (3) *in other relations,* among, between, in; in
among *or* between, in; in among, between; to;
over; along with; (4) *with reflex. pron., of reciprocal
action* (App. §166), with, to, *or* from each other *or*
one another, *as* **inter sē differunt,** differ from one
another; each other, one another, *as,* **cohortātī
inter sē,** encouraging one another.

inter•cēdō, -cēdere, -cessī, -cessum [cēdō, go],
go *or* come between, lie between, intervene, be
between; pass.

inter•cipiō, -cipere, -cēpī, -ceptum [ad + capiō,
take], take *or* catch between (*one point and another*);
interrupt; intercept; cut off.

inter•clūdō, -clūdere, -clūsī, -clūsum [claudō, shut],
shut *or* cut off, separate, hinder; *with* **itinera,**
block.

inter•dīcō, -dīcere, -dīxī, -dictum [dīcō, say],
prohibit, exclude, forbid, interdict; **aquā atque
ignī interdīcere,** *forbid the use of fire and water,*
exile, banish.

intereā, *adv.,* in the meantime, meanwhile.

inter•eō, -īre, -iī, -itum [eō, go. App. §84], perish,
die.

inter•ficiō, -ficere, -fēcī, -fectum [faciō, make],
make away with, kill, destroy.

interim, *adv.,* meanwhile, in the meantime.

interit•us, -ūs, *m.* [intereō, die], destruction,
death.

inter•mittō, -mittere, -mīsī, -missum [mittō, send],
send between; intervene, separate; abate, cease,
let up, discontinue; delay, neglect, omit; let pass.

inter•pōnō, -pōnere, -posuī, -positum [pōnō, put],
place between, interpose; allege; cause; **fidem
interpōnere,** pledge.

interpr•es, -etis, *m. or f.,* interpreter; mediator.

interpretor, 1 [interpres, interpreter], interpret,
explain.

inter•sum, -esse, -fuī, — [sum, be. App. §66], be *or*
lie between, intervene; be present *at,* take part *in;
impers.:* **interest,** it concerns, it is important; there
is a difference *or* an interval; **magnī interest,** it is
of great importance.

intrā, *prep. with acc.* [inter, between], within, inside,
into.

intrō•eō, -īre, -iī, -itum [intrō, within + eō, go. App.
§84], go *or* come in, enter.

intus, *adv.,* within, on the inside.

inūsitāt•us, -a, -um, *adj.* [in + ūsitātus, usual],
unusual, uncommon, strange, startling.

inūtil•is, -e, *adj.* [in + ūtilis, useful], useless,
worthless, disadvantageous.

invent•or, -ōris, *m.* [inveniō, find], inventor, author.

in•veterāscō, -veterāscere, -veterāvī, -veterātum,
grow old; become established.

Iovis, *see* **Iuppiter.**

ipse, ipsa, ipsum, *gen.,* **ipsīus** (App. §59), *intensive
pron.,* self (*as opposed to, someone else*); himself,
herself, itself, themselves; he, she, it, they; *as
adj.,* very; *in gen.,* his, her, its, *or* their own. (*Not
reflexive; for the reflexive pron., compare* **sē,** self,
App. §163.)

ir•rumpō, -rumpere, -rūpsī, -ruptum [in + rumpō,
break], break into, rush into; force a way into,
storm.

is, ea, id, *gen.* **eius** (App. §57), *weak dem. pron.
referring to some person or object named in the
context,* this, that, these, those; he, she, it, they;
the, a; **is locus quō,** a *or* the place where; **ea quae,**
(the) things which; **eō,** *with comp.,* the; **eō magis,**
all the more; **eō . . . quō,** *with comp.:* the . . . the.

ita, *adv.,* so, thus, in this way; as follows; **ut . . . ita,** in
proportion as . . . in such proportion as / as . . . so;
nōn ita, not so very, not very; **ita . . . ut,** just . . . as
/ so . . . that.

itaque, *conj.* [ita, so], and so, therefore.

Itali•a, -ae, *f.,* Italy, *generally Italy below Cisalpine Gaul.*

item, *adv.,* in like manner, so, also, just so.

iter, itineris, *n.* [eō, go], route, road; journey; march;
passage; **iter facere,** march, travel; **magnīs
itineribus,** by forced marches.

iubeō, iubēre, iussī, iussum, order, command, enjoin, bid.

iūdic•ium, -ī, *n.* [**iūdex,** judge], judicial proceedings, trial; opinion, judgement; **iūdicium facere,** express an opinion; **iūdiciō,** by design, purposely.

iūdicō, 1 [**iūdex,** judge], pass judgement on, judge, sentence, decide, determine, think, consider.

iug•um, -ī, *n.* [**iungō,** join], yoke; ridge, crest.

iūment•um, -ī, *n.* [**iungō,** join, yoke], yoke, draft, *or* pack animal, beast of burden.

Iun•ius, -ī, *m.,* Quintus Junius, *a Spaniard who served in Caesar's army.*

Iuppiter, Iovis, *n.* (App. §27), *m.,* Jupiter, *chief god of the Roman state.*

Iūr•a, -ae, *m.,* the Jura *mountains that stretched from the Rhine to the Rhone, separating the Helvetians from the Sequani.*

iūs, iūris, *n.,* human law, law, justice, right; rights, power, authority. *Compare:* **fās,** divine law.

iūs iūrandum, iūris iūrandi, *n.* [**iūs,** right + **iūrō,** swear], an oath.

iūstiti•a, -ae, *f.* [**iūstus,** just], justice, fair dealing, uprightness.

iūst•us, -a, -um, *adj.* [**iūs,** right], in accordance with law *or* right; lawful, valid, just, fair; proper, regular; *with* **fūnera,** appropriate, fitting, proper.

iuvent•ūs, -ūtis, *f.* [**iūvenis,** young], period of youth, *from seventeen to forty-five years*; the youth, the young men.

K.

Kal., *abbr. for* **Kalend•ae, -ārum,** *f.,* the Kalends, *the first day of the Roman month.*

L.

L., *abbr. for* **Lūcius,** Lucius, *a Roman praenomen.*

L., *sign for* **quīnquāgintā,** fifty.

Labiēn•us, -ī, *m.,* Titus Atius Labienus, *Caesar's most trusted lieutenant in the Gallic War. During the Civil War, Labienus fought on Pompey's side, and died in battle against Caesar in Munda (in Spain) in 45 BCE.*

lab•or, -ōris, *m.,* toil, effort, striving, hardship.

lābor, lābī, lāpsus sum, slip; go wrong; **hāc spē lāpsus,** disappointed in this hope.

labōrō, 1 [**lābor,** toil], work hard, toil; be anxious, troubled, *or* perplexed; labor, suffer, be hard pressed.

lacess•ō, -ere, -īvī, -ītum, arouse, harass, provoke, irritate, attack.

lac•us, -ūs, *m.,* lake.

laetiti•a, -ae, *f.* [**laetus,** joyful], joy, rejoicing.

langu•or, -ōris, *m.,* weakness, faintness.

lap•is, -idis, *m.,* stone.

lāpsus, *see* **lābor.**

lātē, *adv.* [**lātus,** wide], widely, extensively; **longō lātēque,** far and wide.

lātitūd•ō, -inis, *f.* [**lātus,** wide], width, extent, breadth.

Latobrīg•ī, -ōrum, *m.,* the Latobrigi, *a Gallic tribe east of the Rhine.*

latrōcin•ium, -ī, *n.* [**latrō,** robber], robbery, brigandage.

lāt•us, -a, -um, *adj.,* wide, broad, extensive.

lat•us, -eris, *n.,* side; wing *or* flank *of an army.*

lāt•us, *see* **ferō.**

laus, laudis, *f.,* praise, commendation; renown, popularity, glory.

lēgāti•ō, -ōnis, *f.* [**lēgō,** delegate], embassy, legation; commission.

lēgāt•us, -ī, *m.* [**lēgō,** delegate], *one with delegated authority*; ambassador, envoy, legate; lieutenant.

legi•ō, -ōnis, *f.* [**legō,** choose], a legion.

Lemann•us, -ī (*often with* **lacus**), *m.,* Lake Lemannus, Lake Leman, *or* Lake Geneva.

lēn•is, -e, *adj.,* gentle, mild, smooth.

Levāc•ī, -ōrum, *m.,* the Levaci, *a Gallic tribe between the rivers Marne and Moselle.*

levi•tās, -tātis, *f.* [**levis,** light], lightness; fickleness, restlessness.

levō, 1 [**levis,** light], lighten, ease, relieve.

lēx, lēgis, *f.,* law, statute.

līber•ī, -ōrum, *m.* [**līber,** free], *the non-slave members of a family or household*; children.

līb•er, -era, -erum, *adj.,* unrestrained, free; undisputed.

līberō, 1 [**līber,** free], make *or* set free, release, deliver.

līber•tās, -tātis, *f.* [**līber,** free], freedom, liberty, independence.

licet, licēre, licuit *and* **licitum est,** *impers.* it is lawful, one has permission, it is permitted, one may, one is allowed; **licet mihi,** I may; **petere ut liceat,** to ask permission.

Liger, -ris, *m.* Loire (*river*).

lignāti•ō, -ōnis, *f.* [**lignum,** wood], the procuring of wood, collecting of wood.

lignāt•or, -ōris, *m.* [**lignum,** wood], one sent to gather wood, wood-forager.

lingu•a, -ae, *f.,* language, tongue.

litter•a, -ae, *f.,* a letter *of the alphabet, a written* sign, mark, *or* character; *pl.:* letters of the alphabet; letter, written message, epistle.

līt•us, -oris, *n.,* seashore, beach, shore.

loc•us, -ī, *m.* (*pl.* **loc•a, -ōrum,** *n.*), place, position, locality, situation; topic, subject; condition, state; rank, family; opportunity; **obsidum locō,** as hostages.

longē, *adv.* [**longus,** long], far, far away, distant, **longē lātēque,** far and wide.

longinqu•us, -a, -um, *adj.* [**longus,** long], far off, distant, remote; long, long continued.

longitūd•ō, -inis, *f.* [**longus,** long], length, extent; long duration.

long•us, -a, -um, *adj.,* distant, long; of long duration; tedious.

loquor, loquī, locūtus sum, speak, talk, converse.

lōric•a, -ae, *f.,* coat of mail; parapet, breastwork.

Lūcān•ius, -ī, *m.* Quintus Lucanius, *a centurion.*

Lūci•us, -ī, *m., a Roman praenomen, abbreviated* **L.**

lūn•a, -ae, *f.,* the moon.

Luteti•a, -ae, *f.,* Lutetia; *city of the Parisii on an island in the Seine river; now called* Paris.

lūx, lūcis, *f.,* light, daylight; **prīmā lūce,** at dawn.

M.

M., *sign for* **mīlle,** one thousand.

M., *abbr. for* **Marcus,** *a Roman praenomen.*

magis, *adv. comp.* [from **magnus,** large], more, rather, in a higher degree; *superl.:* **maximē,** especially, in the highest degree; mostly, mainly.

magistrāt•us, -ūs, *m.* [**magister,** master], public office, magistracy; public official, magistrate.

magn•us, -a, -um, *adj.,* large, big, great (*in size, quantity, or degree*), abundant, much; important, extensive; loud (*voice*); high (*tide*); **magnī** (*gen. sing. n.*), of great importance; **magnīs itineribus,** by forced marches. *Comp.:* **maior;** *superl.:* **maximus.**

maior, maius, *adj.* [*comp. of* **magnus,** large], larger, bigger, greater (*in degree, size, time, etc.*); older, elder; *as noun:* **māiōrēs natū,** elders, old men; **maiōrēs,** ancestors.

magnific•us, -a, -um, *adj.* [**magnus,** large + **faciō,** make], magnificent, splendid.

magnitūd•ō, -inis, *f.* [**magnus,** large], size, large size, greatness, extent; stature (**corporum**); violence (**ventī**); severity (**poenae**); **magnitūdō animī,** courage.

magnopere, *adv.* [**magnus,** large + **opus,** work], *with great effort;* especially, greatly, exceedingly, earnestly.

malefic•ium, -ī, *n.* [**malus,** evil + **faciō,** do], evil doing, mischief, harm, injury.

mandāt•um, -ī, *n.* [**mandō,** command], charge, injunction, order, command; message.

mandō, 1 [**manus,** hand], *give into one's hands,* entrust, commit; enjoin, order, command.

maneō, manēre, mānsī, mānsum, remain, continue, abide, stay.

man•us, -ūs, *f.,* the hand; **in manibus,** near at hand; **manū,** by hand, by art; **ferrea manus,** a grappling hook; **dare manūs,** yield; an armed force, troop, band, gang, company.

Marc•us, -ī, *m., a Roman praenomen.*

mare, maris, *n.,* sea; **mare Ōceanum,** the ocean.

maritim•us, -a, -um, *adj.* [**mare,** sea], of the sea, sea; maritime, naval, on the sea; **ōra,** the seashore.

Mār•s, -tis, *m.,* Mars, the god of war.

mās, maris, *adj.,* male; *as a noun:* a male.

Massili•a, -ae, *f.,* Massilia; *city founded by Greeks in what became the Roman Province (Transalpine Gaul); now called* Marseilles.

māteri•a, -ae, *f.,* material; wood, timber.

mātrimōn•ium, -ī, *n.* [**māter,** mother], marriage, wedlock, matrimony; **in mātrimōnium dūcere,** to marry (*said of the man*).

Matron•a, -ae, *m.,* the *river* Matrona, *now called* the Marne.

mātūrō, 1 [**mātūrus,** ripe], ripen; accelerate, quicken, speed up; hurry up, make haste; hurry, hasten.

maximē, *see* **magis.**

maxim•us, -a, -um, *adj.* [*superl. of* **magnus,** large. App. §42], greatest, largest, biggest.

medeor, medērī, —, cure, remedy.

mediocr•is, -e, *adj.* [**medius,** middle of], ordinary, moderate, average.

medi•us, -a, -um, *adj.,* in the middle of; in the middle, intervening, intermediate; **locus medius utrīusque,** a place midway between the two.

membr•um, -ī, *n.,* limb.

memori•a, -ae, *f.* [**memor,** mindful], the faculty of memory; memory, recollection, remembrance; tradition; **memoriā tenēre,** remember; **patrum memoriā,** in the time of our fathers *or* ancestors.

mēns•is, -is, *m.,* month.

mercāt•or, -ōris, *m.* [**mercor,** trade], merchant, trader.

Mercur•ius, -ī, *m.,* Mercury, *a god especially associated by the Romans with trade.*

mereō *and* **mereor,** 2, deserve, merit, be worthy of; win, earn, incur (**odium**); serve as a *soldier* (*i.e., earn pay*).

Messāl•a, -ae, *m.,* Marcus Valerius Messala, *consul in 61 BCE.*

metō, metere, messuī, messum, mow, harvest, reap.

met•us, -ūs, *m.* [**metuō,** fear], fear, dread, terror, anxiety, apprehension; **metū territāre,** terrify, terrorize; **hōc metū = metū huius reī,** from fear of this.

me•us, -a, -um, *poss. adj.* [*of the pron.* **ego**], my, mine, my own.

mīl•es, -itis, *m.,* soldier, private soldier; infantry (as opposed to **equitēs**); **mīlitēs imperāre,** draft soldiers *from,* levy soldiers *upon.*

mīlia, *see* **mīlle.**

mīlitār•is, -e, *adj.* [**mīles,** soldier], of a soldier, military, martial; **rēs mīlitāris,** military matters, warfare, the science of war.

mīlle, *indecl. num. adj.,* a thousand; *pl.:* **mīli•a, -ium,** *n.,* thousands (*usually followed by a partitive gen.*); **mīlia passuum,** thousands of paces, miles.

Minerv•a, -ae, *f., the goddess* Minerva, *who was associated with wisdom and the liberal arts.*

minimē, *adv.* [**minimus,** least], least, very little; by no means, not at all.

minor, *comp. of* **parvus.**

minuō, minuere, minuī, minūtum [**minus,** less], lessen, impair, diminish; settle (**contrōversiās**); **minuente aestū,** the tide ebbing.

minus, *adv. comp.* [*of* **parvus,** little], less; not at all, too little.

mittō, mittere, mīsī, missum, send, send off, dismiss, let go, dispatch; hurl, discharge.

mōbili•tās, -tātis, *f.* [**mōbilis,** movable], movableness, activity, speed; changeability, fickleness, inconstancy.

moderor, 1 [**modus,** limit], manage, govern, control, guide.

modo, *adv.* [**modus,** measure], *with measure or limit;* only, merely; even, just, at least, but; *of time,* just now, recently; **nōn modo . . . sed etiam,** not only . . . but also.

mod•us, -ī, *m.,* measure, quantity, size; manner, method, style; **ad hunc modum,** in this way; **eius modī,** of such a kind, such; *abl.,* **modō,** *used with a gen.:* in the character of, like.

mol•ō, -ere, -uī, -itum, grind.

moneō, 2, warn, advise, instruct, order.

mōns, montis, *m.,* mountain; mountain range; hill, height.

morb•us, -ī, *m.,* illness, sickness, disease.

Morīn•ī, -ōrum, *m.,* the Morini.

morior, morī, mortuus sum [**mors,** death], die.

moror, 1 [**mora,** a delay], delay, hinder; linger, hang back.

mor•s, -tis, *f.,* death; **sibi mortem cōnscīscere,** commit suicide.

mortu•us, *see* **morior.**

mōs, mōris, *m.,* manner, custom, practice; *pl.:* customs, habits; character; **mōs māiōrum,** the customs of our ancestors, ancestral tradition.

Mos•a, -ae, *m., the river* Mosa, *now called* the Meuse *or* the Maas.

mōt•us, -ūs, *m.* [**moveō,** move], movement, motion; political movement, uprising, disturbance.

multitūd•ō, -inis, *f.* [**multus,** much], a great number, multitude; the multitude, the common people, the populace.

multō, *adv.* [*abl. of* **multus,** much], by far, much.

multum, *adv.* [*acc. of* **multus,** much], much, very, greatly, especially; *comp.:* **plūs,** more; **plūs posse,** be more able *or* powerful; be very powerful *or* influential.

mult•us, -a, -um, *adj.,* much, great; *pl.:* many; *with abl. expressing time when,* late; *as noun,* many persons *or* things; *comp.:* **plūs, plūris,** more; *as noun:* more; *pl.:* more, several, many; *superl.:* **plūrimus, -a, -um,** most; *pl.:* very many.

Munāt•ius, -ī, *m.,* Lucius Munatius Plancus, *a lieutenant of Caesar.*

mund•us, -ī, *m.,* world, universe.

mūniō, 4, defend with a wall, fortify, defend, protect; **mūnītus,** *perf. part. as adj.:* fortified, defended, protected.

mūnīti•ō, -ōnis, *f.* [**mūniō,** fortify], fortifying; fortification, rampart, works, entrenchments.

mūn•us, -eris, *n.,* duty, service, task; present.

mūrāl•is, -e, *adj.* [**mūrus,** wall], pertaining to a wall, mural; **mūrāle pīlum,** mural javelin, *a heavy javelin that was thrown from the top of a wall.*

N.

nam, *conj.,* for.

Nammē•ius, -ī, *m.,* Nammeius, *a member of the Helvetian nobility sent as an ambassador to Caesar.*

nancīscor, nancīscī, nactus sum, get, obtain possession of; meet with, find.

nāscor, nāscī, nātus sum, be born, be produced; rise, spring up, be raised; be found.

nātāl•is, -e, *adj.* [**nāscor,** be born], pertaining to birth, natal; **diēs,** birthday.

nāti•ō, -ōnis, *f.* [**nāscor,** be born], people, tribe, nation.

nātūr•a, -ae, *f.* [**nāscor,** be born], nature; natural disposition, character, constitution.

nāvig•ium, -ī, *n.* [**nāvigō,** sail], a sailing vessel, ship; sailing, navigation.

nāvigō, 1 [**nāvis,** ship], set sail, sail.

nāv•is, -is, *f.,* ship, boat; **nāvis longa,** galley, ship of war; **nāvis onerāria,** transport ship.

nē (App. §188, *b.*) (1), *conj. with the subjunctive,* that . . . not, so that . . . not, in order that . . . not, lest; *after verbs of fearing,* that, lest. (2), *adv.* not; **nē . . . quidem** (*enclosing the emphatic word*), not even.

ne-, nec-, neg-, *inseparable negative prefix.*

-ne, *interrog. enclitic: in direct questions, simply the sign of a question* (App. §213, *a.*); *in indirect questions,* whether; **-ne . . . -ne, -ne . . . an, utrum . . . -ne,** whether . . . or.

nec, *see* **neque.**

necessāri•us, -a, -um, *adj.* [**necesse,** necessary], necessary, requisite, pressing; *with* **tempus,** critical; *as noun:* friend, relative.

necesse, *indecl. adj.,* necessary, unavoidable, indispensable.

necō, 1 [**nex,** death], put to death, kill, murder.

neg-, *see* **ne-.**

neg•legō, -legere, -lēxī, -lēctum [**neg** + **legō,** choose, regard], not heed, not pay attention to, disregard, neglect.

negō, 1, say no, refuse, say . . . not.

negōt•ium, -ī, *n.* [**neg-** + **ōtium,** leisure], concern, business, undertaking; trouble, difficulty, labor; **negōtium dare,** employ, direct; **quid negōtī,** what business; **nihil negōtī,** no difficulty.

nēmō, *acc.* **nēminem,** *m. and f.* [**ne-** + **homō,** human being], no one, nobody.

neque (nec) (App. §188, *a.*), *conj.* [**ne-** + **que**], and not, not, nor; but not; **neque . . . neque,** neither . . . nor.

Nervi•us, -a, -um, *adj.,* of the Nervii; *m. sing. as noun:* one of the Nervii; *m. pl. as noun:* the Nervii, a Belgic tribe.

nēve (neu) (App. §188, *b.*) [**nē** + **ve,** or], and not, nor.

nex, -cis, *f.,* violent death, death, execution.

nihil, *indecl. noun, n.,* nothing; *with gen.,* no, none of; *acc. as adv.,* not, not at all, by no means; **nōn nihil,** somewhat.

nihilō, *adv.,* by no means; **nihilō minus,** nevertheless.

nisi, *conj.* [**ne-** + **sī,** if], if not, except, unless.

nītor, nītī, nīxus sum, rest upon, rely upon, exert oneself, strive, attempt.

nōbil•is, -e, *adj.* [**nōscō,** know], well-known, distinguished, noted; of noble birth, noble; *as noun:* a noble.

nōbili•tās, -tātis, *f.* [**nōbilis,** well-known], fame; noble birth, rank; the nobility.

noceō, nocēre, nocuī, nocitum, harm, injure, hurt; **nocēns,** *pres. part. as noun:* guilty person.

noctū, *adv.* [**nox,** night], by night, at night.

nocturn•us, -a, -um, *adj.* [**nox,** night], at night, nocturnal, nightly.

nōlō, nōlle, nōluī, —, (App. §82) [**ne-** + **volō,** wish], not wish, be unwilling; refuse; *imperat.* **nōlī** *or* **nōlīte,** *with inf.* (App. §219), do not.

nōm•en, -inis, *n.,* name, title; reputation, prestige; **nōmine** *with gen.,* in the name of, as; **suō nōmine,** on his *or* their own account, personally.

nōn (App. §188, *a.*), *adv.,* not; no.

nōndum, *adv.* [**nōn** + **dum**], not yet.

nōn nūll•us, -a, -um, *adj.* [**nōn** + **nūllus,** none], some, several; *pl. as noun:* some, several.

nōn numquam, *adv.* [**nōn** + **numquam,** never], sometimes.

Nōrēi•a, -ae, *f.,* Noreia, *a town in Noricum.*

Nōric•us, -a, -um, *adj.,* pertaining to Noricum (*a territory between the Danube and the Alps*).

nōs, *see* **ego.**

nōscō, nōscere, nōvī, nōtum, learn, become acquainted *or* familiar with; **nōvī,** *perf.,* have learned, *hence* know; **nōtus,** *perf. part. as adj.:* known, well-known, familiar.

nos•ter, -tra, -trum, *poss. adj.,* our, ours, our own; *in pl. as noun:* our men, our troops.

nōt•us, *see* nōscō.

novi•tās, -tātis, *f.* [novus, new], newness; strangeness, novelty.

nov•us, -a, -um, *adj.*, new, novel; unusual, fresh; rēs novae, a change of government, revolution; *superl.*: novissim•us, -a, -um, latest, last; *as noun or with* agmen, those in the rear, the rear.

nox, noctis, *f.*, night; media nox, the middle of the night, midnight; multā nocte, late at night.

noxi•a, -ae, *f.*, crime, offense.

nūdō, 1 [nūdus, bare], strip, uncover, make bare *or* naked, expose.

nūll•us, -a, -um, *gen.* nūllīus, *adj.* [ne- + ūllus, any], not any, no; *as noun*: no one, none; nōnnūllus, some; *as noun*: some, some persons.

nūm•en, -inis, *n.*, divinity, god; divine force *or* will.

numer•us, -ī, *m.*, number, quantity, amount; account; in numerō, *with gen.*, among, as.

nunc, *adv.*, now, at present, at this time.

nūntiō, 1 [nūntius, messenger], announce, send news, report, make known; order, direct.

nūntius, -ī, *m.*, messenger; message, news, report.

nūper, *adv.*, recently, not long ago.

nūt•us, -ūs, *m.* [nuō, nod], nod; sign, command; ad nūtum, at one's nod *or* command.

O.

ob, *prep. with acc.*, on account of, for; *in compounds*, opposed to, to, forward, against; quam ob rem, for which reason, wherefore, why.

obaerāt•us, -a, -um, *adj.* [aes, money], in debt; *as a noun*: debtor.

ob•eō, -īre, -iī, -itum [eō, go. App. §84], go to *or* toward; perform, attend to.

observō, 1 [servō, give heed], observe, mark, watch; regard, obey; celebrate.

ob•ses, -sidis, *m. and f.* [obsideō, blockade], *one who is guarded*, hostage; pledge, security.

ob•sideō, -sidēre, -sēdī, -sessum [sedeō, sit], sit in the way of, obstruct, besiege, blockade.

obsidi•ō, -ōnis, *f.* [obsideō, blockade], siege, investment, blockade; peril, oppression.

obtestor, 1 [testor, witness], call to witness; beseech, entreat.

ob•tineō, -tinēre, -tinuī, -tentum [teneō, hold], hold, retain, possess, maintain; acquire, obtain.

occāsi•ō, -ōnis, *f.* [occidō, fall, happen], occasion, opportunity.

occās•us, -ūs, *m.* [occidō, fall, happen], falling down, setting; *with* sōlis, sunset; the west.

oc•cidō, -cidere, -cidī, — [ad + cadō, fall], fall down, set; happen; be slain, perish; occidēns sōl, the west.

oc•cīdō, -cīdere, -cīsī, -cīsum [caedō, cut], cut down, kill, slay.

occultō, 1 [occultus, secret], hide, keep secret, conceal.

occupō, 1 [ob + capiō, take], take possession of, seize, occupy; engage, employ.

oc•currō, -currere, -currī, -cursum [ob + currō, run], run in the way of, meet; happen upon; go to, come to; oppose, counteract; occur.

Ōcean•us, -ī, *m.*, the ocean.

octāv•us, -a, -um, *adj., ord. num. adj.* [octō, eight], eighth.

offic•ium, -ī, *n.*, service, allegiance, duty; official duty, business; esse, manēre, *or* permanēre in officiō, to remain loyal.

omnīnō, *adv.* [omnis, all], at all; whatever; altogether, entirely, wholly, in all, only.

omn•is, -e, *adj.*, all, every, all the, every kind of, the whole, as a whole; *m. pl. as noun*, all, every one; all the rest; *n. pl. as noun*, all possessions or goods.

onerāri•us, -a, -um, *adj.* [onus, load], equipped for loads *or* fitted for burdens; *with* nāvis, transport, freight ship.

on•us, -eris, *n.*, load, burden; weight, size.

oper•a, -ae, *f.* [opus, work], work, exertion; service; pains, attention; dare operam, give attention, take pains.

opīni•ō, -ōnis, *f.* [opīnor, think], way of thinking, opinion; impression; expectation; reputation; opīniō timōris, impression of cowardice.

oport•et, -ēre, -uit, —, *impers.*, it is necessary, needful, becoming, proper; *when translated as a personal verb*: must, ought.

oportūn•us, -a, -um, *adj.*, fit, opportune, lucky, suitable; favorable, advantageous.

oppid•um, -ī, *n.*, fortified town, town, stronghold.

op•primō, -primere, -pressī, -pressus [ob + premō, press], press down, oppress; overwhelm, overpower, destroy; fall upon, surprise.

oppugnāti•ō, -ōnis, *f.* [oppugnō, storm], a storming, besieging, siege, assault, attack; plan *or* method of storming.

oppugnō, 1 [ob + pugnō, fight], fight against, attack, assault, storm, besiege.

optimē, *superl. of* **bene.**

optimus, *superl. of* **bonus.**

op•us, -eris, *n.,* work, labor; military work *or* works, fortifications, defenses; a work *of engineering or architecture*; **nātūrā et opere,** by nature and art.

opus, *indecl. noun, n.* [*cf.* **opus,** work, deed], need, necessity; **opus est,** it is necessary, there is need; *the thing needed is expressed either by the nom. or the abl.* (App. §146).

ōrāti•ō, -ōnis, *f.* [**ōrō,** speak], a speaking, speech, language, words, address, argument.

ōrāt•or, -ōris, *m.* [**ōrō,** speak], speaker; ambassador, envoy.

orb•is, -is, *m.,* orb, ring, circle; **orbis terrārum,** the world.

ōrd•ō, -inis, *m.,* row, tier, layer; rank, line *of soldiers*; arrangement, order; degree, rank; **prīmī ōrdinis,** centurions of the first rank.

Orgetor•īx, -īgis, *m.,* a Helvetian noble who conspired to become the supreme leader of the Helvetians.

orior, orīrī, ortus sum, arise, begin, spring up, rise, start; be born, descend; **oriēns sōl,** the rising sun, sunrise; the east.

ōrō, 1 [**ōs,** mouth], speak; beseech, entreat.

ort•us, -ūs, *m.* [**orior,** rise], rising.

ōs, ōris, *n.,* mouth; face, countenance.

os•tendō, -tendere, -tendī, -tentum [**obs** + **tendō,** stretch] *stretch before*; present, show, bring into view, reveal; tell, declare; point out, mention.

ostentō, 1 [*freq. of* **ostendō,** show], show frequently; show, exhibit.

P.

pācō, 1 [**pāx,** peace], make peaceful, subdue, pacify; **pācātus,** *perf. part. as adj.*: peaceful, quiet, subdued.

Pad•us, -ī, *m.,* the Padus *river,* the Po, *the biggest river in northern Italy.*

paene, *adv.,* nearly, almost.

palam, *adv.,* openly, publicly.

pār, paris, *adj.,* equal, like, similar; equal to, a match for; *with words of number and quantity,* the same; **pār atque,** the same as.

parcō, parcere, pepercī, parsus [**parcus,** frugal], be frugal *or* economical; spare, do not injure *or* harm.

parēn•s, -tis, *m., f.* [**pariō,** bring forth], parent.

pariō, parere, peperī, partum, bring forth; gain, acquire, win.

parō, 1, prepare, get ready; procure, acquire; prepare for, get ready for; **parātus,** *perf. part. as adj.*: ready, prepared; equipped.

par•s, -tis, *f.,* part, share; (political) faction; direction, side, place; district, area.

partus, *see* **pariō.**

pass•us, -ūs, *m.* [**pandō,** extend], a pace, step, stride, *the distance from where the foot leaves the ground to where the same foot again hits the ground, which Romans standardized as a measure of 4 feet, 10 ¼ inches (= five Roman feet)*; **mīlle passūs** *or* **passuum,** a *Roman* mile (*4,857 feet*).

pate•ō, -ēre, -uī, —, lie *or* be open, be passable; stretch out, extend.

pat•er, -ris, *m.,* father; *in pl.*: forefathers, ancestors; **pater familiae,** father *or* head of a household.

patior, patī, passus sum, endure, withstand, suffer; permit, allow.

pauc•ī, -ae, -a, *adj.* (*rarely used in the sing.*), few; *as noun*: few *persons or things.*

pauci•tās, -tātis, *f.* [**paucus,** few], fewness, small number.

paulātim, *adv.* [**paulus,** little], little by little, by degrees, gradually.

paulō, *adv.* [**paulus,** little], a little, somewhat, slightly.

paulum, *adv.* [**paulus,** little], a little, somewhat, slightly.

paul•us, -a, -um, *adj.,* little; **paulum,** *as noun*: a little; **post paulum,** soon after.

pāx, pācis, *f.,* peace, favor.

pecūni•a, -ae, *f.,* property, wealth; money.

ped•es, -itis, *m.* [**pēs,** foot], foot soldier; *pl.*: infantry.

pedest•er, -ris, -re, *adj.* [**pēs,** foot], on foot, pedestrian; **pedestrēs cōpiae,** infantry.

peditāt•us, -ūs, *m.* [**pedes,** foot soldier], foot soldiers, infantry.

pellō, pellere, pepulī, pulsum, beat, defeat, rout; drive out, expel.

pendō, pendere, pependī, pēnsum, weigh, weigh out; weigh out *money,* pay, pay out; *with* **poenās,** suffer.

per, *prep. with acc.,* through, throughout; by means of, through the agency of, on account of, through efforts *or* influence of; **per sē,** of their own accord, on their own responsibility; *sometimes with intensive force,* in itself, themselves; *in composition,* thorough, very, thoroughly, completely.

per•agō, -agere, -ēgī, -āctum [agō, lead], lead through; complete, finish.

per•currō, -currere, -currī, -cursum [currō, run], run along *or* over.

per•cutiō, -cutere, -cutī, -cussum, strike *or* thrust through, slay, kill.

per•discō, -discere, -didicī, — [discō, learn], learn thoroughly, learn by heart.

per•dūcō, -dūcere, -dūxī, -ductum [dūcō, lead], lead through *or* along, conduct, bring over, bring; construct, extend; influence, win over; draw out, prolong.

perendin•us, -a, -um, *adj.*, after tomorrow.

perequitō, 1 [equitō, ride], ride around, ride about, ride through.

perfacil•is, -e, *adj.* [facilis, easy], very easy.

per•ficiō, -ficere, -fēcī, -fectum [faciō, make, do], make *or* do thoroughly *or* completely; complete, finish; construct, build; achieve, accomplish.

per•fugiō, -fugere, -fūgī, -fugitum [fugiō, flee], flee for refuge, take refuge; desert.

perīcul•um, -ī, *n.*, trial, test, attempt; risk, danger, peril.

perlātus, *see* perferō.

per•legō, -legere, -lēgī, -lēctum [legō, read], read through, read.

per•maneō, -manēre, -mānsī, -mānsum [maneō, remain], stay through *or* to the end, stay, remain; continue, persist.

per•moveō, -movēre, -mōvī, -mōtum [moveō, move], move thoroughly; arouse, incite, excite; affect, influence.

perpauc•ī, -ae, -a [paucī, few], very few, but very few; *m. pl. as noun:* very few.

perpetu•us, -a, -um, *adj.*, continuous, uninterrupted; permanent, lasting, continual; whole, entire; *n. as noun in the phrase* in perpetuum, forever.

per•scrībō, -scrībere, -scrīpsī, -scrīptum [scrībō, write], write out, report, describe.

persev•erō, 1, persist, persevere.

per•spiciō, -spicere, -spexī, -spectum [speciō, look], look *or* see through; view, examine, inspect; perceive, realize, learn, find out, ascertain.

per•suādeō, -suādēre, -suāsī, -suāsum [suādeō, advise], *advise thoroughly, and thus convincingly:* convince, persuade, prevail upon; inculcate; sibi persuādērī, be convinced.

per•terreō, 2 [terreō, frighten], frighten thoroughly; terrify, terrorize.

pertināci•a, -ae, *f.* [pertineō, hold onto], obstinacy, stubbornness, pertinacity.

per•tineō, -tinēre, -tinuī, -tentum [teneō, hold], hold *or* reach to, extend; pertain, have reference to, concern; tend, aim at; eōdem pertinēre, tend to the same purpose *or* result, amount to the same thing.

pertulī, *see* perferō.

perturbō, 1 [turbō, disturb], disturb greatly, throw into confusion, embarrass, disturb; alarm, terrify.

per•veniō, -venīre, -vēnī, -ventum [veniō, come], come through; come to, arrive at, reach; *of property,* fall, revert.

pēs, pedis, *m.*, the foot, a foot (*the Roman measure was 11.65 inches in length*); pedibus, on foot; pedem referre, retreat.

petō, petere, petīvī, petītum, seek, hunt for, aim at, make for, attack, go to, direct one's course to *or* toward; seek to obtain, strive after; ask, request, beseech.

Petrosid•ius, -ī, *m.*, Lucius Petrosidius, *a standard-bearer in Caesar's army.*

pie•tās, -tātis, *f.* [pius, loyal], loyalty, devotion.

pīl•um, -ī, *n.*, heavy javelin, pike.

pīl•us, -ī, *m.*, century *of soldiers*; prīmus pīlus, first century *of a legion*; prīmī pīlī centuriō *or* prīmipīlus, the centurion of the first century, the chief centurion.

pinn•a, -ae, *f.*, feather; battlement, parapet.

Pīs•ō, -ōnis, *f.*, (1) Marcus Puppius Piso Calpurnianus, *consul with Messala in 61 BCE.* (2) Lucius Calpurnius Piso, *killed in the defeat of Cassius's army by the Tigurini in 107 BCE.* (3) Lucius Calpurnius Piso, *Caesar's father-in-law; consul in 58 BCE.* (4) Piso, *an Aquitanian.*

plācō, 1, appease.

Plancus, -ī, *m.*, *see* Munātius.

plēbs, plēbis, *or* plēbēs, plēbeī, *f.*, populace, common people.

plēn•us, -a, -um, *adj.* [pleō, fill], full, whole, complete.

plēr•īque, -aeque, -aque, *adj. pl.*, very many, the most of; *as noun:* a great many, very many.

plērumque, *adv.* [plērusque, the greater part], for the most part, mostly, generally; again and again, very often.

Pleumoxi•ī, -ōrum, *m.*, the Pleumoxii.

plūrimus, *see* multus.

plūs, *see* multus.

poen•a, -ae, *f.,* punishment, penalty.

polliceor, 2 [**prō** + **liceor,** bid, offer], hold forth, offer, promise, pledge.

pollicitus, *see* **polliceor.**

Pompē•ius, -ī, *m.,* (1) Gnaeus Pompeius Magnus, *Pompey the Great, political ally with Crassus and supporter of Caesar in 60 BCE, later joins the Senatorial party against Caesar, is defeated by Caesar in Greece, and murdered in Egypt in 48 BCE.* (2) Gnaius Pompeius, *an interpreter who served under Quintus Titurius Sabinus.*

pōnō, pōnere, posuī, positum, place, put, place over; lay down, set aside; station, post; regard, consider; make, build; *with* **castra,** pitch; *pass.:* be situated; *with* **in** *and the abl.,* depend on, *in addition to the above meanings.*

pōns, pontis, *m.,* bridge.

popul•us, -ī, *m.,* the people, the mass, the crowd, *as opposed to individuals;* a people, a nation.

porrō, *adv.,* farther on; furthermore, then.

port•a, -ae, *f.,* gate.

portō, 1, carry, transport, bring, take.

port•us, -ūs, *m.,* harbor, haven, port.

possum, posse, potuī, — (App. §80) [**potis,** able + **sum,** be], be able, can; to have power *or* influence, have strength, be strong; *with* **quam** *and superl.:* as possible, *e.g.,* **quam plūrimās possunt,** as many as possible; **multum posse, plūs posse,** *and* **plūrimum posse,** *see* **multum.**

post, *adv. and prep. with acc.* (1) *As adv.,* later, afterward; (2) *As prep.,* behind, after; **post tergum** *or* **post sē,** in the rear.

posteā, *adv.* [**post,** after], after this, afterward.

posteā quam, *adv.* [**posteā,** afterward + **quam,** than], after.

poster•us, -a, -um, *adj.* [**post,** after], after, following, next; *in m. pl. as noun:* posterity; *superl.:* **postrēmus** *or* **postumus,** last.

postrēmō, *adv.* [**postrēmus,** last], finally, at last.

pot•ēns, -entis, *adj.* [*pres. part. of* **possum,** be able], powerful, influential.

potes•tās, -tātis, *f.* [**potēns,** powerful], power, ability, authority; control, sway, rule; chance, opportunity, possibility; **potestātem facere,** grant permission, give a chance.

potior, 4 [**potis,** powerful], become master of, get control *or* possession of, obtain, capture.

prae•cēdō, -cēdere, -cessī, -cessum [**cēdō,** go], go before; surpass, excel.

prae•ceps, -cipitis, *adj.* [**caput,** head], headlong; steep, precipitous.

prae•ceptum, -ī, *n.* [**praecipiō,** instruct], instruction, injunction, command.

praed•a, -ae, *f.,* booty, plunder, spoil.

prae•dīcō, 1 [**dīcō,** proclaim], proclaim publicly *or* before others; declare, report, tell of.

prae•ficiō, -ficere, -fēcī, -fectum [**faciō,** make], make before; place over, put in command of, put at the head of, place in charge of.

prae•mittō, -mittere, -mīsī, -missum [**mittō,** send], send before *or* in advance.

praem•ium, -ī, *n.,* distinction, prize, reward.

prae•sēns, -sentis, *pres. part. of* **praesum.**

prae•senti•a, -ae, *f.* [**praesum,** be present], presence; the present moment; **in praesentiā,** for the present; then.

praesertim, *adv.,* particularly, especially.

praesid•ium, -ī, *n.* [**praesideō,** guard], guard, garrison; safeguard, protection; fortification, stronghold; help, aid; safety.

praestō, *adv.,* at hand, ready; *with* **sum,** meet.

prae•stō, -stāre, -stitī, -stātum [**stō,** stand], stand *or* place before; show, exhibit, supply, furnish; be superior, excel, surpass; *impers.* **praestat,** it is better *or* more advisable.

prae•sum, -esse, -fuī, — [**sum,** be. App. §77], be before *or* over, be in command of, rule over, be at the head of; **praesēns,** *pres. part. as adj.:* present, in person; for the present.

praeter, *prep. with acc.* [**prae,** before], before; beyond, past; contrary to; in addition to, except, besides.

praetereā, *adv.* [**praeter,** beyond], beyond this, besides, furthermore.

praeterquam, *adv.,* besides, except.

prae•ūrō, -ūrere, -ussī, -ustum [**ūrō,** burn], burn in front *or* at the end.

premō, premere, pressī, pressum, press, press upon, press hard; oppress, burden, annoy, harass.

prīdiē, *adv.* [**diēs,** day], on the day before.

prīmum, *adv.* [**prīmus,** first], first, at first, in the first place, for the first time; **cum prīmum** *or* **ubi prīmum,** as soon as; **quam prīmum,** as soon as possible, very soon.

prīm•us, -a, -um, *adj. superl.* (App. §43), first, foremost; first part of; *pl. as noun:* the first, the front rank *or* ranks; leaders, chiefs; **in prīmīs,** especially.

prīn•ceps, -cipis, *adj.* [**prīmus,** first], *taking the first place*; chief, most prominent, first; *as noun,* chief *or* principal person, leader, chief.

prīncipāt•us, -ūs, *m.* [**prīnceps,** chief], chief place *or* position; chief authority, leadership.

prīstin•us, -a, -um, *adj.* [*from* **prior,** former], former, original; previous, preceding.

prius, *adv.* [**prior,** former], before, sooner, previously.

priusquam *or* **prius . . . quam,** *conj.,* sooner than, before; until.

prīvāt•us, -a, -um, *adj.,* private, personal, individual; *as noun,* person, individual.

prō, *prep. with abl.,* before, in front of; for, on behalf of; on account of, in consideration of, in return for; as, in the disguise of; in place of, instead of; in proportion to, according to; *in compounds* (*appears as* **prō, pro,** *and* **prōd**), for, before, forward, forth.

probō, 1 [**probus,** good], consider good, approve; prove, show, demonstrate.

pro•cēdō, -cēdere, -cessī, -cessum [**cēdō,** go], go forth *or* forward, proceed, advance.

procul, *adv.,* far off, from afar, in the distance, at a distance.

prōcūrō, 1 [**cūrō,** care], care for, attend to.

pro•currō, -currere, -currī, -cursum [**currō,** run], run *or* rush forward, rush out, charge.

prod•eō, -īre, -iī, -itum [**prō** + **eō,** go, App. §84], go *or* come forth, go forward, advance.

prōd•ō, -dere, -didī, -ditum [**dō,** give], give forth, reveal; betray; give up; transmit, hand down; **memoriā prōditum,** told according to tradition, handed down.

prō•dūcō, -dūcere, -dūxī, -ductum [**dūcō,** lead], lead out *or* forth, bring forth; prolong, protract; produce; *with* **cōpiās,** arrange, draw up.

proelior, 1 [**proelium,** battle], join *or* engage in battle.

proeli•um, -ī, *n.,* battle, contest, engagement; **proelium committere,** join *or* begin battle, risk a fight, engage in battle, fight.

profecti•ō, -ōnis, *f.* [**proficīscor,** set out], a setting out; start, departure.

proficīscor, proficīscī, profectus sum, set out for, start out; go, proceed.

pro•fiteor, -fitērī, -fessus sum [**fateor,** confess], admit, acknowledge, declare, offer.

prōfuī, *see* **prōsum.**

prōgnāt•us, -a, -um, *adj.* [**nāscor,** be born], born; descended, sprung.

prō•gredior, -gredī, -gressus sum [**gradior,** step], step *or* go forward, advance, proceed, go.

prohibeō, 2 [**habeō,** hold], keep from, keep, restrain, prevent, prohibit; keep out *or* away from; protect, guard.

prō•iciō, -icere, -iēcī, -iectum [**iaciō,** throw. App. §7], throw forward *or* away; throw, cast; reject, give up, **sē prōicere,** cast oneself; jump.

proinde, *adv.,* hence, accordingly, therefore.

prō•nūntiō, 1 [**nūntiō,** announce], announce, give out publicly, tell, relate, report, say; give orders; *with* **sententia,** pronounce.

prō•pellō, -pellere, -pulī, -pulsum [**pellō,** drive], drive forward, put to flight, rout; dislodge, drive back.

properō, 1 [**properus,** quick], hasten, hurry.

propinqu•us, -a, -um, *adj.* [**prope,** near], near, neighboring, close at hand; *pl. as noun,* relatives.

propius, *adv. and prep. with acc.* (App. §122, b.) [**prope,** near], nearer.

prō•pōnō, -pōnere, -posuī, -positum [**pōnō,** put], place *or* put forward, present, offer; relate, tell of, explain; purpose, propose; expose.

propter, *prep. with acc.* [**prope,** near], on account of, because of, in consequence of.

proptereā, *adv.* [**propter,** because of], on this account; **proptereā quod,** because.

propulso (1) [**propello,** drive forward], to drive off, repel

prō•sequor, -sequī, -secūtus sum [**sequor,** follow], follow, accompany; pursue; *with* **ōrātiōne,** address.

prō•tegō, -tegere, -tēxī, -tēctum [**tegō,** cover], cover, protect.

prō•vehō, -vehere, -vexī, -vectum [**vehō,** carry], carry forward; *pass.,* be carried forward, sail.

prō•veniō, -venīre, -vēnī, -ventum [**veniō,** come], come forth, grow; be produced, yield (*of grain*).

prō•videō, -vidēre, -vīdī, -vīsum [**videō,** see], see beforehand, foresee; care for, provide.

prōvinci•a, -ae, *f.,* office of *governor of a province*; province, *a territory subject to Rome and governed by a Roman governor; especially* the Province, *the southern part of Gaul along the Mediterranean coast.*

proxim•us, -a, -um, *adj., superl.* (App. §43), nearest, next; last, previous; *with acc.* (App. §122, b.), next to.

pūblic•us, -a, -um, *adj.* [**populus,** people], of the state *or* people, common, public; *n. as noun,* public, public view; **rēs pūblica,** the state, the commonwealth.

puerīl•is, -e, *adj.* [**puer,** child], childish.

pugn•a, -ae, *f.* [**pugnō,** fight], fight, battle, contest; **genus pugnae,** method of fighting.

pugn•ō, 1, fight, engage in battle, contend; strive; *often impers., as* **pugnātur,** it is fought, *i.e.,* they fight.

Pull•ō, -ōnis, *m.,* Titus Pullo, *a centurion in Caesar's army.*

pulv•is, -eris, *m.,* dust.

putō, 1, think, consider, believe.

Pȳrēnae•us, -a, -um, *adj.,* Pyreneian; **Pȳrēnaeī montēs,** the Pyrenaei *or* the Pyrenees Mountains.

Q.

Q., *abbr. for* **Quīntus,** Quintus, *a Roman praenomen.*

quā, *adv.* [*abl. f. of* **quī**], by which way *or* route; in which place, where.

quadringent•ī, -ae, -a, *card. num. adj.,* four hundred.

quaesti•ō, -ōnis, *f.* [**quaerō,** inquire], inquiry; examination, investigation.

quaest•or, -ōris, *m.* [**quaerō,** seek], a quaestor; (1) at Rome, an annually elected official in charge of state revenues; (2) in the Roman army, a quartermaster in charge of money and supplies, and sometimes employed in commanding troops.

quaest•us, -ūs, *m.* [**quaerō,** seek], gain, acquisition.

quant•us, -a, -um, *adj.,* (1) *interrog.,* how much? how large? how great? what? **quantum,** *as adv.,* how much? (2) *rel. pron.,* as much as, as; **quantum,** *as adv.,* as much as, as; **quantō . . . tantō** (*with comparatives*), the . . . the.

quant•usvīs, -avīs, -umvīs, *adj.* [**quantus,** as great as + **vīs,** you wish], as great (large, much, etc.) as you wish, however great.

quārē, *adv.* [**quī,** which + **rēs,** thing], (1) *interrog.,* why? wherefore? for what reason?; (2) *rel.,* on this account, therefore, wherefore.

quārt•us, -a, -um, *adj., ord. num.* [**quattuor,** four], fourth.

-que, *enclitic conj.,* and; **-que . . . -que,** both . . . and.

queror, querī, questus sum, complain, bewail, lament.

quī, quae, quod, *rel. pron.* (*see also* **quis**), who, which, what; *often implying an antecedent,* he, she, *or* it who, those who; *equivalent of the demonstrative,* this *or* that; **quam ob rem,** for which reason (wherefore); **quem ad modum,** in what manner, how, as; **quō,** *with comparatives,* the . . . ; **quō . . . eō,** the . . . the.

quīcumque, quaecumque, quodcumque, *indef.* (*or generalizing*) *rel. pron.,* whoever, whatever; whosoever, whatsoever, any . . . whatever; everyone who, everything that.

quid, *interrog. adv.,* why? *with* **posse,** how? *e.g.,* **quid Germānī possent?** how strong were the Germans?

quīdam, quaedam, quiddam *and* **quīdam, quaedam, quoddam,** *indef. pron.* (App. §62 *and b.*), a certain one, someone; a certain, some, a; a kind of.

quidem, *adv.,* indeed, at any rate, at least, truly; on the other hand; **nē . . . quidem,** not even.

qui•ēs, -ētis, *f.,* quiet, rest, repose.

quiēt•us, -a, -um, *adj.,* in repose, undisturbed, peaceful, calm, quiet.

quīn, *conj.* [**quī,** who *or* how + **ne,** negative], that not, but that; *after negative words of doubt or hindrance,* but that, that, from; to; **quīn etiam,** moreover, but actually.

quīnam, *see* **quisnam.**

quīnquāgintā (L), *card. num. adj., indecl.,* fifty.

quīnque (V), *card. num. adj., indecl.,* five.

Quīnt•us, -ī, *m.,* Quintus, *a Roman praenomen.*

quis, quid *and* **quī, quae, quod** (App. §§61–62), (1) *interrog. pron.,* who? which? what? **quam ob rem,** why? **quem ad modum,** how? (2) *indef. pron., especially after* **sī, nisi, nē, num,** anyone, anything, any; somebody, something, some.

quispiam, quidpiam *and* **quispiam, quaepiam, quodpiam,** *indef. pron.* (App. §62), anyone, any.

quisquam, quicquam, *indef. pron.* (App. §62), any, any person *or* thing.

quisque, quidque *and* **quisque, quaeque, quodque,** *universal indef. pron.* (App. §62), each one, each; everyone, all.

quō, *adv.* [*old dat. case of* **quī,** who, which], *adv.,* (1) *interrog.* to what place? whither?; (2) *rel.,* to which, to whom; to where, whither; toward which; where, wherein; (3) *indef.,* to any place, anywhere.

quō, *conj.* [*abl. case of* **quī,** who, which], in order that, so that, that.

quoad, *adv.* [**quō,** where? + **ad,** to], to where; as long as, as far as; till, until.

quod, *conj.* [*n. acc. of* **quī,** who, which], as to which, in that, that; as to the fact that, insomuch as; because; **quod sī,** but if; **propterea quod,** because.

quoniam, *conj.* [**cum** (=**quom**), since + **iam,** now], since now, since, inasmuch as, because, whereas.

quot annīs, *adv.* [**quot,** as many as + **annus,** year], every year, yearly.

quotiēns, *adv.* [**quot,** how many?], (1) *interrog.,* how many times? how often?; (2) *rel.,* as often as.

R.

rati•ō, -ōnis, *f.* [**reor,** reckon], reckoning, account, estimate; design, plan, strategy, science; method, arrangement; cause, reason; regard, consideration; condition, state of affairs; manner, way; condition, terms; *in pl.,* transactions.

Raurac•ī, -ōrum, *m.,* the Rauraci, *a people along the upper Rhine, north of the Helvetians.*

re- *and* **red-,** *inseparable prefixes,* again, back, un-, re-.

rebelli•ō, -ōnis, *f.* [**rebellō,** renew war], renewal of war, rebellion, revolt.

re•cēdō, -cēdere, -cessī, -cessum [**cēdō,** go], go back, retire.

rec•ēns, -entis, *adj.* recent, late; fresh, new, vigorous.

recess•us, -ūs, *m.* [**re** + **cēdō,** go], go back, retire.

re•cipiō, -cipere, -cēpī, -ceptum [**re** + **capiō,** take], take *or* get back, recover; admit, receive, receive in surrender *or* submission; admit of, allow; *with* **sē,** withdraw oneself, retreat, escape, flee, run back; recover oneself.

recitō, 1, read aloud.

recuperō, 1, recover, regain.

recūsō, 1, refuse, reject; object to, make objections, complain; *with* **perīculum,** shrink from.

red•dō, -dere, -didī, -ditum [**red-** + **dō,** give], give back, return, restore; give *or* return *something due or owed;* make *or* cause to be; render.

red•eō, -īre, -iī, -itum [**red-** + **eō,** go. App. §84], go *or* turn back, return; come; fall to, descend; be referred.

red•igō, -igere, -ēgī, -āctum [**red-** + **agō,** put in motion], bring back, bring under; render, make; reduce.

rediti•ō, -ōnis, *f.* [**redeō,** return], return.

redit•us, -ūs, *m.* [**redeō,** return], returning, return.

re•dūcō, -dūcere, -dūxī, -ductum [**dūcō,** lead], lead *or* bring back; draw back, pull back; extend back.

referō, referre, rettulī, relātum [**re** + **ferō,** carry. App. §81], bear, carry *or* bring back, report; **pedem referre,** go back, retreat; **grātiam referre,** show one's gratitude, make a requital.

re•ficiō, -ficere, -fēcī, -fectum [**re** + **faciō,** make], remake, repair; allow to rest; *with* **sē,** refresh oneself, rest.

re•fugiō, -fugere, -fūgī, -fugitum [**re** + **fugiō,** flee], flee back, retreat; escape.

regi•ō, -ōnis, *f.* [**regō,** keep straight], line, direction; quarter, region, country, territory, place; **ē regiōne,** *with gen.,* opposite.

rēgnō, 1 [**rēgnum,** royal power], reign, rule.

rēgn•um, -ī, *n.* [**rēx,** king], kingly *or* royal authority, royal power, absolute power, sovereignty; despotism, tyranny; kingdom.

regō, regere, rēxī, rēctum, keep straight; guide, direct, control.

re•gredior, -gredī, -gressus sum [**gradior,** step], go *or* come back; turn back, return; march back, withdraw, retire, retreat.

re•iciō, -icere, -iēcī, -iectum [**re** + **iaciō,** throw. App. §7], hurl *or* drive back, repel; cast down *or* off; drive off *or* out.

relegō, 1 [**re** + **legō,** delegate], send away, remove.

religi•ō, -ōnis, *f.,* religion; *in pl.,* religious ceremonies, rites; superstitions.

re•linquō, -linquere, -līquī, -lictum [**re** + **linquō,** leave], leave behind, abandon; *pass.,* be left, remain.

reliqu•us, -a, -um, *adj.* [**relinquō,** leave], left, remaining, the rest, the rest of; future, subsequent; *n. as noun,* remainder, rest.

re•maneō, -manēre, -mānsī, -mānsum [**re** + **maneō,** remain], stay *or* remain behind, remain.

Rēm•us, -a, -um, *adj.,* belonging to *or* one of the Remi; *pl. as noun,* **Rēmī,** *m.,* the Remi, *a Belgic people along the Axona (Aisne) whose main city was Durocortorum (now Reims).*

re•migrō, 1 [**migrō,** move, migrate], move back, return.

re•mittō, -mittere, -mīsī, -missum [**mittō,** send], send *or* dispatch back, return, restore, remit; release, relax, give up; **remissus,** *perf. part. as adj.,* mild.

re•moveō, -movēre, -mōvī, -mōtum [**moveō,** move], move back *or* away, remove, withdraw; **remōtus,** *perf. part. as adj.,* remote, far away.

rēmus, -ī, *m.,* oar.

re•pellō, -pellere, -pulī, -pulsum [**pellō,** drive], bear *or* drive back, repel, repulse.

repentīn•us, -a, -um, *adj.* [**repēns,** sudden], sudden, unexpected, hasty.

reperiō, reperīre, repperī, repertum [re + pariō, procure], procure, find out, discover, ascertain; devise.

reportō, 1 [re + portō, carry], carry *or* bring back, convey.

re•poscō, -poscere, —, — [re + poscō, demand], demand back, exact, ask for.

re•prehendō, -prehendere, -prehendī, -prehēnsum [prehendō (= prendō), seize], hold back; criticize, blame, censure.

repulsus, *see* **repellō.**

rēs, reī, *f., of indefinite meaning; variously translated according to context;* thing, object, matter, event, affair, occurrence; circumstance, case; act, action, deed; reason, ground; **rēs familiāris,** property; **rēs frūmentāria,** supplies; **rēs mīlitāris,** warfare; **novae rēs,** revolution; **rēs pūblica,** state; **rēs actae,** deeds, achievements; **quam ob rem,** *see* **quī** *and* **quis.**

re•scindō, -scindere, -scidī, -scissum [re + scindō, cleave], cut away *or* down, break down, destroy.

reservō, 1 [re + servō, save, keep], keep back, save up, reserve.

re•sistō, -sistere, -stitī, — [sistō, stand], stand back, remain behind, halt, stand still; withstand, resist, oppose.

re•spiciō, -spicere, -spexī, -spectum [re + speciō, look], look back; look at, take notice of; consider, regard.

re•spondeō, -spondēre, -spondī, -sponsum [re + spondeō, promise], reply, answer.

re•stituō, -stituere, -stituī, -stitūtum [re + statuō, set up], set up again, rebuild, renew, restore.

re•tineō, -tinēre, -tinuī, -tentum [re + teneō, hold], hold back, detain, keep; restrain, hinder; detain forcibly, seize; retain, preserve, maintain.

rettulī, *see* **referō.**

re•vertō, -vertere, -vertī, -versum, *used almost exclusively in the perf. tenses, and* **re•vertor, -vertī, -versus sum** [re + vertō, turn], turn back, come back, return.

Rhēn•us, -ī, *m., the river* Rhenus, the Rhine.

Rhodan•us, -ī, *m., the river* Rhodanus, the Rhone.

rīp•a, -ae, *f.,* bank (*of a stream*).

rogō, 1, ask; request, ask for.

Rōmān•us, -a, -um, *adj.* [Rōma], Roman; *as noun,* a Roman.

Rōsc•ius, -ī, *m.,* Lucius Roscius, *one of Caesar's lieutenants.*

rot•a, -ae, *f.,* wheel.

rūm•or, -ōris, *m.,* hearsay, report, rumor.

rūrsus, *adv.* [*for* **reversus,** *from* **revertō,** turn back], again, back, anew; in turn.

S.

Sabīn•us, -ī, *m.,* Quintus Titurius Sabinus, *one of Caesar's lieutenants.*

sacrific•ium, -ī, *n.* [sacer, sacred + faciō, make], sacrifice.

saepe, *adv.,* often, frequently; many times, again and again; **saepe numerō,** often, time and again, frequently; *comp.* **saepius,** oftener, more frequently; time and again, too often.

sagitt•a, -ae, *f.,* arrow.

sagul•um, -ī, *n.* [*dim. of* **sagum,** coat], a small coat; military cloak.

sal•ūs, -ūtis, *f.* [salvus, safe], welfare, security, safety; preservation, deliverance; place of safety; life (*when in danger*).

Samarobrīv•a, -ae, *f.,* Samarobriva (*now* Amiens), *a city belonging to the Ambiani on the river Samara (Somme).*

sanciō, sancīre, sānxī, sānctus, make sacred; make binding, ratify, sanction; **sānct•us, -a, -um,** *perf. part. as adj.,* sacred, inviolable; established.

sap•iō, -ere, -īvī, —, taste; be wise, understand.

satis, *adv., and indecl. adj. and noun,* (1) *as adv.,* enough, sufficiently; rather; very; well; (2) *as adj.,* sufficient; (3) *as noun,* enough.

satis•faciō, -facere, -fēcī, -factum [satis, enough + faciō, make], make *or* do enough for; give satisfaction, satisfy; make amends, apologize, ask pardon.

sauci•us, -a, -um, *adj.,* wounded.

scāl•ae, -ārum, *f.* [scandō, climb], stairs; scaling ladder.

scaph•a, -ae, *f.,* skiff, boat.

scelerāt•us, -a, -um, *adj.* [scelerō, pollute], accursed, infamous; *as noun,* criminal.

sciō, 4, distinguish; know, understand.

scrībō, scrībere, scrīpsī, scrīptum, write, record, *or* make mention *in writing.*

scūt•um, -ī, *n.,* shield, buckler; *oblong, convex (2½ x 4 feet), made of wood covered with leather or iron plates, with a metal rim.*

sē- *and* **sēd-,** *inseparable prefix,* apart, away.

sē, *see* **suī.**

secūt•us, *see* **sequor.**

sed, *conj.,* but, but yet (*a stronger adversative than* **autem** *or* **at**).

sēment•is, -is, *f.* [**sēmen,** seed], sowing.

senāt•us, -ūs, *m.* [**senex,** old], *a body of old men,* senate; *especially, the Roman* Senate.

sententi•a, -ae, *f.* [**sentiō,** think], way of thinking, opinion, sentiment; purpose, design, scheme, plan; decision, resolve; verdict; sentence.

sentiō, sentīre, sēnsī, sēnsum, perceive, be aware of, notice, experience, undergo; realize, know; decide, judge; sanction, adhere to.

septentriōn•ēs, -um, *m.* [**septem,** seven + **triōnēs,** plough oxen], *the seven plough oxen, the stars of the Great Bear (Big Dipper), hence* the North.

septim•us, -a, -um, *ord. num. adj.* [**septum,** seven], seventh.

Sēquan•a, -ae, *m.,* the *river* Sequana, *now called the* Seine. *It flows across much of northern Gaul, and, more famously today, flows through Paris.*

Sēquan•us, -a, -um, *adj.,* of *or* belonging to the Sequani; *pl. as noun,* **Sēquanī,** the Sequani.

sequor, sequī, secūtus sum, follow, follow after, pursue; accompany, attend; follow *in point of time; with* **poena,** be inflicted; **fidem sequī,** seek the protection.

serm•ō, -ōnis, *m.,* conversation, interview, speech.

sērō, *adv.,* late, too late.

serō, serere, sēvī, satum, sow, plant.

servīl•is, -e, *adj.* [**servus,** slave], of *or* like a slave, slavish, servile.

servit•ūs, -ūtis, *f.* [**servus,** slave], slavery, servitude.

servō, 1, save, preserve; maintain, keep; guard, watch; reserve.

serv•us, -ī, *m.,* slave, servant.

sēsē, *see* **suī.**

seu, *see* **sīve.**

sī, *conj.,* if, if perchance; to see whether *or* if; whether; **quod sī,** but if, now if.

sibi, *see* **suī.**

sīc, *adv.,* so, thus, in this manner; **sīc . . . ut,** so . . . that; so . . . as.

sicci•tās, -tātis, *f.* [**siccus,** dry], drought, dryness.

sīcut *or* **sīcutī,** *adv.* [**sīc,** so + **ut(ī),** as], so as, just as, just as if.

sīd•us, -eris, *n.,* star; constellation.

sign•um, -ī, *n.,* mark, sign, signal, watchword; signal for battle, standard, ensign; **ab signīs discēdere,** withdraw from the ranks; **signa īnferre,** advance to the attack; **signa conversa īnferre,** face about and advance to the attack; **signa ferre,** advance *on the march;* direct the attack; **signa convertere,** face *or* wheel about *or* around; **ad signa convenīre,** join the army.

silv•a, -ae, *f.,* forest, woods, a wood.

simil•is, -e, *adj.,* like, similar.

simul, *adv.,* at once, at the same time, thereupon; **simul . . . simul,** both . . . and, partly . . . partly; **simul atque,** as soon as.

simulācr•um, -ī, *n.* [**simulō,** make like], image, statue.

simul•tās, -tātis, *f.,* jealousy, rivalry.

sīn, *conj.,* if however, but if.

sine, *prep. with abl.,* without.

singulār•is, -e, *adj.* [**singulī,** one each], one at a time, one by one; single, alone; singular, remarkable, extraordinary, matchless.

singul•ī, -ae, -a, *distributive num. adj.,* one each, one; one at a time, single, separate; each, every; the several; **in annōs singulōs,** annually.

soc•ius, -ī, *m.* [*compare* **sequor,** follow], companion, confederate, ally.

sōl, sōlis, *m.,* the sun; **ad occidentem sōlem,** toward the setting sun *or* west; **ad orientem solem,** toward the rising sun *or* east.

soleō, solēre, solitus sum (App. §74), be accustomed, be used to.

solvō, solvere, solvī, solūtum, loosen, untie; *with or without* **nāvēs,** weigh anchor, set sail, put to sea.

spat•ium, -ī, *n.,* space, distance, extent, length *of space;* period *or* length *of time, hence* time, opportunity.

speci•ēs, -eī, *f.* [**speciō,** see], seeing, sight; look, appearance, show, pretense.

spectō, 1 [*frequentative of* **speciō,** see], look at, regard; look, face, lie.

speculātōri•us, -a, -um, *adj.* [**speculātor,** spy], of a spy, spying, scouting.

spērō, 1 [**spēs,** hope], hope, hope for, anticipate.

spēs, speī, *f.,* hope, anticipation, expectation.

spontis, *gen. and* **sponte,** *abl.* (*obs. nom.* **spōns**), *f.,* of one's own accord, willingly, voluntarily; by oneself.

stabili•tās, -tātis, *f.* [**stabilis,** firm], firmness, steadiness.

statim, *adv.* [**stō**, stand], *as one stands, hence,* immediately, at once, right away.

stati•ō, -ōnis, *f.* [**stō**, stand], standing *or* stationing; a military post *or* station; sentries, pickets, outposts; **in statiōne esse,** be on guard.

stīpend•ium, -ī, *n.,* tax, tribute.

stō, stāre, stetī, statum, stand, abide by.

strāmentum, -ī, *n.,* covering; straw, thatch; packsaddle.

strepit•us, -ūs, *m.* [**strepō**, make a noise], noise, rattle, uproar.

stude•ō, -ēre, -uī, —, be eager *or* zealous; desire, strive after, devote oneself to; pay attention to; accustom oneself to.

stud•ium, -ī, *n.* [**studeō**, be zealous], zeal, eagerness, enthusiasm, desire; goodwill, devotion; pursuit, occupation.

sub, *prep. with acc. and abl.* (1) With acc., (a) *with verbs of motion,* under, beneath; up to; (b) *of time,* just at, about, toward. (2) With abl., (a) *of position,* under, beneath; toward, near to; at the foot *or* base of; (b) *of time,* during, within; *in compounds,* **sub-** *or* **subs-,** under; up away; from beneath; secretly; in succession; slightly.

sub•dūcō, -dūcere, -dūxī, -ductum [**dūcō**, lead], draw *or* lead up; lead *or* draw off, withdraw; with **nāvēs,** haul up, beach.

sub•eō, -īre, -iī, -itum [**eō**, go. App. §84], come *or* go under, come up to; come up; undergo, endure.

subitō, *adv.* [**subitus**, sudden], suddenly, unexpectedly, of a sudden.

sublātus, *see* **tollō.**

sub•mittō, -mittere, -mīsī, -missum [**mittō**, send], send up, send, send to the assistance of.

sub•moveō, -movēre, -mōvī, -mōtum [**moveō**, move], move away, drive away, dislodge.

sub•sequor, -sequī, -secūtus [**sequor**, follow], follow closely, follow up *or* on, follow.

subsid•ium, -ī, *n.* [**subsideō**, sit near *or* in reserve], sitting in reserve; reserve force, reserves; help, aid, assistance.

sub•sum, -esse, -fuī, — [**sum**, be. App. §77], be under *or* below, be near *or* close at hand.

sub•veniō, -venīre, -vēnī, -ventum [**veniō**, come], come *or* go to help, aid, succor.

suc•cēdō, -cēdere, -cessī, -cessum [**cēdō**, go], go *or* come under; come up to, come up, advance, be next to; succeed, take the place of; succeed, prosper.

suc•cendō, -cendere, -cendī, -cēnsum, set on fire below, kindle, burn.

suc•currō, -currere, -cursī, -cursum [**currō**, run], run to help, aid, assist.

sud•is, -is, *f.,* heavy beam, pile, stake.

suffrāg•ium, -ī, *n.,* vote, ballot.

suī (*gen.*), **sibi** (*dat.*), **sē** *or* **sēsē** (*acc. or abl.*), *reflexive pron.* 3rd person (App. §§163–165), himself, herself, itself, themselves; he, she, it, they, etc.; **inter sē,** *see* **inter** and App. §166.

sum, esse, fuī, —, be, exist, live; stay, remain; serve for; *with gen. in predicate*: be the mark *or* sign of; belong to; *with dat.*: have; *for forms, see* App. §66. **fore=futūrum esse** (*from* **sum**).

summ•a, -ae, *f.* [**summus**, highest], the main thing *or* point, sum total, aggregate, the whole; general management, control, direction; **summa imperī,** the chief command.

summittō, *see* **submittō.**

summoveō, *see* **submoveō.**

summ•us, -a, -um, *adj.* [*superl. of* **superus**, high. App. §44], highest, very high; the highest part of, the top of; preeminent, greatest, chief, supreme; all.

sūmō, sūmere, sūmpsī, sūmptum [**sub + emō**, take], take away, take; assume; *with* **supplic•ium, -ī,** *n.* [**sub + plicō**, bend], humiliation; sacrificing; humble request *or* petition, supplication; punishment, penalty, torture.

sūmptuōs•us, -a, -um, *adj.* [**sūmptus**, expense], expensive.

superō, 1 [**super**, over], go over; overmatch, be superior to, surpass, conquer, master, overcome; prevail; be left over, remain; **vītā superāre,** survive.

superior, -ius, *adj.* [*comp. of* **superus**, high. App. §44], (1) *of place,* upper, higher, superior; (2) *of time,* previous, earlier, former.

super•us, -a, -um, *adj.* [**super,** above], over, above; *comp., see* **superior;** *superl., see* **summus.**

sup•petō, -petere, -petīvī, -petītum [**sub + petō,** seek, obtain], be near *or* at hand; be in store, be supplied, hold out.

supplic•ium, -ī, *n.* [**sub + plicō**, bend], humiliation; sacrificing; humble request *or* petition, supplication; punishment, penalty, torture.

suprā, *adv. and prep. with acc.* (1) *as adv.,* before, previously; (2) *as prep. with acc.,* above; before.

sus•cipiō, -cipere, -cēpī, -ceptum [**su(b)s + capiō,** take], take *or* lift up; undertake, assume, take on oneself; begin, engage in.

suspīci•ō, -ōnis, *f.* [**suspicor**, suspect], suspicion, distrust; surmise.

suspicor, 1 [**suspiciō,** suspect], suspect, distrust; surmise.

sustent•ō, -āre, -āvī, -ātum, to build up; to sustain.

sus•tineō, -tinēre, -tinuī, -tentum [**su(b)s + teneō,** hold], hold up from below; hold up, sustain; hold back, check, restrain; hold out against, withstand, endure, bear; hold out.

sustulī, *see* **tollō.**

su•us, -a, -um, *adj., reflex. pronominal adj. referring to the subject* (App. §§163–167, *a.*), [**suī,** himself, herself, *etc.*], of *or* belonging to himself, herself, *etc.*, his own, her own, its own, their own; his, hers, its, theirs; **sua,** *n. pl. as noun,* one's property; **suī,** *m. pl. as noun,* their men (*friends or countrymen*).

T.

T., *abbr. for* **Titus,** *a Roman praenomen.*

tamen, *adv.* (*opposed to some expressed or implied concession*), yet, nevertheless, notwithstanding, still, however; at least.

tametsī, *conj.* [**tamen,** however + **etsī,** even if], although, though, notwithstanding.

tandem, *adv.*, at last, at length, finally; *in interrog. clauses to add emphasis, as* **quid tandem,** what then?

tantum, *adv.* [**tantus,** so great], so much, so, so far; only, merely.

tant•us, -a, -um, *adj.,* so much, so great, so powerful, such; **quantō . . . tantō,** *with comparatives, see* **quantō.**

Tasget•ius, -ī, *m.,* Tasgetius, *a leader among the Carnutes.*

tegō, tegere, tēxī, tēctum, cover, hide; protect, defend.

tēl•um, -ī, *n., a weapon for fighting at a distance,* missile, dart, spear, javelin.

temerāri•us, -a, -um, *adj.* [**temerē,** rashly], rash, imprudent, reckless.

temerē, *adv.,* rashly, blindly, without good reason.

tēm•ō, -ōnis, *m.,* pole (*of a wagon*).

temperō, 1, restrain *or* control oneself, refrain; **temperātus,** *perf. part. as adj.,* temperate, mild.

tempes•tās, -tātis, *f.* [**tempus,** time], time, season; weather, *usually* bad weather, storm, tempest.

temp•us, -oris, *n.,* a division *or* section of time, a time, time (*in general*); occasion, crisis; **omnī tempore,** always; **in reliquum tempus,** for the future; **ūnō tempore,** at the same time, at once.

teneō, tenēre, tenuī, tentum, hold, keep, occupy, possess, hold possession of; hold in, restrain, bind; **sē tenēre,** remain; **memoriā tenēre,** remember.

tenu•is, -e, *adj.,* slim, thin; slight, insignificant; delicate.

terg•um, -ī, *n.,* the back; **terga vertere,** to flee; **post tergum** *or* **ab tergō,** in the rear.

terr•a, -ae, *f.,* earth, land, soil, ground; region, district; **terrae** (*pl.*) *and* **orbis terrārum,** the world.

terreō, 2, frighten, terrify.

terr•or, -ōris, *m.* [**terreō,** frighten], fright, alarm, panic, terror.

terti•us, -a, -um, *adj., ord. number, adj.,* third.

testimōn•ium, -ī, *n.* [**testor,** be a witness], testimony, evidence, proof.

testūd•ō, -inis, *f.,* tortoise; shed; a testitudo, *a column of men, holding their shields overlapped above their heads* (*which made them look like a giant* tortoise).

time•ō, -ēre, -uī, —, fear, be afraid of, dread; *with dat.,* be anxious about, be anxious for, dread; **nihil timēre,** have no fear.

timidē, *adv.* [**timidus,** fearful], fearfully, cowardly, timidly.

tim•or, -ōris, *m.* [**timeō,** fear], fear, alarm, dread.

Titūr•ius, -ī, *m.,* Quintus Titurius Sabinus, *one of Caesar's lieutenants.*

Tit•us (*abbr.* **T.**), **-ī,** *m.,* Titus, *a Roman praenomen.*

tolerō, 1, bear, endure; hold out; nourish, support; *with* **famem,** alleviate.

tollō, tollere, sustulī, sublātum, lift up, elevate; take on board; take away, remove; do away with, destroy; cancel; **sublātus,** *perf. part. as adj.,* destroyed, elated.

torment•um, -ī, *n.* [**torqueō,** twist], means of twisting; an engine *or* machine *for hurling missiles, e.g., catapults and ballista*; windlass, hoist; device for torturing, *hence,* torment, torture.

torreō, torrēre, torruī, tostum, scorch, burn.

tot, *indecl. adj.,* so many.

tōt•us, -a, -um, *gen.* **totīus** (App. §32), *adj.,* the whole, the whole of; entire, all; *with force of adv.,* wholly, entirely.

trā•dō, -dere, -didī, -ditum [**trāns + dō,** give], give over, give up, surrender, deliver; entrust, commit; hand down, transmit; teach, communicate.

trāgul•a, -ae, *f.,* a javelin, spear, *or* dart *used by the Gauls.*

tra•iciō, -icere, -iēcī, -iectum [**iaciō,** throw. App. §7], hurl across; pierce, transfix.

trāns, *prep. with acc.*, across, beyond, over; *in compounds*, **trāns-** *or* **trā-**, across, over, through.

trāns•eō, -īre, -iī, -itum [eō, go. App. §84], go across *or* come over, cross; march through, pass through; move, migrate; *of time*, pass by.

trāns•ferō, -ferre, -tulī, -lātum [ferō, carry. App. §81], carry *or* bring over, transfer.

trāns•fīgō, -fīgere, -fīxī, -fīxum [fīgō, fix], thrust *or* pierce through; transfix.

trānslātus, *see* **trānsferō**.

trānsportō, 1 [portō, carry], carry across *or* over, bring over, convey, transport.

Trebōn•ius, -ī, *m.*, (1) Gaius Trebonius, *one of Caesar's lieutenants.* (2) Gaius Trebonius, *a Roman of equestrian status.*

trepidō, 1, hurry about in alarm; *pass.*, be disturbed *or* in confusion.

trēs, tria, *gen.* **trium (III),** *card. number, adj.*, three.

III, *see* **trēs**.

Trēv•ir, -erī, *m.*, one of the Treveri; *pl.* **Trēverī,** the Treveri, *a Belgic people near the Rhine.*

tribūn•us, -ī, *m.* [tribus, tribe], tribune; **tribūnus plēbis,** *at Rome, a magistrate elected by the people voting in tribes, originally to defend the interests of the plebs;* **tribūnus mīlitum** *or* **mīlitāris,** a military tribune.

tribūt•um, -ī, *n.* [tribuō, render, pay], tribute, tax.

tulī, *see* **ferō**.

Tuling•ī, -ōrum, *m.,* the Tulingi, *a Gallic tribe east of the Rhine.*

tum, *adv.,* then, at this *or* that time; then, secondly; then, also; **cum . . . tum,** both . . . and, not only . . . but also.

tumult•us, -ūs, *m.* [tumeō, swell], uproar, confusion, disorder, tumult; uprising, insurrection.

tumul•us, -ī, *m.* [tumeō, swell], swelling; mound, hill.

tunc, *adv.,* then, at that time, at this juncture.

turm•a, -ae, *f.,* troop *or* squadron *of about thirty cavalrymen.*

turp•is, -e, *adj.,* ugly, unseemly; shameful, disgraceful, dishonorable.

turr•is, -is, *f.,* tower.

tūtō, *adv.* [tūtus, safe], safely, securely.

tūt•us, -a, -um, *adj.* [tueor, protect], protected, safe, secure.

tu•us, -a, -um, *adj., poss. adj.* [tū, you], your, yours.

U.

ubi, *adv.* (1) *of place,* in which place, where; (2) *of time,* when, whenever; as soon as; **ubi prīmum,** as soon as.

ulcīscor, ulcīscī, ultus sum, avenge; punish, take vengeance on.

ūll•us, -a, -um, *gen.* **ūllīus** (App. §32), *adj.,* a single, any; *as noun,* anyone, anybody.

ulter•ior, -ius, *adj., comp.* [ultrā, beyond. App. §43], farther, more remote, ulterior.

ultim•us, -a, -um, *adj., superl.* [ultrā, beyond. App. §43], farthest, most distant *or* remote; *as noun,* those in the rear.

ultrā, *prep. with acc.,* beyond, on the farther side of.

ultrō, *adv.,* to *or* on the farther side, beyond; of one's own accord, voluntarily, spontaneously, without provocation; besides, moreover; **ultrō citrōque,** back and forth.

ululāt•us, -ūs, *m.,* yell, shriek.

unde, *adv.,* from which place, whence.

undique, *adv.* [unde, whence], from all parts; on all sides, everywhere.

ūnivers•us, -a, -um, *adj.* [unus, one + vertō, turn], turned into one: all together, whole, universal; all *as a mass.*

ūn•us, -a, -um, *adj., gen.* **ūnīus** (App. §32), *card. number, adj.,* one, the same one; single, alone; the sole, the only; the sole *or* only one.

urbs, urbis, *f.,* city; *especially,* the city, Rome.

ūs•us, -ūs, *m.* [ūtor, use], use, experience, practice, skill; service, advantage; need, necessity; **ūsus est,** there is need; **ūsuī esse** *or* **ex ūsū esse,** be of advantage *or* service; **ūsū venīre,** come by necessity; happen.

ut *and* **utī,** *adv. and conj.,* (1) *as interrog. adv.,* how?; (2) *as rel. adv. and conj.,* as, in proportion as, just as; insomuch as; as if; (3) *as conj.* (a) *with the ind.,* when, after; (b) *with the subjunctive,* that, in order that, to; that, so that, so as to; though, although; *after words of fearing,* that not.

uter, utra, utrum, *gen.* **utrīus** (App. §32), *adj.* (1) *as interrog.,* which one *or* which one *of two;* (2) *as rel.,* the one who, *of two,* whichever.

uterque, utraque, utrumque, *adj.* [uter, which *of two*], each *of two,* either *of two;* both.

ūt•or, -ī, ūsus sum, make use of, employ, use, avail oneself of, exercise; have, enjoy, experience, possess, show; adopt, accept; **ūsus,** *perf. part. often translated:* with.

ux•or, -ōris, *f.,* wife.

V.

V, *sign for* **quīnque,** five.

vacāti•ō, -ōnis, *f.* [**vacō,** be empty], exemption.

vad•um, -ī, *n.,* ford, shallow, *i.e., a spot where it is possible to wade across.*

vāgīn•a, -ae, *f.,* sheath, scabbard.

vagor, 1 [**vagus,** roaming], roam around, rove, wander.

valetūd•ō, -inis, *f.* [**valeō,** be strong], health, poor health.

vall•ēs, is, *f.,* a valley

vall•um, -ī, *n.* [**vallus,** palisade], wall *or* rampart *of earth set with palisades;* entrenchments, earthworks.

-ve, *conj., enclitic=***vel,** or.

vel, *conj. and adv.* (1) *as conj.,* or; **vel . . . vel,** either . . . or; (2) *as adv.,* even.

velim, *see* **volō.**

vellem, *see* **volō.**

vēl•ōx, -ōcis, *adj.,* swift, rapid, speedy.

Venet•ī, –ōrum, *m.,* Veneti; *a Gallic people on the western Atlantic coast.*

veniō, venīre, vēnī, ventum, come, arrive, go, advance; **in spem venīre,** have hopes; *pass. often impers. as* **ventum est,** they came, it came, etc.

ventitō, 1 [*frequentative of* **veniō,** come], keep coming, resort; go back and forth, visit.

vent•us, -ī, *m.,* wind.

vereor, verērī, veritus sum, revere; fear, dread, be afraid of.

verg•ō, -ere, —, —, look *or* lie toward, be situated.

vērō, *adv.* [**vērus,** true], in truth, truly, really, indeed; but, however, on the other hand.

versō, 1, turn; deal with; *pass. as deponent,* turn oneself; be, remain; engage in; fight.

versus, *adv.* [**vertō,** turn], turned to; toward.

vers•us, -ūs, *m.* [**vertō,** turn], turning, verse.

Vertic•ō, -ōnis, *m.,* Vertico, *a high-ranking Nervian.*

vertō, vertere, vertī, versum, turn, turn around; **terga vertere,** flee.

Verucloeti•us, -ī, *m.,* Verucloetius, *a Helvetian sent as an envoy to Caesar.*

verūt•um, -ī, *n.,* dart, spear, javelin.

vi•a, -ae, *f.,* way, road, route; journey, march.

vīcēn•ī, -ae, -um, *distributive num. adj.* [**vīgintī,** twenty], twenty each, twenty.

vicis, *gen.* (*no nom. form*), change; *only in the adv. phrase* **in vicem,** alternately, in turn.

victim•a, -ae, *f.,* victim; a sacrificial animal.

vict•or, -ōris, *m.* [**vincō,** conquer], conqueror, victor; *as adj.,* victorious.

victōri•a, -ae, *f.* [**victor,** conqueror], conquest, victory.

vīc•us, -ī, *m.,* village, hamlet.

videō, vidēre, vīdī, vīsum, see, perceive, observe, examine, understand; see to, take care; *in pass.,* be seen; seem, appear; seem proper, seem best.

vigili•a, -ae, *f.* [**vigil,** awake], wakefulness, watching; a watch, *one of the four equal divisions of the night, used by the Romans in reckoning time and organizing guard duty.*

VII, *sign for* **septem,** seven.

vīm•en, -inis, *n.,* a bendable stick, switch, osier.

vinciō, vincīre, vīnxī, vinctum, bind.

vincō, vincere, vīcī, vīctum, conquer, overcome, vanquish, prevail; have one's way *or* desire.

vincul•a, -ae, *f.* [**vinciō,** bind], bond, fetter, chain.

vir, virī, *m.,* man; husband; a man of distinction *or* honor; *compare* **homō,** a human being, *as opposed to lower animals.*

virt•ūs, -ūtis, *f.* [**vir,** man], manliness, bravery, valor, merit, worth, courage, virtue; strength, energy, force; *pl.,* good qualities, merits, virtues.

vīs, vīs (App. §27), *f.,* force, might, energy, strength; violence, severity; authority, power; a force, a great number; *pl.* **vīrēs,** strength, force; **vim facere,** use violence.

vīt•a, -ae, *f.* [*cf.* **vīvō,** live], life; manner of living, lifestyle, living.

vītō, 1, avoid, shun, evade, escape.

vīvō, vīvere, vīxī, vīctum, live; subsist on.

vīv•us, -a, -um, *adj.* [**vīvō,** live], alive, living.

vix, *adj.,* with difficulty, barely, hardly.

vocō, 1 [**vōx,** voice], call, summon; invite.

volō, velle, voluī, — (App. §82), wish, be willing, want, desire; prefer, choose; intend; mean; **quid sibi vellet,** what did he intend *or* mean?

volun•tās, -tātis, *f.* [**volō,** wish], wish, will, desire, inclination; goodwill, favor; consent, approval.

Vorēn•us, -ī, *m.,* Lucius Vorenus, *a centurion in Caesar's army.*

vōs, *see* **tū.**

voveō, vovēre, vōvī, vōtum, vow.

vōx, vōcis, *f.,* voice, tone; outcry, cry, shout; word; *pl.,* words, language, *variously translated according to context, as* entreaties, complaints, tales, etc.

vulgō, *adv.* [**vulgus,** the crowd], commonly, everywhere.

vulg•us, -ī, *n.,* the common people, the multitude, the public, the masses; a crowd.

vulnerō, 1 [**vulnus,** wound], wound.

vuln•us, -eris, *n.,* a wound.

STUDENT EDITION ERRATA

The following refer to the 2012 printing of *A Caesar Workbook*, student edition.

Page	For	Read
4, #10, a	(line 6)	(line 7)
12, #19, a & d	*existimaverunt*	*duxerunt* (line 20)
12, #19, c	infinitive phrase	infinitive
12, #22	In line 20	In line 21
14, #3	lines 12–13	lines 11–12
19	Line 19	Line 20
37, Line 13, 3rd	part of speech is	part of speech of
41, #29, d	the Roman soldiers	the aquilifer
49, Translation	comprehendant	comprehenderant
56	Line 19	Line 18
56	Line 20	Line 19
57	Lines 27–28	Lines 27–29
58, #6	*deicierentur*	*deicerentur*
67	Lines 31–32	Lines 31–34
	Line 34 . . . *citissime*	Line 33
83, Lines 4–7	*iussit*	*dedit*
92	Induitiomarus	Indutiomarus
99, Line 23	*redactum*	*redactam*
102	deferent	deferunt
109, #11, b	they were taking everything they possibly could	they were taking only necessities
165, #1	inexperienced	experienced
178, Line 21	*gratium*	*gratiam*
179, #9	*remittent*	*remittant*
249, orbis	word	world